# Militant Buddhism

Peter Lehr

# Militant Buddhism

## The Rise of Religious Violence in Sri Lanka, Myanmar and Thailand

palgrave
macmillan

Peter Lehr
School of International Relations
University of St Andrews
St Andrews, Fife, UK

ISBN 978-3-030-03516-7     ISBN 978-3-030-03517-4   (eBook)
https://doi.org/10.1007/978-3-030-03517-4

Library of Congress Control Number: 2018964562

This Palgrave Macmillan imprint is published by the registered company Springer Nature
Switzerland AG
The registered company address is: Gewerbestrasse 11, 6330 Cham, Switzerland

# CONTENTS

# CHAPTER 1

# Introduction: Between Dhamma-Ghosa and Bheri-Ghosa

In one of his famous edicts, Maurya Emperor Ashoka (c. 268–c. 232 BCE) declared that under his enlightened Buddhist rule, the sound of war drums (*bheri-ghosa*) had been replaced by the rule of Buddhist law (*dhamma-ghosa*). Since then, a profound pacifism or rejection of violence (ahimsa; lit.: 'do not injure') has been the hallmark of Buddhism and its various traditions—at least from a somewhat naïve and romantic outside perspective. In the West, we are well aware of Christian fundamentalism, Islamist Salafism-Jihadism, militant Judaism, and maybe even of the ultra-nationalist Hindutva movement and militant Sikhism in India. Militant and violent Buddhism, however, features only rarely in Western debates, the current plight of the Rohingya in Myanmar (Burma)[1] notwithstanding. Somehow, the idea of organized Buddhist mob violence targeting non-Buddhists seems to be outright ludicrous. A comment on Facebook which I came across when working on this book brought this scepticism to a point: 'A Buddhist mob: is this really a thing?' Unfortunately, it is indeed 'a thing,' and recent events in Sri Lanka, Burma, and, to a lesser

---

[1] Since June 1989, the official name of the country is *Republic of the Union of Myanmar.* However, I prefer the traditional name *Burma*—not out of political considerations, but to better differentiate between *Burmans* as the majority ethnic group and *Burmese* as the citizens of the state, irrespective of their ethnic origin.

© The Author(s) 2019
P. Lehr, *Militant Buddhism,*
https://doi.org/10.1007/978-3-030-03517-4_1

1

extent, Thailand indicate that in Theravāda Buddhism,[2] a militant, ultra-nationalist strand is on the rise, with prominent Buddhist monks such as Galagoda Aththe Gnanasara Thero in Sri Lanka and Ashin Wirathu or Ashin Parmaukkha in Burma acting as preachers of hate—an expression that so far seemed to have been reserved for Islamists calling for a global Jihad. So, how can the rise of this militant strand of Theravāda Buddhism visible in Sri Lanka, Burma, and Thailand be explained?[3]

We could start the debate with the doctrine of ahimsa, which, on the surface at least, should act as a powerful barrier against acts of violence committed by Buddhists. However, as in any belief system and doctrine, there are exceptions. For example, while expansionist and offensive warfare is prohibited, armed defence is seen as permissible under certain conditions, and even as unavoidable in this current age of suffering (*dukkha*). One such condition would be the impression that Buddhism is under siege by a hostile non-Buddhist enemy. Militant Buddhist violence defined in this way is actually nothing new. In Sri Lanka, Buddhist monks were actively involved in anti-Tamil political violence in 1915 (Sinhalese-Tamil race riots), and then again from the early 1950s onwards. In Burma, monks were actively involved in armed resistance against the British colonial system as early as the 1880s, in the Indo-Burmese riots of 1938, and again in armed resistance against various insurgencies of non-Buddhist ethnic groups after independence. And in Thailand, 'cold war' monks were actively involved in the fight against the communist insurgency of the 1970s. As of today, the most formidable and dangerous 'other' in the eyes of both Buddhist monks and laity in Burma, Sri Lanka, and Thailand are Muslims.

These few examples should suffice to demonstrate that militant, extremist, and ultra-nationalist Buddhist violence with millenarian overtones is not a new phenomenon, but rather an overlooked and under-reported one that was kept hidden for quite a while. In the era of modern media such as global television, Twitter, or YouTube, this is no longer

[2] Since trends and trajectories in Mahāyāna Buddhism and in Vajrayāna (Tibetan) Buddhism are quite different, and since these variants of Buddhism are virtually non-existent in the three countries Sri Lanka, Burma, and Thailand, this study only examines militancy and ultra-nationalism within Theravāda Buddhism.

[3] Cambodia and Laos are also Theravāda Buddhist countries, but due to the communist takeover in 1975, their Sanghas followed a rather different trajectory. Hence, these two countries are not covered here.

possible: militant Buddhist violence and its current Islamophobia are out there for everybody to see. In the case of anti-Muslim violence in Burma, it already led to a backlash: the Taliban in Pakistan, the Indonesian Jemaah Islamiyah (JI), and, more recently, the Islamic State (better known as ISIS) issued statements threatening to attack Burmese Buddhists in retaliation for what they see as the 'state-sponsored murder' of Muslims, while Al Qaeda called upon its followers to support their Muslim brethren in Burma, "financially, militarily, and physically" (SITE 2017). Although at the moment, these threats have not yet been translated into action, terrorist attacks against Buddhist temples have actually occurred over the years—for example, in Bangladesh during October 2012, and on 7 July 2013 in India, targeting the famous Bodh Gaya temple as one of the holiest sites of Buddhism. Hence, the emergence of a tit-for-tat cycle of violence and counter-violence cannot be ruled out (Lehr 2016, 130; 2017).

## APPROACHES: THEORIES AND METHODS

In order to map and compare the trajectories of militant, ultra-nationalist Buddhism in the three main Theravāda countries, namely Sri Lanka, Burma, and Thailand, I explore the commonalities as well as the differences of these movements, also putting them in the proper context: firstly, into the domestic context since, as we shall see, these militant movements usually do not remain unopposed; secondly, in the regional context in the shape of interactions between various strands of Theravāda Buddhism with those of other religions, namely Islam and Evangelical Christianity; and thirdly, in the global context, here defined as the return of religion as a major factor in politics and as a major challenge for secularism. With regard to the underlying theoretical and methodological approach, it is obvious that, as usual in social sciences, mono-causal explanations cannot sufficiently explain these complex interactions. Rather, as Charles Selengut suggests, a holistic approach needs to be adopted, with the assumption that indeed "each particular case will present a unique set of religious, historical, and sociological conditions that set off and, possibly, continue the violence" (Selengut 2003, 228). Hence, it will be assumed as well that "other factors like widespread poverty, grievances, and resentment against governmental authority or strong charismatic leaders" (ibid.) are required to trigger religious violence even if a doctrine justifying religious violence is present. On the other hand, this should not, and does not, allow us to simply ignore the messages and actions of those charismatic preachers such as Ashin Wirathu in Myanmar or Galagoda Aththe Gnanasara Thero in Sri Lanka by reducing them to nothing but politicking. Rather, I agree with Gilles Kepel who, in the context of fundamentalist movements within the three Abrahamic or 'revealed' religions (Judaism, Christianity, Islam) argued that "if we are going to look at these movements, however strange, aberrant or fanatical some of them may seem to us, we have to take seriously both what they are saying and the alternative societies they are trying to build [...]" (Kepel 1994, 11). But I also agree with his follow-on argument: "Taking them seriously does not, however, make us into either their advocates or their fellow-travellers, any more than a person whose eyes had been opened to the condition of the proletariat by reading communist literature had to become a member of the Party" (ibid.).

There are several different methodologies that would have been suitable for this task. I chose a socio-theological approach as defined and explained by Mark Juergensmeyer and Mona Kanwal Sheikh (Juergensmeyer and Sheikh 2013, 620–643) since this allows me to first take a look at the actors' perspectives, and then contrast them with the bigger picture of the socio-political and socio-economic background in the countries under investigation. The first part of this twofold research agenda implies arriving at an understanding or *verstehen* in a Weberian sense of that concept, which, as Juergensmeyer and Sheikh point out, also requires an empathetic immersion as well as relational knowledge, the latter defined as "knowledge that is acquired not through inductive or deductive reasoning but through an interaction of ideas and worldviews with someone whose perspective on the world is quite different than one's own. It is this knowledge that is possible only though [sic] an engagement of worldviews that comes about through informative conversations" (Juergensmeyer and Sheikh 2013, 632). In this context, it is important to note that the various monkhoods (Sanghas) should not be regarded as monolithic blocs: in all three countries, there are hardliners or extremists as well as progressives (for example, environmentalist monks) and moderates, while the majority of monks in all three Sanghas refrain from getting actively involved in politics.

For the case of Hinduism, Marc Gopin (2000, 14) describes the resulting research process in a way that can be easily adapted for my own research, just by switching religion, actors, and locations:

"What, for example, is the inner life of a [Buddhist monk] today in [Sri Lanka, Burma, Thailand] who is dedicated to peace, as opposed to another

[Buddhist monk] who is prepared to destroy a mosque and die in the effort? What are the metaphysical priorities of each, and why do they attach themselves to differing versions of [Theravāda Buddhism]? [...] For example, which sacred phenomena – texts, rituals, or images of [the Buddha] – emerge most often in the minds of the believers who are prone to violence, as opposed to those who are prone to conciliatory approaches?"

The process of 'verstehen' will also allow me to stay as clear as possible from some notional orthodoxical and orthopractical assumptions on what 'authentic' Theravāda Buddhism should look like—which, as a political scientist focusing on political violence, is neither my role nor my intent. In this regard, my approach follows Tessa Bartholomeusz' approach for her impressive study on the relationship between just war ideologies and pacifistic traditions within Sinhalese Theravāda Buddhism (Bartholomeusz 2002), and Rachelle Scott's approach on the relationship between piety and wealth in her important study on the controversial Dhammakāya temple in Pathum Thani, Thailand (Scott 2009).

As regards empathetic immersion, this part of the research process commenced in July/August 2014 with my first stay at a small and remote rural temple in Thailand's Surat Thani province on invitation of a group of thudong (Pali: dhūtanga, lit.: wandering ascetic) monks who chose to stay there for a couple of weeks to teach me the practical basics of being a lay follower or phra khao (phram). It soon turned out that 'understanding' proved to be a somewhat lesser problem than simply 'doing it': I am not really a natural talent when it comes to sitting in the (semi) lotus position or kneeling for lengthy periods. Compared to that, the language barrier (the monks spoke a Southern Thai dialect, while I only speak some limited Central Thai) was less formidable than I feared: with some patience and a good sense of humour, plus occasionally the translations given by one monk and a mae chee (nun) from Bangkok, interesting conversations with monks, some novices, and the odd nun about their lives, their decisions to become monks/novices or nuns, and their daily routines could easily be held. The initial and rather wide-ranging conversations with these thudong monks helped immensely to gain a much better understanding of what wandering ascetic monks are doing day in, day out, as compared to those clerical monks living in big temples in the cities or in the capital, or as compared to those monks who chose to become politically active for one reason or another—the thudong monks called them 'dark monks.' These early-stage empathetic immersions also worked as door openers later on when I began to approach senior monks and abbots in order to conduct in-depth conversations.

## ISSUES: SOME COMMENTS ON THE RESEARCH PROCESS

Self-flattering apart, there is a reason why I mention my travails as a phra khao, and that is the unavoidable 'bracketing': for most of my respondents, I was a more or less devout Theravāda Buddhist—why else would I spend much time with thudong monks in remote rural temples, usually shunning contact with other Westerners flocking to the usual meditation centres? Being identified as a fellow Buddhist had, admittedly, its advantages: the monks were willing to discuss topics they probably would not have discussed that eagerly and freely if I had not been one of 'them'— loosely defined. There were, however, some disadvantages as well. For example, senior monks not so much 'discussed' topics with me, but 'preached' to me,[4] while others encouraged me to immerse myself in meditation, because by doing so, I would gain a deeper understanding of, and answers to, my questions all by myself.[5] Some monks even tried hard to discourage me from meeting what they called 'the dark monks'—that is, those militant monks who actively involve themselves in politics, including condoning and preaching violence. Furthermore, I got treated to the occasional jokes and snide remarks about 'the other' (mainly Muslims). This unfortunate fact raises some ethical issues that Dibyesh Anand, working on a similar project on Hindutva, flagged up quite eloquently:

> How do I conduct fieldwork among actors who indulge in politics I completely disagree with? Should I express my disgust and lose the opportunity to gather ethnographic material? How do we conduct ethnographic research with activists who are in the regular business of dehumanizing a significant section of humanity? When someone glorifies rape or murder, do we challenge him and thus give away the valuable opportunity to get an insight into how they justify it to themselves? Do we laugh at pejorative jokes about

---

[4] Tessa Bartholomeusz reports a similar treatment while conducting interviews for her work on Buddhism and 'Just War.' She says that "[Many] of my informants – monastic and lay alike – closely scrutinized my identity as they framed their answers to my questions" (Bartholomeusz 2002, 17).
[5] Joanna Cook narrates very similar experiences when she carried out research for her book on meditation practices in Thailand (Cook 2014, 20).

Muslim female anatomy and thus get more research material, or do we express our disgust and terminate our research? (Anand 2011, 7)

For Anand, these moral and ethical dilemmas remained unresolved—for me, having cut my teeth many years ago by interviewing pirates and members of various Asian organized crime groups, these dilemmas were firmly put to rest from the very beginning: in my opinion, and even if it sounds like a weak excuse, empathetic immersion requires a certain amount of what a former professor and mentor of mine used to call 'dirt under the fingernails.' Somewhat ironically, my 'double identity' as a Buddhist lay follower and a lapsed Catholic allowed me to approach both the Sangha as well as Catholics as 'one of theirs': while the monks did not care whether there still was some residual 'Catholic-ness' in me, the Catholics never questioned my credentials since I was baptized and confirmed as a Catholic. As we shall see later on, it actually helped me to discover some Catholic finger-pointing and blame-shifting ('it is not us, it is the Evangelicals,' for example) as well as feeble Buddhist attempts at united front-building ('we don't have problems with the Catholics, we only have problems with the Muslims/Evangelicals...').

By now, it should be evident that one pillar of this work is formed by primary data in the shape of wide-ranging personal conversations with Theravāda Buddhist monks on the one hand, and with clerics and activists from the respective 'other' (mainly Muslims, but also some Catholics and Evangelical Christians). I have chosen the term 'conversations' instead of 'interviews' since it turned out, to my scholarly disappointment, that most monks as well as the Sri Lankan Catholic clerics were only willing to speak on the condition of confidentiality—with the effect that I could use only little of what they said verbatim, while everything else had to be heavily paraphrased or hidden behind secondary sources. This also means that, far more than I hoped or expected, other forms of primary data in the shape of booklets, tracts, pamphlets, posters, video clips, or websites formed the second pillar of my research, and were used for further confirmation, to fill in gaps, and to paint a more complete picture in general, if and when necessary. The 'empathetic immersion' stage of the research mainly entailed participant observation, even though there are many helpful academic publications that I read for preparation—for example, Barend Jan Terwiel's brilliant monograph *Monks and Magic* (Terwiel 2012), or Melford Spiro's older but still authoritative work *Buddhism and Society* (Spiro 1982). For the stage of my socio-theological research, that is, contextualizing the actors' perspectives, I made use of secondary sources such as scholarly books and articles, newspaper articles, and government as well as NGO/ INGO documentations and reports. Relevant scholarly publications on various aspects of Theravāda Buddhism, or on religion and violence in general, also helped to put my nagging fear to rest that something could be 'lost in translation': for example, do my findings make sense in the light of established scholarship, or do they 'stand out' like the proverbial 'sore thumb'? And if they stand out, how could that be explained? I am however quite confident that the result of this 'trust is good, control is better' approach vindicates the data garnered in conversations and/or printed sources: there are no major arguments in this research that are supported only by a series of non-verifiable 'confidential interviews' while flying in the face of established knowledge.

## STRUCTURES: THE WAY AHEAD

The book itself is broken down into eight chapters. The following chapter on political theory and the return of religion (Chapter 2: The Sound of War Drums) briefly sets the scene for my research on the rise of militant Theravāda Buddhism. It offers a general discussion of the question why religion in the shape of highly politicized variants of basically all major creeds has made such a comeback at the end of the twentieth and the beginning of the twenty-first centuries. After all, in the second half of the twentieth century at the latest, religion had already effectively been dismissed as a socio-political force with the Nietzschean assertion that "God is dead, God remains dead, and we have killed him" (Nietzsche 2006/1882, Section 125 'The Madman'). Even the majority of those authors who pointed out that religion as such was not necessarily fading away as rapidly as expected agreed that it would survive for the time being only in a much-diminished role as a set of individual ethical guidelines, but its days as 'opium for the people' were well and truly over. In the shape of a review of the main literature, I will explore why the news of religion's demise as a political force or ideology turned out to be somewhat premature.

The next chapter focuses on Theravāda Buddhist discourses on violence and non-violence in theory and practice (Chapter 3: The Age of Suffering). Contrary to modern Western notions of Buddhism as a firmly world-renouncing and pacifist/quietist religion, Theravāda Buddhism, just like nearly all organized religions with the possible exception of Jainism, espouses a certain ambivalence in this regard right from the days of the Lord Buddha himself. And just like those other religions, the command 'thou shalt not kill' comes with a number of qualifiers that turn this strong and, on the surface, unequivocal command into 'thou shalt not kill except...' Mastering this discourse is a prerequisite for understanding why those Buddhist monks and activists in Sri Lanka, Burma, and Thailand came to the conclusion that this is not, in the words of Ashin Wirathu, the time for peaceful meditation but for firm action, and how they translate that into political programmes and actions. For the very same reason, the discourse analysis is followed by a chapter inspecting the manifold roles of monks in traditional as well as transitional societies (Chapter 4: Monks in the Age of Suffering). It will become apparent that modern and contemporary 'political' monks such as U Thuzana, Phra Kitthiwuttho, Ashin Wirathu, or Galagoda Aththe Gnanasara Thero should by no means simply be dismissed as aberrations, or violent exceptions from an otherwise peaceful rule.

Having thus established a firm understanding of the relationship between religion and violence in general, and of Theravāda Buddhism and violence in particular, the next three chapters contain the case studies on Sri Lanka (Chapter 5), Burma (Chapter 6), and Thailand (Chapter 7). Drawing on primary and secondary sources, I will further analyse the justifications for violence by various actors or 'stakeholders,' the constructions of the respective 'other,' and concrete actions taken. This also begs the question of who exactly the actors are, and what kind of role relevant institutions and the government play with regard to condoning or condemning acts of Buddhist violence—and also, which other strands of Buddhist activism can be discerned that do not resort to violence. The perspectives on, and the justifications for, Buddhist violence derived via empathetic immersion will then be contextualized—and criticized—by putting them in context with available macro data on socio-political and socio-economic dynamics in the three countries.

The chapter on saffron armies (Chapter 8: Comparative Analysis) compares the findings from the three case studies in order to highlight common themes. Since the three Sanghas have well-established connections with each other, it is not that surprising that the rhetoric used to construct the respective 'other' is very similar in the case of Sri Lanka and Burma—Burma's foremost firebrand monk Ashin Wirathu, for example, headed a delegation of Burmese monks that visited the Great Sangha Conference organized by the Sinhalese Bodu Bala Sena (BBS; Buddhist Power Army) in Colombo, September 2014, subsequently stating that his own movement, the 969 Movement, would begin cooperation with the BBS. We will however also see that Buddhist violence in Thailand follows different and rather distinctive dynamics and trajectories—another case of the famous Thai expression 'same-same but different.'

The final chapter (Chapter 9: Outlook) will take up themes and issues discussed in the first and second chapters in order to generalize the findings of this book. For example, I will argue that the rhetoric of militant Theravāda Buddhism is very similar to that of political Hinduism, also known as Hindutva, but that it also borrows concepts and rhetoric from the three revealed Abrahamic religions—just as Hindutva does, by the way. Furthermore, I will take a look at the role of global media with regard to disseminating stories of religious violence, and, thus, with regard to help creating mirror images in a 'Samuel Huntington's clash of civilization' flavour.

## REFERENCES

Anand, Dibyesh. 2011. *Hindu Nationalism in India and the Politics of Fear.* New York/Basingstoke: Palgrave Macmillan.

Bartholomeusz, Tessa. 2002. *Defense of Dharma: Just-War Ideology in Buddhist Sri Lanka.* London/New York: Routledge.

Cook, Joanna. 2014. *Meditation in Modern Buddhism. Renunciation and Change in Thai Monastic Life.* Paperback ed. New York: Cambridge University Press.

Gopin, Marc. 2000. *Between Eden and Armageddon: The Future of World Religions, Violence, and Peacemaking.* Oxford/New York: Oxford University Press.

Juergensmeyer, Mark, and Mona Kanwal Sheikh. 2013. A Sociotheological Approach to Understanding Religious Violence. In *Oxford Handbook of Religion and Violence*, ed. Mark Juergensmeyer, Margo Kitts, and Michael Jerryson, 620–643. Oxford: Oxford University Press.

Kepel, Gilles. 1994. *The Revenge of God. The Resurgence of Islam, Christianity and Judaism in the Modern World.* Cambridge: Polity Press.

Lehr, Peter. 2016. Holy Wars Along the Maritime Silk Road: Extremist Islamism, Hinduism, and Buddhism. In *ASEAN Looks West: ASEAN and the Gulf Region*, ed. Wilfried A. Herrmann and Peter Lehr, 115–140. Bangkok: White Lotus Press.

———. 2017. Militant Buddhism Is on the March in Southeast Asia – Where Did It Come from? *The Conversation*, November 7. https://theconversation.com/militant-buddhism-is-on-the-march-in-south-east-asia-where-did-it-come-from-86632

Nietzsche, Friedrich. 2006 (Orig. 1882). The Gay Science. In *The Nietzsche Reader*, ed. Keith A. Pearson and Duncan Large, 207–237. Malden/Oxford/Carlton: Blackwell.

Scott, Rachelle L. 2009. *Nirvana for Sale? Buddhism, Wealth, and the Dhammakaya Temple in Contemporary Thailand*. New York: State University of New York Press.

Selengut, Charles. 2003. *Sacred Fury. Understanding Religious Violence*. Walnut Creek et al.: Altamira Press.

SITE. 2017. Al-Qaeda Central Urges Muslims to Financially, Militarily, and Physically Support Their Brethren in Myanmar. *Country Report Burma*, SITE Intelligence Group, September 19.

Spiro, Melford E. 1982. *Buddhism and Society. A Great Tradition and Its Burmese Vicissitudes*. 2nd expanded ed. Berkeley/Los Angeles/London: University of California Press.

Terwiel, Barend J. 2012. *Monks and Magic. Revisiting a Classic Study of Religious Ceremonies in Thailand*. 4th rev. ed. Copenhagen: NIAS Press.

# CHAPTER 2

# The Sound of War Drums: Political Theology and the Return of Religion

Theravāda Buddhism is, at least in popular perception, a latecomer in the concert of religions or cosmologies that are currently instrumentalized for the achievement of mainly (socio-) political goals. Christianity (the term 'fundamentalism' was originally coined for Protestant movements in the USA), Islam (Salafism-Jihadism à la Al Qaeda and the Islamic State, or militant Shiism à la Iran and Hezbollah, for example), Judaism (for example, the Kach Party), Hinduism (the Hindutva movement that includes mainstream parties such as the BJP or radical movements such as Rashtriya Swayamsevak Sang/RSS), and Sikhism (as espoused by the extremist-terrorist Babbar Khalsa movement) have already been, and still are, used or instrumentalized for this purpose.

Hence, in order to set the scene for the rise of militant Theravāda Buddhism, I commence with a general discussion of why religion in the shape of highly politicized variants of basically all major creeds has made such a comeback at the end of the twentieth and the beginning of the twenty-first centuries after already having been dismissed with the Nietzschean assertion that 'God is dead, God remains dead, and we have killed him' (Nietzsche 2006/1882, Section 125). The return of political theology is so conspicuous that Toft, Philpott, and Shah even speculate that the twenty-first century could be 'God's Century' (Toft et al. 2011). A general discussion of the factors leading to a return or resurgence of religion as "one of the basic forces of the social universe" (Snyder 2011, 1–23) also allows me to situate Theravāda Buddhism in the larger context

© The Author(s) 2019
P. Lehr, *Militant Buddhism*,
https://doi.org/10.1007/978-3-030-03517-4_2

of religion and politics as well as religion and international relations. It also allows me to develop some conceptual questions. For example, how are religious actors—here: the Theravāda Buddhist monkhood (Sangha) in the three countries under discussion—using their influence "to shape politics within states and across states" and why do some of them seem to "legitimate xenophobic nationalism and [...] authoritarianism [...] rather than to promote democracy and human rights?" (Toft et al. 2011, 83). In how far 'the monkhood' can be seen as a monolithic actor would be a logical next question: the case studies will show that there are different factions within 'the monkhood,' whose influences presumably wax and wane over time—dynamics that have to be established and explored in the case studies.

This first chapter also is the place for properly defining the key terms and concepts used in the book: what is religion, for example, and in how far does Theravāda Buddhism qualify as one, given the fact that there is no supreme deity punishing or rewarding the faithful, but an impersonal law based on karma and karmic consequences, that is, the effect of one's actions in life on one's fate as well as one's rebirth? After all, even some leading 'Buddhologists' maintain that Buddhism is not a religion but rather a philosophy—probably being misled by Buddhism's usual willingness to co-exist with other religions (so Gombrich 2008, 25). Furthermore, terms such as 'fundamentalist Buddhism,' 'modernist Buddhism,' 'reformist Buddhism,' 'Protestant Buddhism,' or 'militant Buddhism' will be precisely defined (or dismissed) in this chapter. Defining one's key concepts before using them is not only good academic practice, but, in this case, it also demarcates the epistemic worldview under scrutiny—the first step in the guidelines for a socio-theological analysis as suggested by Juergensmeyer and Sheikh (2013, 629). Hence, in general, this first introductory chapter aims to offer the reader a first insight into the proper context and a first understanding of Buddhism as compared to other religions. The discussion of the roles of religious actors vis-à-vis the state as the political actor should also lead naturally to the next chapter on the role of violence in Buddhist theory and practice.

## DEFINITIONS: RELIGION, VIOLENCE, AND HOLY WARS

Before I delve into the relationship between religion and violence on the one hand, and the conceptually challenging dialectics between violence and non-violence in various religious traditions on the other, a brief discussion of the key terms 'religion' and 'violence' is in order to avoid misunderstandings. For both concepts, numerous definitions are on offer. To start with religion, Martin E. Marty notes, after having discussed 17 different definitional attempts, that "[scholars] will never agree on a definition of religion" (Marty 2000, 11).[1] Many of those that gained wide currency tend to focus on the belief in supernatural beings such as a creator god or gods conceived as supreme deities. One classic definition is the rather short and succinct one suggested by Edward Tylor: religion simply is "the belief in spiritual beings" (Tylor 1871, 424). Many definitions follow Tylor in this regard. *Merriam-Webster Online*, for example, defines religion as "the belief in a god or a group of gods; an organized system of beliefs, ceremonies, and rules used to worship a god or a group of gods; an interest, a belief, or an activity that is very important to a person or group."[2] Arguably, the first two alternatives are too specific—in Theravāda Buddhism, the Lord Buddha is venerated as the teacher who showed the way, but not worshipped as a god—while the third one is too vague: football also is an interest that is very important to many people, but despite some jokes about a 'football god,' nobody would seriously mix it up with religion.

Interestingly, Theravāda Buddhism is rather non-committal regarding the existence or non-existence of god or a group of gods. After all, whether one god or many gods, goddesses, and other supernatural beings exist or not is irrelevant because, according to the Buddha's teaching, they cannot possibly help individuals reaching their salvation in the shape of parinirvāṇa/parinibbāna—this can only be achieved by the individuals themselves, through their own efforts.[3] One of the world's most renowned Buddhist scholars, Richard F. Gombrich, hence describes Theravāda Buddhism as a case of religious individualism. He illustrates this as follows:

> For Buddhists, gods are powerful beings who can grant worldly favours, much like powerful people. Gods form a superhuman power structure, and to discuss the existence or status of a particular god is much like discussing

---

[1] Compared to the difficulty of defining the controversial term 'terrorism,' the attempt to define 'religion' seems to pose a minor challenge: Alex P. Schmid listed more than 200 different definitions of 'terrorism.'

[2] See at http://www.merriam-webster.com/dictionary/religion

[3] This is one of the central doctrinal differences between Theravāda Buddhism and Mahayana Buddhism, or between Theravāda Buddhism and Christianity (Catholic as well as Protestant and Evangelical).

where power lies in strata of human society far above one's own. Buddhists deny the existence of a creator god, or any omnipotent or omniscient deity, or any being in the world who is not subject to decay and death. (Yes, even the gods die in the end.). (Gombrich 2006, 24)

Understanding gods, goddesses, or any other deities and superhuman entities in this way helps to explain why even the most cursory observation of Theravāda Buddhism as practised in Thailand, for example, reveals that many gods from both the Indian and the Chinese pantheon make their appearances on temple grounds, such as Ganesh or Guanyin—the latter venerated by Mahayana Buddhists as a goddess of compassion on the one side, and Bodhisattva (enlightened being) Avalokiteśvara on the other. Furthermore, other supernatural beings such as protector spirits and ghosts and even demons are worshipped as well, especially so in Burma where they are known as 'nats,' and in Thailand where they are called 'phi' (lit. 'Ghost'). If we look a little further, we find that some monks and mediums have expertise in numerology ('lucky numbers,' for the state lottery are ever popular in Thailand) and in astrology, while others are adept in the art of black and white magic, offering rituals of various sorts as well as magically charged amulets that are said to either ward off bad luck and/ or make the wearer invincible, irresistible, or whatever is required.[4] But, as Gombrich points out, as long as these gods, goddesses, deities, nats, phis, demons, and ghosts are not attributed with the power to redeem their worshippers as saviour gods, these practices are not inconsistent with Buddhism (Gombrich 2006, 24). It can thus rather be argued that the 'high' religion of scriptural Theravāda Buddhism fuses with residual animistic forms of worship as well as with 'lower level' religious elements from Hinduism and from Mahayana Buddhism in order to form a 'folk religion' in the shape of 'popular Buddhism,' which is more accessible and more appealing to the average lay followers.

Seen from this perspective, and in the light of the much-reduced role of 'spiritual beings' and gods, both Tylor's and *Merriam-Webster*'s definitions would not really fit. Hence, and to enable us to also focus on religious practice as opposed to religious doctrine, I adopted Emile Durkheim's definition of religion. For him, "[a] religion is a unified system of beliefs

---

[4]On the booming industry around this kind of popular Buddhism, see, for example, Kitiarsa 2012.

and practices relative to sacred things, that is to say, things set apart and forbidden – beliefs and practices which unite into one single moral community called a Church, all those who adhere to them" (Durkheim 1995, 44). These 'sacred things' can be anything in his view: "A rock, a tree, a spring, a pebble, a piece of wood, a house, in a word anything, can be sacred" (Durkheim 1995, 35). Theravāda Buddhism most definitely can be seen as a 'unified systems of beliefs and practices relevant to sacred things,' which makes me reluctant to define it simply as a 'philosophy', as some scholars actually do. What also seems to militate against understanding Theravāda Buddhism as a philosophy is yet another element that it shares with other religions: since it offers an escape from the cycle of rebirth, suffering, and re-death by way of the Four Noble Truths and the Eightfold Path showing the way to enlightenment and nirvana/nibbana (to be discussed in detail in the next chapter), Theravāda Buddhism can be defined as a soteriology—'sōteria' (Greek) meaning 'salvation.' Arguably, this is more than philosophy usually promises—philosophy defined as the 'love of wisdom' in a literal translation. I do however acknowledge that Buddhist Modernists of the late nineteenth and early twentieth centuries actually quite liked to define Theravāda Buddhism as a 'rational' philosophy as opposed to 'superstitious' and 'non-rational' Christian religions in their fight against the encroachment of Western missionaries on their turf—I shall return to this issue later in this chapter as well as in the subsequent ones.

Regarding our second key term, violence, we all tend to have an intuitive understanding of what that entails. However, as Galtung emphasized in his trail-blazing work on violence, there also is something that can be called 'structural violence' that goes far beyond our intuitive understanding of this phenomenon (Galtung 1969). We will encounter structural violence as defined by him later in this book, but I mention this category mainly to draw the reader's attention on the fact that defining violence is somewhat more complicated than it initially appears. I however prefer a narrower understanding of violence more appropriate to the task ahead, and define violence with Mary Jackman as "actions that inflict, threaten or cause injury"—actions further defined as either "corporal, written or verbal," and injuries as "psychological, sociological, or symbolic, as in the case of religious desecration" (Mary Jackman, as quoted in Selengut 2003, 9). Including symbolic violence also allows me to discuss acts of burning of holy books on the lower level and the wholesale destruction of religious sites such as the Bamiyan Buddhas in March 2001 by the Taliban, or of

Nimrod by the Islamic State of Iraq and Syria (ISIS or Daesh according to its Arabic acronym) in April 2015; while including psychological violence enables me to discuss incidents in which monks refused to accept alms offered by lay people, thus depriving them of an opportunity to make merit.

Usually, the first concept that comes to mind in the context of religion and violence is that of 'holy war,' a concept closely associated with the three revealed Abrahamic religions, namely Judaism, Christianity, and Islam, even though, due to the ongoing activities of Al Qaeda, ISIS and various affiliated groups, attention currently tends to focus on Jihad as the Islamic variant of it—or at least on a peculiar narrow interpretation of Jihad (which means 'struggle').[5] Interestingly, as Selengut points out, 'holy war' no longer seems to be a concept solely associated with those three monotheistic Abrahamic religions:

> In the global world of the twenty-first century, holy war has become global and is a phenomenon found all over the world and in religious cultures far removed from Western monotheism and their traditions of holy war. Hinduism, Buddhism, and Zen Buddhism, as well, have now incorporated elements of holy war in their religious outlook. (Selengut 2003, 21–22)

Holy wars are fought either against external enemies, such as societies organized around other religions, or against an internal enemy as the 'enemy within' in the shape of heretics. Examples of Christian holy wars against an external enemy would be the medieval crusades of Catholic Christendom against the Muslim principalities in the 'Holy Land,' ostentatiously to liberate Jerusalem, while the campaigns against the heretic Cathars during the Albigensian Crusade (1208–1241) would be an example for a holy war against an internal enemy. We could further argue that holy wars against external enemies aim at 'spreading (or defending) the faith,' while holy wars against internal enemies ('heretics') aim at ensuring or enforcing religious doctrine (orthodoxy) and conformity (orthopraxy). Of course, this does not mean that spreading or defending the faith was the sole reason for holy wars—for example, Spanish conquistador Bernard

---

[5] On the concept of 'jihad' and its differentiation into a 'greater' jihad as the struggle against one's own shortcomings and a 'lesser' jihad as a holy war, see, for example, Sedgwick 2015.

Diaz famously (and honestly) quipped that he went to the 'New World' "to serve God and his Majesty, to give light to those who were in darkness, and to grow rich, as all men desire to do" (as quoted in Taylor 2001, 58). Hence, McTernan is quite right to point out in the context of crusaders that "[opportunistic] behaviour and greed may well have overshadowed at times the religious intent of their mission" (McTernan 2003, 62). This however does not necessarily imply that the whole notion of 'holy wars' is nothing but a cynical construct or window-dressing to hide far more sinister motives. As McTernan further argues, "[none] the less, an analysis of the Crusaders' songs and writings demonstrates the religious mindset that at least initially motivated them and legitimized their cruel behaviour" (McTernan 2003, 62). I shall return to the concept of holy war later in this chapter, so suffice it to say that, like any concepts or ideas, the concept of 'holy wars' is quite a malleable one.

Furthermore, 'holy wars' do not necessarily entail large numbers of 'believers' and 'unbelievers' clashing with each other as occurred on many occasions during the crusades between Christian and Muslim armies, or between Sunni and Shia levies at the famous battle of Karbala on 10 October 680 (10 Muharram 61 AH). In our times, holy wars may well involve set-piece encounters between large guerrilla units on the one side, and regular army units on the other—the ISIS campaigns against Iraqi and Syrian regular armed forces as well as against Kurdish or tribal militias are examples for that. But on the lowest level, holy wars may be waged in the shape of individual actions of the so-called lone wolves who see themselves as part of a cosmic war between good and evil.[6] One telling example for such 'grass roots' holy wars is the stabbing attack of an ultra-orthodox Jew, Yishai Schlissel, on participants of the Jerusalem Gay Pride Parade on 30 July 2015 during which six people were injured, one of whom later died in hospital—in Schlissel's view expressed before the incident, gays are "evildoers [who] want to have a parade of sin and of all places, in Jerusalem [...] in order to defile its holiness and desecrate its holy name" (Williams 2015). An example from Christian Fundamentalism would be the case of former Presbyterian Minister Paul Jennings Hill who killed the abortion provider Dr John Britton and his bodyguard in Pensacola, Florida, on 29 July 1994. That he was convinced to be part of a holy war can be gleaned from his final words before his execution on 3 September 2003: "If you believe abortion is a

---

[6] On the concept of 'cosmic wars,' see Juergensmeyer 2003, 148–166.

lethal force, you should oppose the force and do what you have to do to stop it. May God help you to protect the unborn as you would want to be protected" (Clarkprosecutor.org, undated).

From the side of Islamist extremism and terrorism, we remember the beheading of Fusilier Lee Rigby in London on 22 May 2013 by Michael Adebolajo and Michael Adebowale who were loosely affiliated with Al Qaeda and Al Shabaab Somalia, or the beheading of Catholic priest Jacques Hamel on 26 July 2016 in his church in Saint-Etienne-du-Rouvray, northern France, by two attackers linked to ISIS, Adel Kermiche and Abdel Malik Nabil Petitjean. Father Hamel was subsequently declared a 'martyr' who "died in odium fidei, that is in hatred of the faith [...] and because of that faith" (Catholic Herald 2016). For Hindu fundamentalism or Hindutva, the most famous example would be that of Nathuram Godse who killed Mahatma Gandhi on 30 January 1948 because the latter was accommodating the 'other' in the shape of Muslims to the detriment of the Hindus as Godse saw it; for Theravāda Buddhism, we could mention the assassination of Sri Lankan Prime Minister Solomon Bandaranaike by Buddhist monk Talduwe Somarama Thero on 25 September 1959, also for giving in to the demands of the 'other' to the detriment of Buddhism.

Examples of small mobs of extremists carrying out killings ostentatiously in the name of God are the spate of killings of atheist bloggers in Bangladesh—for example, of Avjit Roy in February 2015. The BBC reports with typical understatement: "[he] courted controversy by championing atheism and also tackling issues such as homosexuality" (BBC 2015). These examples also serve to highlight that acts of religious violence in the shape of 'grassroots-level' holy wars can be found within all religions, and not only within Christian or Muslim fundamentalism and extremism.

Since I just mentioned 'fundamentalism,' let us define this term as well. Bealey defines it as a "religious position claiming strict adherence to basic beliefs. This frequently results in intolerance towards other beliefs and believers in one's own creed who do not strictly observe and who do not profess to hold an extreme position. [...] A political implication is the tendency of fundamentalists to turn to terrorism" (Bealey 1999, 140). Although I find the definition quite useful, I deem his final statement more than a bit contentious: there is no statistical evidence that fundamentalists as such turn to terrorism or even to political violence in general. Rather, in my opinion, we also need to discern between 'radical' fundamentalists on the one hand, and 'extremist' fundamentalists on the other. With regard to the former, the Latin origin of the word 'radix' or 'root' already points at the right direction: radicals intend to address and rectify the proverbial root of the problem, whatever that may be. But this does not necessarily need to be interpreted as a call to arms. Rather, as a German domestic intelligence agency has helpfully clarified, 'radicalism' should be defined as a term describing political-ideological views or endeavours that aim at solving societal issues and problems with attention to even the most minute detail, which means with zeal and a single-minded uncompromising attitude, without violating the principles of, and the boundaries set by, the constitution (Landesamt für Verfassungschutz Baden-Württemberg 2006, 8). If we broaden this definition to encompass religious or religio-political views and any constitution as the boundary between 'legal' and 'illegal,' this definition can be applied to one set of fundamentalists as well: all those who long for a fundamental and radical change of society without advocating violence or anything else that would be beyond the confines of the respective legal frameworks of the state they are part of. They might, for example, go from door to door hoping to spread the gospel, or simply withdraw from society in general to live their own lives according to their beliefs.

On the other hand, extremism (from Latin 'extremus' or 'utmost') is defined as an activity that violates the boundaries of the constitution (Landesamt für Verfassungschutz Baden-Württemberg 2006, 8–9), thus violating "the norms regulating disputes, protest and dissent" (Wilkinson 2001, 14). Hence, this definition can be applied to those fundamentalists who do instigate, legitimize, and justify the use of violence—those nowadays known as 'preachers of hate,' 'war monks,' or 'war mongers.' And since these fundamentalists condone the use of violence to support their cause, they can also be termed 'militant'—a term of French origin meaning 'fighting,' that I see as a synonym for 'extremist.' Hence, when discussing the political activists amongst the Sanghas, I will frequently refer to the categories of 'moderates,' 'radicals,' and 'extremists/militants,' albeit acknowledging, just as the authors of the German domestic intelligence agency report did, that the boundaries between those groups are indeed fluent. I will however refrain from using the term 'fundamentalist Buddhism,' at least not without further qualification: in my opinion, the case studies reveal that the radical or extremist/militant movements that we will encounter are motivated not only by religious aims and objectives, but also, and inseparably so, by ethno-national considerations. As such,

these Buddhist movements can at best be seen as 'syncretic' fundamentalisms, but not as 'pure' ones as defined by Almond et al. (2003, 93, 110).

## Resurgence: Religion and Politics[7]

Now that we have defined our core concepts, it is time to briefly discuss
the relationship between religion and politics before moving on to that
between religion and violence. The global resurgence of religious faith
appears to have wrong-footed not only leading politicians but also leading
scholars from all human and social science disciplines. Basically, all of them
agreed that secularization would be the order of the day, and that religion,
if it were to survive at all, would become privatized and thus vanish from
public space. Symptomatic for this view is Stalin's famously dismissive
question of "[how] many divisions does the Pope have?" (Higgs 2005).
Even some of the leading scholars of the twentieth century casually dismissed the relevance of religion with the already mentioned Nietzschean
conviction in mind that 'God is dead, God remains dead, and we have
killed him.' Sociologist Peter Berger, for example, predicted that "by the
21st century, religious believers are likely to be found only in small sects,
huddled together to resist a worldwide secular culture" (Berger 1968).
Unsurprisingly, also under the impression that religion as the 'opiate of
the masses' (as Marx famously put it) was gradually fading away in an ever
more secularized and globalized modern world, the three leading paradigms of international relations—realism, liberalism, and constructivism—
pushed it to the margins as well, if it was mentioned at all. Constructivism
would be the approach most amenable to include religion—"after all," as
Barnett points out, "it forcefully argues that ideas, norms, identity, and
culture have a causal significance in world religion" (Barnett 2011, 95).
But these values are usually framed in an utterly secular context: "religion
becomes subsumed under concepts such as identity, norms, and values,
which in turn are nearly always treated as secular phenomena. Religion
becomes a modifier, describing the sources of the identity, the norms, and
the values. But it rarely gets center stage" (Barnett 2011, 95). Or, as
McTernan succinctly puts it, albeit with regard to secularists in general,

---

[7]This and the following chapter are expanded versions of my previous work on 'Holy
Wars' in South and Southeast Asia, in which I compared extremist Islamism, Hinduism,
and Buddhism. See Lehr 2016, esp. 115–122.

"[religion] therefore is seen as an epiphenomenon – it represents some-thing other than what it appears to be – and as such, they maintain, it could not be a real cause for conflict" (McTernan 2003, 23).

Within the realist paradigm, both offensive and defensive realists usu-ally exclude any discussions of religion as a factor. In Snyder's view, "Realists tend to treat religion as hypocritical, marginal, or irrelevant to politics insofar as units of all kinds, whether secular or religious, must act the same way if they are to play an effective role in international politics" (Snyder 2011, 8–9). Shah and Philpott explain why this view prevails:

> At the core of realism, from Machiavelli to Mearsheimer, is the notion of the state as a distinct political body with a distinct end, or 'raison d'état,' as Cardinal Richelieu famously put it. [...] Realists have also been unified by their conception of what the end of states is – namely, security, which can only be achieved through relative power, namely, military power [... Realists] have always viewed the competition for relative power as ubiqui-tous and ends defined by religion or other ideals as either pursued insin-cerely or destined to fail when pursued sincerely. (Shah and Philpott 2011, 35)

Until rather recently, these views made eminent sense. One should not forget that under the impression of the Treaty of Westphalia of 1648, the French Revolution of 1789, the Russian Revolution of 1917, and the birth of new nation states in the late 1940s, the 1950s, and the 1960s as a consequence of the end of the Second World War and the end of European colonial empires, secularization and secularism became global trends, with many of the newly independent states adopting an autochthonous version of nationalism in which religion played a supportive role only—if it was allowed to play a role at all. One example would be Indonesia in the 1950s and early 1960s under Sukarno who espoused a national credo of 'Nasakom'—an eclectic mix of nationalism (the 'Nas' part), communism (the 'kom' part), and religion (the 'a' part for 'agama'/religion). Thus, Shah and Philpott are right to conclude that "[by] the late 1960s, every-one (a term we don't use lightly) believed that the widespread aspiration for political secularism – for a politics and public life free of substantive religious influences – was rapidly becoming reality in virtually all parts of the world" (Shah and Philpott 2011, 46). Interestingly, quite the opposite happened from the 1960s onwards at the very latest, in what Shah and Philpott call "a powerful quantitative shift in the orientation of religious organizations around the world [with the result that] in every major tradition, leaders and key movements abandoned an exclusive focus on spiritual or cultural activity, and took up political activity as an integral part of their religious missions" (Shah and Philpott 2011, 48).

To answer the obvious question of why that might have been the case, Shah and Philpott offer three 'wholesale' explanations: firstly, "some of the dominant political and social trends of the nineteenth and twentieth centuries [such as modernization and political secularization] were not nearly as formidable in their opposition to religion as analysts anticipated"; secondly, "that global democratization greatly increased the opportunity of religious actors to compete freely for political influence"; and thirdly, "that globalization increased the capacity of religious actors to project influence, mobilize resources, and attract followers across national boundaries, greatly enhancing their overall position vis-à-vis nation states" (Shah and Philpott 2011, 48–49). As concerns the first explanation, this is probably the case; otherwise, secularization would simply have marched on. Nevertheless, it is a rather weak one which depends on a case-by-case comparative study. The other two explanations are more convincing in my opinion: indeed, even strong secularizers such as Nasser in Egypt, Atatürk in Turkey, Sukarno and Suharto in Indonesia, or, for that matter, Shah Reza Pahlevi in Persia/Iran found it impossible to entirely suppress Islam as part and parcel of their culture—especially not in the long term. Thus, in all these countries (and some others as well), Islam as one of the fundamental parts of their respective culture was used as a convenient vehicle to rally supporters by tentative opposition movements, biding their time until the old autocrats showed signs of weakness. The erosion of the Shah's power first in the countryside, then in the poorer parts of his towns and cities during the late 1960s and the 1970s onwards is the most striking example in that respect: he simply could not dare to openly move against the powerful clerics around Ayatollah Khomeini by either having all of them thrown into jail or executed.

That globalization offered religious leaders the opportunity to project power and to mobilize resources across national boundaries also is quite a formidable explanation for this quantitative shift: as of today, Al Qaeda's and, even more importantly, ISIS' successful global recruiting efforts on the one hand, and their global reach when it comes to launching terrorist attacks on the other are indeed excellent cases in point. They are supported by a tight network of global media offering 24/7 'real time' television coverage as well as of social media such as Twitter, YouTube, and

Facebook, to name but a few. This also implies that, generally, the awareness of what other religious groups do, or how members of one's own group are made to suffer by them, is much higher than ever before. If one looks at the plight of the Rohingya, for example,[8] until less than a decade ago, only a few regional experts were aware of this issue. But nowadays, due to global media networks such as Al Jazeera, their struggle is as common a knowledge within the World of Islam and beyond as the plight of the Palestinians, and frequent coverage of 'their' stories enables everybody so inclined to vicariously share their suffering—which is why the government of Burma suddenly was faced with sinister threats emanating from the Taliban in Afghanistan, from Al Qaeda and ISIS, and from the terrorist movement Jemaah Islamiyah (JI) in Indonesia.

Shah and Philpott conclude their intriguing article with the argument that "[given] the pervious state of secularization, the resurgence of religion in global politics amounts to an accumulation of anomalies that now calls for a Kuhnian paradigm shift in international relations theory" (Shah and Philpott 2011, 51). But, as they admit, neither does religion fit easily into existing theory, nor do religious aims and objectives (Shah and Philpott 2011, 52). It is questionable whether the events of 9/11 accelerated this expected paradigm shift—but if we look at the usual explanations offered to President Bush's somewhat naïve question of 'why do they hate us so much,' we probably can answer that in the negative. Even when it comes to the atrocities carried out by ISIS today, we must admit that many observers still seem to be in denial that religion matters. A *New York Times* article on the end of Christianity in the Middle East explains why this still seems to be the case: "It has been nearly impossible for two U.S. presidents – Bush, a conservative evangelical; and Obama, a progressive liberal – to address the plights of the Christians explicitly for fear of appearing to play into crusader and 'clash of civilizations' narratives the West is accused of embracing" (Griswold 2015). The article also quotes Philpott as saying that when "ISIS is no longer said to have religious motivations nor the minorities it attacks to have religious identities, the Obama administration's caution about religion becomes excessive" (ibid.). This caution seems to be shared by theorists as well, and it is entirely possible that the long shadow cast by Huntington's much criticized 'clash of civilization'

---

[8] For an overview, see, for example, International Crisis Group 2014 and Ibrahim 2018.

thesis[9] stifles any efforts to adapt international relations theory to these new realities. Hence, a scholarly "theistic theory of international relations" (Barnett 2011, 95)[10] is still lacking. 'Theistic' in this context should not be defined as eschatological or millennial. Rather, it should be seen as a lens through which the world is observed—just as secularism is a lens used by the mainstream approaches. Regarding Islam, Tadjbakhsh, for example, suggests that "Islam as a worldview, as a cultural, religious and ideational variant, has sought a different foundation of truth and the 'good life', which could present alternatives to Western [International Relations Theory]" (Tadjbakhsh 2010, 174). Similarly, Hinduism and Buddhism could also offer convenient lenses, contributing their own normative-ontological understanding of what 'truth' and the 'good life' means, or how the world should be ordered—and so could Confucianism (Escobar 2018) or any other religion. Attempts aiming in that direction however are few and far between, and, as yet, the predominantly Western-oriented secular international relations theory still rules supreme.[11]

## CONCEPTUALIZATIONS: RELIGION AND VIOLENCE

Interestingly, in the much narrower context of the study of terrorism and political violence, Hoffman, as one of its leading voices long before 9/11, pointed at the rise of religious violence and terrorism since the 1980 (Hoffman 1997, 1–15). And in the context of sociology, Berger himself conceded in 1999 that the prediction about the demise of religion had been premature, and that the world was as "furiously religious as it ever was, and in some places even more so than ever" (Berger 1999, 2). Several 'watershed moments' should have made the return of religion as a crucial factor within international relations rather obvious (hindsight is a wonderful thing), for example, the defeat of the Arab nations during the Six-Day War in 1967 that led to a soul-searching with distinct religious undertones, or the ousting of the Shah and the establishment of a theocratic regime in Persia/Iran in 1979. But since 9/11 at the very latest, and international relations theory's foot-dragging notwithstanding, it is more than obvious that religion is far from fading away. Rather, religion seems

---

[9] Introduced in Huntington 1993; expanded in Huntington 1996.
[10] Barnett however is unconvinced with regards to the merits of such an approach.
[11] See, for example, Acharya and Buzan 2010.

to be occupying centre stage again—especially so if one is willing to follow Huntington's 'Clash of Civilizations' thesis, and his argument that "[in] the modern world, religion is central, perhaps *the* central, force that motivates and mobilizes people" (Huntington 1993, 27). That religion takes its place on centre stage again does not need to be a bad thing—after all, religion could, and in many cases it indeed does, act in a peace-making role. Unfortunately, disturbing acts of religious violence more than overshadow all these laudable achievements on this front (which also explains why I am writing this book in the first place). Barnett neatly encapsulates this when he says that "[today] the mere mention of religion summons images of religious fanatics constructing communities isolated from the modern world and producing suicide bombers" (Barnett 2011, 93). To explain this rising phenomenon, we need to revisit the concept of 'holy war' as defined above, to inspect it from the actor's perspective, and Huntington's thesis of a 'clash of civilizations' as well.

With regard to the concept of 'holy wars,' Rubenstein observes that they "rest on a coherent principled rationale" (Rubenstein 2001, 141), which means they are neither random nor haphazard nor 'irrational,' at least not in the Weberian sense of 'Wertrationalität' or 'value rationality'— again a concept that fell prey to secularism's focus on a materialistic 'Zweckrationalität' or 'goal-oriented rationality' unencumbered with difficult-to-measure ballast in the shape of normative-ontological concepts. Selengut provides us with more details about holy wars, leaving no doubt that, seen from the perspective of true believers, their participation is mandatory, not voluntary:

> Holy wars are encounters between good and evil, between truth and falsehood, between the children of God and the offspring of Satan. In this encounter, pious believers are not free agents permitted to choose between violence and non-violence but are drafted into God's infantry to fight the Lord's battles and proclaim his message to all the world. This is not a mantle easily assumed. The burden is heavy and the dangers great, but if believers are to be consistent and faithful to their God, they must answer the call to arms and use every means possible, including murder, assassination, bombings, arson, and collective punishment, to fulfil God's mandate for war. (Selengut 2003, 18)

One telling example of both the 'heavy burden' and the 'every means possible' would be the already mentioned stabbing attack by ultra-orthodox Yishai Schlissel on participants of the Jerusalem Pride Parade on

30 July 2015: it later emerged that Schlissel had been released from prison just a few weeks prior to this event after having served his ten-year sentence for having committed a very similar attack on the Jerusalem Parade of 2005. Nevertheless, Schlissel saw it as his God-ordained duty to rid Jewish society from what he saw as heretics making a mockery out of God's laws—which is why he struck again. That he would have to go to jail again, and this time probably for life, simply was not relevant in this context: God's will is not negotiable, after all. Not surprisingly, Schlissel did not accept the court's verdict, stating that "God, the creator of the world, did not give you authority to judge me" (Bob 2016).[12] Similarly, when on 4 November 1995, ultra-nationalist Yigal Amir assassinated Israel's Prime Minister Yitzhak Rabin, he did so in the firm belief that the prime minister endangered Jewish lives with his pursuit of the peace process—which would have involved ceding Jewish territory to the Palestinians, even though God Himself granted it to the Jewish people in perpetuity. Amir also took it upon himself to fight what he saw as the 'Lord's battle,' notwithstanding the temporal consequences. The case of former Presbyterian Minister Paul Jennings Hill is also quite instructive. As already mentioned, he killed abortion provider Dr John Britton and his bodyguard in Pensacola, Florida, on 29 July 1994, to then calmly wait for the police to arrest him. In his trial, he pleaded 'not guilty,' arguing that he was called upon to kill by the Lord in order to defend unborn life against what he saw as 'mass murder.' Hill also left no doubt that the decision to kill was an agonizing one: "I would be leaving my home, children, and wife, but I felt that God had given me all I had so that I could return it to Him" (Hill 2003). Having failed to convince the judge and the jury, he was sentenced to death on 6 December 1994, and executed by lethal injection on 3 September 2003. In the chapters on Sri Lanka, Burma, and Thailand, we will encounter very similar convictions.

In this context, it is worthwhile to draw attention to the issue of the continuous 'theological reinterpretation,' that is, reframing of how 'holy war' should be understood from within the various religious traditions espousing this concept. The Islamic concept of 'jihad,' and its current narrow interpretation by extremist clerics sympathetic to either Al Qaeda or ISIS, provides a good example. Jihad, which can be translated into 'struggle,' is a complicated concept. First of all, if one takes a look at the history

---

[12] On 26 June 2016, Schlissel was handed a life sentence plus an additional 31 years for one count of murder and six counts of attempted murder (Bob 2016).

of Islam, it becomes clear that the so-called greater jihad or the jihad of the heart and soul as the struggle against oneself and one's shortcomings has always been more important than the 'lesser jihad' or the 'struggle by the sword' against infidels or heretics. Extremist Salafist-jihadist[13] clerics however deny this, claiming that the hadiths[14] usually quoted with regard to the lesser jihad are fabrications or at least misconceptions meant to keep the Muslims weak. Islamist scholar Sayyid Qutb, whose book *Milestones* is heavily used by Al Qaeda to justify their own 'struggle' against the West ('far enemy') and the authoritarian, 'un-Islamic' states in the Middle East ('near enemy'), forcefully argued against any distinction between a 'defensive jihad' and an 'offensive jihad,' arguing that those who try to restrict jihad in the sense of 'jihad by the sword' to the protection "of the 'homeland of Islam' [Dar al-Islam or 'House of Islam' in the original] diminish the greatness of the Islamic way of life" (Qutb 2003, 71). Furthermore, basically all extremist clerics are in agreement that this jihad by the sword is not only a communal obligation (fard al-kifaya) but also an individual one (fard ayn): nobody can escape their individual duty to defend Islam by all means possible against its enemies, wherever they are. Here, Selengut's eloquent formulation of 'being drafted into God's [or in this context rather: Allah's] infantry' is a perfect fit for this reinterpretation of jihad. This reconstruction of the broader concept of jihad into an offensive holy war to be fought with the sword (or whatever weapons available) also demonstrates that what is meant by holy war is quite malleable and prone to theological reinterpretation by charismatic religious leaders (on the role of charismatic leaders within holy wars, also see Selengut 2003, 22–23). As we shall see in the following chapter, this is also the case within Theravāda Buddhism.

When discussing holy wars, it is important to repeat that we are talking about a different kind of rationality here, in the shape of the *Wertrationalität* or value rationality as defined by Max Weber. For secular-minded

---

[13] The Arabic term 'as-salaf as-salih' can be translated as 'pious forefathers,' that is, the Prophet and his earliest followers. Salafists strive to emulate them—however, only extremist Salafists aim at forcing others to adhere to their austere, ultra-orthodox interpretation of Islam as well. Amongst them are the Salafist-Jihadists, who see themselves as engaged in a jihad against internal (heretics) and external (unbelievers) foes.

[14] Hadiths are collections of the sayings of the Prophet. Which of them are deemed to be authoritative and which are not depends on the branches of Islam (Shia and Sunni), and on the different schools of thought within the Sunni tradition.

audiences, especially Western ones, this rationality smacks of 'irrationality' since it is not open to the usual process of negotiating, bargaining, and compromising: from the perspective of the true believers, God's or Allah's command is absolute and irrevocable—which means any attempt to negotiate amounts to heresy and must be opposed. Selengut discusses this issue in a case study on the current holy war between Judaism and Islam in the Middle East in general, and Palestine in particular, pointing out that while for Zionist Jews, the lands of Judea and Samaria (i.e. Palestine) had been given to them by God "as an eternal inheritance" (Selengut 2003, 32), for the extremist Muslims, these regions had been Muslim lands for centuries and are thus "part of an extended Dar al-Islam, which may never be ceded to non-Muslims" (Selengut 2003, 34). His conclusion is telling:

> Moderates and secularists on both sides are willing and able to compromise and work out some political solution akin to the 1947 calls for partition. For them it is a practical matter, a sort of win-win proposition. For the faithful on both sides, however, it is not a matter of politics at all but of divine imperative. The call, now, is for holy war on both sides, for the faithful to destroy and remove the other and realize, finally and totally, God's will. (Selengut 2003, 35)

Selengut's argument is a compelling one—and one that can be generalized to encompass basically all religions whose adherents clash with each other for one reason or another. After all, it is not the case that extremist Islamists have a monopoly of using, or instrumentalizing, their religion for political purposes in the context of a holy war as perceived and defined by them. Interestingly, this is an argument supported by none less than Pope Francis in late July 2016. He was asked by journalists why he never used the word 'Islam' when he talked about terrorism and violence, to which he retorted that equating Islam with violence would be wrong since in nearly every religion, including Catholicism, there is a small group of fundamentalists willing to resort to violence (Spiegel Online 2016)—I prefer to call them extremists or militants, as explained above. Theravāda Buddhism belongs to this group of religions, as we shall see.

Now that we have established the relationship between religion and politics on the one hand, and religion and violence on the other, it is time to revisit the role of charismatic leaders in all this—after all, neither holy wars nor the rather abstract clashes of civilization break out spontaneously.

In later chapters, and following my socio-theological approach, I explore why Theravāda Buddhist monks support violent actions, and, more importantly, "how they [view] the world in such a way that would allow these actions to be carried out" (Juergensmeyer and Sheikh 2013, 627). Hence, it is essential to explain how they do so: how do religious leaders select from Buddhist scripture to justify their actions, how do they mobilize their followers to carry them out, and how do they influence the actions of other stakeholders, such as their own governments, or the 'other' in the shape of the perceived enemy? It is tempting to digress into the territory of mobilization theory here, but in my opinion, it is good enough in this context to fall back on the concept of power that we already mentioned above. More precisely, I shall fall back on a differentiation of power as suggested by Nye in several of his many publications: 'hard' power, and 'soft' power. As Nye explains, "[hard] power can rest on inducements ('carrots') or threats ('sticks'). But sometimes you can get the outcomes you want without tangible threats or payoffs. [...] This soft power – getting others to want the outcomes that you want – co-opts people rather than coerces them. Soft power rests on the ability to shape the preferences of others" (Nye 2004, 5). And further: "Soft power is not merely the same as influence. After all, influence can also rest on the hard power of threats or payments. And soft power is more than just persuasion or the ability to move people by argument, though that is an important part of it. It is also the ability to attract, and attraction often leads to acquiescence. Simply put, in behavioral terms soft power is attractive power" (Nye 2004, 6).

The wielders of both forms of power are, in our context, not states but non-state actors in the shape of Theravāda Buddhist political monks, ranging from moderates and radicals to extremists. The recipients of 'hard power' in the shape of coercive, violent actions are the respective religious and often also ethnic 'others' mainly (but not exclusively) in the shape of Muslim communities, but occasionally also government institutions if they are perceived to be unsupportive. On the other hand, the recipients of 'soft power' are firstly the Buddhist believers, for whose hearts and minds (to use this somewhat tired adage) the political monks are fighting, and secondly the government institutions (law enforcement, for example) and the government itself in order to influence their policies. The 'hearts and minds' issue also hints at one of the findings: the victory of extremist hardliner monks over their moderate or unpolitical fellow monks is not a foregone conclusion.

## RECONSTRUCTIONS: THERAVĀDA BUDDHISM AS A SOCIO-POLITICAL FORCE

So far, I have defined and discussed the key terms that I use in this book, and I have also commented on the relationship between religion and violence in general, and on the question of why religion actually seems to resume its role as one of the main drivers of human actions in the beginning of the twenty-first century rather than fading away as predicted by many during the twentieth century. Now it is time to narrow the discussion down to Theravāda Buddhism as not only a religion but as a socio-political force, in preparation of the in-depth analysis of the current discourse of non-violence versus violence that will follow in the next chapter. This also fulfils the stage of demarcating an epistemic worldview as part of a socio-theological analysis following Juergensmeyer and Sheikh (2013, 629). This is, of course, not the place to engage in a detailed historical discussion of the genesis of Buddhism and its many branches—there are numerous scholarly works that are doing exactly that.[15] Suffice it here to state that Buddhism indeed is an ancient religion, and actually about half a millennium older than Christianity and roughly one millennium older than Islam: Lord Buddha was born in Lumbini (in today's Nepal) either around the year 563 BCE or 480 BCE, depending on one's sources, and died in Kushinagar (in today's Uttar Pradesh, India), attaining parinibbāna or nirvana-after-death, around 483 BCE or 400 BCE, at the age of 80, again depending on one's sources.[16] Even the three leading Theravāda countries differ regarding the question when to place the 'Year Zero' (i.e. the birth year of the Buddha) that started the Buddhist era: for Burma and Sri Lanka, it is the Western calendar equivalent of 544 BCE, while for Thailand, it is 545 BCE. Nevertheless, since the first Sangha or congregation of monks was formed during his lifetime,[17] it is

[15] See, for example, Strong 2015.

[16] On the uncertainty with regard to the Buddha's lifetime including his date of birth and his date of death, see, for example, Gombrich 1992; Bechert 1995; Coningham et al. 2013 (esp. p. 1121).

[17] Originally, females could also be ordained, but the Buddha seemed to have been reluctant at first. Nowadays, this tradition has largely expired within Theravāda Buddhism, although some attempts are made to revive it—against the strong objection of the usually conservative monks and probably the bulk of the lay followers (I shall return to this issue in the case studies). The so-called mae chees, usually translated as 'nuns' (dressed in white and

THE SOUND OF WAR DRUMS: POLITICAL THEOLOGY AND THE RETURN... 33

thus fair to say that Buddhism in general already looks back to a history of 2500 years, which makes it older than Christianity and Islam. With Christianity in general, and the Catholic Church in particular, Buddhism, also defined as a church as explained above, shares one characteristic: to hammer out the correct creed and to weed out the early heterodox troublemakers,[18] several councils had to be held after the Buddha's dead. The origins of what is nowadays known as Theravāda or the 'Teaching of the Elders' can be traced back to the Third Buddhist Council, held in Pataliputra around 250 BCE under the guidance of "proto-Theravādin elder Moggaliputta Tissa" (Allen 2013, 186) and the (probable) patronage of Emperor Ashoka. Hence, it should also be mentioned that Theravāda Buddhism has existed for about 2250 years, making it approximately 100 to 200 years older than the second major branch of Buddhism, Mahāyāna or the 'Great Vehicle.' The third major branch, Vajrayāna or 'Thunderbolt Way' (the Dalai Lama's strand of Buddhism), is the youngest of the three: it can be traced back to the fourth century CE.[19]

At first glance, the long history of Buddhism in general, and of Theravāda Buddhism in particular, allows us to follow Max Weber (1967) and talk of 'Ancient Buddhism.' However, we can only do so in relation to doctrines and scriptures, not necessarily with respect to the Buddhist practice as such. Seneviratne, for example, makes this point, and very convincingly at that. Of course, Weber's sources were limited compared to those unearthed by the new (Western) academic discipline of Indology, with the result that his insights were not at par with those he expressed on Protestant ethics. Seneviratne readily concedes this, but still criticizes that Weber as the "inventor of the ideal type in sociology [...] sometimes put his guard down and let ideal typification become a habit of mind; in such instances he moved back and forth freely between the ideal and mundane worlds, treating the ideal type as if it were the reality" (Seneviratne 1999, 1). In his opinion, "Weber's 'ancient Buddhism' was more of an extrapolation from an essentialized Buddhist doctrine than an abstract of monastic life

also with shaven heads like the monks), are not fully ordained and thus awarded far less respect than the monks themselves.

[18] As I shall explain in Chap. 3, heterodoxy (defined as differences in belief) in Buddhism is less of an issue than heteropractice which relates to different views on monastic practice.

[19] With regard to percentages as of 2010, Mahāyāna is the largest branch of Buddhism with about 53.2 per cent of followers, followed by Theravāda with 35.8 per cent and Vajrayāna with 5.7 per cent according to Johnson and Grim 2013, 36.

as it was actually lived, as far as we are able to reconstruct the latter. His typology of world religions needed an 'otherworldly mysticism,' and he invented one in his conception of 'ancient Buddhism'" (ibid.). The final part of this judgement may well be too harsh, and Weber would probably have objected. By and large, however, the verdict seems convincing. Max Weber was not alone in essentializing Buddhism—as Seneviratne also points out, Emile Durkheim did exactly the same, which even led him to disagree "with Tyler's [sic] 'minimum definition of' religion as 'belief in spiritual beings' by saying that Buddhism has no belief in such beings" (Seneviratne 1999, 45). As we have seen above, the question of whether spiritual beings actually matter is a tricky question in Theravāda Buddhism, but basically all of the Burmese and Thai monks whom I have asked this question were quite reluctant to award those spiritual beings any role central enough to conform with definitions of religion that focus on spiritual, supernatural beings. For this reason, I opted to also 'essentialize' Theravāda Buddhism—albeit only for definitional purposes. After all, my research does not explore Buddhist doctrine as such, but the dialectics of, and tensions between, doctrine and practice.

In the context of tensions between doctrine and practice, I would also like to draw attention on one quite interesting statement hidden in Seneviratne's verdict: the one on 'as far as we are able to reconstruct the latter.' This half-sentence is particularly telling because this word 'we' does not only refer to 'us academics' or 'us Westerners,' but also to 'us monks,' as we shall see, and it also highlights that what we now see as Theravāda Buddhism is a rather modern construction, or better reconstruction, that emerged during the nineteenth century as a result of two 'push-and-pull' factors I already hinted at several times: the advent of Orientalism and the new discipline of Indology on the one hand, and the experience of colonialism and the reactions to it on the other.

With regard to the issue of reconstruction, maybe it is best to start with the stereotypical reactions I encountered whenever I was asked to introduce my current research topic. Most of those taking part in the conversation were somewhat mystified by that: was Buddhism not about non-violence, meditation, and chanting? Was it not about messages of love and peace and the Dalai Lama? Was it not about world-renouncing? Or maybe a harmless pastime or latest craze for certain Hollywood stars? How could Buddhism ever be violent? Of course, we could dismiss all these responses as part of the usual misinterpretation of Buddhism in the

West[20]—quite understandably so given the fact that the current Western discourse on religion and violence tends to nearly exclusively focus on violence committed in the name of Islam due to ISIS- and Al Qaeda-affiliated groups and their actions in the Middle East and beyond. However, as McMahan argues, "many Asian Buddhists – particularly the more educated, cosmopolitan, and affluent – also subscribe to the [popular image that Buddhism is] a religion or philosophy of life that emphasizes meditation, relaxation, exploration of the mind, and compassion" (McMahan 2012, 161).

This idea of what Theravāda Buddhism entails can be depicted as a still reverberating echo from the initial Orientalist rediscovery of Buddhist scriptures, and consequently the 'inadvertent' (McMahan 2012, 161) reconstruction of Buddhism in the nineteenth century. Again, what Seneviratne has to say about the emergence of what he terms a 'Euro-Buddhist canon' is quite instructive:

> For these early western interpreters of Buddhism, there was no question or ambiguity as to the object and focus of their study, which was a select corpus of Buddhist texts. To them any material that did not conform to the imagined Buddhism of this Euro-Buddhist canon was outside Buddhism. Such material were labelled and classified away as pagan cults, animism, folk supernaturalism, idolatry, and so forth. By the process of biblification in the form of printed translations into western languages, they fixed and placed boundaries on this canon, paving the way for a new Buddhist scripturalism. (Seneviratne 1999, 2–3)

Seneviratne's opinion is shared by many other scholars of Buddhism, for example by McMahan who opines that many of the early modern scholars of Buddhism tended to view Buddhism "as a rational, psychological, and ethical philosophy of life." Even more importantly, "[they] saw the essentials of Buddhism as residing in classical texts, from which they selected the writings on philosophy, ethics, and meditation as central, while ignoring the living traditions of Buddhism as peripheral and corrupted" (McMahan 2012, 161). In this 'essentialization,' or in Tambiah's

---

[20] Usually, there was no knowledge about the different branches of Buddhism in the first place, and one person even mixed up Theravāda monks with those Shaolin ones he had seen on TV, saying that he wasn't surprised at all about Buddhist violence, given that the monks were such superb fighters.

parlance, in this 'fetishization' of Buddhism by turning it into a 'high' religion far removed from the 'low' folk religion as actually practised, Western Orientalists, for example Max Mueller or Thomas W. Rhys Davids, inadvertently blazed the way for the emergence of Buddhist Modernism, as already mentioned: their interpretation and (re-) construction of Buddhism was eagerly adopted by a number of Asian reformers, such as the Sinhalese Buddhist revivalist Anagārika Dharmapāla (1864–1933), Burmese nationalist monk U Ottama (1879–1939), or Siamese/Thai monk Vajirayan (1804–1868) who, in 1851, ascended the throne of Thailand as King Mongkut (Rama IV). However, as McMahan emphasizes, "Buddhist modernism began in a context not of mutual curiosity, cultural exchange, and open-minded ecumenical dialogue, but of competition, crisis, and colonialism" (McMahan 2012, 161–162).

This 'Buddhist modernism' does not only limit itself to the scriptures and their (re-) interpretation, 'essentialization,' and 'canonization by imitation' (Almond et al. 2003, 90, 102). Rather, and despite the undeniable fact that the actual practice of Buddhism was largely ignored, it also extended to the (re-) interpretation of the role of the monks as the foremost and highly visible embodiments of Theravāda Buddhism. Again, it is quite instructive to juxtapose Max Weber's position to that of later Orientalist/Western scholars—many of them missionaries, by the way. Weber described Theravāda monks as "cultivated professional monks" (Weber 1967, 192, 229), however opining that at least initially, "the community of Buddha represented the following of a mystagogue, being, in any case, more a soteriological school than an order" (Weber 1967, 216). He also understood why this was the case:

> For salvation from the endless struggle of eternally renewed individuality in order to achieve everlasting tranquillity could be achieved only by giving up every 'thirst' linking man to the world of imperfection and the struggle for existence. Naturally, such salvation was accessible only to the 'homeless' (*pabbajita* that is to say, economy-less) status group, according to parish doctrine only the wandering disciples [...]. (Weber 1967, 214)

Wondering why many of them nevertheless embarked on missionary work that potentially distracted them from their own salvation, and somehow glossing over the fact that the Buddha himself exhorted his followers to go out and spread the dharma (I shall come to that in Chap. 4), he suggested that the Buddhist ethic of compassion (*karuna* as the second virtue after *mettā* or loving kindness and before *mudita* or sympathetic joy and *uppekha* or equanimity) compelled them to do so, aided by an early differentiation of monks into wandering ascetics (*pabbajita*) and residential (*avasika*) monks whose temples and monasteries he likened to church parishes (Weber 1967, 228–230); as a result, these residential monks now catered for their clients in the shape of villagers or town dwellers as "professional holy meditators [...]: priests, preachers, monks" (Weber 1967, 229). This should, however, not be mixed up with the proactiveness of the Christian missionaries who flocked to the countries in question from the sixteenth century onwards in search of 'lost souls' to be converted: Theravāda monks by and large preferred to serve as passive and largely reactive role models, which allowed them to focus on their own salvation. Carrithers cites a modern Sri Lankan monk who likens monks to street lights: just like them, the monks go nowhere and do nothing but enable laypersons to find their ways in a dark world of moral confusion (Carrithers 2007, 134). This view is shared by the vast majority of monks, who usually emphasize that monks should rather focus on spiritual support to people since this would be incomparably better than doing any kind of social work. In any case, Weber's core argument that, initially, the monkhood resembled a soteriological school rather than a monastic order describes the essential trait as well as the original raison d'être of the Sangha quite well.

Such a sympathetic view of the monkhood was notably absent in the descriptions of many other Indologists—especially those hailing from missionary orders who, unlike the 'pure' academics, were able to observe the daily lives and religious practices of both lay followers and monks in those areas they were assigned to, albeit in a rather biased way. Not surprisingly, given the fact that the missionaries and the monks were competitors, the former described the latter with profound disdain—as uneducated, uncouth, lazy, and superstitious parasites who did nothing to improve the lot of what the missionaries saw to be the monks' parishioners—who in their turn were deemed to be "indolent, lazy, childlike, and lower on the evolutionary ladder than the supposedly enlightened Europeans" (McMahan 2012, 162). But even in the few cases in which they awarded individual monks some grudging respect, that did not stop them from building their churches and missionary schools in the direct and immediate vicinity of the local temples, usually aided and funded by the colonial state authorities—after all, theirs was a civilizing mission or mission civilisatrice, as the French called it.

In response to the Western missionaries' challenge, the monkhood not only eagerly adopted the essentialized and rationalized reconstruction of Theravāda Buddhism, but also reinvented themselves along the lines of the missionaries they could observe as 'social activists' and 'social workers.' This is not to say that the monkhood of the three countries in question used to be politically completely inactive prior to the age of colonialism and imperialism—rather, in all three of them, they were one of the pillars of the state as we shall see, on the one hand depending on the patronage of the monarchy, on the other shoring up its authority, while at times also challenging it. In two of these states, in Burma and Sri Lanka, the monkhood even became the sole remaining influential force of the traditional (pre-colonial) order after the monarchy had been defeated and abolished, its institutions dismantled and substituted by alien Western colonial regimes, and its Buddhist culture and values supplanted by secular Western ones—albeit the latter usually came with a distinct Christian flavour. The new self-perception of being political activists and entrepreneurs implies a shift from the previous passiveness as per the 'street light' simile mentioned above to an assertive and self-confident proactiveness previously only found in Christian missionaries. Quite logically, for those monks who became political activists (by no means the majority of them), the natural course of action was to challenge their Christian competitors in a series of discourses and/or pamphlets, in order to roll back the missionaries' impact on local, traditional societies and cultures. Since these monks usually saw themselves in fundamental opposition to the colonial regimes and their values, this also brought many of them, such as the Burmese nationalist monk U Ottama (1879–1939), in close contact with emerging anti-colonial movements and nationalist-chauvinist ideologies, as we shall see in the following chapters as well. However, the proactive course of action that a part of the monkhood took sparked, at times, a fierce normative-ontological and dogmatic debate within the Sanghas, revolving about the key question of what a monk's role should be within modern society, and arguably changed circumstances.[21] As this is a key issue for my own

---

[21] Coincidentally, I worked on this chapter when Mother Teresa was canonized on 4 September 2016—an act that also triggered a debate about what a Catholic monastic is supposed to do. In my opinion, her calm acceptance of, and utter disinterest in, a deeply unfair and flawed system that kept producing high numbers of desperately poor people as well as terminally ill ones puts her on a very similar level as traditional-minded Theravāda monks as opposed to more 'modern,' socially active, and political monks.

research, I shall return to this question in Chap. 4 where I discuss the traditional roles of the monk, and then in the three case studies on Sri Lanka (Chapter 5), Burma (Chapter 6) and Thailand (Chapter 7).

In sum, it can be argued that both traditional Theravāda Buddhism in general and the monkhood in particular were dragged—in the case of the majority of the monkhood probably rather reluctantly—into Buddhist modernity by the dialectics of essentialization and rationalization on the one hand, and the onset of nationalism and chauvinism in response to colonialism on the other. Like basically all transitions to modernity, this protracted process was far from smooth in the three Theravāda nations that themselves as a whole underwent a transition from traditional societies to modern ones, and, in the case of Burma and Sri Lanka, from colonies to independent states. Seneviratne leaves no doubt about the importance of this observation:

> As a rule, in new nations emerging from colonial rule, religious moderniza-
> tion was allied with nationalist resurgence. Far from being the cradle of a
> systematic rationality that embraced all institutions, religious modernity in
> these and similar cases became an ideological force that, in the extreme, as
> in some instances of Islamic resurgence, took fundamentalist and fanatical
> forms. Scripturalism, which could have under favourable circumstances
> channelled the society in the direction of rationalization and civility, here
> opened the path to the fetishization of religion, making it part of the arsenal
> of hegemonization. (Seneviratne 1999, 15)

Again, not all monks were interested in participating in this-worldly activities—many actually took issue with those who are too deeply immersed in such affairs to the detriment of meditation as the path to salvation. The leading and most revered monks of the Thai forest monk tradition, for example, led protracted battles against the new and 'modern' Thai state in the late nineteenth and the early twentieth centuries in order to be left alone and not to be put under a new, strict Sangha hierarchy on the one hand, and not to be instrumentalized as convenient tools for nation-building on the other. Other monks, however, thought nothing of parlaying their charisma and their already existing soft power over numerous lay followers, oftentimes situated in areas not yet under the firm control of the fledgling new (post-colonial) modern state, into lucrative positions in the higher ranks of the now increasingly streamlined clergy. And, once in powerful positions, they also thought nothing of using their new hard power bequeathed to them by the state, for example, to censor or even forcibly disrobe recalcitrant monks who refused to acknowledge their authority, or as a weapon against various 'others,' as discussed above.

Who exactly these 'others' were depends on the state in question, but I will come to that in some detail in the respective chapters on Sri Lanka, Burma, and Thailand. But it shows that 'political monks' come in different flavours, as Suksamran (1982, 54) points out: "first, those that espouse a cause that demands political action, such as campaigning for the under-privileged, Buddhism, or nationalism and, second, those that undertake political action in response to what they conceive of as threats to their personal status, privilege and position." Of course, as he adds, it is at times difficult to clearly define who belongs to which category, in my opinion especially when it comes to nationalist monks, since their actions, ostenta-tiously undertaken to protect Buddhism from a threat, are also geared towards protecting their own role within society—hence, both categories seem to fuse here. By and large, however, it is the first category of monks, those to call for action, which I shall focus on, not those of the established hierarchy only interested in protecting their position at the levers of monastic power against any challengers.

## Conclusion: The Limits of 'World-Renouncing'

To conclude this chapter, it should by now be clear that, like any other religion, Theravāda Buddhism as an ostentatiously world-renouncing reli-gion is not exempt from this-worldly issues. This implies that 'world-renouncing' might not necessarily be the best course of action when it comes to dealing with the essentially socio-political implications of current developments affecting the societies the monks preside over. According to the extremist monk Ashin Wirathu in Myanmar, now is not the time for quiet meditation—now is the time for firm action. On the basis of a self-understanding as political activists and political entrepreneurs, many monks—again, by far not all of them—see themselves called upon to take a stance against developments they deem to be detrimental to society at large. How they do that, and in how far they can be said to be successful, depends on the country in question, and on the respective relationship between monkhood and politics in general, and between religion and vio-lence in particular. In the following chapter, I shall explore these issues further.

## REFERENCES

Acharya, Amitav, and Barry Buzan. 2010. Conclusion: On the Possibility of a Non-Western International Relations Theory. In *Non-Western International Relations Theory. Perspectives on and Beyond Asia*, ed. Amitav Acharya and Barry Buzan, 221–238. London/New York: Routledge.

Allen, Charles. 2013. *Ashoka: The Search for India's Lost Emperor*. Paperback ed. London: Abacus.

Almond, Gabriel A., R. Scott Appleby, and Emmanuel Sivan. 2003. *Strong Religion: The Rise of Fundamentalisms Around the World*. Chicago/London: University of Chicago Press.

Barnett, Michael. 2011. Another Great Awakening? International Relations Theory and Religion. In *Religion and International Relations Theory*, ed. Jack Snyder, 91–114. New York/Chichester: Columbia University Press.

BBC. 2015. Bangladesh Blogger Niloy Neel Hacked to Death in Dhaka. *BBC News Asia*, August 7. http://www.bbc.co.uk/news/world-asia-33819032

Bealey, Frank. 1999. *The Blackwell Dictionary of Political Science*. Oxford: Blackwell.

Bechert, Heinz. 1995. *When Did the Buddha Live? The Controversy on the Dating of the Historical Buddha*. Delhi: Sri Satguru Publications.

Berger, Peter L. 1968. A Bleak Outlook Is Seen for Religion. *New York Times*, February 25.

———. 1999. The Desecularization of the World: An Overview. In *The Desecularization of the World: Resurgent Religion and World Politics*, ed. Peter Berger, 1–18. Washington, DC: Eerdmans/Ethics and Public Policy Center.

Bob, Yonah Jeremy. 2016. Life Sentence for Jerusalem Pride Parade Stabber Who Killed Teen Girl. *Jerusalem Post*, June 26. http://www.jpost.com/Israel-News/Life-sentence-for-Jerusalem-pride-parade-stabber-who-killed-teen-girl-457749

Carrithers, Michael B. 2007. They Will Be Lords Upon the Island: Buddhism in Sri Lanka. In *The World of Buddhism: Buddhist Monks and Nuns in Society and Culture*, ed. Heinz Bechert and Richard F. Gombrich, 133–146. Reprint, London: Thames & Hudson.

Catholic Herald. 2016. Fr Hamel Was Martyred 'in odium fidei', Says Archbishop Fischer. *Catholic Herald*, July 27. http://www.catholicherald.co.uk/news/2016/07/27/fr-hamel-was-martyred-in-odium-fidei-says-archbishop-fisher/

Clarkprosecutor.org. Undated. *Paul Jennings Hill*. http://www.clarkprosecutor.org/html/death/US/hill873.htm

Coningham, R.A.E., et al. 2013. The Earliest Buddhist Shrine: Excavating the Birthplace of the Buddha, Lumbini (Nepal). *Antiquity* 87: 1104–1123.

Durkheim, Emile. 1995. *The Elementary Forms of Religious Life. Translated and with an Introduction by Karen E. Fields.* New York: The Free Press.

Escobar, Pepe. 2018. Will the Putin-Xi Era Supersede the Western Liberal (Dis) order? *Asia Times Online*, March 25. http://www.atimes.com/article/will-putin-xi-era-supersede-western-liberal-disorder/

Galtung, Johan. 1969. Violence, Peace, and Peace Research. *Journal of Peace Research* 6 (3): 167–191.

Gombrich, Richard F. 1992. Dating the Buddha: A Red Herring Revealed. In *The Dating of the Historical Buddha/Die Datierung des Historischen Buddha, Part 2*, ed. Heinz Bechert, 237–262. Göttingen: Vandenhoeck & Ruprecht.

———. 2006. *Theravāda Buddhism: A Social History from Ancient Benares to Modern Colombo.* 2nd ed. Abingdon/New York: Routledge.

———. 2008. Einleitung: Der Buddhismus als Weltreligion. In *Der Buddhismus. Geschichte und Gegenwart*, ed. Heinz Bechert and Richard F. Gombrich, 3rd ed., 15–32. München: Verlag C. H. Beck.

Griswold, Eliza. 2015. Is This the End of Christianity in the Middle East? *The New York Times Magazine*, July 22. www.nytimes.com/2015/07/26/magazine/is-this-the-end-of-christianity-in-the-middle-east.html?_r=3

Higgs, Roberts. 2005. How Many Divisions Does the Pope Have? *The Independent Institute Newsroom*, April 11. http://www.independent.org/newsroom/article.asp?id=1492

Hill, Paul. 2003. *Mix My Blood with the Blood of the Unborn* (unedited version). August. http://www.armyofgod.com/PaulHillMixMyBloodPDF.html

Hoffman, Bruce. 1997. The Confluence of International and Domestic Trends of Terrorism. *Terrorism and Political Violence* 9 (2): 1–15.

Huntington, Samuel P. 1993. The Clash of Civilizations? *Foreign Affairs* 72 (3): 22–49.

———. 1996. *The Clash of Civilizations and the Remaking of World Order.* New York: Simon & Schuster.

Ibrahim, Azeem. 2018. *The Rohingyas. Inside Myanmar's Genocide.* London: Hurst & Company.

International Crisis Group. 2014. *Myanmar: The Politics of Rakhine State.* Asia Report No. 261, October 22, http://www.crisisgroup.org/~/media/Files/asia/south-east-asia/burma-myanmar/261-myanmar-the-politics-of-rakhine-state.pdf

Johnson, Todd M., and Brian J. Grim. 2013. *The World's Religions in Figures: An Introduction to International Religious Demography.* Hoboken: Wiley-Blackwell.

Juergensmeyer, Mark. 2003. *Terror in the Mind of God. The Global Rise of Religious Violence.* 3rd ed. Berkeley/Los Angeles/London: University of California Press.

Juergensmeyer, Mark, and Mona Kanwal Sheikh. 2013. A Sociotheological Approach to Understanding Religious Violence. In *Oxford Handbook of Religion and Violence*, ed. Mark Juergensmeyer, Margo Kitts, and Michael Jerryson, 620–643. Oxford: Oxford University Press.

Kitiarsa, Pattana. 2012. *Mediums, Monks, and Amulets. Thai Popular Buddhism Today*. Chiang Mai: Silkworm Books.

Landesamt fuer Verfassungsschutz Baden-Wuerttemberg/Germany. 2006. *Rechtsextremismus*. Stuttgart, March.

Lehr, Peter. 2016. Holy Wars Along the Maritime Silk Road: Extremist Islamism, Hinduism, and Buddhism. In *ASEAN Looks West: ASEAN and the Gulf Region*, ed. Wilfried A. Herrmann and Peter Lehr, 115–140. Bangkok: White Lotus Press.

Marty, Martin E. (with Jonathan Moore). 2000. *Politics, Religion and the Common Good. Advancing a Distinctly American Conversation About Religion's Role in Our Shared Life*. San Francisco: Jossey-Bass Inc.

McMahan, David L. 2012. Buddhist Modernism. In *Buddhism in the Modern World*, ed. David L. McMahan, 159–176. Oxon: Routledge.

McTernan, Oliver. 2003. *Violence in God's Name: Religion in an Age of Conflict*. Maryknoll/London: Orbis Books.

Nietzsche, Friedrich. 2006 (orig. 1882). *The Gay Science*. In *The Nietzsche Reader*, ed. Keith A. Pearson and Duncan Large, 207–237. Malden/Oxford/Carlton: Blackwell

Nye, Joseph S., Jr. 2004. *Soft Power: The Means to Success in World Politics*. New York: Perseus Books.

Qutb, Sayyid. 2003. *Milestones*. Chicago: Kazi Publications.

Rubenstein, Richard. 2001. The Temple Mount and My Grandmother's Paper Bag. In *Jewish-Muslim Encounters: History, Philosophy, and Culture*, ed. Charles Selengut, 141–164. St Paul: Paragon.

Sedgwick, Mark. 2015. Jihadism: Narrow and Wide: The Dangers of Loose Use of an Important Term. *Perspectives on Terrorism* 9 (2): 34–41. http://www.terrorismanalysts.com/pt/index.php/pot/article/view/417.

Selengut, Charles. 2003. *Sacred Fury. Understanding Religious Violence*. Walnut Creek et al.: Altamira Press.

Seneviratne, H.L. 1999. *The Work of Kings. The New Buddhism in Sri Lanka*. Chicago/London: University of Chicago Press.

Shah, Timothy S., and Daniel Philpott. 2011. The Fall and Rise of Religion in International Relations. In *Religion and International Relations Theory*, ed. Jack Snyder, 24–59. New York/Chichester: Columbia University Press.

Snyder, Jack. 2011. Introduction. In *Religion and International Relations Theory*, ed. Jack Snyder, 1–23. New York: Columbia University Press.

Spiegel Online. 2016. Papst über Terrorismus: 'Nicht richtig, den Islam mit Gewalt gleichzusetzen'. *Spiegel Online*, August 1. http://www.spiegel.de/panorama/papst-franziskus-islam-und-gewalt-nicht-gleichsetzen-a-1105568.html

Strong, John S. 2015. *Buddhisms: An Introduction*. London: Oneworld Publications.

Suksamran, Somboon. 1982. *Buddhism and Politics in Thailand.* Singapore: Institute for Southeast Asian Studies.

Tadjbakhsh, Shahrbanou. 2010. International Relations Theory and the Islamic Worldview. In *Non-Western International Relations Theory. Perspectives on and Beyond Asia*, ed. Amitav Acharya and Barry Buzan, 174–196. London/New York: Routledge.

Taylor, Alan. 2001. *American Colonies: The Settling of North America.* New York: Penguin Press.

Toft, Monica Duffy, Daniel Philpott, and Timothy S. Shah. 2011. *God's Century. Resurgent Religion and Global Politics.* New York/London: W. W. Norton & Company.

Tylor, Edward B. 1871. *Primitive Culture. Researches into the Development of Mythology, Philosophy, Religion, Art, and Custom.* Vol. 1. London: John Murray.

Weber, Max. 1967. *The Religion of India: The Sociology of Hinduism and Buddhism.* Trans. and ed. Hans H. Gerth and Don Martindale. New York/London: The Free Press/Collier-Macmillan.

Wilkinson, Paul. 2001. *Terrorism Versus Democracy: The Liberal State Response.* 1st ed. London: Frank Cass.

Williams, Joe. 2015. Victim of Jerusalem Pride Attack Dies of Injuries. *Pink News,* August 2. https://www.pinknews.co.uk/2015/08/02/victim-of-jerusalem-pride-attack-dies-of-injuries/

# The Age of Suffering: Buddhist Discourses on Non-violence in Theory and Practice

Now that we have linked religion in general and Theravāda Buddhism in particular to both politics and politically motivated violence in rather abstract, terms, it is time for an in-depth exploration of Theravāda Buddhist discourses on violence in theory and in practice. In order to do so, I will start by explaining the central tenets of Buddhism as found in the Tipitaka,[1] to focus on the doctrine of ahimsa, which, at least in theory, should act as a powerful barrier against acts of violence committed by Buddhists. However, as in any belief system and doctrine or ideology, there are exceptions as well as ambiguities. To begin with, and as Tikhonov (2013, 7) reminds us, even "the historical Buddha, realistically enough, never tried preaching non-violence to the kings [...] since war was understood as a part of the king's *dharma*." Rather, the consensus seems to be that while expansionist warfare is prohibited within Theravāda Buddhism, armed defence is deemed to be permissible under certain conditions, and even as

---

[1] The Tipitaka (lit. 'three baskets') contains the Pali canon consisting of the Sutta Pitaka (the 'basket of discourse' with more than 10,000 teachings of the Buddha), the Vinaya Pitaka (the 'basket of discipline' that mainly deals with the monastic rules), and the Abidhamma Pitaka (the 'basket of higher doctrine' with analyses of the Buddha's teachings).

© The Author(s) 2019
P. Lehr, *Militant Buddhism,*
https://doi.org/10.1007/978-3-030-03517-4_3

unavoidable in this current age of suffering (dukkha).[2] One such condition for defensive wars as Buddhist equivalents of 'just wars' would be the
impression that Buddhism itself is under siege by a hostile non-Buddhist
enemy—an impression shared by the Sanghas in Sri Lanka, Burma, and
Thailand.

The logical next step is a discussion of Theravāda Buddhist violence in
practice, focusing both on the micro level (attitude to sporadic violence
committed by individuals) and on the macro level (attitude to organized
violence committed by states in the shape of wars). As regards the former
(micro level), the role of soldiers in Buddhist theory and practice needs to
be scrutinized. I will show that soldiers are not looked upon as outsiders
who should be shunned, but that they rather occupy a respected place
within Buddhist society—however, not necessarily during the lifetimes of
the Buddha himself. As per the original monastic rules (vinaya) as devised
in the times of, and by, the Buddha, soldiers were prohibited to become
monks, while monks were not allowed to preach to soldiers (Tikhonov
2013, 7). Discussing the intentions behind these rules and how they have
been reinterpreted over the centuries and in different regional contexts is
of eminent importance, for example, in the light of the recent phenomenon of 'soldier monks' (*thahān phra*) in the Deep South of Thailand. With
regard to the latter (macro level), the chapter will refer to endemic warfare
between Buddhist kingdoms over the centuries—for example, between
various Burmese and Siamese (Thai) Buddhist empires or between
Buddhist and Hindu kingdoms of Ceylon/Sri Lanka—and the justifications for these wars offered by the respective Sanghas—justifications that
may well amount to a Theravāda version of 'Just War' theories.

The micro-level to macro-level structure of the following debate will be
further broken down as far as possible into (a) the lifetimes of the Buddha,
(b) scriptural Theravāda Buddhism from the times of Ashoka until the
birth of modernist or reformist Buddhism, and, finally (c) modernist/
reformist Buddhism from the late nineteenth century onwards. The reason behind this further categorization that loosely follows Satha-Anand's
'Three Moments in Buddhist History' (Satha-Anand 2014, 175) is that
the perspective on violence and non-violence changed over time by sheer
necessity: during the lifetimes of the Buddha, the Sangha had to function
in an environment still largely defined by Brahmanism, while from the

---

[2] So the opinion of a Buddhist monk interviewed by Juergensmeyer 2003, 114.

times of Emperor Ashoka Maurya onwards, the Sangha operated in a Buddhist realm, usually being used by the kings to shore up the legitimacy of their rule. After the demise of the traditional state (minus the Thai one) during the nineteenth century, the Sangha found itself again in a potentially hostile environment, and in a rather unsettled, chaotic one at that. These changes also required different stances to violence including organized violence—either in the shape of (civil) wars of uprisings against colonial governments or certain ethnic groups associated with such governments.

I shall conclude this chapter with a reflection on absolute values and prima facie duties to argue that Theravāda Buddhism contains elements of a 'Just War' or 'Righteous War' (*dharma yudha*) theory, arrived at via an exegesis and reinterpretation of canonical texts. Again, just as in the discussion of ahimsa, the aim of this discourse is to offer a more nuanced view on the relationship between Theravāda Buddhism and violence, going beyond the one that is usually held in the West where Buddhism in general is usually seen as "a religion of radical world-rejection" (Keyes 2007, 145) with a strong emphasis on meditative contemplation and introspection. Hence, helping the reader to acquire a better understanding of Buddhist discourses on violence is a necessary first step in assessing militant Theravāda Buddhism as of today: as already mentioned, it is not all about quiet meditation and chanting, unfortunately.

## BASICS: THE DIALECTICS OF NON-VIOLENCE AND VIOLENCE

Although this is not a book about Theravāda Buddhism as such but about Theravāda Buddhist violence[3] and militancy, it is still necessary to at least briefly recapitulate the basics of the Buddha's dhamma in order to discuss discourses on violence in theory and practice for the benefit of those readers who are not familiar with them. Basically, the core of the Buddha's teaching consists of the Four Noble Truths and the Noble Eightfold Path. In a nutshell, and as usually rendered, life means suffering (First Noble Truth), suffering comes from attachment (Second Noble Truth), suffering can be stopped when the attachment is stopped (Third Noble Truth),

---

[3] The Vinaya rules make a distinction between intentional and unintentional acts of violence or killing. In the following, I will only discuss intentional violence or killing since unintentional acts are not relevant within my context.

and the Noble Eightfold Path shows how to achieve this (Fourth Noble Truth). If one takes a closer look at the concepts used, and the different possible translations of them, then these somewhat bland, pessimistic, and bleak statements start to make more sense. First of all, for the First Noble Truth, the Pali term *dukkha* has been used by the Buddha. Dukkha can be translated in many ways, especially in a way that leads us from a narrow understanding of suffering as purely physical pain. After all, as we know, life is not always painful, but it can be pleasant as well. The point is that the pleasure is impermanent and does not last, making way for disappointment and discontent. Hence, I would prefer to translate dukkha as 'incapable of satisfying,' which then gives the First Noble truth the broader meaning of 'life is unsatisfactory.'[4] The Second Noble Truth illuminates the origins of this suffering, explaining that it comes from being attached to desire, or clinging to/craving something or somebody. As Ajahn Sumedho elaborates, there are three kinds of desire: *kama tanha* or the craving for sense pleasures (for example, eating, drinking, sexual pleasures), *bhava tanha* or the desire to become something other than what one is at the moment (for example, getting a better job, becoming a better meditator, becoming a monk, getting enlightened), and *vibhava tanha,* that is the desire to get rid of something (for example, getting rid of being jealous, fearful, angry, or of suffering altogether) (Sumedho n.d., 28–29). Many Buddhist proverbs revolve around this, always advising that it is better to let go to be free from such cravings which, in the end, are simply delusions.

This brings us to the Third Noble Truth of the cessation (or *niroda*) of suffering. In the words of Ajahn Sumedho (n.d., 36), "[the] whole aim of the Buddhist teaching is to develop the reflective mind in order to let go of delusions" as only this can bring an end to suffering, to the production of kamma, and, as a result, to a never-ending cycle of rebirth and re-death. The question of how to learn to let go is answered by the Fourth Noble Truth, which states that the Noble Eightfold Path (see Sumedho n.d., 48–69) of right view, right intention, right speech, right action, right livelihood, right effort, right mindfulness, and right concentration will lead to a cessation of suffering, thus breaking the cycle of rebirth and re-death.

---

[4] Some eminent scholars such as Strong (2015, 137) translate *dukkha* as 'stress,' which means life is stressful. This also is a good way to steer clear from focusing on purely physical experiences as well.

The first two steps of this sequential path (right view, right intention) belong to the wisdom (*pañña*) group, the next three (right speech, right action, right livelihood) to the group of moral virtues (*sīla*), and the final three (right effort, right mindfulness, right concentration) to the meditation (*samadhi*) group. In the Theravāda tradition, the goal of this eightfold path is to achieve the status of an arahant (Pali, Sanskrit: *arhat*), which can be translated as 'perfected person' or 'one who is worthy,' thus having attained nibbāna, however, without having necessarily gained full Buddhahood. This sets the Theravāda tradition apart from the Mahāyāna tradition, which posits that somebody who follows the path to its end does indeed achieve full and perfect Buddhahood. From a doctrinal perspective, the difference is not trifling: while a full Buddha can help others to achieve nibbāna, an arahant cannot (Harvey 2000, 123–125). But since this would lead us into a complicated discussion of whether it is possible at all for one being a saviour for others (possible in Mahāyāna, rather not possible in Theravāda), I shall leave that issue open: it is not relevant in our context.

More important in this context is the concept of *karma* (Sanskrit) or *kamma* (Pali), which can be translated as 'action,' 'deed,' 'work,' or (executed) 'intent,' and the Buddha's reconceptualization of it. Gombrich opines that this was done purposely as a response to Brahmanism that linked one's duties, and by extension one's karma, to the social strata one was born into (Gombrich 2006, 67–73). A good example for this Brahmanic cosmic point of view can be found in the famous Bhagavad Gita[5] (lit. 'Song of the Lord'), an epos of 700 verses that was probably composed between the fifth to second century BCE—although in Hindu traditions, it is deemed to be far older, with the date of origin assumed to be in the fourth to third millennium BCE. If we accept the later date, that is fifth century BCE, then the Bhagavad Gita would have been written in the lifetime of the Buddha himself. This does not necessarily imply that he knew the epos, but he was definitely familiar with the song's core arguments. One of them dealt with one's duty, which depends on one's birth, given the Brahmanic idea of the four varnas or colours (castes), which are those of the priests (Brahmans); warriors (Kshatriyas); peasants, artisans and (later) merchants (Vaisyas); and labourers (Shudras). Every caste has its own duties and responsibilities that need to be attended to, with the

---

[5] See, for example, Mascaró 2003 or Easwaran 2007.

warriors' main duty obviously to fight—not as an aim for itself but to establish or to defend the right order (*dharma*) by fighting a righteous war (*dharma yudha*).

This is illustrated by a dialogue between Pandava prince Arjuna and his advisor and charioteer Lord Krishna (one of the major deities of Hinduism), which takes place on the eve of the climactic battle between the Pandavas and the Kauravas. In the 46 verses of the Prathama Adhyaya (usually translated as 'The Distress of Arjuna'), Arjuna is worried by the prospect of having to kill relatives and friends in the battle, and hence asks Lord Krishna for advice. For Krishna, an incarnation of Vishnu, the answer is clear: Arjuna is a warrior, and thus fight he must, as this is his duty. If he does not fulfil his duty as good as he can, then he will never attain liberation from the cycles of rebirth. In Brahmanic terms, this liberation is known as moksha. It is equivalent to the Buddhist concept of nibbāna.[6] In the 43 verses of the Karma Yoga (usually translated as 'Virtue in Actions'), Krishna then teaches Arjuna that it is only the correct performance of his duties that matters, not their results. The Bhagavad Gita is not the only source that sees the concept of karma linked to the importance of proper action in and for itself without a care for possible consequences: as Gombrich explains, Pūrana Kassapa (Kāśyapa), a contemporary of the Buddha, taught exactly the same, asserting that whether one would kill everyone in sight or only carry out acts of charity would not matter at all for one's fate since there was no moral causality (Gombrich 2006, 68).

Obviously, in the Brahmanic view, one's dharma and karma depended on the social group one was born into, as well as on one's actions no matter what results came from them. Right actions also included carrying out the proper rituals for one's social group both individually in one's household and communally in one's temple since these rituals were meant to be able to appease the gods and to thus improve one's karma. With regard to the Buddhist version of karma, Gombrich argues as follows:

> [The] most important step the Buddha took was to turn the doctrine of *karman* on its head. He ethicized it completely, made morality intrinsic, and so denied all soteriological value to ritual and all ultimate value to social distinctions. In place of a highly particularistic view of duty he propounded

[6] It is actually a bit more complicated than that, depending on the school in question. See Loy 1982.

a simple and universal ethical dualism of right and wrong. He put it succinctly: 'It is the intention that I call *kamma*.' (Gombrich 2006, 68)

I should probably hasten to add that without suitable action, intention
remains just that: a mind game only without consequences. This potential
problem, however, is soundly resolved in the Noble Eightfold Path. As
mentioned above, right view about karma and rebirth and right resolve or,
in our context, right intention need to be followed up with right speech
and right action—again, interpreted as refraining from killing, stealing, or
sexual misconduct. Hence, we could argue that this universal ethical dualism of right and wrong is based on right action as a result and consequence
of right intention. And this, in my opinion, is exactly the point where
some moral ambiguity creeps in—but to defend and explain this, some
further definitional work is required, starting with yet another look at
some relevant parts of the Noble Eightfold Path.

As already noted, 'right action' requires a Buddhist to refrain from killing, stealing, and sexual misconduct: "And what is right action with effluents, siding with merit, resulting in acquisitions? Abstaining from killing,
from taking what is not given, and from illicit sex" (translated by Thanissaro
Bhikkhu 2008). These particular 'right actions' are the first three of the
so-called *pañca sikkhāpada* or five precepts that form the basics of Buddhist
ethics for lay followers, the remaining two being refraining from incorrect
speech (lying) and from intoxicating drinks and drugs since they lead to
carelessness (Bullit 2005). Furthermore, 'right livelihood' requires one
from abstaining from professions that are deemed to be wrong: "And
what is the right livelihood that is noble, without effluents, transcendent,
a factor of the path? The abstaining, desisting, abstinence, avoidance of
wrong livelihood in one developing the noble path whose mind is noble,
whose mind is without effluents, who is fully possessed of the noble path"
(translated by Thanissaro Bhikkhu 2008). As Harvey emphasizes citing
the Anguttāra Nikāya or 'Numerical Discourses' (v. 177), 'right livelihood' also requires one to refrain from pursuing such livelihoods that
could cause others to suffer—amongst those 'wrong' livelihood being
"trade in arms" (Harvey 2000, 249). And if the intrinsic morality and
complete ethicality of the Buddha's teachings are not yet clear enough,
then one could also look at the four Buddhist virtues or 'Divine Abodes'
(*Brahmavihāra*) which I already mentioned: *mettā* (meaning loving kindness), *karuna* (compassion), *mudita* (appreciative joy or sympathetic joy),
and *uppekha* (equanimity). In this context, *mettā* or loving kindness usu-

ally is defined as "the wish that all sentient beings, without any exceptions, be happy," while *karuna* or compassion is defined as "the wish for all sentient beings to be free from suffering" (both quotes from Buddha Dharma Education Association/Buddhanet 2008). All of this quite naturally begs the following question: how can violence, be it individual in the shape of battery, manslaughter, or murder or organized in the shape of war, be justified within Theravāda Buddhism as a notionally non-violent religion? After all, the *Dhammapada*, as one of the best-known collection of the Buddha's sayings, in a couple of verses in its *Dandavagga* (Violence) section, explicitly exhorts the readers to refrain from violence and from killing:

> All tremble at violence; all fear death. Putting oneself in the place of another, one should not kill nor cause another to kill. All tremble at violence; life is dear to all. Putting oneself in the place of another, one should not kill nor cause another to kill. (Dandavagga, Dhammapada verses 129 and 130, as translated by Buddharakkhita 1996)

Next, the Dandavagga describes the consequences of the resort to violence for one's own life:

> One who, while himself seeking happiness, oppresses with violence other beings who also desire happiness, will not attain happiness hereafter. One who, while himself seeking happiness, does not oppress with violence other beings who also desire happiness, will find happiness hereafter. (Dandavagga, Dhammapada verses 131 and 132, ibid.)

Again then, how can the use of violence, and even the act of killing, ever be justified within Theravāda Buddhism? To start with, this is probably a good time to add some other feature of Theravāda Buddhism: the rather strict institutional compartmentalization of traditional[7] ethics into one set for the lay followers and another one for the monks (Jackson 2003, 60). The former, *lokiya-dhamma* ('mundane' Dhamma), is geared towards those lay Buddhists who pursue this-worldly activities with all their imperfections, impurities, and temptations, thus unlikely to end the circle of rebirth and re-death. Since the aim is, simply put, to improve one's kamma

---

[7] This strict compartmentalization of traditional Theravāda Buddhism is far less pronounced in reformist and modernist interpretations, as we shall see.

(karma) via good and meritorious deeds, thus improving one's chance of a better 'next life,' Spiro calls this practice "kammatic Buddhism" (Spiro 1982, 12). The latter, *lokuttara-dhamma* ('supra-mundane' Dhamma), as the path of renunciation or world-renouncer, aims exactly at ending this circle and its related suffering by achieving *nibbāna* via meditation and the study of scripture, traditionally only deemed possible for monks who did not need to care for this-worldly affairs since they gained the necessities of life from their lay followers; Spiro calls this "nibbanic Buddhism" (Spiro 1982, 12).[8] The *Samaññaphala Sutta* as part of the *Dīgha Nikāya* (lit.: 'Long Discourses') illustrates this compartmentalization quite nicely:

> A householder or householder's son, hearing the Dhamma, gains conviction in the Tathagata [Pali, lit.: one who has thus gone' – a term that the Buddha used when referring to himself] and reflects: 'Household life is confining, a dusty path. The life gone forth is like the open air. It is not easy living at home to practice the holy life totally perfect, totally pure, like a polished shell. What if I were to shave off my hair and beard, put on the ochre robes, and go forth from the household life into homelessness?' [After having done so:] When he has thus gone forth, he lives a life restrained by the rules of the monastic code, seeing danger in the slightest faults. Consummate in his virtue, he guards the doors of his senses, is possessed of mindfulness and alertness, and is content. (Samaññaphala Sutta, as translated by Thanissaro Bhikkhu 1997a)

Implicit in this is the acceptance that a lay follower's (or 'householder's) life is by sheer necessity an imperfect one: as much as one might wish to follow the Eightfold Noble Path, the demands imposed by one's environment might well interfere—a realization that leads us straight back to the aforementioned question: can violence actually be avoided in this current age of suffering or *dukkha*? Even some monks (like the one quoted in Juergensmeyer 2003, 114) would actually answer this in the negative, for example, drawing on the *Sakkhapañha Sutta* (lit.: 'Sakkha's Questions') to support their view. In this sutta, the Buddha explains that even though men (as well as deities and demons) want to live "free from hostility, free from violence, free from rivalry, free from ill will, free from

---

[8] Spiro (1982, 12) also sees a third form of Buddhist practice: 'apotropaic Buddhism' as a non-soteriological variant focusing on the protection from danger, illness, demons, and so on. In the present context, however, this variant is not relevant to the discussion.

those who are hostile," they nevertheless live under these conditions due to what he calls "envy and stinginess" (both quotes from SakkhaPañha Sutta, as translated by Thanissaro Bhikkhu 1999b). The Buddha's explanation of violence, which was in any case endemic during his lifetime (Premasiri 2006, 80), clearly echoes the First and the Second Noble Truth: life is suffering, and suffering comes from attachment or craving. Harvey, one of the leading authorities on Buddhist ethics, eloquently sums this up as follows:

> The Buddhist path aims at a state of complete non-violence, based on insight and inner strength rooted in a calm mind. Yet those who are not yet perfect, living in a world in which others may seek to gain their way by violence, still have to face the dilemma of whether to respond with defensive violence. Pacifism may be the ideal, but in practice Buddhists have often used violence in self-defence or defence of their country – not to speak of sometimes going in for aggressive violence, like any other group of people. (Harvey 2000, 249–250)

The term 'Buddhists' Harvey uses in his insightful definition requires some deconstruction in order to better examine their relation to violence. Obviously, the term refers first to 'the people' as such who might use violence to achieve their temporal aims and objectives, and then to 'the country'—here, the Buddhist realm—that might need to be defended against foreign encroachment. The only element missing of the triad 'people, state and religion' that constitutes the Buddhist realm is the Sangha, that is, the monks either as a body or as individuals. In the following, I shall discuss Theravāda Buddhist perspectives on violence on the micro and macro levels as committed (a) by monks, (b) by the people in general, (c) by soldiers as a specialized subset of the people in general, and (d) by the state.

## PATHWAYS: MONKS, HOUSEHOLDERS, AND VIOLENCE

Starting with the monks as individuals who are, unlike the householders, firmly on the path of the renunciation and restrained by the monastic code, the Buddha's teachings are unequivocal and unambiguous: "He is not a true monk who harms another, nor a true renunciate who oppresses others" (Dhammapada 184, as translated by Buddharakkhita 1996)—this is what the Buddha says in the Ovādapātimokkha as the first set of rules for monks.[9] Hence, Harris is quite right to point out that "[no] compromises were made concerning violence when it came to the monk" (Harris 1994, 24). Harris draws on the *Kakacupama Sutta* ('The Simile of the Saw') that contains a key phrase regarding the monk's expected attitude in the face of violence or abuse, a key phrase repeated several times in this sutta, accompanied by different examples of abuse the monks could encounter:

> In any event, you should train yourselves: 'Our minds will be unaffected and we will say no evil words. We will remain to that person's welfare, with a mind of good will, and with no inner hate. We will keep pervading him with an awareness imbued with good will and, beginning with him, we will keep pervading the all-encompassing world with an awareness imbued with good will equal to the river Ganges – abundant, expansive, immeasurable, free from hostility, free from ill will.' That's how you should train yourselves. (Kakacupama Sutta, as translated by Thanissaro Bhikkhu 1997b)

Finally, the Buddha exhorted them to also remain calm and unperturbed in the face of physical violence:

> Monks, even if bandits were to carve you up savagely, limb by limb, with a two-handled saw, he among you who let his heart get angered even at that would not be doing my bidding. Even then you should train yourselves: 'Our minds will be unaffected and we will say no evil words.' (as quoted in ibid.)

Here, it is clear how he expected monks to react to abuse and violence meted out to them. When it comes to monks themselves committing the ultimate form of (individual) physical violence, intentional killing, there is no ambivalence. The code of monastic discipline (*Bhikkhu Pātimokkha*) for (male)[10] monks lists the intentional killing of a human being as one of the four 'Disrobing Offences' or *Pārājikas* ('Defeat,' lit. 'making the doer defeated').[11] As extreme violations of the monastic code, they will lead to

---

[9] Recitation of the Ovādapātimokkha is one of the central parts of the ceremonies surrounding the 'Great Festival of Offering' (*maha puja* in Pali, *Makha Bucha* in Thai), usually held on a day in February depending on the lunar calendar.

[10] There is also a code of monastic discipline for female monks, the *Bhikkhunī Pātimokkha*, but since in the Theravādin tradition, female monkhood is no longer recognized (nuns are not on the same level as monks), it is not relevant in the context of this research.

[11] The other Pārājika offences are sexual intercourse, theft, and claiming to have achieved a superior human state.

an automatic expulsion from the Sangha without the chance to "simply re-ordain after a period of grace" (Brahmavamso 1996). The rule reads as follows:

> Should any bhikkhu intentionally deprive a human being of life, or search for an assassin for him, or praise the advantages of death, or incite him to die (saying,): "My good man, what use is this evil, miserable life to you? Death would be better for you than life," or with such an idea in mind, such a purpose in mind, should in various ways praise the advantages of death or incite him to die, he also is defeated and no longer in affiliation. (Pārājika 3, Bhikkhu Pātimokkha, translated by Thanissaro Bhikkhu 2007)

Arguably, intentionally depriving a human being of life, or assassinating a human being, is a rare offence for monks, but they do occasionally happen. One rather well-known example I have already mentioned in the first chapter—that of Sinhalese monk Talduwe Somarama Thero who shot and killed the then Sri Lankan Prime Minister Solomon Bandaranaike in the latter's residence on 26 September 1959, ostentatiously for 'country, race and religion.' What is of importance in the present context is that Somarama appeared at court dressed not in the saffron monk robes but in the white of a lay follower, and later, a couple of weeks before his execution, he even converted to Anglicanism (Jeyaraj 2014), allegedly in order to not besmirch Buddhism.

If a monk deprives any other (non-human) living being of its life, this is seen as a lesser offence that does not result in being automatically dispelled once and for all from the Sangha, but still one that requires expiation: "Should any bhikkhu intentionally deprive an animal of life, this is to be confessed" (Pācittiya 61, Bhikkhu Pātimokkha, translated by Thanissaro Bhikkhu 2007). The same is the case for "making use of water containing living [sic]" (Pācittya 62, ibid.) or "the damaging of a living plant" (Pācittiya 11, ibid.). Physical violence between monks is also covered and deemed to be an offence in need of confession: "Should any bhikkhu, angered and displeased, give a blow to (another) bhikkhu, it is to be confessed" (Pācittiya 74, ibid.), and "[should] any bhikkhu, angered and displeased, raise the palm of his hand against (another) bhikkhu, it is to be confessed" (Pācittiya 75, ibid.). That such acts of violence occasionally occurred even in the lifetime of the Buddha is reflected in the first two Dandavagga verses I quoted above: they are basically the Buddha's reaction to a violent fight between two groups of monks triggered by a dispute over the ownership of a temple. Deegalle points out that the sequence 'tremble at violence' used in most translations should actually better be translated as 'tremble at the rod' (Deegalle 2006, 5–6)—a feeling shared by quite a few inattentive or unruly novices even nowadays.[12]

Be that as it may, contrary to the cases of the people in general, the soldiers as a specialized subset of them and the state as such, these monastic rules pertaining to violence committed by the monks themselves have not been diluted over the centuries by reinterpretation or adaptation to changing circumstances. If we recall that Max Weber saw Theravāda Buddhism as a 'soteriology' rather than a religion (Weber 1967, 216), and that Gombrich categorized it as 'religious individualism' (Gombrich 2006, 73–80), this makes eminent sense: the Buddha, not overly concerned with the world at large, showed a path towards nibbāna, and laid out clear rules for those who chose to walk along that path; these rules were, and still are, independent from any specific socio-political or socio-cultural backdrop. However, as we shall see, the Buddha's exhortation to say no evil words and to be imbued of good will at all times has occasionally fallen by the wayside—otherwise, there would be no need for a study on how militant and ultra-nationalist monks of our times justify and condone acts of violence committed by others in defence of Buddhism. We will encounter some examples of that later in the chapter, and then again in the chapters on Sri Lanka, Burma, and Thailand.

The people as such—defined as all those who do not belong to the Sangha either as monks, novices, or nuns and are also not part of the state administration—are the easiest to examine with respect to their relation to violence. Of course, there are the Noble Eightfold Path's exhortations that one should refrain from acts of violence, such as killing, stealing, sexual misconduct, but this, like similar exhortations or commandments in other religions, is more or less what people should aspire to do—this is compulsory only for members of the Sangha who will be disrobed and dispelled for committing such offences. In Harvey's words:

---

[12] On 19 August 2018, a senior monk from a temple in Kanchanaburi was disrobed and charged with manslaughter after having beaten an unruly nine-year-old novice with a wooden stick so severely that the novice fell in a coma and later died in hospital. See, for example, Chongcharoen 2018.

Ordinary Buddhists may feel that they are not yet capable of the totally non-violent response, particularly as they are still attached to various things which they feel may sometimes need violence to defend. Of course they could give these up, by becoming a monk or nun, but they may not feel ready for this level of commitment. (Harvey 2000, 250)

Nevertheless, the commitment to *ahimsa*, a term best translated as 'non-harm' or 'non-injury' and not 'non-violence' as it is usually rendered (Jenkins 2011, 311; Jerryson 2018, 458), is something even Buddhist lay people should at least earnestly aspire to, and there are many suttas warning against taking lives or committing any other acts of violence against living beings. The *Cula-kammavibhanga Sutta*, for example, bluntly states:

[Some] woman or man is a killer of living beings, murderous, bloody-handed, given to blows and violence, merciless to living beings. Due to having performed and completed such kammas, [...] after death, he reappears in a state of deprivation, in an unhappy destination, in perdition, in hell. If [...] after death, instead of his reappearing in a state of deprivation, in an unhappy destination, in perdition, in hell, he comes to the human state, he is short-lived wherever he is reborn. This is the way that leads to a short life, that is to say, to be a killer of living beings, murderous, bloody-handed, given to blows and violence, merciless to living beings. (as translated by Nanamoli Thera 1994, v. 5)

Hence, Harris seems to state the obvious when she explains "[that] lay people should never initiate violence where there is harmony or use it against the innocent is very clear" (Harris 1994, 28). Then, however, Harris raises the question whether this implies that non-violence should consequently be seen as an absolute value within Buddhism. To shed some light on the importance of this question, she examines the various shades of grey that can creep in when it comes to the use of violence:

For instance, is a father, as head and protector of the family, justified in using violence against a person forcefully entering his house with the intention to kill? Has an elder sister the duty to protect a younger brother if he is attacked violently, by using similar violence? Has a group of citizens the right to kill a dictator if, by doing so, they might save the lives of oppressed minorities to whom the citizens feel a duty? Should the terrorist gun be challenged with similar methods? These are areas where absolutes seem to break down. (Harris 1994, 27–28)

The questions Harris asks would put the absolute morals of any religion or philosophy of any age to the test, with the one on terrorism of particular current interest against the backdrop of ISIS-related terror attacks in our cities, be they Paris, Brussels, Berlin, Manchester, London, Barcelona, Istanbul, Lahore, or Bangkok, Yangon, and Colombo for that matter. In the case of Theravāda Buddhism, Harris points out that there are at least guidelines about the consequences of violence—consequences in the shape of karmic (*khammic*) retribution that have to be taken into account whenever violence is used. Again, we can return to the Four Noble Truths and the Eightfold Noble Path as laid out by the Buddha: wrong action based on wrong intent simply perpetuates suffering, and the circle of rebirth and re-death, as described above. In the words of Harris:

> He or she has to be aware that there is a dynamism within hatred and violence when the causal chain has not had its nourishment removed. Such a person needs to evaluate motives in the knowledge that violent tendencies are rooted in the defilements of *lobha, dosa* and *moha,* and in the obsessions generated by *papanca*.[13] Yet that person might still judge that the risks are worth facing to prevent a greater evil. Whether the assassination of Hitler would have prevented numerous innocent deaths is still an open question. (Harris 1994, 28)

In order to shed further light on this question, Gethin examines the commentaries to the Tipitaka, the so-called *atthakatās,* that were put in writing at the same time as the Tipitaka itself; hence, his argumentation pertains to the Second Moment, not to the lifetime of the Buddha. Gethin explains that according to the commentaries, the seriousness of an act of killing depends on three factors: first, the size of the being that is killed (more relevant for animals, for example, a mouse compared to an elephant), second, the being's virtue (the more virtuous, the more serious the act of killing), and third, the intensity of the wish to kill together with the effort that had been made to carry out the killing (Gethin 2004, 172). He illustrates this by juxtaposing the murder of a 'sweet old lady' with the killing of a notorious criminal, and an imagined assassination of Hitler or

---

[13] Lobha, dosa, and moha (Pali terms) are known in Theravāda Buddhism as the 'three unwholesome roots.' Their meanings are as follows: lobha = attachment, (sexual) desire, greed, lust, sensuality; dosa = aversion, hate, moral corruption; moha = confusion, delusion, dullness, ignorance. Prapanca means 'conceptual proliferation.'

Stalin as compared to the actual assassinations of Mahatma Gandhi and Martin Luther King. Seen from this perspective, the questions asked by Harris above are far easier to answer since the *atthakatās* seem to add the element of proportionality as regards violence in general, and killing in particular. It could even be argued that under certain circumstances, acts of killing might even be seen as acts of compassion (*karuna*). This perspective however is not shared by all scholars of Theravāda Buddhism; Gethin himself strongly argues against it, concluding that from a doctrinal point of view, killing is always wrong in Theravāda Buddhism. He adds a telling warning regarding the 'virtue' aspect just mentioned: he sees an act of killing based on one's virtue as

> a more morally dangerous if not positively morally repugnant idea because it might be taken as allowing us to conclude that those whom we consider as morally degenerate are somehow morally less valuable, and so can be disposed of with impunity. (Gethin 2004, 173)

In a similar vein, Harris also comes to the conclusion that from a doctrinal point of view, Theravāda Buddhism sees the resort to *metta* or loving kindness in the face of violence as the superior path. But still she concedes that "[absolutes] of that kind cannot be found or perhaps should not be sought for in a teaching which spoke of the danger of claiming of a view, 'this alone is truth, all else is falsehood'" (Harris 1994, 28). Finally, Harvey (who also discusses Harris' arguments) states that "[if] violence is used, it is something that Buddhism may *understand* but not actually *approve of*" (Harvey 2000, 252).

## AMBIGUITIES: SOLDIERS, KINGS, AND VIOLENCE

With regard to soldiers as a specialized subset of the people in general, the use of violence is, by the very nature of their profession, part and parcel of their duty. This was well understood in Brahmanism and Hinduism, as I already explained: to fight is the duty of the warrior, and, by extension, the professional (or semi-professional, for the duration of a campaign) soldier. But, as just discussed, Theravāda Buddhism has a completely different understanding of the khammic aspects of carrying out this duty than that expressed in the Bhagavad Gita. Furthermore, we are probably safe to assume that if 'trade in arms' has been explicitly mentioned as 'wrong livelihood' (as mentioned above), then a professional 'use of arms' should be even more prohibited (Harvey 2000, 249, 253–254). Indeed, the Buddha made his own view on that matter very clear, as, for example, the *Yodhajiva Sutta* demonstrates. Yodhajiva, a headman of soldiers and professional warrior, approached the Buddha with a question: are warriors killed in battle reborn in heaven and in the company of divine beings (devas) who were also killed in battle? Subscribing to a Brahmanic view of the world as regards battle, the headman seemed to expect an answer in the positive. To his consternation, the Buddha refused to answer the question, telling the headman quite bluntly: "Enough, headman, put that aside. Don't ask me that." But after the headman insisted, repeating his question twice, the Buddha finally answered, obviously not mincing his words:

> Apparently, headman, I haven't been able to get past you by saying, 'Enough, headman, put that aside. Don't ask me that.' So I will simply answer you. When a warrior strives and excels himself in battle, his mind is already seized, debased, and misdirected by the thought: 'May these beings be struck down or slaughtered or annihilated or destroyed. May they not exist.' If others then strike him down and slay him [...], after death, he is reborn in the hell called the realm of those slain in battle. But if he holds such a view as this: 'When a warrior strives and exerts himself in battle, if others then strike him down and slay him [...], after death, he is reborn in the company of devas slain in battle,' that is his wrong view. Now, there are two destinations for a person with wrong view, I tell you: either hell or the animal womb. (Yodhajiva Sutta, as translated by Thanissaro Bhikkhu 1998)

The Buddha even went further than just condemning professional soldiers either to hell or to a rebirth as animals: he also did not allow active or former soldiers including deserters to become monks, nor did he allow his monks to watch military parades, visit soldiers, or stay in their camps more than three nights: all these were Pācittiya offences (Pācittiya 48–50, Bhikkhu Pātimokkha, translated by Thanissaro Bhikkhu 2007). As Tikhonov argues, by doing so, the Buddha intended to "effectively [detach] his community from the ubiquitous state violence – without ever trying to effectively contain it in practical terms" (Tikhonov 2013, 7). However, as Gombrich points out, there also were some distinctly this-worldly and 'realpolitikal' considerations behind the Buddha's attempts to detach his community from violence in general and soldiers in particular: he was explicitly warned by King Bimbisāra of Magadha, his earliest and most important benefactor, "that kings would not take kindly to seeing soldiers desert by joining the Sangha" (Gombrich 2006, 83). Obviously, the Buddha heeded this warning, which even in his lifetimes allowed some ambiguity to creep in, as I already suggested: although he had no qualms to condemn individual soldiers to hell or a rebirth as animals for their use of deadly violence as part of their duty, he did not censor kings quite as openly even though their incessant wars were largely responsible for the actions of the soldiers he condemned.

Arguably, the Buddha's unequivocal condemnation of soldiers for the violence they committed in their line of duty lost some of its sting during the Second Buddhist Moment, that is, from the times of Emperor Ashoka Maurya onwards when Buddhist realms emerged. From that moment, political realities required Buddhist kings to field armies in order to protect their kingdoms via defensive wars—or to wage offensive wars against neighbours, be they Buddhist or not. This also implies that most of the soldiers were Buddhists as well, and probably educated enough in the basics of Theravāda Buddhism to be aware that their duty clashed with the Buddhist version of the well-known 'Thou Shalt Not Kill' command. Hence, Yodhajiva's question reappeared in the now Buddhist socio-political context, probably putting at least some monks in a quandary: on the one hand, there was the Buddha's clear and unambiguous condemnation of soldiers to hell or a rebirth as animals, but on the other, there were periods in which warfare was endemic, and, by implication, not much of a choice for the monks' lay followers who were conscripted into their overlords' feudal levies whether they liked it or not. Summarily condemning them all to hell thus was not really an option, apart from the fact that challenging kings never was a good idea, not even for monks; as I shall discuss in the following chapter, various kings of Sri Lanka, Burma, and Siam/Thailand did indeed meddle in the affairs of their respective Sanghas, including purifying them and forcefully disrobing and dispelling, or, in a few cases, even executing those who did not toe the official line. Obviously, a more moderate stance was now the order of the day.

Interestingly, and by way of a (short) digression, a reinterpretation of the Buddha's words was made possible after the Buddhist canon was written down about three centuries after the Buddha's death. During the Buddha's lifetime, and also during several centuries after his death, the canon was basically an oral tradition; hence, it had to be memorized by the monks either in its entirety (only a few achieved that) or in parts. The Buddha himself was a strict literalist in that regard: he clearly stated in the *Mahāparinibbāna Sutta* (part of the *Dīgha Nikāya*) that if the monks would encounter a disputed statement, they would have to compare it with the *suttas* as his recorded words and with the rules laid down in the *vinaya* or 'book of discipline' with the patimokkha at its heart. If the disputed statement could not be found in either, it had to be discarded. After the canon had been written down and thus become a literary tradition, this purely literalist approach was by and large put aside in favour of a hermeneutic approach that also considered whether a disputed statement was in accordance with the doctrine and patterned after the Dhamma. As Jackson explains:

> The principle that scriptural interpretations should be patterned after the Dhamma amounts to a recognition that in literal tradition faithfulness to the Buddha's teaching no longer necessitates a strictly literal adherence to his actual words but may also be based upon views which follow the spirit of the Buddha's teachings. (Jackson 2003, 84)

Opting to follow the Buddha not necessarily in word but in spirit made certain concessions towards soldiers possible. Still, the starting point of their exegesis was the position that killing constituted wrong action based on wrong thinking and wrong intent, thus leading to wrong results in the shape of negative khamma and a rebirth in hell or as an animal as the logical consequences —just as the Buddha had said. This is where the Buddha left it, and, arguably, so did most of the monks of the following Sanghas. Some however went further, for example, by examining the intent behind individual acts of killing: was the intent negative, say, based on greed or lust? If so, then the perpetrator would face the consequences as lined out by the Buddha. Or was the intent a positive one, for example, protecting the lives of innocents by way of defending them with the sword? Or maybe protecting the Buddhist religion by destroying a non-Buddhist opponent or invader? In such cases, the act of killing still produced negative khamma; however, this could be mitigated by the positive khamma produced by protecting innocents or the religion as such. Here, the above-mentioned *atthakatās* or comments, especially the ones regarding the virtue of those being killed and the intensity of the act of killing itself, can easily be applied in order to not necessarily justify but at least relativize certain acts of violence via some inspired moral reasoning or casuistry, with all the negative connotations of that term.

In the current times of the Third Buddhist Moment, that is of modern nation states featuring mass conscript armies, Yodhajiva's question still is prominent on the mind of Buddhist soldiers, and monks still face the problem of finding a solution that on the one hand does not fall foul of the Buddha's own words but on the other offers the (not always willing) conscripts some consolation. As Gombrich puts it (albeit in the entirely different context of the consecration of a Buddhist image in Sri Lanka), "some accommodation of the doctrinally ideal to the empirically convenient" (Gombrich 1966, 28) has to be found. Again, one aspect of the Buddha's stance seems to be ignored in order to achieve this: in Sri Lanka, Burma, and Thailand, monks do actually preach to armed soldiers, also visiting them in their camps—in Sri Lanka, even to the point of inducting monks into the armed forces as chaplains, carrying the rank of a captain/army (Bartholomeusz 2002, xix). Furthermore, former soldiers now may ordain as monks, and, allegedly, in the Deep South of Thailand, even serving soldiers have been reported to temporarily ordain as monks while keeping their arms; however, since this is a rather complicated issue with plenty of qualifiers such as 'allegedly,' I shall examine it later. In any case, the problem posed to the monks of the modern Theravāda states can be exemplified by a comment of Venerable Anandavamsa, a Sinhalese monk interviewed by Daniel Kent in 2005:

> We wouldn't say, 'May you have strength. May you defeat the enemy!' We can't pray for that! If monks were to pray for that there, they would face problems with the rules of monastic discipline. A monk never can tell someone to kill. In the same way, they can't say that killing is good... That is why monks don't have any blessing for killing. We say: 'May soldiers be protected! May they be free from sickness and suffering! May they live lives without accidental harm!' (Kent 2010, 161)

In a very similar vein, a thudong monk who I interviewed in August 2015 in a temple in the South of Thailand said, "I can tell him to be a good person and to incessantly strife to do good – I cannot tell him to be a good soldier and to shoot people."[14] For the soldiers themselves, trying to minimize the negative khamma generated by the act of killing according to the way described in the *atthakatās* still is the best way forward—although whether the intention is to defend innocents and/or the religion and hence less bad or offensive, or driven by greed and aggression and thus bad probably lies in the (very subjective) eyes of the beholder. Gethin's

[14] Personal communication in a rural temple in the South of Thailand.

warning in this regard is quite poignant. Apart from this, and as Harvey suggests, a "Buddhist soldier may also try to dilute the evil of his killing by the performance of counteractive good actions" (Harvey 2000, 255).

Regarding the state, in olden days usually personified by a king or an emperor, Harvey mentioned the need to occasionally defend itself in acts of self-defence against enemies. As I will argue in the following chapter, the monarch as the (ideal type) *dhammaraja* or 'righteous ruler' and *cakkavattin* (Sanskrit: 'chakravartin,' lit.: 'Turner of the Wheel [of Dhamma]') was meant to be the protector of the religion or *sāsanā* in general, and the Sangha in particular. Very few exceptions apart (such as Emperor Asoka Maurya's decision to refrain from warfare after his violent conquest of Kalinga), the rulers of Buddhist realms did indeed see it as part and parcel of their royal duties to defend the religion with the sword if the need arose. With regard to keeping armies at the ready in order to defeat enemies, Buddhist kings could, amongst others, draw on verses from the *Cakkavatti Sīhanāda Sutta* (lit.: Discourse on the Lion-Roar of the Wheel-Turner) in which the Buddha answers the question about the duties of a 'wheel-turning' monarch as follows:

> It is this, my son: Yourself depending on the Dhamma [...], you should establish guard, ward and protection according to Dhamma for your own household, your troops, your nobles and vassals, for Brahmins and householders, town and country folk, ascetics and Brahmins, for beasts and birds. Let no crime prevail in your kingdom, and to those who are in need, give property. [...] That, my son, is the duty of the Ariyan wheel-turning monarch. (Cakkavatti Sīhanāda Sutta, DN26:61, as translated by Walshe 1995, 396–397)

Again, the need to wage defensive war in order to protect the religion is something that Theravāda Buddhism may well understand but may not necessarily approve of: as before, in the case of individual violent actions, organized violence in the shape of war is acknowledged as being, at least at times, unavoidable—but non-violence is seen as superior.[15] The *Saṅgama Sutta*, for example, contains two examples that nicely illustrate the Buddha's view on warfare—a view that probably can be summed up in

---

[15] It should be noted that the following discussion draws heavily on Harvey's argumentation (Harvey 2000, 250–251), adopting the same structure while also quoting Khantipalo Bhikkhu.

'violence begets more violence.' Both examples refer to a (defensive) battle of King Pasenadi of Kosala (Sanskrit: Prasenajit, sixth century BCE, contemporary, patron, and lay follower of the Buddha) against his nephew King Ajātasattu (Sanskrit: Ajatashatru). Pasenadi defeats Ajātasattu and confiscates the remains of the latter's army, but refrains from executing Ajātasattu. When the Buddha heard of this event, he said:

> Monks, King Ajatasattu has evil friends, evil comrades, evil companions, whereas King Pasenadi has fine friends, fine comrades, fine companions. Yet for now, King Pasenadi will lie down tonight in pain, defeated. Winning gives birth to hostility. Losing, one lies down in pain. The calmed lie down with ease, having set winning and losing aside. (Sangama Sutta SN 3.14, as translated by Thanissaro Bhikkhu 2001)

The meaning of the Buddha's comment is quite clear: by resorting to arms in order to defeat Ajātasattu, he continues the cycle of 'wrong action,' which will lead to 'wrong results.' The Buddha's second comment on this event further clarifies this:

> A man may plunder as long as it serves his ends, but when others are blundered, he who has plundered gets plundered in turn. A fool thinks 'Now's my chance,' as long as his evil has yet to ripen. But when it ripens, the fool falls into pain. Killing, you gain your killer. Conquering, you gain one who will conquer you; insulting, insult; harassing, harassment. And so, through the cycle of action, he who has plundered gets plundered in turn. (Sangama Sutta SN 3.15, as translated by Thanissaro Bhikkhu 1999a)

Khantipalo Bhikkhu, a leading (former) Western Theravāda monk and scholar, puts this into a modern Western context to help us understand this crucial issue even better:

> The Buddha could not dissuade King Ajātasattu from his campaigns [but he] saw how fruitless would be Pasenadi's action in confiscating the army of his troublesome nephew. The effect that it had was to harden Ajātasattu's resolve to conquer Kosala, which he did eventually do. In our times the huge reparations demanded of Germany after the First World War is another good example – our revenge is followed by their revenge as seen in Hitler and the Second World War. Patterns of war and revenge for wars, as seen in the past with England and Scotland, or between the former with France [...] never solve anything, but only exacerbate the bias and tension to provoke new trouble. (Khantipalo Bhikkhu 1986)

That wars never solve anything but only exacerbate issues, thus perpetuating the cycle of 'wrong action' leading to 'wrong results,' which again lead to renewed 'wrong action'—this is the message, or, rather, warning, of the Buddha to King Pasenadi. The Buddha perfectly understood the pressure the king was under, the secular duties he was required to fulfil (Premasiri 2006, 83), and the political realties he had to face (Harris 1994, 3, 5). After all, the Buddha hailed from the same warrior caste as the king, and would have lived a very similar life under different circumstances. Hence, the Buddha did not unequivocally condemn the king for his conduct and, unlike in the case of the individual soldier, did not refer to a rebirth in hell or as an animal. And, as already mentioned, he never even attempted to preach non-violence to kings, although he occasionally tried hard to dissuade them from embarking on war, such as King Ajātasattu, and always tried to teach them about the consequences of their resort to violence—the message being 'violence begets violence.' We could even ask with Harvey for the Second Buddhist Moment, that is, the times of Buddhist kingdoms, "whether one who 'gives up victory and defeat' can remain a king, or would need to be ordained as a monk to pursue purely spiritual concerns to practice his ideal" (Harvey 2000, 251)—a question which is soundly and convincingly answered in the negative by Tambiah for the reigns of Indian Emperor Ashoka Maurya and Sinhalese King Dutthagāmani:

> Kings must be good killers before they can turn to piety and good works. Asoka's alleged conversion and his pious pillar edicts followed the victorious wars that made possible the largest empire India had known until the arrival of the British. Dutha Gamini [Dutugāmunu or Dutthagāmani], the Sinhalese hero, indulged in successful violence and blood spilling in his defeat of the Tamils before he could build his monuments and accumulate his credit of merit. (Tambiah 1976, 522)

## Justifications: Towards a 'Righteous War' Doctrine

By now it should be clear that Buddhist scripture is not unequivocally condemning violence including warfare: although ambiguous to a certain extent, even the Buddha himself seemed to acknowledge that under certain conditions, warfare was unavoidable, and that violence was part and parcel of the society he lived in. After his lifetimes, the Sanghas of the Theravāda kingdoms that came into being over the centuries had even less compunction to justify the kings' resort to violence, including warfare. Furthermore, what constitutes 'defensive' and 'offensive' to a large degree lies in the eyes of the beholder—yet another ambiguity that offers warlike kings enough room to manoeuvre, supported by a wide-enough range of scriptures that condone (at least in the sense of not outright condemning) what they are doing. However, kings, especially strong kings, were not necessarily content with carefully selecting suitable verses and comments from various suttas. They went farther than that, as Tambiah explains: "strong kings do creatively interpret sacred traditions, which are alleged to be transmitted unchanged from the past" (Tambiah 1976, 187). Against the backdrop of the discussion of 'essentialized Buddhism' that we had in the previous chapter, it can thus be argued that these strong kings did basically the same as the Western scholars we encountered, such as Max Müller, Thomas Rhys Davids, and Max Weber—they went back to what they saw as uncontaminated sources, and interpreted them according to their requirements, and to the "standards of truth, relevance, and veracity of the later period" (Tambiah 1976, 187), "and in cases where they did not agree they were to be altered in order to restore what was believed to be the original text" (Tambiah ibid., quoting Wenk 1968), just that their aims and objectives were different. In their quest to defend the religion or *sāsanā* from enemies, real or imaged, the kings could count on a sympathetic view of their activities by the Sangha.

One way to justify and condone warfare as the epitome of violence is to develop a theory of 'Righteous War' or 'Just War,' as, for example, Christian theology did. The *Cakkavatti Sīhanāda Sutta*, already mentioned above, provides some initial insights in this regard since it sketches out an ideal society free of crime and poverty, ruled and protected by a righteous ruler, that is, the *Cakkavattin* or Wheel-Turner. Although it does not directly refer to warfare, it does refer to armies, and it also contains exhortations on how this righteous ruler should conquer his kingdom, and presumably neighbouring ones as well: without the use of force, solely by the use of the Dhamma. Again, this is an ideal type that we encounter, not a realistic proposition: even for celebrated Emperor Ashoka, world conquering by the sword came first, compassion and world renouncing after the conquests had been completed came later. As Tambiah said, kings must indeed be good killers before they can turn to piety and charity; although, in defence of Ashoka, I should hasten to add that he converted to Buddhism only after, and under the impression of, his campaigns during which thousands of people perished; while on the other hand, Dutugāmunu was already a Buddhist and thus familiar with the Dhamma and the expectations towards a Cakkavattin when he went to war. In any case, a theme that I shall further develop in the following chapter becomes clear: the righteous ruler is depicted as the protector of the people as well as of the Dhamma—both tasks he cannot possibly accomplish alone but only with the help of the people themselves who are needed to fill the ranks of the king's forces in times of war. For the specific case of Sri Lanka, Bartholomeusz sums this up nicely by stating that the "[the] Sinhalese king protects the Sinhala people, who in turn protect the island, which itself is shelter to the dharma" (Bartholomeusz 2002, 21). In my opinion, this can be generalized into 'the king protects the people, the people protect the realm, and the realm is shelter to the Dhamma.'

Since the bulk of current 'Just-War' theory arguably harks back to Christian roots, a frequently referred-to quote of St Augustine helps to illustrate the problems Theravāda Buddhism faces here. In a letter to Boniface, the Byzantine governor of Africa, he wrote in the early fifth century: "Do not imagine [...] that no one can please God while he is engaged in military service" (Davis 1991, 31; also quoted in Bartholomeusz 2002, 36). As Davis explains, St Augustine wrote this letter to assuage the fears of the governor that "military command may hinder him from fulfilling the demands of Christian life" (Davis 1991, 31). St Augustine, or, more precisely (since he was made a saint only after his death) Augustine, bishop of the diocese of Hippo-Regius (today Annaba/Algeria), did, however, not only try to put the governor's unease to rest but also included a number of recommendations pertaining to the conduct of war—one of them rather similar to the 'right thinking, right intention' part of the Noble Eightfold Path:

> If it is supposed that God could not enjoin warfare, because in after times it was said by the Lord Jesus Christ, 'I say unto you, That ye resist not evil: but if any one strike thee on the right cheek, turn to him the left also,' the answer is, that what here [in war] is required is not a bodily action, but an inward position. The sacred seat of virtue is the heart. (Augustine of Hippo, undated)

Hence, St Augustine argues on the basis of the Old Testament that Moses' killing of Egyptians was not a sin; rather, it would have been a sin not to do so because God ordered it since "the Egyptians were in open rebellion against God, for they [worshipped] idols [...] and they had

grievously oppressed strangers [the Israelites] by making them work without pay" (ibid.). As we remember, this 'God Wills It' theme was turned
into a battle cry during the crusades. Of course, in Theravāda Buddhism,
a similar construction could not emerge since there is no creator God
whose will one has to carry out whether one likes or not. And, arguably,
in the canon itself, there are only very few references to warfare, and most
of them are ambiguous: as I already mentioned when discussing the
*Cakkavatti Sīhanāda Sutta*, the king was described as having an army—a
'four-fold' army consisting of elephant corps, cavalry, charioteers, and foot
soldiers, to be precise—but ideally, he was meant to rule, and to conquer,
without recourse to violence, since this would only lead to more violence.
Consequently, another part of the sutta drastically describes the bleak consequences of a rule unfettered by the Dhamma, culminating in "the
destruction of human life" (Bartholomeusz 2002, 66). This notwithstanding, Bartholomeusz finds the very mention of an army significant, and
comes to the following conclusion:

> [While] it is clear in the canonical texts that non-violence has priority over
> violence, the military presence in the texts might suggest that the obligation
> to be non-violent is not absolute, contrary to the argument of some scholars
> of Buddhism. (Bartholomeusz 2002, 47)

Nevertheless, she concedes that Theravāda Buddhism requires very
convincing arguments for the resort to violence (ibid.). And here, we
return to the 'right thinking, right intention' theme of the Noble Eightfold
Path, and arguably to St Augustine as well: a war fought for the right reasons, for example, in order to defend the religion and possibly also to
spread the faith while doing so was seen as justifiable—not during the
lifetimes of the Buddha, but from the emergence of Buddhist realms and
the 'Second Buddhist Moment' onwards. Having said all that, I find these
justifications rather contrived and awkward; basically, they are a nod to
realpolitik. The awkwardness of Theravāda justifications of war becomes
even more apparent if we compare them to justifications of 'Just War' or
'Righteous War' (*dharma yudha*) as they appear in the Indian epic
Mahabharata, which with about 100,000 verses and 1.8 million words is
"the longest poem ever written" (Lochtefeld 2002). Put into writing
around 400 BCE, it contains clear recommendations for fighting a 'Just
War,' recommendations that revolved around the topic of proportionality
that we already encountered, but in a much more specific and unapolo-

getic military context: for example, a just cause for going to war should be established prior of doing so, people in distress should not be attacked, poisoned or barbed arrows should not be used, and prisoners of war should be treated fairly (Robinson 2003, 117). The first criterion, establishing a just cause, is similar to the modern international law category of *jus ad bellum* (right to go to war), while the others belong to the modern category of *jus in bello* (right conduct in war). Theravāda Buddhism as a notionally non-violent religion committed to 'non-injury' or 'non-harm' (Jerryson 2018, 458) never went that far in justifying war. One might even be tempted to argue following Premasiri that "[the] idea of a just or righteous war involving the use of weapons of war and violence is conspicuously absent in the Buddhist canon" (Premasiri 2006, 81). In my opinion, the Buddha's stance of 'understanding' but not 'approving of' war still reverberates through the Dhamma and its interpretations. But I shall come back to this issue later in this chapter, and in more detail in the chapters on Sri Lanka, Burma, and Thailand, since there are variations of how far the Sanghas (or rather, individual monks) are prepared to go in order to defend the controversial idea of a Buddhist 'Just War' or *dharma yudha* in Sinhalese-Buddhist discourses; as we shall see, Premasiri's view appears to be a bit too optimistic.

There is, however, yet another possibility to justify killing. It is well known that one way of circumventing moral obstacles (not only Buddhist ones) standing in one's way can be found in the age-old 'demonizing' or 'othering' of the enemy—a practice well known and established across all times and cultures. For the requirements of war and the organized, large-scale killings that it represents if we strip the concept of 'war' to its very core, this 'othering' works best in the shape of dehumanizing the enemy. For example, during the Second World War, German soldiers usually saw their Russian counterparts as 'sub-humans,' while US-American soldiers saw the Vietcong irregulars or the North-Vietnamese army soldiers they fought against during the Second Indochina War as 'gooks.' Arguably, denying the 'other' his or her humanity makes the task of killing them somewhat easier. And this is exactly what those monks tended to do who were asked by a king for advice either before or in the aftermath of a battle. In our context, the earliest of such interpretations can be found in the Sinhalese *Mahāvamsa* or 'Great Chronicle,' a chronicle that Gombrich calls the "charter of Sinhalese Buddhist nationalism" (Gombrich 2006, 141). I shall return to the Mahāvamsa and its importance in this regard later in the chapter on Sri Lanka. In the present context, it is of relevance that this chronicle also covers a series of wars waged by Sinhalese kings against Tamil kings—both local ones and invaders from South India. In one such battles, the Sinhalese-Buddhist prince Dutugāmunu (Dutthagāmani, r. 161 BC–137 BC) defeated Tamil King Ellalān (Elara), thus establishing his own dynasty. After the battle that took place in 161 BC somewhere near Anuradhapura, the newly crowned King Dutugāmunu expressed an Asoka-like (so Gombrich, ibid.) remorse for the manifold deaths he had brought about, including that of King Ellalān himself. The monks he asked for advice, however, responded as follows:

> That deed presents no obstacle on your path to heaven. You caused the deaths of just one and a half people, O king. One had taken the Refuges, the other the Five Precepts as well. The rest were wicked men of wrong views who died like (or: are considered as) beasts. You will in many ways illuminate the Buddha's Teaching, so stop worrying. (Mahāvamsa XXV, 108–11, as quoted in Gombrich 2006, 141)

This means that, basically, the king and his troops mainly killed 'beasts,' not humans, with just one and a half exceptions. It also implies that killing was excusable as long as the intention behind it was the defence of the religion, or the spread of it, which in my opinion also opened the door to offensive warfare: arguably, there were many more 'wicked men of wrong views' outside of the boundaries of a Buddhist realm. Interestingly, Bartholomeusz seems to see that as an example of 'Just War' reasoning since, according to the Mahāvamsa, Dutugāmunu fought a defensive war to protect the Dhamma, and a limited one at that, thus also fulfilling the *jus in bello* criteria (Bartholomeusz 2002, 55). This is, however, not very convincing. I would rather side, on this occasion, with Walpola Rahula who dismisses this contrived justification both as "religio-patriotism" and as "diametrically opposed to the teaching of the Buddha" (Rahula 1974, 21, 22). Similarly, Harvey denounces it as "a rather perverse reflection of the doctrine that it is less bad to kill an unvirtuous person than a virtuous one" (Harvey 2000, 256). For modern times, the most blatant case of 'othering' a perceived enemy is Thai Monk Phra Kittiwutthō's reconstruction of fellow-Thai communist insurgents in the 1970s as embodiments of *mara* (evil) trying to destroy the Thai triad of nation, religion, and monarchy—basically evil-minded beings who were 'not complete persons.' Thus, killing them was not demeritorious but was the sacred duty of all Thai people. Again, I will discuss these religio-patriotic constructions and their justifications as well as the rejection they receive from within the three Sanghas in the chapters on Sri Lanka, Burma, and Thailand later in this book.

## CONCLUSIONS: THE UNAVOIDABILITY OF VIOLENCE IN THE AGE OF DUKKHA

It should be clear by now that the notion that "violence is the antithesis of a supposedly *authentic* Buddhism" (Abeysekara 2001, 2) unfortunately has to be rejected as incorrect. Neither is violence a "dark underside" of Buddhism, attributable to history rather than to Buddhism itself (so Gananath Obeyesekere, as quoted in Abeysekara 2001, 3). Rather, in the current age of *dukkha* or suffering, violence should be seen as unavoidable; if we follow Galtung, it is even woven into the very fabric of our societies as 'structural violence,' defined as 'social injustice' (Galtung 1969, 171). By extension, this means that it is indeed questionable whether it is possible, at least for lay followers, to follow the Noble Eightfold Path and the five precepts to the letter at all times and under any circumstances. Quite interestingly, even the Dalai Lama himself speculated that pacifism as an absolute value may well be an unachievable goal in this world. Questioned on his views on the justification of violence against Tamils by Sinhalese-Buddhist monks, and challenged that "the kind of pacifism [the Dalai Lama] advocate[s] doesn't work in the real world, and that to let the enemy destroy Buddhist monuments and temples and kill Buddhists without fighting back is simply intolerable," the Dalai Lama admitted:

> [I]f the situation was such that there was only one learned lama or genuine practitioner alive, a person whose death would cause the whole of Tibet to lose all hope of keeping its Buddhist way of life, then it is conceivable that in order to protect that one person it might be justified for 10 enemies to be eliminated – if there was no other way. I could justify violence only in this extreme case, to save the last living knowledge of Buddhism itself. (as quoted in Thurman 1997)[16]

However, before admitting that under certain circumstances, violence might be justifiable, the Dalai Lama cautioned that even if it were justifi-

---

[16]Also quoted in Bartholomeusz 2002, 29, which is how this interview of the Dalai Lama came to my attention.

able, "nevertheless once you commit violence, then counterviolence will be returned" (ibid.). In the chapters on Sri Lanka, Burma, and Thailand, we will encounter very similar attitudes expressed by Theravāda monks. In the present context, all we need to do is to accept that even within Buddhism as the epitome of non-violence, the use of violence can be justified under particular circumstances and as a last resort. This argument brings us back to the comments or *atthakatās* and the notion of proportionality that I discussed earlier in this chapter. It also indicates that, like any other religion, Theravāda Buddhism evolved over the centuries and the 'Three Buddhist Moments.' It is indeed questionable whether the Buddha himself would have accepted such an argumentation—all that he did was acknowledge that violence existed, however, without ever condoning or justifying it. As we remember, he was not too concerned with this-worldly activities but with showing the way to nibbāna. From the moment Buddhist kingdoms emerged, this absolute morale theory steeped in non-violence or *ahimsa* had to change to accommodate new realities.

With regard to this evolving stance, Hallisey argues that "[we] would do better to begin any investigation of Buddhist ethics with a common-sense expectation that any historical tradition worth its salt will inevitably display evidence that its practitioners and intellectuals have resorted to more than one kind of moral theory" (Hallisey 1996, 35). Then, however, he asks an interesting question: "is [it] possible that Buddhists approached their ethical concerns without any ethical theory at all, but instead adopted a kind of ethical particularism[?]" (Hallisey 1996, 37). To answer his own question, Hallisey refers to W. D. Ross' concept of prima facie duties[17] that "does not suggest that some moral principles are more important than others [and] also eschews any attempt to discover any consistency in the things we take to matter morally" (Hallisey 1996, 38–39). Hallisey refers to the well-known *Mangalasutta* (lit.: 'Discourse on Blessings') as an example: the sutta itself is with 12 verses that are rather short, but it has been interpreted and discussed in numerous comments, one of the largest being the sixteenth-century 500-page Thai text *Lamp on the Meaning of Auspiciousness* (Hallisey 1996, 39). As Hallisey explains, the sutta contains

[17] A 'prima facie' duty is a duty that is obligatory unless it is overridden or trumped by another duty. As Garrett (2004) explains, "[an] example of a prima facie duty is the duty to keep promises. 'Unless stronger moral considerations override, one ought to keep a promise made.'"

a list of 38 prima facie duties, including some common-sense recommendations such as living in a suitable locality, supporting mother and father, as well as caring for one's wife and children; some other geared towards the Noble Eightfold Path, for example, to associate with the monks, abstain from intoxicants, and to lead a chaste life (Mangalasutta, as translated by Narada Thera 1994). Very interestingly, as Hallisey observes, some of the recommendations of this short sutta contradict themselves: arguably, the recommendation to live a chaste life is difficult to reconcile with the one on caring for one's wife and children. Hence, Hallisey draws the following conclusion:

> It is precisely this inclusiveness that prevents us from taking the items on the list as together providing a portrait of an ideal moral agent, such as we might find in a virtue-theory of ethics. [...] Indeed, rather than the outline of any particular underlying ethical theory, the impression that one takes away from this list [...] is that all sorts of things matter [...] but in a way that is not structured by systematic consistency. (Hallisey 1996, 39–40)

Hallisey offers more examples from the body of Theravāda commentarial literature on the Mangalasutta in which the Buddha himself seems to be inconsistent in his actions as well as in his recommendations, to then argue that it is the context of these stories and the admonitions they contain that matters when it comes to charting out an ethical course of action, not an overarching general ethical theory:

> The diversity of stories associated with each one of the duties included in the Mangalasutta encourages us, in turn, to respond to the rich particularity of each situation before us without holding ourselves to a standard of moral consistency generally associated with taking guidance from a single ethical theory. (Hallisey 1996, 42)

Interpreting these stories against the backdrop of a given situation does not only "help us to negotiate the conflicts that inevitably occur among *prima facie* duties" (Hallisey 1996, 42) but also allows us (or in the context of my study and this particular chapter: the monks) to reinterpret the Buddha's sayings and to adapt them to make them fit into an environment that the Buddha could not possibly foresee and probably was not even interested in. On the negative side, this also allows a certain ambiguity to creep in, and it does also open the door to some clever casuistry, as, for example, the one used by explaining away the casualties of King Dutugāmunu's battle against his Tamil foe as 'wicked men of wrong views who died like beasts.' Jerryson (2018, 459) sums up this what he calls 'hermeneutical ambiguity' by stating that the question whether violence (Jerryson speaks of murder in that context) is ethically permissible or not depends on the intentions behind it (i.e. pure or not), the nature of the victim (i.e. human or not), and the status of those who carry out the act of violence (i.e. king, soldier, layperson). All taken together, it is evident that Hallisey's 'theory of an ethical particularism' helps us immensely in the chapters on Sri Lanka, Burma, and Thailand to make sense out of the different interpretations of the same suttas in order to either justify and condone violence, or to categorically dismiss it as based on wrong thinking, wrong intent, and wrong action.

## REFERENCES

Abeysekara, Ananda. 2001. The Saffron Army, Violence, Terror(ism): Buddhism, Identity, and Difference in Sri Lanka. *Numen* 48 (1): 1–46.

Augustine of Hippo (St Augustine). undated. Contra Faustum Manichæum, Book 22. 69–76. *Early Church Texts*. http://www.earlychurchtexts.com/public/augustine_war_contra_faustum.htm

Bartholomeusz, Tessa. 2002. *In Defense of Dharma: Just-War Ideology in Buddhist Sri Lanka*. London/New York: Routledge.

Brahmavamso, Ajahn. 1996. Vinaya: The Four Disrobing Offences. *Newsletter*, April–June. Perth, Australia: The Buddhist Society of Western Australia. http://www.budsas.org/ebud/ebsut019.htm

Buddha Dharma Education Association/Buddhanet. 2008. Unit Six: The Four Immeasurables. *Buddhist Studies, Secondary Level*. http://www.buddhanet.net/e-learning/buddhism/bs-s15.htm

Buddharakkhita, Acharya. 1996. Dandavagga: Violence. *Dhammapada: The Buddha's Path of Wisdom*. Access to Insight: Readings in Theravāda Buddhism. http://www.accesstoinsight.org/tipitaka/kn/dhp/dhp.10.budd.html

Bullit, John. 2005. The Five Precepts: *pañca-sila*. Access to Insight: Readings in Theravāda Buddhism. http://www.accesstoinsight.org/ptf/dhamma/sila/pancasila.html

Chongcharoen, Piyarach. 2018. Battered Young Novice Dies. *Bangkok Post*, August 24. https://www.bangkokpost.com/news/crime/1527714/battered-young-novice-dies

Davis, S. 1991. 'Et Quod Vis Fac.' Paul Ramsey and Augustinian Ethics. *The Journal of Religious Ethics* (Special Focus Issue: The Ethics of Paul Ramsey) 19 (2): 31–69.

Deegalle, Mahinda. 2006. Introduction. In *Buddhism, Conflict and Violence in Modern Sri Lanka*, ed. Mahinda Deegalle, 1–21. London/New York: Routledge.

Easwaran, Eknath, trans. 2007. *The Bhagavad Gita*. Tomales: Nilgiri Press

Galtung, Johan. 1969. Violence, Peace, and Peace Research. *Journal of Peace Research* 6 (3): 167–191.

Garrett, Jan. 2004. *A Simple and Usable (Although Incomplete) Ethical Theory Based on the Ethics of W. D. Ross*. August 10. http://people.wku.edu/jan.garrett/ethics/rossethc.htm

Gethin, Rupert. 2004. Can Killing a Living Being Ever Be an Act of Compassion? The Analysis of the Act of Killing in the Abhidhamma and Pali Commentaries. *Journal of Buddhist Ethics* 11: 167–202.

Gombrich, Richard F. 1966. The Consecration of a Buddhist Image. *Journal of Asian Studies* 26 (1): 23–36.

———. 2006. *Theravāda Buddhism: A Social History from Ancient Benares to Modern Colombo*. 2nd ed. Abingdon/New York: Routledge.

Hallisey, Charles. 1996. Ethical Particularism in Theravāda Buddhism. *Journal of Buddhist Ethics* 3: 32–43.

Harris, Elizabeth J. 1994. *Violence and Disruption in Society. A Study of the Early Buddhist Texts*. The Wheel Publication No. 392/393. Kandy: Buddhist Publication Society.

Harvey, Peter. 2000. *An Introduction to Buddhist Ethics: Foundations, Values and Issues*. Cambridge: Cambridge University Press.

Jackson, Peter A. 2003. *Buddhadāsa: Theravada Buddhism and Modernist Reform in Thailand*. Bangkok: Silkworm Books.

Jenkins, Stephen. 2011. On the Auspiciousness of Compassionate Violence. *Journal of the International Association of Buddhist Studies* 33 (1–2): 299–331. http://archiv.ub.uni-heidelberg.de/ojs/index.php/jiabs/article/view/9284

Jerryson, Michael K. 2018. Buddhism, War, and Violence. In *Oxford Handbook of Buddhist Ethics*, ed. Daniel Cozort and James M. Shields, 453–478. Oxford: Oxford University Press.

Jeyaraj, D.B.S. 2014. The Assassination of Prime Minister S. W. R. D. Bandaranaike 55 Years Ago. http://dbsjeyaraj.com/dbsj/archives/33515

Juergensmeyer, Mark. 2003. *Terror in the Mind of God. The Global Rise of Religious Violence*. 3rd ed. Berkeley/London: University of California Press.

Kent, David W. 2010. Onward Buddhist Soldiers: Preaching to the Sri Lankan Army. In *Buddhist Warfare*, ed. Michael K. Jerryson and Mark Juergensmeyer, 157–177. Oxford/New York: Oxford University Press.

Keyes, Charles F. 2007. Monks, Guns, and Peace: Theravāda Buddhism and Political Violence. In *Belief and Bloodshed. Religion and Violence Across Time and Tradition*, ed. James K. Wellman, 145–163. Lanham et al.: Rowman & Littlefield.

Khantipalo Bhikkhu. 1986. *Aggression, War, and Conflict: Three Essays*. Bodhi Leaf No. 108. Kandy: Buddhist Publication Society. http://www.bps.lk/olib/bl/bl108-p.html

Lochtefeld, James G. 2002. *The Illustrated Encyclopedia of Hinduism: A-M*. New York: Rosen Publishing Group.

Loy, David. 1982. Enlightenment in Buddhism and Advaita Vedanta: Are Nirvana and Moksha the Same? *International Philosophical Quarterly* 23 (1): 65–74. http://buddhism.lib.ntu.edu.tw/FULLTEXT/JR-AN/26715.htm

Mascaró, Juan, trans. 2003. *The Bhagavad Gita*. Reprint, London et al.: Penguin Books.

Nanamoli Thera. 1994. Cula-kammavibhanga Sutta: The Shorter Exposition of Kamma. *Tipitaka, Majjhima Nikaya*. Access to Insight: Readings in Theravāda Buddhism.    http://www.accesstoinsight.org/tipitaka/mn/mn.135.nymo.html

Narada Thera. 1994. Mangalasutta: Blessings. *Tipitaka, Khuddakapatha*. Access to Insight: Readings in Theravāda Buddhism. http://www.accesstoinsight.org/tipitaka/kn/khp/khp.5.nara.html

Premasiri, P.D. 2006. A 'Righteous War' in Buddhism? In *Buddhism, Conflict and Violence in Modern Sri Lanka*, ed. Mahinda Deegalle, 78–85. London/New York: Routledge.

Rahula, Walpola. 1974. *The Heritage of the Bhikkhu: A Short History of the Bhikkhu in Educational, Cultural, Social, and Political Life*. New York: Grove Press.

Robinson, Paul F. 2003. *Just War in Comparative Perspective*. London/New York: Ashgate.

Satha-Anand, Suwanna. 2014. The Question of Violence in Thai Buddhism. In *Buddhism and Violence: Militarism and Buddhism in Modern Asia*, ed. Vladimir Tikhonov and Torkel Brekke, paperback ed., 175–193. New York/London: Routledge.

Spiro, Melford E. 1982. *Buddhism and Society. A Great Tradition and Its Burmese Vicissitudes*. 2nd expanded ed. Berkeley/London: University of California Press.

Strong, John S. 2015. *Buddhisms: An Introduction*. London: Oneworld Publications.

Sumedho, Ajahn. n.d. *The Four Noble Truths*. Hemel Hempstead: Amaravati Publications.    https://web.archive.org/web/20150325013823/http://www.buddhanet.net/pdf_file/4nobltru.pdf

Tambiah, Stanley J. 1976. *World Conqueror and World Renouncer. A Study of Buddhism and Polity in Thailand Against a Historical Background*. Cambridge et al.: Cambridge University Press.

Thanissaro Bhikkhu. 1997a. Samaññaphala Sutta: The Fruits of the Contemplative Life. *Dīkha Nikaya: The Long Discourses*. Access to Insight: Readings in Theravāda    Buddhism.    http://www.accesstoinsight.org/tipitaka/dn/dn.02.0.than.html

———. 1997b. Kakacupama Sutta: The Simile of the Saw. *Majjhima Nikaya: The Middle-length Discourses*. Access to Insight: Readings in Theravāda Buddhism. http://www.accesstoinsight.org/tipitaka/mn/mn.021x.than.html

———, trans. 1998. Yodhajiva Sutta: To Yodhajiva (The Warrior). *Samyutta Nikaya: The Grouped Discourses*. Access to Insight: Readings in Theravāda Buddhism. http://www.accesstoinsight.org/tipitaka/sn/sn42/sn42.003.than.html

———, trans. 1999a. Sangama Sutta: A Battle (2). *Samyutta Nikaya: The Grouped Discourses*. Access to Insight: Readings in Theravāda Buddhism. http://www.accesstoinsight.org/tipitaka/sn/sn03/sn03.015.than.html

———. 1999b. Sakkha-Pañha Sutta: Sakkha's Questions. *Digha Nikaya: The Long Discourses*. Access to Insight: Readings in Theravāda Buddhism. http://www.accesstoinsight.org/tipitaka/dn/dn.21.2x.than.html

———, trans. 2001. Sangama Sutta: A Battle (1). *Samyutta Nikaya: The Grouped Discourses*. Access to Insight: Readings in Theravāda Buddhism. http://www.accesstoinsight.org/tipitaka/sn/sn03/sn03.014.than.html

———, trans. 2007. Bhikkhu Pātimokkha: The Bhikkhus' Code of Discipline. *Vinaya Pitaka: The Basket of the Discipline*. Access to Insight: Readings in Theravāda Buddhism. http://www.accesstoinsight.org/tipitaka/vin/sv/bhik-khu-pati.html#pr

———, trans. 2008. Maha-cattarisaka Sutta: The Great Forty. *Majjhima Nikaya: The Middle-length Discourses*. Access to Insight: Readings in Theravāda Buddhism. http://www.accesstoinsight.org/tipitaka/mn/mn.117.than.html

Thurman, Robert. 1997. The Dalai Lama on China, Hatred, and Optimism. *Mother Jones*, November/December. http://www.motherjones.com/politics/1997/11/dalai-lama

Tikhonov, Vladimir. 2013. Introduction. In *Buddhism and Violence: Militarism and Buddhism in Modern Asia*, ed. Vladimir Tikhonov and Torkel Brekke, 1–12. New York/London: Routledge.

Walshe, Maurice. 1995. *The Long Discourses of the Buddha. A Translation of the Dīgha Nikāya*. Somerville: Wisdom Publications.

Weber, Max. 1967. *The Religion of India: The Sociology of Hinduism and Buddhism*. Trans. and Ed. Hans H. Gerth and Don Martindale. New York/London: The Free Press/Collier-Macmillan.

Wenk, Klaus. 1968. *The Restoration of Thailand Under Rama I, 1782–1809*. The Association for Asian Studies: Monographs and Papers, No. XXIV. Tucson: The University of Arizona Press.

# CHAPTER 4

# Monks in the Age of Suffering: World Renouncers and World Conquerors

A discussion of Buddhist discourses on violence in theory and practice naturally leads to a discussion of the relationship between the Sangha and the state on the one hand, and, more generally but of utmost importance in our context, of the relationship between the Sangha and the people on the other, with the purpose to assess the Sangha's role within society. Observing monks and their interactions with rulers and ruled in both traditional and transitional societies will assist in arriving at a better understanding of the changes that affected the Sanghas, and it also helps putting the activities of today's 'political,' 'radical,' and 'extremist' monks in perspective. As we shall see in this chapter, political monks are by no means completely new and aberrant variations of an otherwise traditionally apolitical Sangha solely focused on meditation, and neither did they emerge only after the advent of Buddhist modernism. It will, however, also become clear that these modern avatars of political monks do indeed differ from their pre-modern, traditional predecessors to a certain extent.

Hence, in this chapter, I will first explore what monks are supposed to do, and what roles they are meant to play in a society that usually awards them high respect, using their own monastic rules as well as tradition as benchmarks for both aspects. Then, I will turn to investigating how and why they were gradually transformed into political actors and what being 'political actors' entailed in traditional, pre-modern societies. I define 'they' in this context, first, as the Sangha in general, and, second, as individual temples, but not yet as individual monks since the available sources

© The Author(s) 2019
P. Lehr, *Militant Buddhism*,
https://doi.org/10.1007/978-3-030-03517-4_4

do not always allow us to go into such levels of detail. Since I am dealing here with developments in three different countries over hundreds of years, my argumentation will by sheer necessity gloss over many otherwise interesting details that country specialists might deem to be important, to arrive at some easily generalizable findings. In my opinion, this approach can be justified by the aims and objectives of this chapter, these being (a) to dispel the impression that the Sanghas did not embark on politics until recently, and (b) to also show that the nature of politics, and hence the political culture of the Sanghas, has changed after the collapse of traditional societies. Doing so will enable us to better contextualize the findings of the case studies which will follow this chapter.

I shall start with a short recapitulation of the main findings of the previous chapter where we examined Theravāda Buddhist discourses on violence, to then contrast these theoretical discourses to the real political practice from the Second Buddhist Moment onwards. I argued that a defensive war fought to protect the faith was deemed to be permissible and explained how extendable and malleable the idea of 'defence' could be when it came to serve the 'national interest,' or at least the interest of kings and their dynasties. So, obviously, when it comes to non-violence, there is at least some room to manoeuvre—as in any religion, and in any doctrine or scripture, I should hasten to add. Theravāda Buddhist scripture tends to be ambiguous for a variety of reasons, including issues of transcription and translation, the possibility of multiple meanings of a chosen term, and suchlike. And then there is the usual and inescapable difference between theory and practice. This truism brings us to the human actors involved in turning theory in the shape of scripture and doctrine into (pious) practice: the Sangha in general as well as individual monks, and their interactions with laypersons, be they rulers or the ruled.

## IDEALS: BEING A MONK IN THEORY AND PRACTICE

In the light of the common Western stereotypical image I mentioned earlier on about what 'proper' Buddhist monks are supposed to do and what not, it is probably a good idea to start with the assertion that there are, indeed, day-to-day interactions between most of the monks of the three Sanghas in question, and the laity. I am emphasizing this point because there still seems to be a misconception about what being a monk entails, especially in the West: usually, it is assumed that monks as archetypical world renouncers spend most of their days in deep meditation without much of a care for mundane matters. Over the years I have met many Westerners who went on retreats in various Burmese or Thai Buddhist temples, and even a few who ordained as monks, or, if they were female, joined as a mae chee (i.e. as a nun). Most of them initially held the same idea, and consequently were in for quite a disappointment. Except for those presumably better-informed individuals who wisely opted to join a forest monastery that actually does focus on meditation, they shared my own observation that temples, even small ones, are no 'oases of tranquillity' but rather busy and noisy places in which many a menial task needs to be done, and many a visitor attended to. Depending on the size and location of the temple in question, these tasks include cleaning, washing, raking, repairing, accounting, counselling and advising, dealing with domestic and foreign visitors (and translating for the latter), or just chatting with villagers or townsfolks dropping by. And then there are the frequent invitations to various ceremonies in the lay followers' homes or businesses which the monks have to deal with.

Although it is of course always possible for individual monks to retreat for a week to a jungle, a cave, or a mountain top (depending on the location) in order to meditate without disturbance (indeed the first important duty of a monk), or at least a couple of hours per day to one's hut in order to study scripture (the second important duty of a monk), obviously not everybody can do that at the same time. This means that often there is simply not enough time for oneself,[1] and even if there is, the background hubbub might make it difficult to concentrate, especially for the beginners (including junior monks and novices) who are not yet well versed in the art of meditation. Hence, I fully agree with Schedneck's (2011, 328) finding that "[the] first challenge for Westerners is to negotiate their romanticist ideas about the tranquil, meditative lives of Asian monastics, with the responsibilities they must hold in the Thai monasteries." Even experienced monks occasionally complain that there is not much time left for their own meditation when they are done with their assigned duties and with the study of Pali chants that they need for the

---

[1] Being the first Westerner ever (or at least the first for a decade or two) in a rural temple can be especially taxing as everybody comes to see, and chat with, the unexpected guest. On the negative side, this means that progress with regard to meditation can be excruciatingly slow, on the positive it provides one with interesting insights into the ordinary peoples' lives—apart from drastically improving one's language skills.

various rituals they have to attend (the same observation was already made by Tambiah 1970, 118; for the case of Burmese monks, see Spiro 1982, 307, fn 3). That such lively and regular monk-laity interactions are no coincidence or aberration but were intended from the very beginning becomes clear if we look at the Buddha's exhortation to his disciples to go out and preach the Dhamma:

> Go ye now, O Bhikkhus, and wander, for the gain of the many, for the welfare of the many, out of compassion for the world, for the good, for the gain, and for the welfare of gods and men. Let not two of you go the same way. Preach, O Bhikkhus, the doctrine which is glorious in the beginning, glorious in the middle, glorious at the end, in the spirit and in the letter; proclaim a consummate, perfect and pure life of holiness. There are beings whose mental eyes are covered by scarcely any dust, but if the doctrine is not preached to them, they cannot attain salvation. They will understand the doctrine. (Mahāvagga, Vinaya Pitaka[2])

The Buddha went further than just exhorting his disciples as the first, original Sangha (community) to spread the Dhamma: he also explicitly forbade them to turn down invitations to preach and to teach, and he even told them to do so in the vernacular language of the people they went to. Although this can indeed be seen as a detraction from the monks' personal quest to attain nibbāna, and thus as a set of conflicting, contradicting aims and objectives, the main reason behind that command obviously was to ensure the survivability of the Sangha and the Dhamma: without new recruits in the shape of either novices or fully ordained monks, the Sangha would not have endured, nor Buddhism as such. Furthermore, since the monks depend on the goodwill and support of the laity to survive (I will come to that later), a willingness and preparedness to always preach and teach is the least that should be expected from the monks in return.[3]

---

[2] Many different translations of this exhortation exist. The one I have chosen is from Rhys David and Oldenberg 1881, 112–113.

[3] To a large extent, these exhortations were however side-stepped by ascetic hermit monks who shunned contact with the outside world. A disciple of the Buddha, Venerable Batkula (or Bakkula), is the first known example for this practice and also a good example for the unease with which such individuals are treated in scripture: while some sources see him positively, others describe him rather negatively as 'selfish' and 'aloof.' See, for example, Nānamoli Bhikkhu and Bodhi Bhikkhu 2005, 985–988; Strong 1983, 255. See also Anālayo 2007 and Anālayo 2010.

Now that we have established the fact that there is a lively interaction between the monks and the laypeople, let us take a closer look at it. In the first chapter, I referred to the 'street light' simile from a contemporary Sri Lankan monk mentioned by Carrithers: he said that just like street lights, the monks would go nowhere and would do nothing but enable layersons to find their ways in a dark world of moral confusion (Carrithers 2007, 134). Although at first glance, it seems to directly contradict the Buddha's exhortation, it actually tries to explain the role of the monk(s) resident in an already established monastery, and it also illustrates the differences between Theravāda monks and Catholic priests or Protestant vicars, for example. Gombrich elaborates on this difference as follows:

> [He] does not function like the English village vicar. Villagers who need a monk to conduct mortuary rites must by custom invite him [...], and he must accept; but these are the only rites for which such a presumptive link is recognized, even though the villagers feed him and his fellows, and generally use the local temple for most of their 'merit-making'. In other words, they are responsible for him, not he for them; he is not a pastor, a shepherd to his people. His twin functions [...] have traditionally been to teach and to preach. (Gombrich 2006, 146)

Gombrich's argument made for the case of Sri Lankan monks and villagers can be generalized to encompass the monkhood-laity relations in all Theravāda Buddhist countries: monks are available for teaching, preaching, and conducting certain ceremonies and rites, which we shall explore later, but it is up to the lay followers to come to the temple, or to invite the monks. And even then, the participating monks should not be seen as officiating, but as preaching and consoling—a point Gombrich emphasizes as well to further highlight the crucial differences between priests and vicars as Christians know them and a typical, traditional Theravāda monk (Gombrich 2006, 125). For the case of the Sangha in Burma, Smith comes to a very similar conclusion:

> The Buddhist monk is not a priest and has no direct spiritual authority over the layman. The latter is not dependent on the monk for the absolution of sins or the administration of sacraments. The Buddhist clergy has no power to excommunicate the erring layman. (Smith 1965, 103)[4]

---

[4] This is actually not completely true: Buddhist monks can refuse alms donated by lay followers by turning their alms bowls over. This approach was taken by the Burmese monks

Spiro adds more details on this relationship by breaking down the monks' functions into two categories: those carried out for the benefit of the laity and those carried out for the benefits of the monks themselves. Having interviewed a sample of 20 monks, he states that "in response to the question 'What are the functions of a monk?' not even one monk listed services to laymen as a major, let alone *the* major monastic function" (Spiro 1982, 285 [emphasis in the original]). As he elaborates, the major functions listed by the monks are to meditate, to study, and to strive for nibbāna. The six monks who mentioned it at all saw serving the laity as a secondary function—and here, it was the teaching of Buddhism that was deemed to be important, while the task of performing religious rituals was mentioned by only one monk (Spiro 1982, 284–286). Although his rather small sample of only 20 monks is not representative, it does nicely illustrate Gombrich's more theoretical argumentation.

Spiro's arguments also reinforce Weber's position that "the community of Buddha represented the following of a mystagogue, being, in any case, more a soteriological school than an order" (Weber 1967, 216), as well as Gombrich's categorization of Theravāda Buddhism as 'religious individualism' (Gombrich 2006, 73–80), both of which we discussed in the first chapter. Indeed, as Spiro reminds us, "the monk can do nothing to assist laymen to achieve salvation because each [Theravāda] Buddhist must save himself" (Spiro 1982, 286). Spiro illustrates this with a telling passage in the *Questions of King Milinda*, in which the king asks the venerable monk Nāgasena, "What is the object, Sir, of your renunciation, and what the summum bonum at which you aim?," to which the monk answers, "Why do you ask? Our renunciation is to the end that this sorrow may perish away, and that no further sorrow may arise; the complete passing away, without cleaving to the world, is our highest aim" (Spiro 1982, 286–287; Rhys Davids 1890, 49). Here, between the lines, Nāgasena himself reveals the religious individualism (note that this is a modern academic term) that underlies Theravāda Buddhism, and that makes the monks concentrate on their own salvation. However, Nāgasena also reveals that not all monks joined for the laudable reason to strive for nibbāna: when the king asks whether all monks have joined the order for the high reasons Nāgasena mentioned, the latter readily concedes that this was not necessarily the

---

involved in the *Saffron Revolution* of August and September 2007 in an (unsuccessful) attempt to face down the military regime.

case: "Certainly not, Sire. Some for those reasons, but some have left world in terror at the tyranny of kings. Some have joined us to be sa. from being robbed, some harassed by debt, and some perhaps to gain a livelihood" (Rhys Davids 1890, 49–50). But I shall return to the composition of the early Sangha and the wider implications of that later in this chapter. In any case, Spiro arrives at an even more pointed conclusion than Gombrich about the relationship between monk and laity:

> Whereas in Christianity, for example, it is the duty of the priest, by his sacramental functions, to assist the layman to achieve salvation, in Buddhism it is the recognized duty of the layman to assist the monk to achieve salvation. (Spiro 1982, 287)

This verdict, as interesting as it sounds, is however not entirely justified since it seems to have the already mentioned 'English village vicar' in mind: whereas monasticism in Protestantism is notably absent, in Catholicism and the various Orthodox churches, there is a clear differentiation between the roles of (mainly) secular priests and that of monks belonging to monastic orders. Such a differentiation does not exist in Theravāda Buddhism, however: monks routinely fulfil both roles, with the flagged-up limitations.[5] This observation leads us to the term 'monk' that I have used here so far without any qualification. 'Monk' is just one possible translation of the original Pali term *bhikkhu*. That there are many possible other translations becomes apparent when we look at the description of the term as it appears in the *Suttavibangha* section of the Vinaya Pitaka.[6] It reads as follows:

> *Monk* means: he is a monk because he is a beggar for alms, a monk because he submits to wandering for alms, a monk because he is one who wears the patchwork cloth, a monk by the designation (of others), a monk of account

---

[5] However, we will see later in this and some of the following chapters that while some monks specialize in meditation without much contact with lay followers (forest monks), others focus on scripture as well as on clerical aspects of Buddhism (city monks). Hence, it could well be argued that although the distinction does not exist in theory, it does so in practice and depends on the inclination of the monk in question.

[6] Literally, the 'Basket of the Discipline' as one part of the Tipitaka or 'Three Baskets' that form the core of the Theravada Buddhist canonical texts.

of his acknowledgment; a monk is called 'Come, monk,' a monk is endowed
with going to the three refuges, a monk is auspicious, a monk is the essential, a monk is a learner, a monk is an adept, a monk means one who is
endowed with harmony for the Order, [...], with actions (in accordance
with dhamma and the discipline), with steadfastness and the attributes of a
man perfected, this one is a *monk* as understood in this meaning. (Horner
1938, Vol. I, 42 [emphasis in original])

Here, the choice of 'monk' as a translation for the original term *bhikkhu*
is consciously made by Horner as the translator, who prefers this translation to 'mendicant,' 'almsman,' 'brother,' or 'friar.' As he explains,
although the first two translations would be historically correct, they put
too much emphasis on just one aspect of the monk's daily life, while
'brother' and 'friar' would be historically incorrect (Horner 1938, Vol. I.,
xl–l). 'Monk' seems to be the best fit for him since both *bhikkhus* and
(Western) monks represent "the outcome of certain and definite historical
tendencies"—but he admits that Christian and Buddhist understandings
of the term "although comparable in meaning, are not synonymous"
(Horner 1938, Vol. I., xliv). Spiro (1982, 279–281) is less sanguine in this
regard, but nevertheless concedes, after some debate, that "it is not
stretching the term unduly to render *bhikkhu* as 'monk'"—a verdict that I
am happy to accept: in my opinion, the terms 'mendicant,' 'almsman,' or
even 'beggar' not only overemphasize just one aspect of the monk's existence, but even verge on denigrating them. On the other hand, 'brother'
(in a religious context) and 'friar' suffer from too many Christian connotations and expectations to be helpful. Hence, let us settle for the more
neutral term 'monk.'

The monks' overall conduct and their monastic life are painstakingly
controlled and governed by the *patimokkha* (literally 'towards liberation';
Sanskrit: prātimoksa).[7] This section of the *Vinaya Pitaka* contains the dis-
ciplinary code in the shape of 227 major rules that the monks must
observe, while a commentary on them can be found in the latter's *vib-
hanga* section. Over the centuries, new commentaries and interpretations
have been added that differ from Sangha to Sangha and country to country, but these differences need not be discussed in our present context.
Suffice it to say then that according to the Vinaya Pitaka in all its different
interpretations, the monks are understood to be outsiders to the society

[7] On the monastic life of Theravāda monks, see Wijayaratna 1990.

which they had left on their own accord, and ideally meant to be ascetic, peripatetic seekers of their own salvation and that of others. They are supposed to only possess the Eight Requisites[8] or *asta pariskāra*, that is their robes (up to three sets), begging bowls, a belt, a razor for shaving their hair (and in Thailand their eyebrows), a needle, a toothpick, a strainer, and a staff (Lamotte 2007, 56–57). Nowadays, monks usually also carry a so-called *klot*, that is a large umbrella fitted with a mosquito net, plus, times being as they are, mobile phones to stay in touch with each other and their followers. Furthermore, monks are not allowed to build their own houses except for the temporary lean-tos, huts, or tents (which explains the klot which serves as a tent-like shelter), or to farm in order to produce their own food supply—the latter to prevent them from accidentally killing the fauna living on and below the ground, but also to enable the laity to make merit by donating food during the monks' morning alms rounds. This implies that the monks depend on the generosity of the people, who in return depend on the monks for their preaching of the Dhamma and for allowing them to make merit (tam boon in Thai) by accepting their donations. Carrithers describes this as a 'moral economy of poverty': "If the monks received something of value from the laity, the laity received something of value from the monks: 'the gift of the Teaching is the best gift'" (Carrithers 2007, 134). Very similarly, Gombrich calls it 'reciprocal generosity,' saying that "the Sangha gave the Dhamma, the laity gave material support, rather disparagingly termed 'raw flesh'" (Gombrich 2006, 116).

The patimokkha also regulates monk-layperson interactions. For example, being alone with women is strictly forbidden for the monks as celibates, and so is touching them or accepting anything directly from the hands of a woman; hence, a present given to a monk by a woman has to be put on a piece of cloth first before the monks can accept it. Monks also cannot accept gold, silver, jewellery, or money, although the latter is usually deemed to be acceptable if handed over in an envelope—after all, even monks have bills to pay. Regarding food, the monks usually have to accept whatever is offered to them during their morning alms rounds or *pindapāta* (binderbaht in Thai, usually starting at daybreak around 6 am)[9] or when

---

[8] In earlier tradition, only four were mentioned: the monk's robes, his begging bowl, medicine, and shelter.
[9] Michael Symes, who visited the Kingdom of Ava (Burma) in 1795 as part of a diplomatic mission sent by the Governor General of India, reports that "[during] their walk they never

lay followers visit the temple during Buddhist holidays, festivals, or the so-called four monthly 'monk days' (uposatha days; wan phra in Thai, following the lunar calendar), which implies that the monks are not required to be strict vegetarians since the food they receive normally includes some chicken curry, fish, pork, and sometimes beef. However, they must not eat such dishes if there is a suspicion that the animals in question were slaughtered explicitly to feed the monks. I could observe this rule in its actual interpretation on a rural market in Southern Thailand where a nun and I were sent to buy some fresh fish: all fish that were still moving and thus obviously still alive were ineligible for that very reason.

## EXCHANGES: MONKS AND LAITY

There are many more rules regulating the minutiae of the monk's daily life, including the way monks are supposed to walk and talk, exhorting them to always carry themselves with a humble, correct, and dignified composure. As Lamotte opines, all these rules and obligations are meant to guide the monks, not to turn them into mere machines devoid of their own thinking (Lamotte 2007, 57–58) and, thus, without agency of their own. The original intention behind these rules as expressed in the Buddha's First Sermon was to steer a middle course between comfort and discomfort to prevent the monks from becoming distracted from seeking their own enlightenment (Gombrich 2006, 95). In any case, it is the duty of the monks to observe these rules, and they are repeated and affirmed twice per month in an assembly of all monks, including visiting monks, staying in a given monastery. However, all these rules and regulations tend to ignore the other side of this moral economy of poverty based on the exchange of material goods for spiritual ones, and that is

cast their eyes to the right or to the left, but keep them fixed on the ground; they do not stop to solicit, and seldom even look at the donors, who appear more desirous to bestow, than the others to receive." Symes also comments that they normally received much more than they could possibly consume, with the positive side effect that "the surplus [was] disposed of as charitably as it was given; to the needy stranger, or the poor scholars [he probably means temple boys] who daily attend them, to be instructed in letters, and taught their moral and religious duties" (Symes 1800, 211). This is still the same today. I could observe one occasion at a temple in the South of Thailand where I stayed as a lay follower where a young English lad down on his luck received a large meal consisting of rice and various curries prepared for him by the nuns (mae chees), and even some money to help him on.

the laity and its expectations, wishes, and hopes. After all, the best way to make merit in this life in the hope to gain a more auspicious rebirth and, thus, a better next life, is by making donations to temples and monks as "the best field for karmic fruitfulness" (Harvey 2000, 21–22)—a laudable practice that can, in some cases, put the strict adherence to the patimokkha to the test.

Consider, for example, a temple in an urban setting, in a town or a city. For monks residing in such a temple, interactions with townspeople or city dwellers are of a frequent nature and basically occur on a day-to-day basis. People come to pray, but also for advice—which means the urban monk functions more as a this-worldly teacher and advisor than as a world-renouncing meditator (Carrithers 2007, 134). Donations and gifts for the temple and/or for individual monks will be frequent too, and oftentimes rather valuable in order to accrue as much merit as possible.[10] Furthermore, monks will be invited to attend many functions at the homes of laypeople, for example, presiding over, and chanting at, weddings, funerals,[11] and blessing ceremonies. Not surprisingly, many city temples acquire immense wealth over the decades and centuries, especially if they are home to a famous relic, a 'foot print' of the Buddha, or a statue said to be imbued with magical power. Some monks even gain celebrity status due to their eloquent sermons, the auspicious amulets they offered, the black magic they allegedly can perform, or their alleged ability to predict lucky (lottery) numbers. A few of them become rather wealthy themselves in the process. Nowadays, 'celebrity' monks possessing expensive cars and owning real estate (even though the vow of poverty should prevent this from happening) are common occurrences, and reasons for endless gossip and sensational news stories.

Of course, it is only human that some monks would abuse the position of (moral) trust and (spiritual) authority in which they found themselves due to circumstances not necessarily under their control. This issue is hard to avoid as it basically comes as a largely unanticipated side-effect of the peculiar relationship between the nominally peripatetic, ascetic monks and

[10] On the central concept of merit in Burmese Buddhism, see, for example, Spiro 1982, 92 passim; for current Thai Buddhism, see Scott 2009.

[11] Gombrich (2006, 125) notes that participating in a funeral "is quite logical for [the monk] to do [since death] is the perfect occasion for preaching on impermanence and the inevitability of suffering."

the lay followers in which the former provide moral and spiritual advice, while the latter offer material support. Carrithers astutely comments on this relationship as follows:

> [This] perfect moral economy has probably always been less the norm than the ideal, practised only by a very few. Even in the ancient canonical writings it appears chiefly in exhortations and pious reminiscences, while the more circumstantial account suggests that, even then, laymen invited monks for meals, gave them robes, and built them shelter [...]. The relationship between monks and laymen [...] might reasonably be phrased as a long-term exchange: spiritual goods for material support. The history of the Sangha is the gradual unfolding of the implications of this exchange. (Carrithers 2007, 134)

As just mentioned, it goes without saying that the laity is aware of this flip side: breaking news about scandals involving monks, sometimes rather senior ones, is rather frequent nowadays, covering anything from alcohol and/or drugs abuse, sexual misconduct, financial fraud, and suchlike. For the case of Thailand, and against the backdrop of a manifest decline in ethical standards, Cook points out that "[the] personal ethics of the individual monk are of great concern to the laity [because it] is only by donating to spiritually pure monks that alms donations may be meritoriously accumulative" (Cook 2014, 43). Hence, lay followers at times travel great distances to make donations to an individual monk who is seen as a paragon of virtue—and for this reason as well, there is a Thai saying to the effect that people respect the robe but not necessarily the individual wearer of it.

During my research, I could witness these wider implications of the monkhood-laity interactions in practice, and on an admittedly low and innocent level, when I followed some ascetic monks in Thailand: whether they liked it or not, these forest monks were seen as persons of moral and spiritual purity wherever they went. Of course, they received plenty of food from the inhabitants of the villages they passed through during their wanderings even though it was clear that they would not stay in the vicinity. And when the people of a certain village deep inside a lesser-known Southern Thai national park realized that the monks had occupied a long-vacant monastic residence (officially a hermitage, not a temple), they immediately came to visit to make merit. Of course, they expected the monks to offer morning and evening chants as long as they were staying, and to preach to them and to teach them the dharma. But they also asked the monks for advice on how to deal with the more mundane problems of their daily lives. When it became obvious that the ascetic wandering monks would stay for a while, the delighted villagers went to great lengths to make the lives of the monks more comfortable by repairing the dilapidated temple buildings and by reconnecting the temple to running water. On top of that, a 'Buddha tree' or Bodhi tree[12] was planted as well, both to adorn the residence and to elevate its significance. Again, it should be kept in mind that making donations to a temple and its monks is the best way to make merit and ensure a better rebirth. But unlike in urban areas with their numerous temples populated by dozens or even hundreds of monks, in some remote rural regions monks are scarce, especially in those regions that can be reached only by foot or after an arduous hours-long drive in a 4 × 4 vehicle along rather dubious dirt tracks. And since modernity with its different rhythm of life has caught up with the Theravāda countries as well, the number of fully ordained 'professional' monks is in decline, which is why the countryside is dotted with many vacant temples—similar to Western European rural areas with their closed-down churches. So, the fact that the small group of ascetic monks chanced upon this small monastic residence in the middle of nowhere was a stroke of sheer luck for the villagers: now, they were finally able to donate food in the morning or visit the temple every day if they were so inclined instead of having to venture out of their valley to the next town temple once per week.

This example from a rather remote rural village at least one-hour drive away from the main roads is as innocent as it gets: neither are there any riches to be gained, nor are the ascetic monks even remotely interested in such things. But the example illustrates that there is, by sheer necessity and human nature, a give and take between two parties: the monks and the laity. This also implies that, as Gombrich observed, even the most ascetic monk "is constantly nudged back to normal comforts by the 'relentless piety' of the laity who shower him with donations" (Gombrich 2006, 156). In a different setting, say a wealthy urban centre, this process of give and take might involve more actors on both sides, and a higher quality of goods to be exchanged as well: on the one side, the laity could make much more valuable donations, while on the other, the temple could dispatch

---

[12] The Buddha is said to have gained enlightenment sitting under such a tree. The Bodhi tree is also known as 'sacred fig' tree, ficus religiosa in Latin.

more, and especially more senior, monks for blessing ceremonies and chanting, thus imbuing them with more spiritual power than that on offer by just one senior monk and some junior ones in my example. It is thus probably permissible to argue that it is not necessarily malice or human fallibility and greed that lead individual temples as well as individual monks astray from the path of poverty in general, and certain patimokkha rules in particular. Rather, there seems to be a complicated set of push-and-pull factors at work, with one driver behind this being the expectations of the laity, as just illustrated.

With regard to these push-and-pull factors, it is interesting to note how deeply intertwined the monkhood and the laity are in Burma and Thailand: unlike in Sri Lanka, where, for a variety of reasons, it is difficult for monks to leave the monkhood to become a layman again, it still is the norm in Burma and in Thailand that males should temporarily join the temple as a novice[13] or a fully ordained monk at least once in their lives for some weeks or months, most auspiciously during Buddhist Lent. As Bechert explains, the Buddha "left it to the members of the Sangha to withdraw from the Order at any time if they did not feel equal to the spiritual life. Anyone who left the Sangha of his own accord, and not because of an offence against the basic rules during his life as a monk, could be ordained again without difficulty" (Bechert 2007, 154). Although in an urban environment, this practice of temporary ordination seems to be in decline, it is very much alive and well in a rural setting where men who have not yet been monks are usually deemed to be not yet 'ripe,' and thus not full members of their rural societies.[14] By extension, that obviously also implies that all those who did so are deemed to be full-fledged members of their rural societies, and the longer they stayed within the monkhood, usually measured in *pansa* or Buddhist Lent cycles, the higher their prestige. This practice also implies that the boundaries between laity and Sangha tended to be blurred in the sense of an ebb-and-flow 'revolving door' effect tied

[13] One needs to be 20 years of age to become a fully ordained monk; males that enter the monastery between 8 years and 20 years can be ordained as novices (śrāmanera (Sanskrit) or sāmanera (Pali), Thai version: samanen; lit.: 'small renunciate'). Before the age of 8, ordination is not possible.

[14] This fact, plus the peer pressure within a village, occasionally even leads non-Buddhist young males to temporarily ordain as monks. Since a renunciation of their beliefs, or a conversion to Buddhism, is not required, this is easily done and seen as a kind of 'social service' rather than a religious one.

to the seasons: during the rainy season that coincides with the Buddhist Lent (mid-July/early August to mid-October/end of October depending on the lunar calendar) when not much work in the fields can be done, many males ordain as monks or as novices depending on their age, to disrobe and leave again when the Buddhist Lent is over.

Apart from allowing lay followers to make merit, a temple fulfils several other important functions as well. First of all, the temple serves as a community centre, not unlike the parish church in a Western setting, or the mosque in Muslim countries. Here, ceremonies are undertaken, and temple festivals held that bring the villagers together, thus reinforcing the community. Since villages in the three countries normally are far-flung habitations, consisting of only loosely linked farm houses with wide fields or jungles separating them, which is very unlike our Western ideas of a tight group of houses huddled around the parish church, this is quite an important function. In these get-togethers, issues of common interest are also discussed, with the senior monk or the abbot having a say as well—again not unlike the village priest or vicar in a Western setting. Furthermore, in pre-modern times, the temples also served as free schools where the villagers or towns folks learned the basics of the Dhamma, of reading, writing, and calculating, some practical skills (depending on the location), and what we would nowadays call 'citizenship.' Michael Symes, who as a lieutenant colonel took part in a diplomatic mission of the Governor-General of India to Burma (the Kingdom of Ava, to be more precise) in 1795, reported on that as follows:

> All [...] monasteries, whether in town or country, are seminaries for the education of youth, in which boys of a certain age, are taught their letters, and instructed in moral and religious duties. To these schools the neighbouring villagers send their children, where they are educated gratis, no distinction being made between the son of a peasant and him who wears the [...] string of nobility. (Symes 1800, 194–195)

The assertion that no distinction was made between the sons of commoners (who required only basic training anyway due to their menial occupations, mostly as farmers or artisans) and the sons of the nobility (who required a more profound education since they were supposed to occupy administrative positions) is not entirely credible. I would rather side with Tambiah who states, with respect to Thailand, "[before] the spread of state-sponsored education [...] the monasteries not only trained sons of nobility as novices for a limited period of time to fill public positions but, perhaps equally importantly, made accessible diverse kinds of knowledge other than strictly religious to monks who spent a long time in robes (from novicehood to ordained monk), which they were able to put to good use when they disrobed" (Tambiah 1976, 208). We could compare this to modern school systems: the longer the pupils or students stay, the higher the qualification they achieve. However, one caveat needs to be made here: unlike modern secular schools, the temple-based school system did not aim at providing general education per se to enable the students to become useful and productive members of their society. Rather, as Turner emphasizes in the case of Burma, "its purpose was to preserve the *sāsana* and create good merit for both the boys and their parents" (Turner 2014, 49).

Although the secular state has now taken over schools as important early vehicles not only for basic education but for socialization and for nation-building, many temples still offer basic religious instruction and, for the poorer families, the opportunity to enrol their (male) children as temple boys or as novices in exchange for free food and accommodation. A few temples also continue to offer higher education, but only of a religious kind, such as advanced studies in Pali which are essential for those monks who choose a scholarly path or are interested in an ecclesiastical career. As in the modern secular educational system, diplomas are now routinely awarded in order to certify such achievements, some of which entitle the holder to an honorific, such as 'Maha' in Thailand for those successfully concluding Level 3 (Parian Tham Sam Prayok) Pali studies (starting with Level/Parian 1, and ending with Level/Parian 9). Furthermore, in all three countries, several Buddhist universities, usually centred on a major temple, offer further education up to postgraduate degree level mainly for monks who follow the 'vocation of learning' (*pariyatti*) more than the 'vocation of practice' (*patipatti*)—the latter being the monastic aspect that the ascetic monks focus on.

From all this we can glean that temples and monks never only fulfilled ceremonial, ritual, and religious functions. Rather, they played, and still play, an important role when it comes to communal politics—again very similar to village priests and vicars in a Western rural setting. In modern times, this role has been somewhat weakened by other sources of readily available authority such as the district-level civil administration or, regarding the enforcement of law and order, the police. In pre-modern times, however, and prior to state-building efforts such as highway and railroad construction, temples and monks used to be the only sources of authority that linked remote villages to the government residing in the faraway capital. Ascetic forest monks even acted as trailblazers in this regard—not necessarily on purpose, though: often, a hermitage of a renowned monk morphed into a proper temple populated by monks and novices following him, which then attracted lay followers as well who settled as farmers or temple servants. Hence, as Kasetsiri (quoted in Tambiah 1984, 69–70) argues, temples became "a binding force which tied the population together" and thus also became "one of the basic concerns of the rulers in the area." This explains why these governments had by sheer necessity an interest in controlling the activities of the monkhood, and to turn them into agents of the state in the absence of, or in addition to, other sources of the state's authority. How this worked, and what it meant for the monkhood, will be discussed next. The best way to start with that is to examine how temples and monks acquired political power that went beyond mere communal matters in the first place. And here, donations again play a major role since they are at the heart of what Carrithers called the moral exchange of poverty and its implications for the Sangha.

## PILLARS: MONKS AND TRADITIONAL POLITICS

When it comes to such major donations, it is typical for a traditional agricultural society that substantial parts of them do not come as money or any other valuables, but in the shape of land donations. This was, understandably, even more the case in pre-modern societies in which the use of money either was still not yet practised or at least not yet widespread enough to reach remote villages.[15] Nowadays, many villagers are landowners in their own right, whereas in the olden days, the nobility and rich merchants formed the bulk of landowners. Carrithers comments on the implications of this as follows:

> At the most modest this meant that the monk became the incumbent of a small dwelling with the surrounding ground, and his food and his robes might have been seen to, as in poor rural temples today, by the arrangement of a rota among his villagers. At the least modest the Sangha became lords

---

[15] There is some evidence that in the city-based society the Buddha hailed from, money was already in use to facilitate organized long-distance trade.

and heirs of vast estates, encompassing not only land and villages, but also irrigation, reservoirs, canals and plantations. (Carrithers 2007, 136)

As I already mentioned, the patimokkha rules explicitly forbid the monks to work on their own fields or have someone else to do it for them, and neither should they handle uncooked food since all this would undermine the 'begging order' nature of the Sangha: after all, they are supposed to receive their food and robes as well as other necessities of life from the laity who, by donating these things, would accrue merit (Carrithers 2007, 136). However, it can be argued that the Sangha fell victim to its own success: alms rounds in the morning as the sole base for the monks' sustenance may work well for small groups of peripatetic, ascetic monks, but it does not work, or is at least not very practical, when it comes to dozens, or even hundreds, of settled monks staying at a major temple. If all its resident monks, or just a substantial part of them, were to descent on the villagers of those habitations surrounding the temple every morning, this would not necessarily endear the former to the latter—and probably much less so at a time when villagers struggle hard to put food on the table for their own families. Several such cases are mentioned in the Tipitaka, for example, in the Suttavibangha (see the translation of Horner 1938, Vol. I, 26). The villagers' donations would probably also not have been enough to guarantee the long-term existence of a given temple. Hence, some other way needed to be found to ensure the longevity and survivability of both the temple and the resident monks in the shape of food, donations, and other suitable support. In modern times (in this narrow context defined as post-Second World War), the increasing popularity of both the Samadhi and Vipassanā meditation practices amongst laypeople in the three countries[16] and beyond, and the resulting proliferation of temples that offer such meditation courses to hundreds of lay followers, also meant that additional sources of income had (and still have) to be found. Hence, as Gombrich states, "[to] survive, the Sangha immediately and constantly requires material support" (Gombrich 2006, 150).

---

[16] In Myanmar, Vipassanā meditation was popularized by meditation master Mahasi Sayadaw (1904–1982) in the 1950s, and in Thailand at roughly the same time by Phra Phimolatham (1903–1989) who was deeply influenced by the former's meditation techniques (Cook 2014, 26–27).

From a doctrinal point of view, the potential patimokkha violations were quickly defused by appointing middlemen (either monastery servants or ārāmika, or trusted lay followers or upāsaka) who administered the worldly affairs of the temple, including the handling of the money, on behalf of the monks. Even the Buddha seemed to have condoned this practice—albeit probably only somewhat reluctantly so.[17] Of course, this could be interpreted as a blatant case of hypocrisy, but I would rather see it as a realpolitik decision to react to unintended consequences of the Sangha's success. On the other hand, the practice of owning land and growing their own food that gradually crept in created yet another unintended side effect: loosening, or at least weakening, the bonds of the 'moral economy of poverty' to the detriment of both sides, monkhood and laity. After all, the senior monks and abbots of the land-owning temples by default acquired a new, additional role that went far beyond that of a preacher, teacher, and advisor: as land owners in a feudal society, they now were on a similar hierarchical level as the land-owning feudal nobility, which also means that they were heavily involved in this-worldly politics at least on the local level, but in some cases on the regional level as well, depending on the size and the wealth of a given temple. Occasionally, it also meant that temples found themselves embroiled in legal disputes with other temples, with the laity, or even with the king due to conflicting property interests, as Tambiah (1984, 62–63) points out for the case of the Burmese Pagan dynasty. This is not a thing of the past, by the way: disputes around questions of ownership of a particular strip of land between temples and the state, or temples and citizens, can often be found in the local or even regional media.[18]

Carrithers and Gombrich develop their compelling arguments mainly for the case of Sri Lanka, but similar mechanism can be observed in the pre-modern societies and realms of the Southeast Asian countries Myanmar and Thailand as well: many temples gained control over vast tracts of land via royal patronage or via that of other influential actors such as rich merchants, and with that, they also gained control over those who tilled this

---

[17] See the interesting discussion on this in Gombrich 2006, 94–95, 104–105.

[18] Legal ownership can be quite a murky affair. For example, in 2014, I visited a rural temple in Thailand where the temple ground belonged to the temple, but the rubber trees that had been planted there when the temple was unoccupied for many years belonged to the farmer, who was not too keen to sell his trees even though they stood in the way of urgent renovations.

land which, due to the perennial under-population of vast tracts of Southeast Asia in pre-modern times, was even more important than the control of the land itself. This also means that, by default, these temples could turn into powerful political actors in their own right as well,[19] occasionally even challenging the ruling dynasty in times of civil rebellion or wars between various contenders for the crown. And even if the abbots of these influential temples were not interested in this-worldly things at all, the very fact that ever more arable, and thus taxable, land was controlled by someone else than the ruling dynasty meant that the ruler of the day lost substantial parts of his tax base. Unsurprisingly, some powerful rulers found excuses that allowed them to divest those temples which had become too wealthy and powerful of the bulk of their real estate and, thus, their income and their power base.[20] Carrithers comments on the ensuing implications of this as follows:

> So the Sangha – or at least the monks of the capital – meddled with kings. But kings meddled with the Sangha, drawing it deeper into political matters and changing its internal constitution. (Carrithers 2007, 141)

From the perspective of the monkhood, this meddling in worldly affairs probably was unavoidable even in the lifetimes of the Buddha and the original Sangha. And it was as unavoidable as it was for other founders of religions, such as Jesus Christ and Prophet Mohammed: the very fact that they were, unlike many other contemporaries trying to do exactly the same, successful in establishing a new faith and in attracting numerous followers, invariably brought them to the notice of the power holders of their times who may not necessarily have regarded them kindly: whatever the soteriological merit of the new faith may have been, in the 'here and now,'

---

[19] Again, this transition from world renouncer to world conqueror in the shape of a feudal lord is nothing really novel: in other times and other regions, similar processes were at work—one example would be the Catholic prince bishops and prince abbots who emerged after the collapse of Imperial Roman power from the fourth century onwards in those parts of Western Europe that later formed part of the Holy Roman Empire of German Nations. Arguably, in Buddhism this practice started very early on in the lifetimes of the Buddha: King Bimbisāra, for example, is said to have handed over individuals and even whole villages to work for the temples associated with them, after having asked the Buddha for permission to do so.

[20] This point is also made by Tambiah (1984, 63), who also cites several other publications that focus on aspects of statecraft and administration in pre-modern Southeast Asia.

these founders of faith were first of all troublemakers when seen from a political, law-and-order perspective since they challenged the established order. After all, in pre-ideological times, religion served as a powerful mobiliser and as a rallying point—sometimes used by the authorities of the day for their own purposes (I already mentioned crusades and jihad in that regard), or employed against them, usually in the shape of peasant rebellions led by a charismatic leader who, in many cases, professed to be clerics or monks. Even nowadays, religion is a powerful and dangerous weapon, potentially able to seriously challenge governments. I already touched upon Al Qaeda and Islamic State of Iraq and Syria (ISIS), but on a lower and far less dangerous level, this also explains why the government of the People's Republic of China banned the rather harmless and small Falun Gong ('Dharma Wheel Practice') sect and detained many of its leaders: a brief look at Chinese history shows that many uprisings originated from such religious movements.

In any case, it must have been obvious to the Buddha from the very beginning that if his teaching would turn out to be too successful in the sense that the broad masses chose to become world renouncers, then the society as he knew would have collapsed. After all, monks are supposed to be celibates, not meant to embark on physical labour, and depend on the support of the laity as I explained earlier in this chapter—which presupposes the existence of a laity in the first place (Spiro 1982, 283). In his usual flourish, Spiro follows that for these reasons, Buddhism must by sheer necessity be a 'virtuoso religion' as he calls it, and that "a Buddhist society consists of a small core of world-renouncing religious virtuoso surrounded by a large mass of the religiously unmusical, who although living in the world cherish and support this otherworldly minority" (Spiro 1982, 283).

Now, in basically all societies, not everyone is interested in becoming a world renouncer.[21] The same holds true for the society that formed the backdrop to the Buddha's life and his teaching. There is some evidence that, even though at least in theory, everybody could become a monk, the Buddha's teaching mainly appealed to the higher strata of society, namely

[21] This is true even if, at times, overzealous governments try to force the populations under their control to live their lives as saintly as possible, contemplating the greatness of God or any other deity without fail or let-up. Current examples would again include the Taliban's regime in Afghanistan, and ISIS' attempts to regulate daily life in the areas under their control down to the most minute detail.

Brahmins, Kshatriyas, and Vaisyas. Gombrich points at this, using Gokhale's findings about the composition of the early Sangha[22]: from a sample of 328 well-enough documented monks, 209 apparently came from the Brahmin (priests) and Kshatriya (warrior) castes, and thus from the upper strata of their society. Gombrich draws a convincing conclusion: "If these figures have any foundation, they show that Buddhism, though it admitted anyone to the Sangha, was not primarily a religion of the downtrodden" (Gombrich 2006, 56–57). Rather, the composition of the first Sangha appears to be a bit elitist. In my opinion, Gombrich thus is entirely justified to argue that "[to present the Buddha] as a sort of a socialist is a serious anachronism" (Gombrich 2006, 30). His argument gets even more convincing if we look at the 'in theory' qualification I just made: neither slaves nor soldiers could join the Sangha. As mentioned in the previous chapter, this has not only to do with the soldiers' use of violence and the Buddha's strategy to insulate the Sangha from such this-worldly actions he deems to be deeply wrong, but also with the fact that, just like ordaining slaves, ordaining soldiers would undermine society and the security of the state.

Again, Gombrich's argumentation in this regard is quite convincing: after pointing out that it was not only the Buddha who advised kings but, at times, also kings who advised the Buddha, he narrates an encounter (real or not) between the Buddha and his greatest and most powerful supporter, King Bimbisāra of Magadha, during which the latter bluntly told the Buddha "that kings would not take kindly to seeing soldiers desert by joining the Sangha" (Gombrich 2006, 83). Obviously, the Buddha heeded this sage advice, and so did his followers: in Thailand, for example, one of the questions that need to be answered by a candidate during his ordination ceremony is whether he is exempt from government service. Another question is about personal debt, by the way, thus rendering it impossible for a debtor to simply escape into the monkhood instead of paying back what he had borrowed. For the Buddha himself, these concessions probably were only minor ones. After all, his teaching was not about reforming the society, let alone destabilizing it, but about leaving it as a first step on the way to nibbāna, and eventually leaving the sorrowful world of dukkha altogether when personal enlightenment was achieved, and the personal circle of rebirth and re-death was finally stopped. The

---

[22] Gombrich mainly refers to Gokhale 1965.

Buddha's fundamental disinterest in politics or in any social consequences of his teaching still has resonance in the contemporary Sanghas, which offers us a first hint at why contemporary political monks, despite their vociferousness, face an uphill struggle when it comes to being accepted by the majority of their respective Sanghas.

Meddling in the sense of direct interference with politics was, however, rather rare for the Sanghas of the pre-modern societies since the direct secular power in the shape of arms and armies was challenged only at the monks' peril—again Burma being a very telling case in point: as we will see, Gombrich's remark that "[the] theory may be that kings are protectors, but the reality is that they are predators" (Gombrich 2006, 83) is entirely justified. The more usual case was that, due to the monks' high status and their ready access to kings, court, and officials, the monks could influence decisions in their favour, or in favour of those individuals on whose behalf they acted. Spiro, for example, mentions monks successfully interceding for prisoners condemned to death and facing execution, or interceding to protect peasants from being extorted by greedy officials (Spiro 1982, 380). Furthermore, when it comes to the kings and their actions themselves, monks usually did not fail to remind them of their duty to uphold and defend the faith, which also entailed to act accordingly. After all, from the days of the Buddha, and as explained in the previous chapter, the king was meant to be both a *cakkavattin* (Sanskrit: chakravartin), that is, the 'turner of the wheel of Dhamma' and a *dhammaraja*, which means a righteous ruler. Perceiving kings as righteous rulers meant that the monks not only remonstrated with errant kings and their officialdom time and again, but also acted as supporters of them, basically being one pillar of the traditional Buddhist polity, with the kingship being the second, and the people the third (Tambiah 1978, 111–112). This was also a matter of eminent self-interest: after all, the monks could go on their daily alms rounds only if a certain amount of law and order existed. The valuable support that the Sanghas offered to the various kings does explain to a large extent why Theravāda Buddhism was treated as a (quasi-) state religion, and why the monks were showered with royal favours, including new temples and stupas, monthly allowances, special ecclesiastical courts, and titles and rewards for scriptural achievements, such as learning and mastering Pali. Seen from this perspective, the relationship between various dynasties and the Sangha was indeed "close and reciprocal" (Spiro 1982, 380–381): the king needed them as loyal supporters of his rule legitimizing his rule mainly via the integrative system of

Buddhist values they had to offer, especially so in remote villages where they usually were the only source of authority, while the Sangha needed the king to guarantee a stable and peaceful environment that allowed them to focus on learning, meditating, teaching, and preaching without too much trouble.

On the other hand, precisely because they were the defenders of the religion as cakkavattin and dhammaraja, kings saw it as their right to interfere with their respective Sanghas in order to reign them in and 'purify' them, also using this opportunity as a convenient excuse to claw back at least some of the land donated to the temples in earlier reigns. In order to purify and renew traditions and practices of village- and towns-based monks deemed to be errant in their ways, various rulers of historical Sri Lanka, Burma, and Siam/Thailand often made use of their 'pure' ascetic forest monks active in remote parts of the kingdom, and thus not tainted by corruption and other forms of moral decay. Tambiah (1984, 68–69, 72–73) hence sees these forest monks as a ruler's convenient and effective counter-weight against the power of monasteries and cults who had become too influential. On other occasions, rulers drew on the help of Sanghas outside of their own realm to purify their own monkhood. Spiro, for example, mentions Burmese King Narapatisithu (Sithu II, Pagan Dynasty, ruled 1174–1211) under whose influence the Sangha decided to follow Sri Lanka's (Ceylon's) more orthodox Mahavihara Nikaya ('school') instead of the somewhat less orthodox Mon-influenced Thaton school (also see Harvey 1925, 56), and King Dhammazedi (Hanthawaddy Kingdom, r. 1471–1492), who used to be a monk before he became king (Spiro 1982, 382). With regard to Ceylon, Harvey draws attention to a mission of Burmese monks sent by King Anawratha (Pagan Dynasty, r. 1044–1077) to King Vijayabahu I. (Kingdom of Polonnaruwa, r. 1055–1110) on the latter's invitation to re-establish the Sinhalese Sangha, while Gombrich adds the contribution of Sri Lankan King Parākramabāhu I. (Kingdom of Polonnaruwa, r. 1153–1186) who reunified a Sangha split into three factions, and the purification and reordaining of the Sinhalese monastic order (which had nearly become extinct by then) in 1753 during the reign of King Kirti Sri Rajasinha (Kandy Dynasty, r. 1747–1782) with the help of Thai monks who founded the Siyam Nikaya—one of the three monastic orders that still exist in Sri Lanka (Gombrich 2006, 158).[23]

---

[23] These episodes also are quite indicative as regards the close relations between the three different Sanghas even in these early days.

Finally, Tambiah reports a series of purifications and purges for the reign of Siamese King Rama I (Chakri Dynasty, r. 1782–1809), the last occurring as late as 1801 (Tambiah 1976, 183–188). In most cases, such purifications became necessary after a prolonged time of (civil) war, during which many temples were looted, books were burnt, and monks were forced to flee, as was, for example, the case after the sack of Ayutthaya in 1767 by the Burmese (Tambiah 1976, 183).

Just how much the power balance was tilted in favour of the king in the monarchy-Sangha relationship can be gleaned from the fact that time and again, kings did not just purge the Sanghas but all but annihilated them—usually without triggering an uprising against their rule. Burmese King Thohanbwa (Kingdom of Ava, reigned 1527–1542), for example, regularly plundered temples and pagodas on the excuse that they had no religious meaning and were nothing but treasure chambers. Monks who dared to stand in his way, he executed without moral qualms. Since he saw monks as potential rebels and was weary of the huge number of followers they could attract and mobilize, he held the opinion that they should all be killed anyway. This was not only rhetorical bluster: in 1540, he invited more than 1300 monks of the cities Ava, Sagaing, and Pinya to a festival, just to have them surrounded and put to the sword by his troops. According to Harvey, 360 monks, including 30 senior monks renowned for their learning, perished in this massacre, while the survivors fled to Toungoo, a city not under his control (Harvey 1925, 107). Thohanbwa, labelled by Harvey "a full-blooded savage" for this reason (ibid.), was not an exception: about three centuries later, Burmese King Alaungpaya (Konbaung Dynasty, reigned 1752–1780) had 3000 Mon monks executed in May 1757 at the end of the long siege of Pegu because they had supported the Mon resistance against his attempts to incorporate their kingdom into his own empire. Of course, these cases could be seen as brutal exceptions that prove the rule mentioned above: that there was, in normal times, a close and reciprocal relationship between the monarchy and the Sangha because both needed each other. Nevertheless, the point was made, and the lesson was obviously learnt. Envoy Michael Symes, for example, informs us that when he visited the Kingdom of Ava in 1795, the monks stayed out of politics:

In the various commotions of the empire, I never heard that the [monks] had taken any active share, or publicly interfered in politics, or engaged in war: by this prudent conduct they excited no resentment: the Birmans and the Peguers professing the same religion, who ever were conquerors, equally respected the ministers of their faith. (Symes 1800, 212)

That the rather frequent purifications and other interferences of kings in the affairs of the Sangha were not necessarily caused by religious issues but quite often by substantial political considerations is also pointed out by Tambiah. After a detailed assessment of such purifications in Sri Lanka's history, he raises some interesting questions that, if we could answer them, would further illuminate the reciprocal, and at times even symbiotic, relationship between Sangha and kingship. Indeed, it would be good to know how many monks there were and from which social segments they hailed since knowing this would allow us to better assess their political weight in a given situation. Also, it would be interesting to know in how far the monks were able to mobilize the lay followers they employed, given the fact that they had to depend on middlemen in that regard (Tambiah 1976, 173)—middlemen who may well have had different interests. Furthermore, against the backdrop of the existence of various monk factions centred around an influential temple, gaining a better knowledge about the intensity of the competition between these factions for royal favours in the shape of land grants or material gifts would also be helpful for a deeper analysis of their role as political actors (Tambiah 1976, 173–174). When it comes to the monarchy, it would be important to know how much a given king depended on the Sangha's support in order to defend his throne or to win it against another contender, and it would be also important to know how the Sangha's spiritual (soft) power compared to the king's coercive (hard) power in the shape of his access to armies and weapons (Tambiah 1976, 174). Hence, with regard to the relationship between the Sangha and the kingship as the two pillars of the traditional state, much is still left to conjecture, and we are only able to paint a rather crude picture.

## ENTREPRENEURS: MONKS IN A TIME OF TRANSITION

To sum up this argumentation, and with the caveat in mind that I just made, in pre-modern monarchic societies notionally (that is at least in theory if not in practice) ruled by a dhammaraja whose role involved protecting the Dhamma and the Sangha,[24] a certain balance of power existed: on the one hand, the kings supported the monkhood by building temples

---

[24] His own realm's Sangha, strictly speaking: in the frequent wars between Burma and Siam, the other side's temples and their treasures were seen as fair game and spoils of war (Tambiah 1976, 162).

and pagodas, by making lavish gifts, and by awarding them with titles and elevated positions, while also defending the faith itself—time and again quite literally against contenders professing a different creed, be it Hinduism, Islam, or Christianity. On the other, the monkhood, thus secure in their elevated position in society, supported the state by reconciling the ruled with their ruler by constructing the latter as the righteous king who had to be obeyed. Since Buddhism reigned supreme (although other religions were at least tolerated, as we shall see in the case studies), and since nobody challenged the position of the monks within the society, there was no need for proactive politicking or any attempt at social change: with regard to society as such, everything was as it should be in the sense of 'it always has been thus,' and since the goal was to leave society behind and to reach nibbāna, any attempt to change it was futile and irrelevant. This age-old equilibrium was destroyed by the actions of exterior, in our case Western, powers that abolished the traditional monarchies, supplanting them with their own secular colonial regimes. Hence, in Burma as well as in Sri Lanka (Ceylon), the Sanghas lost their royal patron as well as their pre-eminent position in the now quickly changing societies, with the consequence that the time-honoured "traditional relationship between church and state collapsed" (Spiro 1982, 383). The influx of Christian missionaries, mostly of a protestant variant, came as an additional aggravating factor that convinced many monks, especially younger monks, to become more proactive in order to defend the Dhamma. This was also the case in Siam/Thailand which was not colonized and whose monarchical system remained in place, but which also felt the power and influence of the neighbouring colonial regimes in Burma (British) and Laos and Cambodia (French). Mainly in response to the Western missionaries' proselytizing efforts, many of the younger monks not only eagerly adopted the essentialized and rationalized reconstruction of Theravāda Buddhism as a powerful counter to the 'superstitious' Christians, but also reinvented themselves along the lines of the missionaries they could observe as 'social activists' and 'social workers,' or as 'political entrepreneurs.' In the case of Sri Lanka, for example, Anagārika Dharmapāla as the founder of Buddhist modernism in that country encouraged monks to develop traits such as "methodism, punctuality, cleanliness, orderliness, time-consciousness, dedication, and 'non-consciousness'"—all of them "derived from contact with Christianity, its organizational structure, its social teachings and, above all, its idea of ministering to a flock" (Seneviratne 1999, 27). Seneviratne's conclusion is quite telling, and nicely depicts the change from a passive upholder of tradition to a proactive agent of change:

> The monk came to think of himself as an empowered political activist and an entrepreneur, in addition to being a caretaker of the flock. (Seneviratne 1999, 27)

The expression 'the monk,' however, should not mislead us to think that it was the majority of the monks that underwent this transition. This was, and, as I shall demonstrate, still is, most empathically not the case. The majority of monks still would support the statement of an abbot of a monastery in Mandalay, Myanmar, interviewed by Spiro in the 1970s. In the context of reaching nibbāna, the abbot said:

> It is like a log floating on a river – if there are no obstacles, it will eventually float to the ocean. These [politically active, PL] monks will have a hard time getting to the ocean [nirvana] because their political organizations are an obstacle. In fact, not only will they not get to the ocean for a very long time, but it is even more likely that they will become waterlogged and sink to the bottom of the river. Instead of getting to the ocean, they will end up in hell. (as quoted in Spiro 1982, 393)

This is, of course, a very stark statement that the politically active monks dispute in equally strong terms. Such diametrically opposed positions within the three different Sanghas beg one question: how come that expressing them is possible at all without being expelled? This is due to the fact that despite the new modern state's attempt to reign in and control the monkhood, for example, by appointing suitable pro-government senior monks to the position of Supreme Patriarch, the Sangha does not normally speak with one voice, and does not function as "a wholly united and monolithic entity" (Tambiah 1992, 102). In comparison with other religions, Theravāda Buddhism is far more comparable with loosely organized Sunni Islam than with the more centralized Shia Islam, and much nearer to Protestantism and its various streams than to Roman Catholicism unified under the Pope. To provide an example for this, the practice of some wandering ascetic monks I observed in Thailand to find a vacant temple and occupy it either for a couple of days or even for years without bothering to ask for permission from the Sangha hierarchy first would be impossible for Catholic monks or priests: reopening a church or a convent can only be done with explicit permission of, and on order by, the hierarchy—not by some individual monks' or priests' own initiative. Furthermore, as Gombrich, one of the leading scholars on Buddhism, explained, for the Sangha of early and medieval India, a Buddhist monastery should not be understood as a spiritual hierarchical organization. Rather, it constitutes a collection of individuals striving for their own salvation and the salvation of others. Gombrich concludes that "[one] corollary of this is the principle that decisions on matters of monastic discipline should be taken unanimously; another is that monks owe no obedience" (Gombrich 2007, 81). Indeed, within the different Theravāda Sanghas, it is more about orthopraxy or the right conduct than about orthodoxy or correct belief (Kirsch 1975, 9). In a sense, this focus on 'right conduct' as opposed to 'right belief' reflects the Noble Eightfold Path's emphasis on 'right action,' which then would lead to 'right results' (Jackson 2003, 19). Hence, as Spiro points out, as long as a monk complies with the rules of the vinaya, that means as long as he behaves like a monk, he is a monk (Spiro 1982, 391)—which also implies, as Jackson points out, that the "concern with heresy has been relatively unimportant in Buddhist countries" (Jackson 2003, 17).

In consequence, it is rather difficult, albeit not entirely impossible as we shall see in the case studies, to discipline, left alone to disrobe and dispel errant monks from the Sangha just for the beliefs they express. To be forcefully disrobed—and then usually rather swiftly[25]—and forbidden to ever enter the Sangha again, a monk has to violate one of the so-called *four parajikas* (Four Defeats) as the most serious transgressions of the patimokkha: having sexual intercourse, taking what is not given (stealing), intentionally bringing about the death of a human being, and deliberately lying to others that he has attained a superior spiritual state, for example being an arahant/arhat or 'perfected person' who has already achieved nibbāna. For the case of Sri Lanka, Seneviratne points at the consequences

[25] Nowadays, disrobing disgraced monks is a quick affair usually conducted in the office of the abbot of their temple, or the abbot of the temple nearest to the location where monks who were caught in the act, or were found stealing, or were driving under the influence, either by the police and/or villagers (who don't have much patience with errant monks) and had been arrested. In the late 1795 in Burma, Symes reports that such monks were publicly disgraced by daubing their head black and white, putting them on the back of an ass, and parading them through town or village, preceded by a drummer. Such elaborate practices were rare, however, he admits (Symes 1800, 211).

of not enforcing orthodoxy and settling for orthopraxy: "[The] Sangha has no overarching and unifying social structures that would make it into a powerful elite endowed with a gnawing class consciousness, [and that by] its very nature the Sangha cannot be a power. It can only be a hand-maiden of power" (Seneviratne 1999, 17). Against the background of a usually loose organizational structure of the various Sanghas in question, it is not difficult to understand why factions with diametrically opposed convictions towards this-worldly issues exist in each of them, and why there are clashes—occasionally even violent ones—between extremist, radical, and moderate factions in the same country.

## EVALUATIONS: TRADITIONAL MONKS AND CONTEMPORARY MONKS

To conclude this chapter, I argue following Carrithers that with regard to their conduct, today's political monks are not that different from the tra-ditional monks in as far as the latter also occasionally engaged in politics (Carrithers 2007, 146). And it is also probably true to say that contempo-rary monks still tend to wield their newly acquired secular powers in the political arena "by virtue of prestige and through personal ties" (ibid.). These superficial similarities however hide some rather significant differ-ences lurking below the surface. First of all, and quite obviously, the pro-cess of democratization opened the field for anyone with a political message, hence also for individual monks interested in such mundane mat-ters. Unlike traditional societies built around the concept of kingship, ide-ally along the just-mentioned meritorious 'world conqueror/world renouncer' pattern, the political arena of modern democratic/semi-democratic societies is a much bigger one, allowing for a plethora of con-flicting opinions and discourses including such that are diametrically opposed to traditional Buddhist values, thus giving room to a wide range of political actors. Arguably, this makes it easier for interested monks to enter this arena as well: even though they can be sure that, by doing so, they may antagonize the more traditionally inclined of their followers (i.e. those who see the monks as 'street lights'), they will most certainly appeal to many others who are convinced that in modern times, monks should actively defend the faith, which is often perceived to be under threat, as we shall see in the subsequent chapters.

In my opinion, we can also see a second and even more important difference: unlike their predecessors living, teaching, and preaching in traditional societies of old, contemporary political monks tend to see themselves as social activists and political entrepreneurs in quite a departure from the more traditional role understanding of their predecessors who saw themselves as teachers and preachers, showing, on request, the path to nibbāna, that is, a path out of this world and its endless cycles of rebirth and, if you like, 're-death' (Sanskrit: punar-mrtyu). In this regard, I agree with Gombrich's compelling argument on the Buddha not being a social reformer:

> Certainly, in consenting to preach and then establishing an Order of monks to do likewise, he showed his great compassion and concern for mankind. Moreover, he was supremely kind and understanding towards everyone, so far as we can tell. But his concern was to reform individuals and help them to leave society forever, not to reform the world. [...] Though it could well be argued that the Buddha made life in the world more worth living, that surely was an unintended consequence of his teaching. (Gombrich 2006, 30)

Although this argument is contested as Gombrich himself concedes, it is difficult to find fault with the examples he added to illustrate and defend his position: indeed, and as already discussed, the Buddha made no effort to combat the manifest inequalities in his own times, for example, by fighting against the oppressive caste system or against slavery (Gombrich 2006, 30); as we shall see, the fight against inequalities is high on the agenda of reformist political monks, for example, those preaching a Buddhist socialism. Neither did the Buddha take position against other religions, however, or other ethnic groups, since his path to nibbāna was open to everyone—but as we shall see, these fights are high on the agenda of contemporary radical and extremist monks in Sri Lanka, Burma, and Thailand.

## References

Anālayo, Bhikkhu. 2007. The Arahant Ideal in Early Buddhism – The Case of Bakkula. *Indian International Journal of Buddhist Studies* 8: 1–21.
———. 2010. Once Again on Bakkula. *Indian International Journal of Buddhist Studies* 11: 1–28.

Bechert, Heinz. 2007. 'To Be a Burmese Is to Be a Buddhist': Buddhism in Burma. In *The World of Buddhism: Buddhist Monks and Nuns in Society and Culture*, ed. Heinz Bechert and Richard F. Gombrich, 147–158. Reprint, London: Thames & Hudson.

Carrithers, Michael B. 2007. They Will Be Lords upon the Island: Buddhism in Sri Lanka. In *The World of Buddhism: Buddhist Monks and Nuns in Society and Culture*, ed. Heinz Bechert and Richard F. Gombrich, 133–146. Reprint, London: Thames & Hudson.

Cook, Joanna. 2014. *Meditation in Modern Buddhism. Renunciation and Change in Thai Monastic Life*. Paperback ed. New York: Cambridge University Press.

Gokhale, Balkrishna Govind. 1965. The Early Buddhist Elite. *Journal of Indian History* XLII (2): 391–402.

Gombrich, Richard F. 2006. *Theravāda Buddhism: A Social History from Ancient Benares to Modern Colombo*. 2nd ed. Abingdon/New York: Routledge.

———. 2007. Buddhism in Ancient India: The Evolution of the Sangha. In *The World of Buddhism: Buddhist Monks and Nuns in Society and Culture*, ed. Heinz Bechert and Richard F. Gombrich, 77–89. Reprint, London: Thames & Hudson.

Harvey, Godfrey E. 1925. *History of Burma: From the Earliest Times to 10 March 1824*. London: Frank Cass & Co.

Harvey, Peter. 2000. *An Introduction to Buddhist Ethics: Foundations, Values and Issues*. Cambridge: Cambridge University Press.

Horner, I.B., trans. 1938. *The Book of the Discipline (Vinaya-Pitaka): Suttavibangha*. Sacred Books of the Buddhists. 3 vols., vol. XXIII, ed. Rhys Davids. London: Humphrey Milford.

Jackson, Peter A. 2003. *Buddhadāsa: Theravada Buddhism and Modernist Reform in Thailand*. Bangkok: Silkworm Books.

Kirsch, Thomas A. 1975. Modernizing Implications of Nineteenth Century Reforms of the Thai Sangha. *Contributions to Asian Studies* VIII: 8–23.

Lamotte, Etienne. 2007. The Buddha, His Teachings, and His Sangha. In *The World of Buddhism: Buddhist Monks and Nuns in Society and Culture*, ed. Heinz Bechert and Richard F. Gombrich, 41–58. Reprint, London: Thames & Hudson.

Nānamoli Bhikkhu, and Bodhi Bhikkhu. 2005. *The Middle Length Discourses of the Buddha: A Translation of the Majjhima Nikāya*. 3rd ed. Somerville: Wisdom Publications.

Rhys Davids, Thomas W., trans. 1890. *The Questions of King Milinda. Part I*. Sacred Books of the East, ed. Henry E. Palmer and F. Max Müller, vol. 35. Oxford: Clarendon Press. http://www.sacred-texts.com/bud/milinda.htm

Rhys Davids, Thomas W., and Hermann Oldenberg, trans. 1881. *Vinaya Texts Part I: The Patimokkha, The Mahāvagga, I–IV*. Oxford: Clarendon Press. Part of the Series *The Sacred Books of the East* Palmer (published 1879, series editors Henry E. Palmer and F. Max Müller). Online at https://archive.org/details/1922707.0013.001.umich.edu

Schedneck, Brooke. 2011. Constructions of Buddhism: Autobiographical Moments of Western Monks' Experiences of Thai Monastic Life. *Contemporary Buddhism. An Interdisciplinary Journal* 12 (2): 327–346.

Scott, Rachelle L. 2009. *Nirvana for Sale? Buddhism, Wealth, and the Dhammakaya Temple in Contemporary Thailand.* New York: State University of New York Press.

Seneviratne, H.L. 1999. *The Work of Kings. The New Buddhism in Sri Lanka.* Chicago/London: University of Chicago Press.

Smith, Donald Eugene. 1965. *Religion and Politics in Burma.* Princeton: Princeton University Press.

Spiro, Melford E. 1982. *Buddhism and Society. A Great Tradition and Its Burmese Vicissitudes.* 2nd expanded ed. Berkeley/Los Angeles/London: University of California Press.

Strong, John S. 1983. *The Legend of King Aśoka.* Princeton: Princeton University Press.

Symes, Michael. 1800. *An Account of an Embassy to the Kingdom of Ava, Sent by the Governor-General of India, in the Year 1795. By Michael Symes, Esq. Lieut-Col. In His Majesty's 76th Regiment* (electronic book). London: Printed by W. Bulmer and Co. Cleveland-Row, St. James's; and sold by Messrs. G. and W. Nicol, Booksellers to his Majesty, Pall-Mall; and J. Wright, Piccadilly.

Tambiah, Stanley J. 1970. *Buddhism and the Spirit Cults in North-East Thailand.* Cambridge Studies in Social Anthropology, No. 2. Cambridge: Cambridge University Press.

———. 1976. *World Conqueror and World Renouncer. A Study of Buddhism and Polity in Thailand Against a Historical Background.* Cambridge et al.: Cambridge University Press.

———. 1978. Sangha and Polity in Modern Thailand: An Overview. In *Religion and Legitimation of Power in Thailand, Laos and Burma,* ed. Bardwell L. Smith, 111–133. Chambersburg: Anima Books.

———. 1984. *The Buddhist Saints of the Forest and the Cult of Amulets.* Cambridge Studies in Social and Cultural Anthropology. Cambridge: Cambridge University Press.

———. 1992. *Buddhism Betrayed? Religion, Politics, and Violence in Sri Lanka.* Chicago/London: University of Chicago Press.

Turner, Alicia. 2014. *Saving Buddhism. The Impermanence of Religion in Colonial Burma.* Honolulu: University of Hawai'i Press.

Weber, Max. 1967. *The Religion of India: The Sociology of Hinduism and Buddhism.* Trans. and Ed. Hans H. Gerth and Don Martindale. New York/London: The Free Press/Collier-Macmillan.

Wijayaratna, Mohan. 1990. *Buddhist Monastic Life: According to the Texts of the Theravāda Tradition.* Cambridge et al.: Cambridge University Press.

# CHAPTER 5

# Sri Lanka: "This Is the Country of Us Sinhala People"

For visitors arriving by air, the dominant role of Buddhism in Sri Lanka becomes obvious as soon as they leave Bandaranaike International Airport: the Buddha, in the form of statues, seems to be omnipresent, and so are temples and monks. All these visual impressions drive home the fact that the history of this island has been deeply influenced and shaped by the teachings of the Buddha. Two major sources shed light on its early history: the Mahāvamsa (lit. 'Great Chronicle') and its continuation, the Cūlavamsa (lit. 'Lesser Chronicle'). As K. M. de Silva (1981, 3) states, both chronicles

> were the work of bhikkhus [Buddhist monks] and, naturally enough, were permeated by a strong religious bias [...]. The central theme was the historic role of the island as a bulwark of Buddhist civilisation, and in a deliberate attempt to underline this, it contrives to synchronize the advent of Vijaya [legendary founding father of Sri Lanka] with the parinibbāna (the passing away of the Buddha).

After narrating the Vijaya legend that the Buddha himself chose Sri Lanka as the country where his religion should be established, de Silva (1981, 4) says that

> [this] was to become in time the most powerful of the historical myths of the Sinhalese and the basis of their conception of themselves as the chosen guardians of Buddhism, and of Sri Lanka itself as 'a place of special sanctity for the Buddhist religion'. This intimate connection between the land, the

© The Author(s) 2019
P. Lehr, *Militant Buddhism*,
https://doi.org/10.1007/978-3-030-03517-4_5

'race' and the Buddhist faith foreshadowed the intermingling of religion and national identity which has always had the most profound influence on the Sinhalese.

Indeed, this notion of an intimate relationship between the Sinhalese, the Buddhism, and the land reverberates through the Sinhalese historiography even today to the detriment of all those who are neither Sinhalese nor Buddhists. Chandrika de Silva, for example, quotes a monk who likened the relationship between the Sinhalese and Buddhism as that between a bark and a tree, the message being that the tree (the Sinhalese) would neither survive nor prosper without the bark (Buddhism)—after all, the Sinhalese nation "had an extraordinary civilization because of Buddhism" (as quoted in Chandrika de Silva 1998, 54). I encountered very similar opinions, albeit not always as eloquently expressed, during my own research. In particular, I found that Buddhism was one identity marker that defined 'Sinhala-ness,' the other two being Sinhalese ethnicity and Sinhalese language.[1]

The perception of Sri Lanka being the sanctuary and bulwark of Buddhism, and of the Sinhalese as "the Buddha's chosen people [inhabiting a] Buddhist promised land" (Bartholomeusz 2002, 20), was reinforced over the centuries by various missions dispatched by Burmese and Siamese (Thai) kings to Sri Lanka, inviting Sinhalese monks to assist them in purifying and reorganizing their own congregations, which they deemed to have succumbed to corruptive influences.[2] Thus, when the island emerged as an independent nation on 4 February 1948 after three and a half centuries of being first under the Portuguese, then the Dutch, and finally the British colonial rule, this myth of Sri Lanka chosen by the Buddha himself was still very much alive in the minds of the Sinhalese who with 74.9 per cent (2012 census; 1981 census: 73.8 per cent) form the majority of the approximately 22 million population of Sri Lanka. The mainly Hindu Sri Lankan Tamils (those whose families have lived for centuries on the island) constitute about 11.1 per cent (2012 census; 1981 census: 13.9 per cent) and mainly Hindu Indian Tamils—those who had been brought to the island in the nineteenth century by the

---

[1] Interestingly, Obeyesekere (1975, 238) only mentions Sinhalese language and Buddhism as the "two distinct markers of Sinhalese identity."

[2] This was no one-way relationship, however: as I have mentioned in the previous chapter, in 1753, King Kirti Sri Rajasinha (Kandy Dynasty, r. 1747–1782) welcomed a group of fully ordained Siamese (Thai) monks whose task was to help re-establishing his own Sangha which was in terminal decline at that time. These Siamese monks founded the Siyam Nikaya—one of the three monastic orders that still exist in Sri Lanka (Gombrich 2006, 158).

British as plantation workers—constitute another 4.1 per cent (2012 census; 1981 census: 4.6 per cent). In all, 9.3 per cent (2012 census; 1981 census: 8.3 per cent) of the people are Muslims ('Moors'), and the rest are the so-called Burghers (mainly Christian Sri Lankans of European descent) and aboriginal Veddas. In other words, the Buddhist Sinhalese enjoy a majority ratio of 4:1 over all other religious and ethnic groups combined, and should thus feel quite safe in the knowledge that Buddhism will keep flourishing in their country. However, this is not the case—rather, the Buddhist majority feels to be under siege, facing the threat of sooner or later being marginalized in their own country. Since this self-perception of being an 'imagined minority' is quite important in the context of Sinhalese militant Buddhism, this issue needs to be explained.

## FOUNDATIONS: SINHALESE BUDDHISTS AS AN IMAGINED MINORITY UNDER SIEGE

To begin with, a look at a map reveals that the teardrop-shaped island of Sri Lanka is situated just off the south-eastern tip of the Indian subcontinent, and, more precisely, off the federal state of Tamil Nadu as part of the Indian Union. The Palk Strait between Sri Lanka's north-eastern coast and the coast of Tamil Nadu is, at its narrowest, only about 33 miles (or 53 km) wide. In this area, officially called Adam's Bridge but also known as Rama's Bridge, the sea is rather shallow and dotted with many sandbanks, which makes crossing it rather easy. Some sources even claim that until the end of the fifteenth century, Adam's Bridge was above sea level and passable without the using the boats (Garg 1992, 142). In the early history of Sri Lanka, several waves of Tamil invaders crossed this bridge in order to establish their own kingdoms on the island. This is the context of the battle of 161 BCE between the army of Sinhalese-Buddhist prince Dutugāmunu (Dutthagāmani, r. 161 BC–137 BC) and that of Tamil King Ellalān (Elara), already mentioned in the third chapter when I discussed the mechanics of 'othering' the enemy: according to the Mahāvamsa, the troops of victorious King Dutugāmunu—who had been accompanied by no less than 500 ascetic monks, by the way—killed mainly 'beasts' or 'wicked men of wrong views' but only very few 'real' people, that is Buddhists. This battle, and many other battles between the Buddhist Sinhalese and the Hindu Tamil levies[3] have not been

---

[3] As usual, a closer look at the events reveal that the differences were never as clear-cut as they are constructed nowadays for political reasons. For example, Dutugāmanu's forces also included Tamil units fighting on his side—nationalism as we know it now did not yet exist in

forgotten. As of today, the Indian federal state of Tamil Nadu has a population of about 74 million, with about 88 per cent of them being Hindus, 6
per cent Christians, 6 per cent Muslims, 0.1 per cent Jains, and 0.3 per cent
with either no religious affiliation or an (unreported) other religious affiliation. From a militant Sinhalese-Buddhist perspective, this means that to the
'avant-garde' of the Hindu Tamils and Muslims of a combined four million
already present on the island, roughly 70 million more need to be added
who seem to stand by just over the horizon—out of sight, but most definitely not out of mind. Seen from this perspective, the 4:1 majority the
Sinhalese seem to enjoy in their own country turns into a 7:2 minority.
Harvey describes that feeling rather well, using the (imagined) viewpoint of
a British Christian:

> If an Ireland-sized Britain (cf. Sri Lanka) and the Scandinavian Peninsula (cf.
> South-east Asia) were islands of Christianity (cf. Buddhism) facing a Europe
> which had predominantly turned Muslim (cf. Hinduism in India), after hav-
> ing once been a stronghold of Christianity, then the presence of a Muslim
> enclave in South-east Britain might cause some concern, especially if there
> had been a history of invasions from Muslim Europe! If, moreover,
> Christianity in a Protestant form (cf. Theravāda Buddhism) *only* now existed
> in Britain and Scandinavia, this would increase the concern. (Harvey 2000,
> 258–259)

In her impressive work on Just-War ideology in Sri Lanka, Tessa
Bartholomeusz quotes a 1998 letter to the editor of the *Daily News* which
illustrates that Harvey's imagined viewpoint does indeed exist. The writer
of this letter eloquently expresses the uneasy feeling of being under siege
as follows:

> Rome is sacred to the Catholics, so is Jerusalem to the Jews and so is Mecca
> to the Muslims. The tiny island in the Indian Ocean ... where the Sinhalese
> lived for over 25 centuries ... is the hallowed land of Sinhala Buddhists. (as
> quoted in Bartholomeusz 2002, 20)

If we take the myth of Sri Lanka being the country chosen by the
Buddha himself into consideration, and also the feeling of being under

those times. Also, some Tamil kings turned out to be great benefactors for Buddhism in
general and some major temples in particular.

siege, then it is hardly surprising that in independent Sri Lanka, Buddhist monks have (re-) emerged as eminent political actors, targeting non-Buddhist minority groups that raise political demands seen as challenging the special status of Buddhism on the island. Recent examples of such monks would be Gangodawila Soma Thero, who was one of the most vociferous anti-(Christian) conversion monks in the 1990s and early 2000s (his untimely death in December 2003 resulted in a wave of violence against Christian Sinhalese; see the polemical article of Perera 2008), and, especially since the riots of April 2012 focusing on the Dambulla mosque (on the incident, see, for example, Riza 2012), Inamaluwe Sri Sumangala Thero: both regularly included the theme of being under siege by hostile others, especially so by the Muslims, in their sermons (Holt 2016b, 204). It is also hardly surprising that a version of Theravāda Buddhism emerged that can well be called 'fundamentalist' as discussed and problematized in the first chapter, or even more precisely "Sinhala-Buddhist fundamentalism" (Bartholomeusz 1999, 175).

Perhaps even more importantly with regard to the future of Sinhalese Buddhist monks as political actors, in February 2004, the more activist part of the monkhood was also instrumental in forming a political party, the *Jāthika Hela Urumaya* (National Sinhala Heritage, JHU). The JHU is a staunchly Sinhalese-nationalist party that included in its original platform the demand that the Liberation Tigers of Tamil Eelam (LTTE) be wiped out, and also included the demand for a prohibition of conversions—which originally targeting Evangelical missionaries but nowadays also attempts of Muslim clerics to proselytize Sinhalese Buddhists. One of their leaders, Athuraliye Rathana Thero, could even be seen as the first Sinhalese Buddhist 'preacher of hate' of international renown, as we shall see. However, he is just one of the numerous Buddhist preacher of hate we will encounter in this chapter, and there are also political parties and nationalist movements organized and run by monks such as the just mentioned JHU, or the *Sinhala Ravaya* ('Roar of the Sinhalese'), the *Ravana Balaya* ('Ravana's Force'), and the *Bodu Bala Sena* ('Buddhist Defence Force')—the latter a group that broke away from the JHU in 2009 and formally established itself on 7 May 2012 (Silva 2016, 120). On the other hand, there are also moderate and apolitical factions in the Sinhalese monkhood cautioning against mindless violence, and calling for a return to the temples. Hence, there are many voices to listen to in order to 'understand' in the tradition of Max Weber. But let me start with a look at the (revivalist) reconstruction of modern

Sinhalese Buddhism before I turn to more modern, and probably more nationalist and violent, strands of it.

## RECONSTRUCTIONS: THE RISE OF POLITICAL MONKS

I have already introduced the Mahāvamsa and the Cūlavamsa earlier in this chapter. However, focusing on these chronicles in order to shed light on current Sinhalese Buddhism would actually be a mistake. This is not to deny that both of them, especially the former, play a central role in understanding Sinhalese Buddhism. But the way these chronicles are interpreted and contextualized nowadays in itself depends very much on the respective agendas of monks and activists—as any text, scripture or chronicle, the contents of both chronicles is malleable with regard to its meaning. For the extremist monks, for example, the Mahāvamsa is a powerful tool for the justification of their political demands, and even for acts of political violence. Apart from running the risk of falling into the nationalist trap, accepting the Mahāvamsa as one's point of departure would also imply that there were no breaks in the historical relationship between 'the state' (then represented by kings, now by presidents) on the one hand, and the Sangha on the other. More to the point, it would ignore the fact that current Sinhalese Buddhism is a rather modern construct going back not much further than the late nineteenth century (Bartholomeusz 1999, 174)— a construct that borrows much from the Sinhalese monks' reaction to the encroachment of Western missionaries on their 'turf,' and from their more or less uncritical adoption of a basically Western-Orientalist interpretation of Theravāda Buddhism as such, and the role of the monks within it. I already pointed at Max Weber and Emile Durkheim in this context, for whom Buddhism was "an ideal type [that expressed] itself as an empirical reality" (Seneviratne 1999, 1–2). This 'essentialization' of Theravāda Buddhism was facilitated by the tendency of the early Western Orientalists to canonize or 'biblify' it (Seneviratne 1999, 3) by focusing on a select corpus of scripture while dismissing observable Buddhist practice as an irrelevant and idolatrous heterodoxy at best. In Sri Lanka, then still a British colony known as Ceylon, the close interactions between a growing nationalism and the works of the Western Orientalists that gave birth to Buddhist modernism are more obvious than in the other two cases. Tambiah, for example, argues that "[the] most vivid and consequential formulation of Sinhala Buddhist revivalism with nationalist overtones is to be witnessed in the anti-Christian movement begun by monks like Migettuwatte Gunananda and Hikkaduwe Sumangala in the mid-nineteenth century, then given an institutional and propagandist basis by the Theosophists, notably by Colonel Olcott as their leader in the 1880s, and taken to its ideological limits by the charismatic Anagarika Dharmapāla" (Tambiah 1992, 5).

The fact that the Sangha had lost all the political power it enjoyed in the traditional Sinhalese kingdoms to a new and mainly European-educated Christian elite was nothing novel then: the gradual erosion of their power started as early as 1597 when the king of Kotte, Dharmapāla, surrendered his kingdom to the Portuguese. It was complete in 1815 when the British occupied the last independent Sinhalese-Buddhist kingdom, the kingdom of Kandy, during the Second Kandyan War. Even though the so-called Kandyan Convention that terminated the war in March 1815 stipulated that the "religion of the Buddha is declared inviolable and its rights to be maintained and protected," and despite a guarantee by British Governor Brownrigg that neither proselytizing nor mission schools would be allowed, the reality was a different one: aided by modern technology such as steam ships (which made overseas travel more reliable than the vagaries of voyages by sailing ships), a network of modern roads and even some railways (which made inland destinations far more accessible than before), the rotating press (which made the production of pamphlets and tracts much cheaper), and a system of Western education based on the English language (which made those pamphlets and tracts accessible to a rising literate middle class), Christian missionaries descended on the island in great numbers and with great missionary zeal. Hence, within a couple of decades after the signing of the convention, not only mission schools[4] but churches as well had been constructed even in remote villages, and often in close proximity or even within the sacred precinct of Buddhist temples. The Christian missionaries routinely depicted the monks living in those temples as superstitious, idolatrous, uncouth, uneducated, and unenlightened. Not very surprisingly, the incensed monks started to fight back, using the same modern technology to organize themselves, and to reach out to ever wider audiences.

Two of the leading monks in this fight have already been mentioned: Migettuwatte Gunananda Thera (1833–1890) and Hikkaduwe Sri

---

[4] As Walter Wijenayake claims, "[the] missionary schools overtook the Pirivena or the Buddhist temple schools by 1827" (Wijenayake 2008).

Sumangala Thero (1827–1911).[5] Unfortunately, although several articles cover their lives, the articles read more like hagiographies than like credible, impartial biographies, rendering it somewhat difficult to see through the hyperbole. There can be no doubt, however, about the role both of them played with regard to Sinhalese Buddhist revivalism. Migettuwatte Gunananda Thero (also known as Mohottiwatte Gunananda Thero)[6] in his early youth allegedly toyed with the idea of becoming a Catholic priest before ordaining as a Buddhist monk. As it turned out, the Catholic Church's loss was the Sangha's gain, for Gunananda Thero rapidly made a name for himself as a gifted and eloquent orator. Hence, he was one of the Sangha's representatives in the five public debates held with Christian (Protestant) missionaries in 1865 (Baddegama and Waragoda debates), 1866 (Udanwita debate), 1871 (Gampola debate), and 1873 (Panadura debate). As Wijenayake explains, the "debate ranged from the nature of God, the Soul and resurrection on the one hand, to the concept of Karma, Rebirth, Nirvana and the principle of Paticca-Sumupadda or dependent origination" (Wijenayake 2008). Again, it is quite difficult to cut through the hyperbole, but it seems that Gunananda knew far better how to appeal to the audiences than the more learned but rather staid Protestant delegates. Mohottiwatte Gunananda Thera's rhetoric, well preserved in pamphlets summarizing the debates, also had a deep impact on Colonel Sir Henry Steel Olcott, the co-founder of the Theosophical Society. In the words of yet another hagiographer of Mohottiwatte Gunananda Thera, C. V. Rajapakse, the colonel saw him as "the most brilliant Polemic Orator of the Island, the terror of the missionaries, with a very intellectual head, most brilliant and powerful champion of the Sinhalese Buddhism" (Rajapakse 2003).

Hikkaduwe Sri Sumangala Thero is the second key figure with regard to Sinhalese Buddhist revivalism. Considered the most influential monk at the time of the great debates, and having taken part in the final debate at Panadura, it was he who taught Colonel Olcott the basics of Buddhism as well as Pali. Sri Sumangala Thero also was instrumental for the creation of a network of Buddhist schools and colleges to counter the predominance

[5] 'Thera' or 'Thero' can be translated into 'Venerable,' and is used as an honorific for fully ordained monks. 'Theri' is the female version of it, used not for nuns but for female monks (bhikkhsuni) if and where they exist.
[6] The first part of a monk's name usually refers to the village he came from; in his case, the village was known as Migettuwatte or as Mohotiwatte.

of English-language schools, for example, the influential Vidyodhaya Pirivena in 1873, which "turned out to be the premier seat of Buddhist and oriental learning and was also instrumental in spearheading the revival and renaissance of Buddhism, Sinhala Language, Literature and the lost heritage" (Peiris 2006). Furthermore, he also established a Buddhist newspaper titled *Lankaloka* that disseminated suitable publications to a wider audience. In both the efforts, he was supported by the third key figure—Colonel Sir Henry Steele Olcott, one of the spiritual leaders and founders of the already mentioned Theosophical Society.[7] His contributions to Sinhalese Buddhist revivalism are at least fourfold: firstly, he collected the original Buddhist scriptures as soon as they had been discovered and translated, usually by Western Indologists. Secondly, on the basis of these scriptures, he composed a 'Buddhist Catechism' as probably his most important contribution to Sinhalese Buddhism: originally written in 1881, this catechism belonged to the core texts of Sri Lanka's schools until the 1970s, or maybe even the 1990s.[8] Thirdly, he sponsored the establishment of a network of Buddhist schools and colleges, for example, the Ananda College in Colombo or the Dharmaraja College in Kandy, in order to break the dominance of the English school system on the island. And fourthly, he also sponsored an international organization that aimed at revitalizing Buddhism outside of Sri Lanka/Ceylon as well: the Maha Bodhi Society founded by Anagārika Dharmapāla, who even went as far as saying that "what is now called the Buddhist revival dates from the year 1880, when Colonel Olcott and the late Mme. Blavatsky first visited Ceylon, and the former delivered a series of addresses to the Sinhalese people" (Dharmapāla 1893, 1).

The colonel did not content himself with passively collecting original scriptures in order to arrive at an 'essentialised' form of Buddhism. Rather, as Prothero points out, "Olcott creatively adapted [the religious tradition of mentors such as Hikkaduwe Sumangala] to his circumstances. And then he went out, like any good missionary would, to inculcate, through preaching and teaching, that new faith in the people of Ceylon" (Prothero 1995, 285). And this new (or rather, reconstructed) faith was a practical and moral one for Olcott—not a ritualistic exercise but a system of ethics.

---

[7] Founded in New York, November 1875, by Olcott, famous Russian occultist Mme Helena Petrovna Blavatsky and William Quan Judge.

[8] For the former view, see Obeyesekere 1970, 46. For the latter, see Prothero 1995, 285.

Hence, as Prothero emphasizes, in this modernist Buddhism, "a Buddhist was not someone who believed in Buddhist ideas or practiced Buddhist rituals but one who followed Buddhist precepts. Monks were monks not by virtue of tradition but through their exhibition of traditional virtues" (Prothero 1995, 295). Furthermore, in order to counter the frequent claims coming from Christian missionaries that Buddhism was nothing but superstation and idolatry, he strove to prove that Buddhism was, indeed, compatible with modern science: in the words of Prothero again, "[he] devoted an entire section of his *Buddhist Catechism* to demonstrating that Buddhism was a 'scientific religion' – that it coincided with evolution and psychology far better than did the 'revealed religion' of Christianity" (Prothero 1995, 286–287).

What Olcott wisely refrained from was getting drawn into the emerging anti-colonialism, neo-nationalism, racism, and chauvinism that also tended to express themselves in 'othering' adherents of other religions (Prothero 1995, 297)—in this case the Tamils, who had already served as convenient bête noirs in the Mahāvamsa, and now even more so due to the advent of a Tamil-Hindu revivalist movement that also claimed Sri Lanka as their home in a direct challenge to the Buddhist Sinhalese nationalism (Nuhman 2016, 20). Playing the nationalist card was Anagārika Dharmapāla's prerogative as the 'culminator' of Sinhalese Buddhist Nationalism: in the words of Obeyesekere, he created an "intellectual climate that made it possible for Sinhalas to see the total otherness of their Tamil neighbors" (Obeyesekere 1991, 237), despite the fact that until then, Sinhalese and Tamils had largely lived peacefully together (Nuhman 2016, 19). Unfortunately, Dharmapāla's intolerant and exclusivist view of Buddhism proved to be stronger and more appealing than Olcott's tolerant and inclusivist version (Prothero 1995, 298). Dharmapāla's exclusivism, however, can be understood as a mirror image of the Christian missionaries' stance: they also were not prepared to accept other religions, or even other Christian creeds, as 'sister cults,' the way Olcott did with regard to Brahmanism and Buddhism (Prothero 1995, 298). That not much love was lost between Christian missionaries and Sinhalese Buddhists can be gleaned from a rather vitriolic exchange in which the former denigrated the Sinhalese as "[natives] so sodden in vice, so wedded to their idols ..., so dull of head and slow of heart," while the latter retorted that "[the] diabolism known as ecclesiastical Christianity has its paid professors in theological seminaries, where in incubation are hatched half-trained idiots who are sent to civilized people to disseminate the insane views enunciated in theological asylums" (as quoted in Sarkisyanz 1965, 117).

In any case, Tambiah characterizes Dharmapāla quite well when he states that "[if] out of all this fervour and turmoil a notable personality emerged in Ceylon, it was a militant and devoted Buddhist called Anagārika Dharmapāla, who manifested the dual aspects of a colonial product – the rational puritanism of the missionaries interpreted in terms of Buddhism, which he combined with an intense hatred of the religion and culture of the Western rulers" (Tambiah 1976, 218–219). Not only of the Western rulers, though: especially after independence, but also occasionally before that, this 'intense hatred of the religion and culture' also manifested itself in communalist (sectarian) clashes, the most notorious of such incidents being the Sinhalese-Tamil race riots of 1915 which resulted in the death of more than one hundred people on both sides of the divide. They also demonstrate that violence against Tamils, backed up with religious motivations and supported by monks, is nothing new but has a tradition that is a century old by now.

When independence finally arrived on 4 February 1948, the nascent Sinhalese Buddhist nationalism was quickly instrumentalized by conservative Sinhalese politicians trying to establish a credible conservative-Buddhist counter-weight to the secular parties of the left and the right. Solomon West Ridgeway Dias Bandaranaike (SWRD Bandaranaike for short) emerged as the first Sinhalese politician to successfully instrumentalize the issues of Buddhism, Sinhalese language, and Sinhalese culture as well as the Sinhalese feeling to be encircled by the more than 50 million Tamil-speaking people then inhabiting the present-day Tamil Nadu (India) and parts of their own 'Sinhalese' island (De Silva 1981, 512). Buoyed by the rise of Buddhist Sinhalese nationalism, Bandaranaike won the 1956 elections against the more moderate incumbent Prime Minister Sir John Kotelawala, on a decidedly anti-Tamil platform. He promised, for example, to make Sinhalese the sole official language within 24 hours after taking office. Playing on the feelings of the largely rural Sinhalese-Buddhist voters, Bandaranaike's Sri Lanka Freedom Party (SLFP) and its allies managed to capture 51 seats of the 95-member parliament. As Narayan Swami (2004, 10) comments, "Bandaranaike kept his word. He brought forward a three-clause bill which came to be known as the 'Sinhala Only Act' – a monumental faux pas which sowed the seeds of Tamil separatism. [...] Simultaneously, the first Tamil-Sinhalese riots erupted." Shocked by the growing violence between the Sinhalese and the Tamils, Bandaranaike made belated efforts to force the genie back into the bottle. His attempts to find a compromise between the Sinhalese and the Tamil interests ultimately cost him his life: on 25 September 1959, he was assassinated by Thalduwe Somarama Thero, a Buddhist monk, for betraying Buddhist values.

Bandaranaike's widow Sirimavo Bandaranaike continued the 'Sinhala Only' politics of her late husband. When she lost power in the elections of March 1965, Tamil politicians gained fresh hope after newly elected Prime Minister Dudley Senanayake promised a modicum of autonomy by way of setting up district councils in Tamil-dominated regions. However, as soon as Senanayake sensed that the Sinhalese resistance to these moves could cost him his power, he abrogated the accord (Narayan Swami 2004, 10). Even worse was in stock for the Tamils when Sirimavo Bandaranaike was re-elected in May 1970: having campaigned on a stridently anti-Tamil platform, and after having crushed a Marxist-inspired uprising of the *Janatha Vimukti Peramuna* (People's Liberation Front, JVP) in 1971, Bandaranaike pushed a new constitution through the parliament and changed the name of the country from Ceylon to Sri Lanka, the latter being the Sinhala version of the more neutral former. The new republican constitution cemented all bills passed under the Sinhala Only Act which, amongst others, stated that "the Republic of Sri Lanka shall give to Buddhism the foremost place and accordingly it shall be the duty of the state to protect and foster Buddhism" (as quoted in Narayan Swami 2004, 19). The Tamil parties reacted to this creation of what Peter Schalk (1990) calls a 'dharmacracy' by forming the Tamil United Front (TUF) on 14 May 1972 to be able to counter this latest provocation with one voice. However, the Tamil politicians had already missed the boat: according to the Buddha's warning that violence begets violence, a younger generation of Tamils, disillusioned with the politicians' lack of progress, had already taken up arms.

Although Tamil militancy can be traced back to the early 1960s, it is the formation of LTTE on 5 May 1976 that stands out: led by the ruthless and charismatic leader Velupillai Prabhakaran, it quickly crushed all other Tamil militant movements, monopolized the Tamil struggle for a separate state, and waged a merciless guerrilla war against the Sinhalese state that only ended more than three decades later on 18 May 2009 when the LTTE could finally be crushed. Although the LTTE was a secular movement, it also attacked Buddhist temples as well as monks, novices, and nuns. In 1984, for example, "an LTTE commando force stormed the premises of the Sri Mahabodhi sacred area in Anuradhapura and massacred

135, many of which were [Buddhist nuns]," while later in the same year, 30 monks travelling on a bus "were unceremoniously offloaded by another squad of Tamil Tigers before their throats were slit and their bodies left strewn about the roadside" (Holt 2016b, 202). In early 1998, a Tamil Tiger squad even bombed the Temple of the Tooth (Dalada Maligava) in Kandy. In Holt's opinion, the "attack on the Dalada Maligava, like the attack on Sri Mahabodhi, was a calculated assault on Buddhist religious culture, especially on how Buddhism has traditionally functioned as a legitimator of the Sinhala nation-state" (Holt 2016b, 203).

The Sri Lankan Armed Forces responded in kind, destroying mosques, Hindu temples, and Christian churches in Tamil regions in a merciless tit-for-tat action. Even after the LTTE were finally defeated, the hostility towards the Tamils, no matter whether Hindu or Muslim, remained: especially from 2012 onwards, a series of attacks mainly against mosques but also against Evangelical Christian churches occurred. At the moment, in the current "era of postwar political triumphalism" (Silva 2016, 119), the strident anti-Tamil violence as part and parcel of Sinhalese Buddhist nationalism as originally preached by Dharmapāla seems to be too deeply entrenched to be meaningfully addressed. A telling example for this includes the activities of the Bodu Bala Sena (BBS), an organization that in Kalinga Tudor Silva's words "may be seen as a rabble-rousing effort aimed at targeting the Muslim minority" (Silva 2016, 119).

## STRANDS: ANAGĀRIKA DHARMAPĀLA, WALPOLA RAHULA, AND *JATHIKA CHINTANAYA*

In order to better understand the role of extremist monks in the current political violence, we need to take a look at the foundations of their ideology. Basically, there are three different ingredients: firstly, the exclusivist Sinhalese Buddhist ultra-nationalism as developed by Anagārika Dharmapāla (1864–1933) and built on by Walpola Rahula (1907–1997); secondly, the *Jathika Chintanaya* or 'Nationalist Thought' ideology that emerged as the most modern manifestation of Sinhalese Buddhist nationalism in the 1970s; and, thirdly, the discussions revolving around a Buddhist 'Just War' doctrine. To start with Anagārika Dharmapāla,[9] his contribution to Buddhism in general, and

---

[9] Dharmapāla meaning 'Defender of the Faith,' Anagārika meaning 'Homeless One' and denoting a status between monk and lay follower.

Sinhalese Buddhism nationalism in particular, is immense. Regarding the former, Seneviratne (1999, 28) states that "[to] talk about the political and social developments in Sri Lanka since his time up to now without reference to his work is to ignore the spring of these developments. No major Sinhala thinker or writer after him has escaped his influence, directly or indirectly." In the narrower context of the reconstruction of Sinhalese Buddhism, Bartholomeusz opines that he was "the first person in the modern period to link his nation's role to the preservation of Buddhism," drawing attention to Dharmapāla's own comment on that mission: "Ceylon, the home of the Dhamma, sacred to the Buddhists, hallowed by the touch of the blessed feet of the all-compassionate Lord, has become the beacon of light to future Humanity" (as quoted in Bartholomeusz 1999, 175).

Central to Dharmapāla's fundamentalist-nationalist reconstruction of Sinhalese Buddhism is the notion of a 'holy land' or 'promised land,' imagining Sri Lanka as the *Dhammadīpa*, that is, the 'Island of the Dharma' (Bartholomeusz 1999, 175–176). From this perspective, only the Buddhist Sinhalese, understood by Dharmapāla as a descendant of the "Aryan race" (Grant 2009, 73), could conceivably be the rightful inheritors of the island. All others he saw as invaders who corrupted its Buddhist heritage and its values, and who, by extension, had to be driven out— especially the Tamils, both Hindu and Muslim, who Dharmapāla "specifically listed [...] among other 'foreign' plunderers of the sacred Buddhist island" (Bartholomeusz 1999, 176). His description of Tamil Muslims in 'rivers of blood' article written shortly before the Sinhalese-Tamil riots of 1915 (and thus preceding British parliamentarian Enoch Powell's infamous speech of 20 April 1968 more than five decades) is particularly devastating:

> The Mohammaden [sic], an alien people by Shylockian method, became prosperous like the Jews. The Sinhalese sons of soil, whose ancestors for 2358 years had shed rivers of blood to keep the country free from alien invaders ... are in the eyes of the British only vagabonds. ... The alien South Indian Mohammaden comes to Ceylon sees the neglected villager without any experience in trade ... and the result is that the Mohammedan thrives and the son of the soil goes to the wall. (as quoted in Nuhman 2016, 29)

Dharmapāla did not only turn against Tamil Muslims living on his 'sacred island,' rather, he also blamed Muslims in general for wiping out Buddhism from India:

Superstition again took hold of the thought, and in an evil hour the Mohammedan conquerors entered India. The vestiges of Buddhism were destroyed by this inhuman, barbarous race. Thousands of Bhikkhus were killed, temples were destroyed, libraries were burned and Buddhism died in India. (as quoted in Nuhman 2016, 29)

Despite all his other laudable contributions to Buddhism, Dharmapāla would now probably be called a 'preacher of hate': even though he never openly called for acts of violence against the Muslims, he certainly prepared the grounds for such violence via anti-Muslim diatribes, thus acting as a fire starter. Hence, well before independence, the Buddhist cultural heritage was consciously weaponized not only against the Western intruders, but also against the Tamils who also claimed a birth right to the island.

Regarding Dharmapāla's foremost audience, this mainly consisted of the Sinhalese rural poor as well as the working-class Sinhalese in the colony's towns and ports. To reach out to them, he made good use of his genuine hostility towards the colonial regime in general, and the aggressive Christianity that seemed to be part and parcel of it, in particular for the purpose of cajoling the Sinhalese to change their behaviour. For example, Dharmapāla frequently railed against the abuse of alcohol and illicit drugs and its negative effects on Sinhalese morals, as can be gleaned from the following excerpt of one of his speeches:

Buddhism prohibits alcoholic drinks and drugs, and in Ceylon where the religion has flourished for nearly 2000 years, since the British advent, we see old traditions being wiped off by the introduction of Western abominations … Consequently, we see the noble Religion of the Tathagata [Buddha] slowly disappearing from the Island where it had so long flourished. There is no way to prevent it, and as long as the religion of the pagans influences the Sinhalese Buddhists, so long will Buddhism decline and not prosper. (as quoted in Bartholomeusz 1999, 175)

In virtually all of his speeches on that matter, Dharmapāla left no doubt that a return to superior Buddhist morality would be the first step to restore the Sinhalese nation, its freedom, and, of course, the central role of Sinhalese Buddhism. Hence, Seneviratne (1999, 32) is quite right to state that for Dharmapāla, "purity, morality and unity are different manifestations of the same wholesome state," and that he believed that "with a return to the righteous Buddhist way of life, progress will occur, and the country will be prosperous."

Dharmapāla's ultra-nationalist reconstruction of Sinhalese Buddhism that saw Sri Lanka as the 'Island of the Dhamma' and a 'beacon of hope' obviously required the cooperation of the Sinhalese monks, who in his view were to play a central role as educators and leaders of their largely rural flock. The vast majority of Sinhalese monks however rejected this new activist role, much to the annoyance of Dharmapāla who upbraided these apolitical monks in no uncertain terms as immoral, pompous, "lazy and confined to sleepy monasteries" (Seneviratne 1999, 37), overseeing their equally lazy flocks of traditional villagers. That Dharmapāla took to describing monks in such denigrating terms shows that he faced a formidable uphill struggle when it came to mobilizing the Sangha to fulfil his aim of Sinhalese Buddhist nation-building. Even long after independence, the obstacles faced by monks who are willing to embark on a 'career' as political entrepreneurs and activists are considerable. Buddhist scholar Karunadasa, for example, steadfastly refused a political role by saying that the "monk is a path shower, a philosopher and friend of the layman, but it is not his task to institute a pattern of activity about the worldly affairs of laymen" (as quoted in Seneviratne 1999, 34). But this was exactly what Dharmapāla tried to establish: a proactive monkhood that tended to their flock just like the Christian priests he had encountered both in Sri Lanka and during his travels around the world. Dharmapāla made this connection abundantly clear when he stated that "[many] padres from England and America leave their country and their loved ones and go to Africa where there very fierce and uncivilized people, and to Australia which is situated far to the south, to propagate the Christian dharma. But it is greatly saddening to find our monks practicing indifference, and have no intention of propagating Buddhism in the provinces" (as quoted in Seneviratne 1999, 38).

Despite the reticence of the majority of the Sangha, Dharmapāla's conceptualization of the monks as proactive religio-political entrepreneurs gradually gained traction, especially amongst the *dhammakathika* (village-dwelling monks) as opposed to the *pamsukulika* (forest-dwelling ascetic monks), mainly due to the fact that the formers' links with the laity were closer than those of the latter (Seneviratne 1999, 32–33). In particular, he found a kindred spirit in a scholar monk Walpola Rahula, who, in 1946, on the eve of independence, published his influential book *Bhiksuvage Urumaya*, later (in 1974) also published in English as *The Heritage of the Bhikkhu*. As Grant argues, "[this] combative, pungently argued book maintains that before the arrival of European colonizers, the *Sangha* had been socially engaged and actively concerned about the welfare of the people" (Grant 2009, 84). Just like Dharmapāla, Rahula draws on the Mahāvamsa to develop his ideas, yet there are important differences between his Sinhalese Buddhist nationalism and that of Dharmapāla, as Seneviratne highlights:

> First the Dharmapalite monk is an inspiring activist, who though accorded a high place in the village, is an ascetic and humble soldier. In contrast, the monk depicted in Rahula's writings [...] is a powerful kingmaker who is heavily endowed or salaried and lives in comfort. [...] Second, whereas the Dharmapalite monk is an honoured and able leader, the Rahulite is much more: he is supremely powerful. Rahula's ancient monk is much involved in politics [...] Third, the Dharmapalite monk is a rural activist involved with the peasantry. [...] In contrast to this the monk of Rahula's work is an urbanite, as indeed his ancient counterpart was. (Seneviratne 1999, 191)

Seneviratne adds regarding both Dharmapāla's and Rahula's critique of the passive monkhood that in "Rahula's *The Heritage,* the intention of the critique is *empowerment* of the monk, which is *political,* whereas in Dharmapāla's [...] it is the *enablement* of the monk to render service to society, which is *economic"* (Seneviratne 1999, 301). That may well be the case, but in my opinion, this distinction depends on how we define what 'political' means as opposed to 'economic.' Interestingly, Rahula (1974, 120), deploring the "idea that *bhikkhus* should not participate in political activities," goes to great lengths in his *Bhiksuvage Urumaya* of 1946 (I quote the English-language version of 1974) to define 'politics'—in particular in a way that makes involvement in politics palatable for the majority of monks who still remained aloof:

> According to Buddhism, politics is a righteous deed. [...] Politics is connected with life. So is religion. The two can never be separated. What the mind is to the body, religion is to politics. Politics bereft of religion becomes sin and evil. What is meant by religion here is not external rites and ceremonies of established or institutionalized religion, but the development of moral and spiritual character through the cultivation of such qualities as love, compassion, and wisdom. Political activities undertaken by those who, lacking such sublime thoughts and virtuous qualities, have no character, can only spell disaster instead of prosperity to the world. (Rahula 1974, 122–123)

Rahula praises those "pious and virtuous" monks who engage in social and political work, claiming that such monks "must necessarily possess nobler and more exalted virtues and qualities than a *bhikkhu* living by himself and meditating in retirement in a forest" (Rahula 1974, 127). Although he concedes that there may be monks engaging in social and welfare activities who are of impure mind and impure character, he still insists in his argument, even trying to cajole the reluctant monkhood into political activism by challenging their integrity just as Dharmapāla did:

> It is unthinkable that the present-day *bhikkhu* population of over 15,000 will, all of them, retire to the forest for meditation. Are they all to continue to live this meaningless and lazy life both in respect of themselves and of others, which is just another burden to the country and the nation? This is not merely a religious question. This is a very grave question of religious, national, economic, and social import. (Rahula 1974, 127)

Despite his (and Dharmapāla's) best efforts, the real breakthrough of the idea of monks as political activists, however, came with the creation of an independent Ceylon (since 1972, Sri Lanka) on 4 February 1948: arguably, the political arena of the post-independence democracy is a much vaster one than that of the colonial period, with the effect that a much wider variety of political actors emerged, including secular politicians playing the 'Buddhist card' to appeal to their Sinhalese rural voters, and activist monks following in Dharmapāla's footsteps. Hence, Carrithers (2007, 145) is both right and wrong at the same time when he argues that "these changes bore on the Sangha affairs in many ways, of which two may be singled out: a new idea of the monk's political responsibilities was born; and therewith the idea of the monk's social responsibilities was expanded": while it is certainly true that the monks' social responsibilities were expanded, it is not necessarily the case that the monks' political responsibilities were born after independence—this happened much earlier, prompted by Dharmapāla.

Interestingly, but unsurprisingly, given the international context and similar developments in post-independence Burma, the first bout of organized activism of political monks came with a distinctive left-wing flavour in the shape of Buddhist socialism. In a sense, that brought the fight against British, or generally Western, colonialism and imperialism to a logical (and ideological) conclusion—after all, all Western-origin ideologies such as capitalism or liberalism were tainted because of their Western origin in the eyes of the colonial 'natives.' From this perspective, it made eminent sense to 'marry' an indigenous belief system (i.e. Buddhism) with a non-Western ideology (i.e. socialism and Marxism). As regards Sri Lanka, this fusion between Buddhism and Marxism was propagated most vehemently in a book written by D. C. Vijayavardhana, titled *Dhamma Vijaya or the Revolt in the Temple*, that denounced Western societies as 'sick societies,' "disintegrating under the impact of the advancing technology" (Sarkisyanz 1965, 194). According to Vijayavardhana, democracy was conceptualized as follows:

> [Democracy is] a leaf from the book of Buddhism, which has ... been torn out and, while perhaps not misread, has certainly been half emptied of meaning by being divorced from its Buddhist context and thus has been made subservient to reactionary forces. The democracies today are obviously living on spiritual capital; we mean clinging to the formal observances of Buddhism without possessing its inner dynamic. (Vijayavardhana 1953, 595–596)

But it is not only democracy that can thus be linked with Buddhism but also Marxism, which is also described as "a leaf taken from the book of Buddhism – a leaf torn out and misread" (Vijayavardhana 1953, 596). Although there seems to be a whiff of hyperbole, the notion of Buddhist Marxism certainly had some appeal in those days. Even before independence, in 1935, a socialist party had been founded—the Marxist *Lanka Sama Samaja Party* (LSSP). Although the LSSP was a secular party, Seneviratne (1999, 131) states that a "group of monks who had followed Dharmapāla to Calcutta and had been exposed to Indian nationalism there [...] became openly associated [by the mid 1940s] with Marxism in general and the LSSP in particular." Since their exposure to socialism only was a superficial one, their Sinhalese Buddhist socialism gradually became "more 'Buddhist' than socialist, and by the mid 1950s [...] turned into a hegemonic Sinhala Buddhist chauvinism" (Seneviratne 1999, 131). This did not mean that the idea of Buddhist socialism was dead—but it now expressed itself in the shape of a right-wing ideology that fused the struggle against 'others' such as Tamils or Christian Evangelical missions with 'green' politics such as the ban of harmful pesticides, an end of deforestation, and, quite in Dharmapāla's tradition, a 'temperance' policy as regards alcohol that also includes a shutdown of liquor stores. The JVP, founded on 14 May 1965, was the first party that made use of this ideology, and that also enlisted monks as members—many of whom took part in the two JVP-led insurrections of 1971 and 1987–1989.[10]

Currently, the most modern ideological manifestation of Sinhalese Buddhist nationalism is *Jathika Chintanaya* or 'National Thought' (also translatable into 'National Consciousness,' 'National Identity')[11] which emerged during the 1970s, developed first by Gunadasa Amarasekara and then elaborated on by Nalin De Silva (a scholar), Patali Champika Ranawaka (a politician), Wimal Weerawansa (also a politician), and Athuraliye Rathana Thero (a monk) (Dewasiri 2016, 8). In essence, this ideology aims to offer an autochthonous and alternative ideology to the Western-developed reigning paradigms of capitalism and Marxism, and can basically be seen as "a sophisticated version of Sinhala nationalist ideology" (Nuhman 2016, 38). Jathika Chintanaya owes much to the foundational works of Dharmapāla and Rahula, and, as the culmination of their works, depicts Sri Lanka "as the land of the Sinhala Buddhists and not as a multiethnic and multireligious country; minorities are aliens, latecomers, troublemakers, and the enemies of Sinhala Buddhist civilization" (Nuhman 2016, 38). Regarding its impact, I agree with Dewasiri (2016, 8) who opines that although it "was only an intellectual movement and was not capable of directly mobilizing the masses, it had a powerful impact on young political activists"—including young activist monks.

Finally, it is time to take a look at the justification and legitimization of Buddhist violence in Sri Lanka—after all, neither Dharmapāla nor Rahula did so in their constructions of Sinhalese Buddhist nationalism. Ironically, and courtesy of the Mahāvamsa as the "charter of Sinhalese Buddhist nationalism" (Gombrich 2006, 141), this is easier to explain than the genesis of Sinhalese Buddhist ultra-nationalism. We remember that King Dutugāmunu expressed an Ashoka-like (Gombrich 2006, 141) remorse for the deaths and the suffering he caused in his victorious battle against the Tamil King Ellalān in 161 BCE. However, he was told by the monks (eight arhats or Buddhist saints, to be precise; Keyes 1999, 1) he asked for advice that he would not need to worry:

---

[10] On the JVP, see, for example, Gunaratna 1995; Chandraprema 1991.

[11] Fernando (2013, 115 fn 7) says that 'Jathika' "can be translated as both 'racial' and 'national,'" and also refers to Peter Schalk who sees the term as corresponding to the German term 'völkisch.'

That deed presents no obstacle on your path to heaven. You caused the deaths of just one and a half people, O king. One had taken the Refuges, the other the Five Precepts as well. The rest were wicked men of wrong views who died like (or: are considered as) beasts. You will in many ways illuminate the Buddha's Teaching, so stop worrying. (Mahāvamsa XXV, 108–11, as quoted in Gombrich 2006, 141)

As I already discussed, this means that the king and his troops mainly killed 'beasts' not humans, with just one and a half exceptions—and as I explained in the third chapter as well, from a doctrinal point of view, the killing of non-humans (however defined) is a lesser sin than the killing of humans. Hence, as Keyes (1999, 2) points out, after his death, Dutugāmunu "was said to have been reborn in the Tusita heaven where he became the first disciple of Maitreya (Mettaya), the future Buddha." This justification of violence also implies that killing was excusable as long as the intention behind it was the defence of the religion. As I already mentioned in Chap. 3 (The Age of Suffering), Bartholomeusz thus interprets the monks' justification of the king's resort to violence as an example of 'Just War' (Dhamma Yudha) reasoning—after all, according to the Mahāvamsa, Dutugāmunu fought a defensive war to protect the Dhamma, and a limited one at that, thus also fulfilling the *jus in bello* criteria (Bartholomeusz 2002, 55). On the other hand, Walpola Rahula dismisses the Mahāvamsa's contrived justification as "religio-patriotism" which is "diametrically opposed to the teaching of the Buddha" (Rahula 1974, 21, 22). However, he seems to reluctantly accept a certain rationale behind it:

Working for the freedom and uplift of the religion and the country was recognized as so important and noble that the Sinhalese in the 5th century A.D., both laity and *Sangha,* seemed to have believed that *arahants* themselves had accepted the idea that even the destruction of human beings for that purpose was not a very grave crime. What is evident from this is that the *bhikkhus* at the same time considered it their sacred duty to engage themselves in the service of their country as much as in the service of their religion. (Rahula 1974, 22).

Rahula's argumentation seems to echo the German political theorist Carl Schmitt's suggestion of the existence of an *Ausnahmezustand* or 'state of exception' (Jerryson 2018, 459) that justifies even the most violent action free from any legal restraints—with the notable difference that in Rahula's version, an element of proportionality is added: although the resort to violence, and in particular the act of killing, still produces negative khamma, this can be mitigated by the positive khamma produced by protecting innocents, or the religion as such. As such, and in the special case of Sri Lanka, the lesson from the Mahāvamsa can easily be applied in order to relativize certain acts of violence via some inspired moral reasoning or casuistry, with all the negative connotations of that term. Unlike Dharmapāla and Rahula, this is exactly what the current extremist monks do, driven by the firm conviction that Buddhism is under threat. It should however also be noted that according to Obeyesekere (1975, 236), the Mahāvamsa story "is the only instance in the Ceylon chronicles where there is an explicit justification for war and killing in terms which perhaps better fit the *Bhagavata Gita* than the Buddhist *suttas*" and that he had "heard historians of Ceylon argue that this was simply a lone exception in the history of Ceylon." He does however concede that "though this may be the case statistically, the mythic significance of the episode totally outweighs its statistical importance" (Obeyesekere 1975, 237).

## INTERPRETATIONS: ANTI-MUSLIM RHETORIC AND THE (IMAGINED) EXTINCTION OF THE SINHALESE RACE

When it comes to current justifications and legitimizations of violence put forward by extremist Sinhala Buddhist nationalist monks, it is best to start with a political party organized and run by monks, the JHU. The JHU is a Sinhalese-nationalist party that fights for the establishment of a righteous state or *dharma rājyayak udesā vū pratipatti pūjāva*—a state they define in their first of 12 points as a Sinhala Buddhist state, even though the rights of other religions should be safeguarded (Deegalle 2004, 94–95). The JHU also included in its original platform the demand that Sri Lanka should be "a unitary state that cannot be divided" (point 2; Deegalle 2004, 95), but a decentralized one in which village-level communes should play a central role (point 6; Deegalle 2004, 95–96). This decentralization was deemed to be preferable to a devolution of power which would eventually lead to a "separate state for Tamils and [...] to the creation of fanatical religious beliefs and conflicts within Sri Lanka" (Deegalle 2004, 96). Furthermore, the JHU demands that the government "should control and monitor" the activities of foreign NGOs because they feared that these organizations would "undertake evangelical activities of converting poor Buddhists and Hindus to Christianity in the guise of providing technical education" (point 5; Deegalle 2004, 95). It is thus obvious that the

JHU stands in the tradition of Dharmapāla and Rahula, firstly as regards their Sinhala Buddhist nationalist platform, and secondly as regards their self-perception as political activists fighting against the "power-hungry Sinhala lay-politicians [who] have betrayed the Sinhala and Buddhist rights of the majority population of the country" (Deegalle 2004, 96). One of their leaders during their first years, Athuraliye Rathana Thero (ousted from JHU in 2017), also one of the key thinkers of the *Jathika Chintanaya* ideology, could even be seen as the first Sinhalese Buddhist 'war monk.' This is mainly due to his vigorous defence in 2008 of the then raging war of the Sri Lankan Army against the LTTE, and his rejection of renewed peace negotiations as suggested by the Western observers:

> Peace negotiations simply made the LTTE stronger. [...] We mustn't talk to them, we can crush the LTTE. It is like surgery. I don't like war, we need peace. But the LTTE is killing people every day. The West fights terrorism in Afghanistan and Iraq and, like them, we have to fight it here. It simply has to be finished. We can't go on and on. (as quoted in Sunday Herald Colombo 2008)

Athuraliye Rathana Thero then emphasized that even the Dalai Lama "once had an army [...] and that the Buddha did not prohibit his followers from defending themselves" (Sunday Herald 2008). Unsurprisingly, this realpolitikal statement earned him some notoriety as well as the epithets of 'war monk' or 'war monger' in the Sri Lankan press. In the same interview, he however promised that after the war, the Tamils would be well treated. Several years later, and against the backdrop of anti-Tamil violence, he clarified that "[we] have never stood against the Tamils and it was our sincere intention to defeat terrorism since it would lead both Sinhala and Tamil communities towards disaster and we do not have a feeling of hatred towards the Tamils as Buddhist priests" (Roshanth 2015).

Athuraliye Rathana Thero is by far not the only monk who could be called a 'war monk.' I already mentioned the riots of April 2012 that commenced with an attack on the Dambulla mosque, and the role the senior monk of two major local temples, Inamaluwe Sri Sumangala Thero, played in this regard. Hence, let us take a look at what this monk actually preached. First of all, it should be noted that Sumangala Thero has a media network of his own, the *Rangiri Dambulu Media Network*, that includes a newspaper and a radio station, with a television station being prepared, and also founded a union of monks (*Sangha Sabhā*) that "comprised 170 monks from various temples in and around Dambulla" (Heslop 2014, 22, 30). This means that the he can reach out to far wider audiences than those who come to his temples to listen to his sermons. Luke Heslop, who happened to be in Dambulla on the day the mosque was attacked, reports that Sumangala Thero "told a large crowd that Muslim terrorists (*Mussal Waroo Trusthawāthi*) are wiping out the Buddhist heritage in the whole of Asia," and also "that Muslims are 'an inhumane/animal-like race of people who can cut the neck of a living cow'" (Heslop 2014, 23, 33)— the latter a not-so-subtle reference to the practice of halal slaughter, which is time and again used by extremist monks as a 'proof' for the Muslims' penchant for violence—Farook points out that there are billboards in Sri Lanka exhorting readers to end the practice of halal and the slaughter of the "milk giving mother" (Farook 2012). In Burma, Ashin Wirathu explicitly uses this link as well, as we will see. To return to what Heslop calls 'caustic diatribe,' Sumangala Thero also claimed that the Dambulla mosque had been set up illegally in a Buddhist sacred area, and that he himself would lead the protest march to the mosque—which he did, while also including a small Hindu temple in his procession to make the same claim there (Heslop 2014, 23, 24). As Heslop further reports, the marching crowd chanted *may Sinhala, apigay ratay*, which Heslop translates as "this is the country of us Sinhala people" (Heslop 2014, 23). Apart from this very obvious othering of Muslims as well as Hindus by Sinhalese Buddhists, Sumangala Thero employs a pattern with which we already are familiar: firstly, he draws on the 'Buddhism under siege theme' by claiming that Muslims intend to wipe out Buddhism in the whole of Asia in order to justify his intended action (the removal of the mosque); secondly, he dehumanizes them by calling them 'animal-like creatures.' As we already know, according to Buddhist scripture, committing acts of violence against other than humans is a much lesser evil than comparable acts against humans—especially so if these acts are committed in defence of the religion.

As the April 2012 Dambulla riots demonstrate, the anti-Muslim rhetorical violence of these extremist monks is readily translated into physical violence by their equally extremist followers. Another telling example would be the anti-Muslim riots of 15–17 June 2014 that were triggered by an alleged attack of some Muslims on a Buddhist monk followed by an anti-Muslim rally organized by the BBS—a Sinhala Buddhist movement that "presents itself as a moral police force with a responsibility for direct intervention whenever they feel there is reportedly immoral conduct or threats for moral integrity and monoculture of the Sinhala-Buddhist nation," as Silva (2016, 123) puts it. During these riots affecting Aluthgama and neighbouring Dharga Town, three Muslims were killed and 80 more injured, while dozens of Muslim-owned houses and shops were either burnt down or severely damaged by a Sinhalese Buddhist mob (BBC 2014a). The police, mainly composed of Sinhalese-Buddhist officers, did not interfere. In the aftermath of the riots, various Sinhalese Buddhist organizations including the BBS brazenly blamed the Muslims for the outbreak of the riots, thus turning the victims into perpetrators (Nuhman 2016, 51–52).

Of particular interest is the rhetoric of one of the leading BBS monks, Galagoda Aththe Gnanasara Thero, on the eve of the riots. On 15 June, the monk who openly and proudly claims to be a racist and an extremist (Colombo Telegraph 2014) gave a sermon to a Sinhalese Buddhist crowd in Aluthgama that, according to the Colombo Telegraph (2014), could well be called "inciteful and fear mongering." Among his exhortations was the following one: "if one marakkalaya (Muslim) lays a hand on a Sinhalese that will be the end of all of them" (ibid.)—in my opinion, a very carefully formulated exhortation that avoids committing the Pārājika offence pertaining to the deprivation of human beings of their lives (Pārājika 3, Bhikkhu Pātimokkha, translated by Thanissaro Bhikkhu 2007) while still being clear enough to be understood by the monk's followers. The Colombo Telegraph summarizes his sermon as follows:

> He threatened to destroy Muslim businesses at Aluthgama, Beruwala and other places. He instructed his listeners to grab any bags with Halal signs and throw them on the ground. He asked his audience to fight against the minorities. Part of the audience shouted back saying yes, they will do it. The monk called the President of Sri Lanka Mahinda Rajapaksa a brainless person and asked whether any person with brains would appoint a Muslim to be a Minister of Justice. He told the crowd that party politics have destroyed Sinhalese and urged the crowd to unite and take things into their own hands. (Colombo Telegraph 2014)

His vicious verbal diatribes against Muslims that whipped his audience into a frenzy finally forced the state to react: in 2017, the police opened investigations against him for inciting hatred, but he was swiftly granted bail after he surrendered himself to the authorities: as the BBC (2018) reports, it is indeed very rare in Sri Lanka that monks are convicted to prison sentences. In June 2018, however, he was finally "sentenced to two six-months terms, to be served concurrently" for personal threats against the wife of a political cartoonist who disappeared in 2010. But again, Buddhist monks are rarely brought to justice, and as regards the combative monks, "[this] is the first time Gnanasara has been jailed, although he has previously accused of hate crimes and anti-Muslim violence" (BBC 2018). It is quite unlikely, however, that he changes his ways as a result of the sentence: like other ultra-nationalist monks, he is prepared to even go to jail for his convictions.

Apart from mosques, extremist monks and their equally extremist followers also attack other visible manifestations and customs of Islam, with the *hijab* probably being the most formidable red flag (so to speak). Nuhman (2016, 51), for example, mentions that the BBS ridiculed Muslim women opting to wear a hijab as *goni billa*, meaning 'sack devil'—with the effect that these Muslim women often found themselves bullied and even physically attacked by Sinhalese Buddhist nationalists aligned with the movement. That these targeted Muslim women preferred to stay at home for fear of being attacked, bullied, and insulted again was the intended aim of this campaign, ensuring Buddhist dominance and the Buddhist hegemonic discourse by making the 'other' less visible. The same can be said for the extremist Buddhists' attempt to ban the Muslim practice of *halal* slaughtering—attempts that go back to the early years after independence but returned with a vengeance due to the activities of the BBS which, as Nuhman points out, "tried to take direct field action by creating tension among Muslims, especially during the *Haj* festival time" (ibid.).

It should also be noted that the systematic bullying campaign of the BBS does not target only Muslims, but also anyone who dares to openly criticize them and their actions—including other Buddhist monks. A case in point would be Watareka Vijitha Thera, a moderate monk and the secretary general of the *Jathika Bala Sena* (National Power Force, JBS) which promotes peace and co-existence. Since he is an outspoken and fearless critic of Sinhala Buddhist nationalists, and especially the BBS, he is regularly denounced as a traitor of both his (Sinhala) nation and his religion, and frequently threatened and attacked (Forum Weltkirche, undated). Sri Lankan journalist Megara Tegal, for example, reports that in the aftermath of the Aluthgama riots, Vijitha Thera was "kidnapped, disrobed and assaulted [after having] been threatened and attacked on previous occasions after having spoken against the BBS for spreading hate and inciting communal disharmony" (Tegal 2014; also see BBC 2014b). The attempts to force the outspoken monk into silence did not stop with that: when he was released from hospital, he was arrested and charged of having fabricated the abduction and assault (BBC 2014c). Although the charges later were dropped, this demonstrates the wide influence that the BBS enjoys, and the price that its critics have to pay if they dare to publicly censor the movement.

The anti-Muslim battle is not only fought on the rhetorical front, and also not only expressed via mob violence or systematic bullying. Rather, it also expresses itself via Buddhist symbolism as another form of an essentially hegemonic discourse, in particular the construction of Buddha statues and temples—a programme of visible religious dominance that is in itself not new but has gained a new urgency after the war against the Tamil LTTE had been won in May 2009. Obeyesekere, who sees this practice as an imitation of the long-established habit of Sri Lankan Catholics to 'mark' their territory with statues of Christ, the Virgin Mary, and various saints, comments on that as follows:

> [Symbolic] representations of the Buddhist-ness of the nation were happening long before we won the war, but, alas, it would seem to lose the peace, when in the aftermath, Buddha images have begun to sprout in Muslim areas [...] in the Western Province and in the areas in the Eastern Province where the dominant population is Muslim or Hindu. As the north has begun to open up, Buddhist temples and statuary have begun to be erected in the heartland of the Tamil country. (Obeyesekere 2011, xvi)

Obeyesekere deplores this practice, calling it a "cultural invasion [...] symbolically expressing the triumphalism and the possible emergent cultural conquest of the Tamil and Muslim periphery and the beginnings of the creation of a Buddhist nation" (ibid.). For the future, the current wave of 'discovering' the remains of 'ancient' Buddhist temples in the Tamil heartlands does not augur well in that regard, especially not when seen against the backdrop of mob attacks on mosques, in particular against newly established mosques which are seen as "bunkers of jihad" by the BBS (UNHCR 2014, Annexs 1, 26): indeed, it seems that Sri Lanka is losing the peace, sooner or later triggering a new wave of Tamil counterviolence. As the Buddha said: "Killing, you gain your killer. Conquering, you gain one who will conquer you; insulting, insult; harassing, harassment. And so, through the cycle of action, he who has plundered gets plundered in turn" (Sangama Sutta SN 3.15, as translated by Thanissaro Bhikkhu 1999). Unfortunately, these stark but inconvenient warnings from the Buddha himself seem to have fallen by the wayside for the time being.

There is one crucial difference between the militant monks of today and their predecessors: while the latter had to depend on 'word of mouth' in order to spread their messages of hate, today's militant monks, or preachers of hate, can reach out to a vastly larger audience, courtesy of social media. Just like in many other countries, posts on Facebook, Twitter, or YouTube facilitate the spread of anti-Tamil and anti-Muslim propaganda and rumours, nowadays called 'fake news.' As Silva (2016, 124) puts it, "[with] the emergence of Facebook, Twitter, mobile phones, and other forms of social media, gossip and rumour have received a new lease of life and an ability to fast-track the slow process of information flows typically associated with word of mouth." But it is not only the spreading of propaganda, gossip, and rumours, or the brutal trolling of critics, that is facilitated by social media platforms—rather, they enable interested parties to form groups, either open or closed, with which to organize and orchestrate actions carried out on the basis of the propaganda, be they peaceful protests or violent attacks. Taub and Fisher (2018), for example, report on "Sinhalese-language Facebook groups, goaded on by extremists with wide followings on the platform [that] planned attacks on Muslims, burning a man to death." Taub and Fisher (ibid.) also draw attention to a reconstruction of the anti-Muslim riots of 26 February to 10 March 2018 starting in the town of Ampara which found that "Facebook's newsfeed played a central role in nearly every step from rumour to killing." They illustrate this with a telling example—that of a rumour that "the police had seized 23,000 sterilization pills from a Muslim pharmacy in [the town of] Ampara" (ibid.). Harris (2018) calls this rumour a 'viral lie' that lay dormant for a while. But then, he says,

> everything exploded after an incident in one of the town's [Muslim owned] restaurants. A Sinhalese customer found something in his food and claimed it was one of the supposed pills, put there by the owners. What happened next was filmed on a smartphone: 18 innocuous-looking seconds in which a disembodied voice raged on and on; and, wrongly understanding the complaint to be about a lump of flour, one of the owners replied, in broken Sinhalese: "I don't know. Yes … we put?" (Harris 2018)

As Taub and Fisher (2018) state, "[in] an earlier time, this might have ended in Ampara." But not so in our modern time: the restaurant owner's seeming admission of guilt was recorded with a smartphone, and disseminated country-wide within hours via a popular Sinhalese Facebook group, the Buddhist Information Centre, "presenting it as proof of long-rumoured Muslim plots" (Taub and Fisher 2018). The Muslim restaurant owner was comparatively lucky: although he was beaten up by the angry mob, he survived—unlike other victims of similar mob violence. His restaurant, however, was torched, and so was a nearby mosque. We will return to the Ampara riots and more of their context later.

## Evaluation: The Characteristics of Sinhalese Militant Buddhism

When it comes to evaluating the rise of Sinhalese militant and ultranationalist Buddhism in Sri Lanka, we need to briefly revisit the terms that I have used so far. First of all, after having looked at the history of militant Buddhism in Sri Lanka, it is abundantly clear by now that this is not a recent phenomenon: due to modern international media, it may well have come to our (Western) attention only fairly recently, but Buddhist militancy and religious violence can be traced back at least to the late nineteenth century. Secondly, it also became abundantly clear that this militant Buddhism goes hand in glove with Sinhalese nationalism, which means it would be better to use the term 'Sinhalese Buddhist Nationalism,' with the adjectives 'ultra,' 'extremist,' or 'militant' put in front to draw attention on the violent means this nationalism expresses itself. The discussion of the relevant works of Anagārika Dharmapāla and Walpola Rahula on the one hand and of *Jathika Chintanaya* or 'National Thought' on the other further clarified this connection, well expressed in the popular stickers *me gauthama buddha rajyayayi* or 'this is the realm of the Gauthama Buddha'—a political sticker that also hints at an 'ideal political order' to be established (Dewasiri 2016, 3). As Dewasiri (2016, 3–4) further elaborates, the "political message that is carried by the sticker […] forms the core of the Sinhala-Buddhist political imagination. In this imagination, Sri Lanka is a land that belongs to Sinhala-Buddhists; the other non-Sinhala-Buddhists are allowed to live here without any problem as long as they recognize this exclusive right of Sinhala-Buddhists." It is not surprising then that Buddhist monks as 'political entrepreneurs' or at least as activists play a leading role within this Sinhalese Buddhist nationalism, just as prop-agated by Dharmapāla and Rahula. Here, I would like to add that Dharmapāla's construction of this Sinhalese Buddhist nationalism was, strictly speaking, both exclusivist (i.e. there is truth only in Buddhism) and exclusionist (it is for the Sinhalese only).

In the context of exclusivism and exclusionism, I argued that Dharmapāla created an "intellectual climate that made it possible for Sinhalas to see the total otherness of their Tamil neighbours" (Obeyesekere 1991, 237)—despite the fact that until then, Sinhalese and Tamils had largely lived peacefully together (Nuhman 2016, 19). Obeyesekere's argu-ment is certainly not wrong. However, if we were able to take a much more detailed look at the political history of Sri Lanka, then it would become apparent that the target groups of the Sinhalese Buddhist nation-alists, and the extremist monks, change over time.[12] In the beginning, that is in the era of the Mahāvamsa, it was the Tamil Hindus as the original 'others' who had to be defeated. In the late nineteenth century, the most formidable 'other' that sparked the emergence of modern Sinhalese Buddhism were the Christian missionaries, especially the Protestants who came after the British conquest of the island. Another target group of the late nineteenth century included the Muslims, much vilified by Dharmapāla, as we have seen. Inciting anti-Muslim hate resulted in outbreaks of com-munalist violence pitting Sinhalese Buddhists against Tamil Muslims, as, for example, in the race riots of 1915. At that time, Tamil Hindus were not usually seen as a major threat, even though the communalist violence occasionally spilt over to affect them as well. This changed after indepen-dence when a much more formidable threat arose which overshadowed the (largely imaginary) ones posed by Christians and Muslims: the threat posed by secular Tamil ethno-nationalism and, from the 1970s on, the LTTE which challenged the very survival of the state for about three decades until 2009. Interestingly, as Dewasiri argues, although the

---

[12] Benjamin Schonthal offers a set of target groups which is slightly different to mine: "In the first period (1940s–1970s), one sees a configuration of Buddhist nationalism concerned predominantly with Catholic agents, colonial legacies, and education; in the second period (1970s–2009), one sees a configuration of Buddhist nationalism concerned predominantly with Tamil separatists, 'new' Western religious and aid organizations, and territorial unity; in the third period (after 2009), one sees a configuration concerned predominantly with Islam and winners and losers in the island's postwar capitalistic economic climate" (Schonthal 2016, 98–99).

"military defeat of the LTTE was particularly a decisive victory for the Sinhala-Buddhist imagination, [at] the same time [it] posed a major existential threat to Sinhala-Buddhist nationalism, because the former was the pivotal antagonistic other of the latter" (Dewasiri 2016, 5). Efforts to keep the threat of Tamil separatism alive via theories revolving around alleged international pro-Tamil conspiracies proved to be unconvincing. Thus, a new 'other' had to be found—or rather, resurrected:

> It was against this backdrop that the new extremist Buddhist organizations make [sic] their presence felt in the Sinhala-Buddhist South, by opening up a new frontier in the Sinhala-Buddhist nationalist politics, viz. the threat from Muslim and Christian fundamentalism to the existence of Buddhism in Sri Lanka. (Dewasiri 2016, 6)

In the case of the Christians, this 'othering' did not so much target the established churches but mainly the Evangelicals "who were passionately and enthusiastically engaged in conversion efforts, especially among poor Sinhala-Buddhists," as Dewasiri (ibid.) further explains. In 2014, for example, members of the extremist Buddhist organization *Ravana Balaya* ('Ravana's Force') interrupted more than 20 Evangelical prayer meetings in Polonnaruwa, demanding "that pastors stop converting Buddhists and Hindus in the area," as Henri Cimatu from Ecumenical News reports (Cimatu 2014). In defence of these actions, the general secretary of the group, Ittekande Saddhatissa Thero "said that Ravana Balaya had received hundreds of complaints from Buddhists and Hindus that the pastors offer gifts and money to convert Buddhists." Cimatu quotes the general secretary of the National Christian Evangelical Alliance as saying that "[many] pastors have been beaten and threatened to halt their prayer meetings" during 2013 and 2014, also mentioning an incident in January 2014 in Hikkaduwa during which Evangelical churches were attacked by 30 monks and around 200 lay followers belonging to the *Bodu Bala Paura* or 'Buddhist Shield' organization who burnt the Christian literature they found, while also destroying computers and furniture (Cimatu 2014). These are just a few examples—similar incidents happen rather regularly, also targeting Jehovah's Witnesses (Colombo Page 2013), and not all of them are reported. Interesting in this context is that the established Christian churches also see the activities of Evangelical groups in Sri Lanka as a threat rather than as fellow Christians in need of support. I realized this during my conversations with a number of Catholic Sinhalese (including a high-ranking cleric) who, assuming that I am a Catholic as well, always made a point of emphasizing that it 'is not us (Catholics) but them (Evangelicals) who are the trouble makers – we are in this together with the Sinhalese Buddhists.'

By comparison, as Dewasiri (ibid.) also mentions, the Muslims "were easy to demonize." The events of 9/11 and the rise of Al Qaeda saw to that: in 2003, for example, Patali Champika Ranawaka, one of the developers of *Jathika Chintanaya* but at that time also a Sinhalese cabinet minister affiliated with the JHU, published a highly polemical pamphlet titled *Al Jihad Al Quaida* [sic] in which he argued that Muslim extremism and jihadism were on the rise in Sri Lanka as well (Dewasiri 2016, 7). This pamphlet turned out to be so popular that a second edition was printed in 2013 (Ranawaka 2013). As of now, Muslims still form the main target group when it comes to extremist Buddhist violence.[13] In my opinion, two interlinked themes are behind this construction of the 'Muslim threat.' The first one revolves around the argument I just mentioned that in the times of Al Qaeda, and now also of Islamic State of Iraq and Syria (ISIS), Muslim extremism is on the rise in Sri Lanka, with all new mosques basically being 'bunkers of jihad.' The second one is that of a steady rise of the Muslim population on the island due to a higher birth rate on the one hand and inter-marriages plus conversions on the other, while the percentage of Sinhala Buddhists is slowly declining. As Silva explains, this theme of the impending extinction of the 'Sinhala race' is constructed by the BBS and other extremist organizations via a "highly selective reading of census information, anecdotal evidence of the researchers, speculative reasoning, and building on the legacy of the Anagarika Dharmapāla" (Silva 2016, 126). She quotes from a BBS pamphlet titled *Wamsayaka Vinasaya Abimuwa* ('Approaching the Extinction of a Race') that reads:

> Various opinions have been expressed to the effect that Musalmans will overcome the Sinhalese due to existing patterns of population growth in time to come. [...] The basic truth is that Muslims are propagating at an unprecedented rate. This miserable development and misfortune will not

---

[13] In early October 2017, even a small group of 31 Muslim Rohingya refugees from Burma who ended up in Mount Lavinia were attacked by a Buddhist mob mainly from the *Sinhala Raya* organization. Its leader, Ven. Akmeemana Dayarathana Thero, was briefly arrested in the aftermath of the incident (Ariff 2017).

happen overnight. But we have to be alert to this possibility and the resulting political reality. (as quoted in Silva 2016, 127)

As the Ampara riots of February and March 2018 show, such arguments find ready believers who are eager to turn the monks' rhetorical
violence into physical violence without any qualms: as I explained, it was
the rumour that a Muslim-owned restaurant put sterilization pills in the
food made for their Sinhalese Buddhist customers that sparked this outbreak of religio-political violence. The pamphlet contains yet another message: that Sinhala Buddhism is under threat, and that 'something needs to
be done' to stop this threat. If we revisit Galagoda Aththe Gnanasara's
rather chilly remark that "if one marakkalaya (Muslim) lays a hand on a
Sinhalese that will be the end of all of them" (Colombo Telegraph 2014),
then it becomes clear that physical violence is a major part of this 'something.' After all, it is the right even of notionally peaceful Buddhists to
defend themselves and their religion.

Regarding the legitimization of such violence by current extremist
monks, we cannot possibly escape the legacy of the Mahāvamsa and the
advice offered to King Dutthagamani that he killed mainly 'beasts' or
'wicked men of wrong views' but only one and a half 'real' (i.e. Buddhist)
people. Hence, what the king had done was (a) in defence of his realm
only, (b) for the benefit of the Sinhalese race and the religion, and (c)
mostly affecting non-humans, the killing of which is a lesser sin in any
case. As Seneviratne points out, it is thus not only the current monks who
should be censored for using this example as a ready-made legitimization,
or excuse, for violence meted out against non-Buddhists—rather, it is the
monkhood of the days of King Dutthagamani as well who created this
convenient 'realpolitikal' excuse in the first place. Seneviratne very power-
fully argues as follows:

> Whether fictional or true, what the story reflects on the Sangha is clear: its
> culture did not have effective mechanisms for imbuing itself with the univer-
> salist values of tolerance, nonviolence, and pluralism that we readily infer
> from the ethical theories of Buddhist compendia and celebrate as the
> achievement of the Asokan Buddhist state. Thus, in the Sangha or at least in
> a decisive section of its membership in the Buddhist state as it blossomed in
> early medieval Sri Lanka, we are able to isolate a crucial variable inhibitive of
> the development of civility. (Seneviratne 1999, 21)

The persistent efforts to legitimize and justify violence of militant monks on the basis of the Mahāvamsa are however not accepted by all of the Sinhalese monkhood, the majority of whom remain strictly apolitical and also rather silent on all things political—which also includes the choice of not commenting on the activities of the politically active ones. Some, however, speak out against the misuse or, at the very least, selective use of Buddhist scriptures and traditions. One of them is quoted by Seneviratne (1999) on the frontispiece of his book:

> While this [Buddhist] Sangha, based on the ancient Sangha, has democracy [as its base] it has neither special country nor nation nor caste. To such a society which has no special country, nation, or caste, every human being is the same... If a given Buddhist is moral, wise, and just, that Buddhist can commit no crime for country, language, or nation. If a Buddhist commits a crime for whatever reason, that Buddhist is no Buddhist. Those who fight against the Tamils are not Buddhists. (Ven. Naravila Dhammaratana)

A Sinhalese senior monk whom I interviewed (he prefers to remain anonymous) wondered whether these extremist monks ever listen to themselves when they preach at least twice per day about mettā (loving kindness), karuna (compassion), mudita (sympathetic joy), uppekha (equanimity), because they are not following these cherished values.[14] Regarding the monk's request for anonymity, it should be emphasized again that speaking out publicly against the extremist Buddhist monks and their justification of violence on the one hand, and their instigation of such violence on the other, is not without risk. Watareka Vijitha Thera, for example, was abducted and assaulted for doing so. 'Othering' him also was rather easy: for his opponents, he is neither a 'true Buddhist' nor a real monk who should command respect, but a traitor of his race (the Sinhalese) and his religion who has no right whatsoever (from the extremists'' perspective) to wear the saffron robes of a monk.

After having assessed the justifications for (defensive) violence, we also need to take a look at the wider picture—after all, in the introduction to this book, I argued following Selengut (2003, 228) that "other factors like widespread poverty, grievances, and resentment against governmental authority or

---

[14] Personal communication by phone, August 2015.

strong charismatic leaders" (ibid.) are required to trigger religious violence even if a doctrine justifying religious violence is present. To begin with, we can draw on Holt who warns with regard to Buddhist violence that there "has been no specifically Buddhist religious rationale appealed to, or formulated, that is consonant with ethical or doctrinal understandings." Rather, he argues, "all of the reasons actually articulated by Buddhists for their actions have been economic, political, or social in nature" (Holt 2016a, 8). He further explains that movements such as the BBS "may be led or orchestrated by Buddhist monks, but their aims are almost purely economic and political in nature" (Holt 2016a, 9). That such movements come with a very distinct Buddhist flavour can basically be explained by the political culture of Sri Lanka: as he says, "there is a well-worn adage that 'the country exists for the sake of the religion'" (ibid.)—at least as seen from the perspective of the Sinhalese majority, I would like to add. He does however concede that "it is just impossible not to consider the religious factor as central to what has been transpiring, especially when considering how moments of ritual observance, its venues and its temporal occasions, and predominate symbols of religious identity have figured in the unfolding dynamic of contestation" (Holt 2016b, 197). Holt developed this argument against the backdrop of the anti-Muslim violence since 2012, which he clearly sees as "instigated by Buddhist nationalist groups"—before these events, he had been sceptical regarding the role of Buddhism in such communalist violence. Similar to Holst but with an emphasis on the motif of 'being under siege,' Almond, Appleby, and Sivan characterize Sinhalese Militant Buddhism in the times of the war against the LTTE (when Hindu Tamils constituted the main target group[15]) as follows:

> Sinhala Buddhist extremism is not a religious mobilization against modernization and secularization but rather a movement among the Sinhala-Buddhist majority against the threat of the Hindu Tamils emigrating from South India. It is much more a political movement than a religious one, concerned with domination of the Sinhala state and the Sri Lankan territory. [The Sinhala Buddhists'] readiness to resort to violence on a large scale separates them from their own Buddhist heritage. (Almond et al. 2003, 111).

[15] The fact that the majority of the supporters of the LTTE were Hindu Tamils has more to do with demographics than with religion: the LTTE was a secular, vaguely Marxist movement, not a religious (Hindu) movement. On that, see, for example, Schalk 2017.

Basically, this quote consists of three arguments: one on the nature of the movement, another one on its aims and objectives, and a final one on the willingness of the movement to use political violence in order to achieve its aims and objectives—and doing so contrary to the teachings of the Buddha. To start with the first one, this defines militant Sinhalese Buddhism not as a 'pure fundamentalism' but as a 'syncretic fundamentalism,' that is a fundamentalism "in which ethnocultural or ethnonational features take precedence over religion or are inseparable" (Almond et al. 2003, 93, 110). I argue that at least from the perspective of the monks participating in movements linked to this 'syncretic' fundamentalism, the defence of Buddhism is inseparable from ethno-cultural, ethno-national, and even territorial (or 'ethno-territorial') aspects such as language and ethnicity that may well have had precedence for Sinhalese secular actors such as the leading politicians of the most relevant parties. Hence, seen from the monks' point of view, and again following Almond, Appleby, and Sivan, 'their' syncretic fundamentalism was an 'ethno-religiously pre-emptive' one seeking "to limit, suppress, or expel from the national community other ethnoreligious groupings" (Almond et al. 2003, 94).

Furthermore, my discussion of the sacred nature of Sinhalese territory, and the swiftness with which the previously LTTE-controlled parts were symbolically taken back and purified from alien (Hindu Tamil or Muslim Tamil) contamination by either erecting new Buddhist temples or 'discovering' old temples and even 'long-lost' relics, also allows me to argue that this syncretic Buddhist fundamentalism does indeed have millennial overtones (Almond et al. 2003, 97). However, this millennial element is somewhat less pronounced than that observable in the border area of Burma and Thailand inhabited by ethnic Karen. In that region, a *Buddhadesa* or 'Buddha Land' version of Buddhism has developed, propagated amongst others by charismatic monk U Thuzana (himself a Karen), that aims as the creation of a 'pure land' or 'holy land' as the necessary precondition for the appearance of Buddha Maitreya as the next Buddha (I will discuss that further in Chapter 8: Comparative Analysis). This is not (yet) the case in Sri Lanka; hence, Holt is quite right to remind us that despite the Buddhist trappings of anti-Tamil violence, the aims are very secular indeed.

Regarding the political nature of this movement, it is, however, prudent to add a caveat—that of Seneviratne, who, in the context of the Sinhalese Sangha developing into a supra-local power, however, one with "no overarching and unifying social structure that would make it into a powerful elite endowed with a gnawing class consciousness," cautions that "[by] its very nature the Sangha cannot be a power [but] only be the handmaiden of power." Seneviratne adds that this "is well understood by perceptive members of the culture who call the Sangha a 'tool of politics' (*despalana atakolu*)" and "stage props" (*vedika sarasili*) (Seneviratne 1999, 17, 279). In my view, Seneviratne's characterization of the Sangha as the 'handmaiden of politics' still is a very perceptive one—even though I would like to point out with a nod to anthropology's notion of the 'agency of things' that this 'tool of politics' is very much aware of its power, thus also influencing its wielder and by no means detached and uninterested in the effects of its use. We should thus not commit the mistake to completely disregard the agency of the monks themselves by reducing them to nothing but 'useful tools' mindlessly serving other players' interests. After all, nationalist monks in the tradition of Anagārika Dharmapāla and Walpola Rahula do not only fight *against* something but also *for* something: a higher Sinhalese Buddhist moral, for example, based on the Five Precepts, and a righteous state—as, for example, enshrined in the JHU's programme. We are hence well-advised to take them seriously, just as Giles Kepel demanded: "we have to take seriously both what they are saying and the alternative societies they are trying to build [...]" (Kepel 1994, 11). In my opinion, there still is a tendency to explain that away by unduly focusing on all the secular aims and objectives—a tendency or reluctance with the undertone of 'unlike others, Buddhists don't do such things' that may well stand in the way of a proper understanding of these conflicts. Interestingly, denouncing these extremist and nationalist monks as 'Buddhist Taliban' as Perera (2008), for example, does seems to involuntarily acknowledge the existence of a religio-political agenda. I shall come back to these issues in the final chapter where I discuss the findings of the case studies.

## References

Almond, Gabriel A., R. Scott Appleby, and Emmanuel Sivan. 2003. *Strong Religion: The Rise of Fundamentalisms Around the World*. Chicago/London: University of Chicago Press.

Ariff, Yusuf. 2017. Ven. Akmeemana Dayarathana Thero Arrested. *Adaderana*, 2 October. http://www.adaderana.lk/news/43336/ven-akmeemana-dayarathana-thero-arrested

Bartholomeusz, Tessa. 1999. First Among Equals: Buddhism and the Sri Lankan State. In *Buddhism and Politics in Twentieth-Century Asia*, ed. Ian Harris, 173–193. London: Continuum.

————. 2002. *In Defense of Dharma: Just-War Ideology in Buddhist Sri Lanka*. London/New York: Routledge.

BBC. 2014a. Sri Lanka Muslims Killed in Aluthgama Clashes with Buddhists. *BBC News Asia*, June 16. http://www.bbc.co.uk/news/world-asia-27864716

————. 2014b. Sri Lanka Moderate Monk Critical of Anti-Muslim Violence Beaten. *BBC News Asia*, June 19. http://www.bbc.co.uk/news/world-asia-27918343

———— 2014c. Sri Lanka Charges Moderate Monk Critical of Anti-Muslim Violence. *BBC News Asia*, June 25. http://www.bbc.co.uk/news/world-asia-28023701

————. 2018. Sri Lanka Hardline Monk Gnansara Jailed for Intimidation. *BBC News Asia*, June 14. https://www.bbc.co.uk/news/world-asia-44479610

Carrithers, Michael B. 2007. They Will Be Lords Upon the Island: Buddhism in Sri Lanka. In *The World of Buddhism: Buddhist Monks and Nuns in Society and Culture*, ed. Heinz Bechert and Richard F. Gombrich, 133–146. London: Thames & Hudson (reprint).

Chandraprema, C.A. 1991. *Sri Lanka, the Years of Terror: The J.V.P. Insurrection, 1987–1989*. Colombo: Lake House Bookshop.

Cimatu, Henri R. 2014. Buddhist Extremists Accused of Persecuting Sri Lankan Christians. *World-Wide Religious News*, July 25. https://wwrn.org/articles/43062/

Colombo Page. 2013. Buddhist Extremists Group in Sri Lanka Overpower Evangelical Christians. *Colombo Page News Desk*, June 16. http://www.colombopage.com/archive_13A/Jun16_1371391544KA.php

Colombo Telegraph. 2014. Unedited Full Video: BBS Gnansara's Pre-Riots Speech [Video]. *Colombo Telegraph*, June 19. https://www.colombotelegraph.com/index.php/unedited-full-video-bbs-gnanasaras-pre-riots-speech/

De Silva, K.M. 1981. *A History of Sri Lanka*. London: C. Hurst.

De Silva, Chandra R. 1998. The Plurality of Buddhist Fundamentalism: An Inquiry into Views Among Buddhist Monks in Sri Lanka. In *Buddhist Fundamentalism and Minority Identities in Sri Lanka*, ed. Tessa J. Bartholomeusz and Chandra de Silva, 53–73. Albany: State University of New York Press.

Deegalle, Mahinda. 2004. Politics of the Jathika Hela Urumaya Monks: Buddhism and Ethnicity in Contemporary Sri Lanka. *Contemporary Buddhism. An Interdisciplinary Journal* 5 (2): 83–103. https://doi.org/10.1080/1463994042000319816.

Dewasiri, Nirmal Ranjith. 2016. *New Buddhist Extremism and the Challenge to Ethno-Religious Coexistence in Sri Lanka*. Colombo: International Centre for Ethnic Studies, October. http://ices.lk/wp-content/uploads/2016/12/New-Buddhist-Extremism-and-the-Challenges.pdf

Dharmapāla, Anagarika. 1893. Introductory Note to *The Kinship Between Hinduism and Buddhism: A Lecture Delivered in the Town Hall, Calcutta, Oct. 24th, 1892*, by Henry Steel Olcott. Calcutta: Maha Bodhi Society.

Farook, Latheef. 2012. Attack on Dambulla Mosque: Latest Hooliganism Under Organized 'Hate Muslim' Campaign. *Colombo Telegraph*, April 29. https://www.colombotelegraph.com/index.php/attack-on-dambulla-mosque-latest-hooliganism-under-organized-hate-muslim-campaign/

Fernando, Jude Lal. 2013. *Religion, Conflict and Peace in Sri Lanka: The Politics of Interpretation of Nationhoods*. Berlin et al.: LIT Verlag.

Garg, Ganga Ram. 1992. Adam's Bridge. *Encyclopaedia of the Hindu World, A-Aj*. New Delhi: South Asia Books.

Gombrich, Richard F. 2006. *Theravāda Buddhism: A Social History from Ancient Benares to Modern Colombo*. 2nd ed. Abingdon/New York: Routledge.

Grant, Patrick. 2009. *Buddhism and Ethnic Conflict in Sri Lanka*. Albany: State University of New York Press.

Gunaratna, Rohan. 1995. *Sri Lanka: A Lost Revolution? The Inside Story of the JVP*. 2nd ed. Kandy: Institute of Fundamental Studies.

Harris, John. 2018. In Sri Lanka, Facebook's Dominance Has Cost Lives. *The Guardian*, May 6. https://www.theguardian.com/commentisfree/2018/may/06/sri-lanka-facebook-lives-tech-giant-poor-countries?CMP=share_btn_fb

Harvey, Peter. 2000. *An Introduction to Buddhist Ethics: Foundations, Values and Issues*. Cambridge: Cambridge University Press.

Heslop, Luke A. 2014. On Sacred Ground: The Political Performance of Religious Responsibility. *Contemporary South Asia* 22 (1): 21–36. https://www.tandfonline.com/doi/abs/10.1080/09584935.2013.870975

Holt, John C. 2016a. Introduction. In *Buddhist Extremists and Muslim Minorities: Religious Conflict in Contemporary Sri Lanka*, ed. John C. Holt, 1–17 (E-book Version). New York: Oxford University Press.

———. 2016b. A Religious Syntax to Recent Communal Violence in Sri Lanka. In *Buddhist Extremists and Muslim Minorities: Religious Conflict in Contemporary Sri Lanka*, ed. John C. Holt, 194–210 (E-book Version). New York: Oxford University Press.

Jerryson, Michael K. 2018. Buddhism, War, and Violence. In *Oxford Handbook of Buddhist Ethics*, ed. Daniel Cozort and James M. Shields, 453–478. Oxford: Oxford University Press.

Kepel, Gilles. 1994. *The Revenge of God. The Resurgence of Islam, Christianity and Judaism in the Modern World*. Cambridge: Polity Press.

Keyes, Charles F. 1999. Political Crisis and Militant Buddhism in Contemporary Thailand (Revised Edition, Original Version Published in *Religion and Legitimation of Power in Thailand, Burma and Laos*, ed. Bardwell Smith, 147–164. Chambersburg: Anima Books 1978). http://www.academia.edu/8987102/Political_Crisis_and_Militant_Buddhism_in_Contemporary_Thailand_rev_1999_

Narayan Swami, M.R. 2004. *Tigers of Lanka, From Boys to Guerrillas*. Colombo: Vijitha Yapa Publications.

Nuhman, M.A. 2016. Sinhala Buddhist Nationalism and Muslim Identity in Sri Lanka: One Hundred Years of Conflict and Coexistence. In *Buddhist Extremists and Muslim Minorities: Religious Conflict in Contemporary Sri Lanka*, ed. John C. Holt, 18–53 (E-book Version). New York: Oxford University Press.

Obeyesekere, Gananath. 1970. Religious Symbolism and Political Change in Ceylon. *Modern Ceylon Studies* 1 (1): 43–63.

———. 1975. Sinhalese-Buddhist Identity in Ceylon. In *Ethnic Identity: Cultural Continuities and Change*, ed. George de Vos and Lola Romanucci-Ross, 231–258. Palo Alto: Mayfield Publishing.

———. 1991. Buddhism and Conscience: An Exploratory Essay. *Daedalus* 120 (3, Summer): 219–239.

———. 2011. Foreword. In *In My Mother's House: Civil War in Sri Lanka*, Thiranagama, Sharika (author), xi–xvi. Philadelphia: University of Pennsylvania Press.

Peiris, Gopitha. 2006. Most Venerable Hikkaduwe Sri Sumangala Nayaka Thera Remembered. *Daily News Online*, April 29. www.archives.dailynews. lk/2006/04/29/fea05.asp

Perera, Ajith P. 2008. As Buddhists, Should We Further Milk Local Talibans? *Dare to Be Different* (Blog), September 12. https://bandaragama.wordpress.com/tag/ven-gangodawila-soma-thero/

Prothero, Stephen. 1995. Henry Steel Olcott and 'Protestant Buddhism'. *Journal of the American Academy of Religion* LXIII (2, Summer): 281–302.

Rahula, Walpola. 1974. *The Heritage of the Bhikkhu: A Short History of the Bhikkhu in Educational, Cultural, Social, and Political Life*. New York: Grove Press.

Rajapakse, C.V. 2003. Ven. Migettuwatte Gunanada Thera, the Indomitable Orator. *Daily News*, January 25. www.archives.dailynews.lik/2003/01/25/fea05.html

Ranawaka, Patali Champika. 2013. *Al Jihad Al Qaeda Islam muladharmavadaye varthamanaya ha anagataya*. Mudungoda: Tharanga (original ed. 2003). https://www.scribd.com/document/226004818/Al-jihad-Al-Qaeda

Riza, Raashid. 2012. Bigoted Monks and Militant Mobs: Is This Buddhism in Sri Lanka Today? *Groundviews. Journalism for Citizens*, April 23. http://groundviews.org/2012/04/23/bigoted-monks-and-militant-mobs-is-this-buddhism-in-sri-lanka-today/

Roshanth, M. 2015. We Have Never Been Anti-Tamil Ven. Athuraliye Rathana Thera. *Daily Mirror (Sri Lanka)*, March 16. https://www.pressreader.com/sri-lanka/daily-mirror-sri-lanka/20150316/281698318226334

Sarkisyanz, Emanuel. 1965. *Buddhist Backgrounds of the Burmese Revolution*. Amsterdam: Springer.

Schalk, Peter. 1990. Articles 9 and 18 of the Constitution as Obstacles to Peace. *Lanka* 5 (December): 280–292.

———. 2017. The LTTE: A Nonreligious, Political, Martial Movement for Establishing the Right of Self-Determination of Ilattamils. In *The Cambridge Companion to Religion and Terrorism*, ed. James R. Lewis, 146–157. New York: Cambridge University Press.

Schonthal, Benjamin. 2016. Configurations of Buddhist Nationalism in Modern Sri Lanka. In *Buddhist Extremists and Muslim Minorities: Religious Conflict in Contemporary Sri Lanka*, ed. John C. Holt, 97–115 (E-book Version). New York: Oxford University Press.

Selengut, Charles. 2003. *Sacred Fury. Understanding Religious Violence*. Walnut Creek et al.: Altamira Press.

Seneviratne, H.L. 1999. *The Work of Kings. The New Buddhism in Sri Lanka*. Chicago/London: University of Chicago Press.

Silva, Kalinga Tudor. 2016. Gossip, Rumour, and Propaganda in Anti-muslim [sic] Campaigns of the Bodu Bala Sena. In *Buddhist Extremists and Muslim Minorities: Religious Conflict in Contemporary Sri Lanka*, ed. John C. Holt, 119–137 (e-book version). New York: Oxford University Press.

Sunday Herald (Colombo). 2008. Rise of 'War Monk' Sparks Fear of Bloodier Conflict. *Herald Scotland*, March 2. http://www.heraldscotland.com/news/12768721.Rise_of__apos_war_monk_apos__sparks_fears_of_bloodier_conflict/

Tambiah, Stanley J. 1976. *World Conqueror and World Renouncer. A Study of Buddhism and Polity in Thailand Against a Historical Background*. Cambridge et al.: Cambridge University Press.

Tambiah, Stanley J. 1992. *Buddhism Betrayed? Religion, Politics, and Violence in Sri Lanka*. Chicago/London: University of Chicago Press.

Taub, Amanda, and Max Fisher. 2018. Where Countries Are Tinderboxes and Facebook Is a Match. *New York Times*, April 21. https://www.nytimes.com/2018/04/21/world/asia/facebook-sri-lanka-riots.html

Tegal, Megara. 2014. The Burning Fires of Aluthgama. *The Sunday Leader*, June 22. http://www.thesundayleader.lk/2014/06/22/the-burning-fires-of-aluthgama/

Thanissaro Bhikkhu, trans. 1999. Sangama Sutta: A Battle (2). *Samyutta Nikaya: The Grouped Discourses*. Access to Insight: Readings in Theravāda Buddhism. http://www.accesstoinsight.org/tipitaka/sn/sn03/sn03.015.than.html

Thanissaro Bhikkhu, trans. 2007. Bhikkhu Pātimokkha: The Bhikkhus' Code of Discipline. Vinaya Pitaka: The Basket of the Discipline. Access to Insight: Readings in Theravāda Buddhism. http://www.accesstoinsight.org/tipitaka/vin/sv/bhikkhu-pati.html#pr

UNHCR. 2014. *Violations of Muslims' Civil & Political Rights in Sri Lanka. Annex 1 – Attacks Against Muslims. Stakeholder Report*, UN Human Rights Committee, Secretariat for Muslims, September 9. http://tbinternet.ohchr.org/Treaties/CCPR/Shared%20Documents/LKA/INT_CCPR_CSS_LKA_18205_E.pdf

Vijayavardhana, D.C. 1953. *Dharma-Vijaya (Triumph of Righteousness) or The Revolt in the Temple*. Colombo: Sinha Publications.

Wijenayake, Walter. 2008. Ven Migettuwatte Gunananda. *The Island Online*, September 20. www.island.lk/2008/09/20/features3.html

# CHAPTER 6

# Burma: "You Cannot Sleep Next to a Mad Dog"

'To be Burmese means to be Buddhist'—this slogan of the Burmese independence movement still enjoys wide currency against the backdrop of the ongoing nation-building or *Myanmafication* (as Houtman 2000 labels it) in this multi-ethnic state, indicating the fundamental role that Buddhism plays for the majority of the Burmese.[1] We are not talking only about personal piety, however; rather, "Buddhism was undoubtedly the most integrative influence in Burmese society and culture" (Smith 1965, 83), and "the common factor that held this society together, providing a worldview, a cosmology [...] and even a sense of identity as a people and a nation" (Matthews 1999, 27–28). Gravers (2015, 3) even goes as far as stating that "Buddhism is synonymous with Myanmar culture and a corporate identity." Indeed, this crucial element of 'Burmeseness' or 'Being Burmese' (the other is speaking the Burmese language) is well reflected in the statistics: the vast majority of all Burmese, about 87.9 per cent, are Theravāda Buddhists. The small remaining non-Buddhist minority consists of 6.2 per cent Christians, 4.3 per cent Muslims, 0.5 per cent Hindus, and 0.8 per cent animists (Republic of the Union of Myanmar 2016). How central the role that Buddhism plays within the country is easy to see when travelling through it: even more than in the case of Sri Lanka, pagodas and temples are omnipresent here, not only in the vast space of Bagan, a former capital and now nominated as a UNESCO world heritage, that

---

[1] 'Burmese' here defined as the citizens of Burma irrespective of their ethnicity.

© The Author(s) 2019
P. Lehr, *Militant Buddhism*,
https://doi.org/10.1007/978-3-030-03517-4_6

features nearly 4000 Buddhist monuments (Ei Ei Thu 2017). Equally ever-present, not only but especially during the early morning alms round, are monks and novices, quietly walking in a single file, just like their counterparts in Sri Lanka and Thailand. Among the three Theravāda countries examined in this book, Burma leads the way as regards the percentage of the country's gross domestic product (GDP) donated by private persons to monasteries or individual monks. Burma also has the highest percentage of monks in relation to the population as a whole of the three countries: depending on the season, it is estimated that there are about half a million monks and novices populating its monasteries, large and small. Again, we might be inclined to think that these numbers speak for themselves, and that both the religion and the Sangha are safe and secure in Burma. But just like in the case of Sri Lanka, there are outspoken activist monks who beg to differ, and who also see themselves under siege by an implacable enemy intent on wiping out Buddhism, and to take over the country in the name of another religion—and that is Islam.

Indeed, it is not difficult to find militant monks who vociferously espouse a reactionary, xenophobic ultra-nationalism, very similar to the 'preachers of hate' known from other religions. One of the leading protagonists in this regard is Ashin Wirathu, who famously argued that this is not the time for calm meditation but for firm action, against what he sees as Muslim intruders: "You can be full of kindness and love, but you cannot sleep next to a mad dog. If we are weak, our land will become Muslim" (as quoted in Beech 2013). Against the backdrop of rapid socio-economic and socio-political change in Burma on the one hand, and the killing of a monk in Meiktila by Muslims in early 2013 on the other, it is not surprising that his message finds resonance among the Buddhist mainstream—he at least offers an easy-to-understand explanation for these unwelcome changes, and a convenient scapegoat on top of that. But this is only part of the answer (as it is in the case of Sri Lanka and, later, in the case of Thailand), since he firmly believes in what he says, even to the point of going to jail for his convictions—just like Galagoda Aththe Gnanasara Thero in Sri Lanka.

Obviously, Ashin Wirathu and the many like-minded monks who warn against a hostile takeover of Burma by Muslims are very different from those monks such as U Gambira who participated in the famous and utterly peaceful *Saffron Revolution* of August and September 2007. Hence, in order to understand and explain this dramatic change from peaceful resistance as a leading part of a pro-democracy movement to a nationalist-chauvinist militancy targeting Muslims, I will explore the relationship between the Sangha as the religious actor and the various Burmese governments as the political one. I will show that like in Sri Lanka, Buddhist militancy is nothing new in Burma: Buddhist monks were actively involved in armed resistance against the British colonial system prior to independence, as early as the 1880s, and against various insurgencies of non-Buddhist ethnic groups different from the dominating Burmans (Bamar) that ended up within Burmese borders after independence against their wish: the Chin, Kachin, Karen, Kayah, Mon, Rakhine, and Rohingya—the latter seen as foreigners and denounced as 'Bengali' as we will see. However, as usually the case when it comes to human nature and human interactions, there is more than black (Ashin Wirathu) and white (U Gambira). Hence, the analysis will have to go beyond providing a historical narrative, to include issues such as socio-economic and socio-political changes. But, as in the previous chapter on Sri Lanka, I shall start by discussing the theme of 'Buddhism under siege,' which can be found in Burma as well.

## CONTEXT: BURMESE NOTIONS OF NATIONALISM AND OF BUDDHISM UNDER SIEGE

In the previous chapter on Sri Lanka, I pointed out that one chronicle, the Mahāvamsa, plays a central role in positioning the country as an exemplary Theravāda country, and as a lead narrative for contemporary political monks. Very similarly, Burma has its own chronicle that illuminates the early history of Buddhism in the country from the third century BCE to 1885 in the shape of the *Sasanāvamsa*, that is the Chronicle of the Religion. Unlike its Sri Lankan counterpart, however, its factual accuracy (as far as such chronicles cared for that) is highly suspect, and even the identification of this Suvannabhumi or 'Land of Gold' to which a mission under the lead of famous monk Moggaliputta Tissa (ca. 327–247 BCE) travelled as Burma is contentious: the country in question could also be Central Thailand instead of Lower Burma (Gombrich 2006, 137–138, also see Lieberman 1976). Although Mahāyāna Buddhism seems to have spread in Burma in the early centuries of the current era, Theravāda Buddhism as such can be traced back with certainty only to the times of the Mon kingdom of Thaton and, thus, the ninth to the eleventh century CE. With the conquest of this kingdom by King Anawratha as the first ruler of the Pagan dynasty (ruled 1044–1077), and his relocation of the surviving Mon monks to the core of his empire, Theravāda, successfully established itself as the mainstream religion—on top of, but not replacing, animism, ghost or *nats* worship, or traces of Brahmanism and Hinduism.

Thant Myint-U takes great care to juxtapose the rise of Theravāda Buddhist Pagan with the wider development in the then rapidly shrinking Buddhist world. Indeed, as he says, during the time of the Pagan dynasty, the centres of Buddhist learning in India (including the vast monastery and university of Nalanda) were sacked and destroyed by several waves of Muslim armies between the eleventh and thirteenth centuries, while the South Indian Chola dynasty as fervent Shivaites threatened the survival of several Buddhist kingdoms of Sri Lanka, while also all but destroying the Buddhist sea power of Srivijaya centred on the Straits of Malacca. In the meantime, Buddhism had started to decline in China as well, driven back by a rise of Neo-Confucianism. In Thant Myint-U's opinion, this had the consequence that the "people of Pagan, as fervent practitioners of Buddhism and increasingly of Theravada Buddhism, saw themselves more and more as the defenders of a threatened faith and an island of conservative tradition in a hostile and changing world" (Thant Myint-U 2007, 59). Thant Myint-U elaborates both themes a bit more for the Pagan dynasty and its times:

> Once Burma had been part of a far-flung and dynamic conversation, a component of the Buddhist world that linked Afghanistan and the dusty oasis towns of the Silk Road with Cambodia, Java, and Sumatra, with scholar-officials in every Chinese province, and with students and teachers across India. Now the conversation was shrinking. Burma's Buddhism would become ever more impassioned. Not part of Christendom, the Islamic world, or the cultural worlds of Hindu India and Confucian China, Burma, proud and resolutely Theravada, would be left largely to talk to itself. (Thant Myint-U 2007, 59)

Thant Myint-U's argumentation is quite interesting, especially when read against the backdrop of current events within Burma that also revolve around the 'Buddhism under siege' theme. But then again, as any historian would warn us, historians are products of their own times and thus prone to project current assumptions and values back into the 'olden days'— including the feeling of Buddhism under siege on the one hand, and more than a passing nod to Huntington's 'clash of civilisations' theory on the other. Hence, we are well advised to take such evaluations with a pinch of salt. For example, this fervent Theravāda Buddhism did not lead to a prohibition of other religions that found their way into the country via trade. In the times of the Kingdom of Ava, for example, Hindus, Muslims, and Christians were present in the country and could freely pray in their own mandirs, mosques, and churches, respectively. Lieutenant-Colonel Michael Symes, part of a British delegation dispatched from British India to Ava in 1795, mentions this: "The Birmans never trouble themselves about the religious opinions of any sect, or disturb their ritual ceremonies, provided they do not break the peace, or meddle with their own divinity Gaudma [sic]" (Symes 1800, 215). In the times of the traditional monarchy in Burma (as in Ceylon and Siam), Theravāda Buddhism enjoyed the status of a (quasi-) state religion. Hence, a relaxed stance towards other religions was possible. Symes (ibid.), however, adds an interesting and rather telling caveat which also is of eminent interest in our context: "[But] if any person commit [sic] an outrage, which the Mussulmen, in their zeal for the true faith, will sometimes do, the offender is sure to be put in the stocks, and if that does not calm his turbulent enthusiasm, they bastinado him into tranquillity." In a sense, and with the wisdom of hindsight, we could call this a glimpse of the shape of things to come—firstly, the relationship of the Sangha with Muslims on the one hand, and Christian missionaries on the other in the decades of colonial administration, especially after the traditional monarchy had been abolished by the British colonial administration; secondly (and more importantly), the Sangha's position vis-à-vis non-Buddhist minorities, especially the Muslim Rohingya, after Burmese independence in 1948 onwards. The Rohingya actually were one of the main reasons why the mission led by Lieutenant-Colonel Symes visited the Kingdom of Ava: basically, they were on a fact-finding mission, as we would call it nowadays. Arakan, the coastal region between Burma and modern-day Bangladesh had only been conquered by the armies of King Bodawpaya in 1784 as a response to repeated Arakanese incursions into Burmese territory and remained far from settled. Several uprisings of the mostly Muslim population had to be dealt with by punitive expeditions which resulted in waves of refugees streaming towards Cox's Bazaar, and with that on British-Indian territory. Unsurprisingly, the colonial administration based in Calcutta wanted to know what was going on—hence the mission. Although this is of little consolation for current victims, it can thus be said that Rohingya fleeing from their region in great numbers due to Burmese oppression has a history of more than 200 years by now.

After the British occupation of the whole of Burma in three campaigns between 1824 and 1885, the socio-political as well as the socio-economic position of Muslims within Burma initially improved, mainly due to the secular character of the colonial administration. The influx of Indian Muslims into Burma, however, and their general ability to secure better-paid work than the majority of the Burmese, had rather detrimental results, at least in the long term: the preferential treatment the Indian Muslims seemingly enjoyed by a harsh and decidedly non-Buddhist colonial regime was not forgotten by the various activists fighting for independence. Regarding the Muslim Rohingya in particular, the alleged preferential treatment of Muslims is not the only issue that had serious consequences for them: due to an administrative error, the Rohingya were not listed in the census of 1911 as 'indigenous Arakanese group' as they should have been, but as an 'Indian ethnicity' (Ahmed 2017)— and thus mistakenly labelled as foreigners. This clerical oversight was reason enough for the governments of independent Burma to also describe the Rohingya as a non-Burmese ethnic group. In the *Burma Citizen Law* of 1982, for example, eight ethnic groups were listed as Burmese citizens: the Kachin, Kayah, Karen, Chin, Burman, Mon, Rakhine, and Shan. Also included were "ethnic groups as have settled in any of the territories included within the State as their permanent home from a period anterior to 1185 B.E., 1823 A.D." (UNHCR Refworld undated). The Rohingya were not listed, and also, from a Burmese legal position, not included in the 'anterior to 1823 A.D.' provision. Not even the term 'Rohingya' has found acceptance: officially, the Rohingya are described as 'Bengali,' and thus as foreigners—as unwanted and persecuted foreigners, to be precise, who have been targeted by several military operations since independence with the aim of evicting them. An example would be *Operation Nagamin* (Dragon King) of 1978 that resulted in a wave of more than 200,000 Rohingya fleeing to Bangladesh.

The merciless persecution of the Rohingya[2] that has the appearance of a genocide (UNHCR 2018, 16) can be explained in four steps: firstly, the Rohingya alone represent nearly half of all Muslims in Burma. Secondly, in their area of settlements in the Rakhine State (Arakan), they form a sizeable minority of 42.7 per cent, not necessarily threatening but at least challenging the political dominance of the 52.2 per cent of Buddhist

---

[2] For a historical overview, see, for example, Ibrahim 2018.

Rakhines. Thirdly, their areas of settlement are adjacent to the Burmese-Bangladeshi border, which means they have direct access to the Darul Islam (House of Islam). All taken together, this means that, fourthly, they are perceived by Burmese nationalists, including ultra-nationalist monks, not as the minority that they are, but as the avant-garde of a Muslim jihad bent to destroy Buddhism in Burma, and to turn Burma into yet another Muslim state. Buddhism, obviously, is under siege again. Earlier, I already referred to Thant Myint-U's argument that "[the] people of Pagan, as fervent practitioners of Buddhism and increasingly of Theravada Buddhism, saw themselves more and more as the defenders of a threatened faith and an island of conservative tradition in a hostile and changing world" (Thant Myint-U 2007, 59). If we simply swap 'people of Pagan' for 'Burmese people,' then it becomes clear that this nationalist and xenophobic trait Thant Myint-U flagged up manifests itself in the case of the Rohingya again. What also becomes clear again is the theme of being an 'imagined minority' as is the case in Sri Lanka. Thus, the socio-cultural roots of the conflict are basically the same in both countries, even though the targets groups are broader in Sri Lanka's case since Hindus frequently are targeted as well.

## Activists: The Rise of Political Monks

Earlier, I already mentioned the British fact-finding mission of 1795 tasked with establishing why the area around Cox's Bazaar was flooded by streams of refugees from Arakan. What prompted the British to finally declare war on Burma about three decades later were the interventions of Burmese King Bagyidaw in Assam on behest of a contender of the local crown between 1817 and 1823: this is where Burmese and British imperial designs clashed. In three campaigns (1824–1826, 1852–1853, and 1885), British troops defeated the still formidable Burmese armies with unexpectedly heavy losses of their own, occupied the kingdom, and annexed it to British India whose backwater it became. The monarchy was summarily abolished, and the last king, Thibaw Min, forced to abdicate on 29 November 1885 and exiled to Ratnagiri on the Indian west coast. However, it soon turned out that defeating and abolishing the traditional monarchy was one thing—establishing law and order was another[3]:

---

[3] As the defeat of Saddam Hussein's regime and its armies in the Iraq war showed, or the defeat of Gadhafi's regime and armed forces in Libya, for that matter, such lessons have to be relearned again and again.

numerous uprisings against the new colonial order had to be dealt with during the pacification campaigns in the years 1886–1890, and during the following decades as well, basically up until the outbreak of the Second World War.

For the Buddhist population, and especially for the Sangha, the end of the traditional kingdom came as a shock. After all, as imperfect as the 'real' king had been when compared to the ideal of a Cakkavattin, he nevertheless was the rightful ruler and the patron of the Dhamma and the Sangha. Now that he was gone, the monkhood and the Buddhist laity looked forward to an uncertain future. The feeling of uncertainty and unease was so pronounced that even some members of the new colonial administration noticed it—for example, financial commissioner D. Smeaton who wrote that the "Burman cannot conceive of a religion without a Defender of the Faith – a king who appoints and rules the Buddhist hierarchy" (as quoted in Smith 1965, 45). From the perspective of the Sangha, this 'end of days' feeling is well reflected in a poem written by the Zibani Sayadaw[4]:

> No more the Royal Umbrella. No more the Royal Palace. And the Royal City, no more. This is indeed an Age of Nothingness. It would be better if we were dead. (as quoted in Thant Myint-U 2007, 25)

From a traditional point of view, it was actually worse than an 'age of nothingness': with the British colonial administration and their secular way of doing things also came new ideas of how to govern for the benefit of the governed. Hence, after the colonial system had securely established itself in this new province of British India, general welfare policies were inaugurated that covered issue areas such as public health, sanitation, agriculture, and education (Turner 2014, 13). Regarding education, the British administrators initially had high hopes that the traditional temple schools could adapt to the new requirements to teach a modern science-based curriculum on top of the religious instruction—after all, temple schools already taught reading and writing as well as some basic arithmetic, so the changes required would not be too difficult to

---

[4] Sayadaw means 'royal teacher' and originally was reserved for senior monks teaching the Burmese kings. Nowadays, it is a title conferred to senior monks or abbots of major monasteries. It is usual to refer to such senior monks with this combination of title and name of monastery. Hence, Zibani Sayadaw can be rendered as Abbott of the Zibani Monastery.

implement. To the dismay of those administrators keen to transform temple schools into a kind of secular basic schools, the monks demurred: as already mentioned in the fourth chapter, the main purpose of education at the temple was the preservation of the religion, not the teaching of worldly matters.[5] Unfortunately for the temple schools, many Burmese, especially those situated in the cities of Rangoon and Mandalay with their vibrant economies, voted with their feet: studying a modern curriculum including maths and English offered them the chance to get a well-respected and well-paid 'white collar' job within the colonial administrative system.[6] It is thus indeed fair to say that the decline of Buddhism in Burma during colonial rule had much more to do with the impact of modernization than with British meddling in religious affairs (Smith 1965, 38).

As in the case of Sri Lanka, the modernizing activism on the educational front was not only supported by the notionally secular and religiously neutral[7] colonial government itself, but also by the Christian (Protestant) missionaries who arrived in the wake of British troops and spread all over the country to make converts and to set up missionary schools (Sarkisyanz 1965, 110–119). And also as in the Sri Lankan case, laypeople as well as mainly younger monks took it upon themselves—in the absence of a dhammaraja whose task this would otherwise have been—to try to stem the tide, and the decline of Buddhism, by borrowing from both the colonial administration and the missionaries. From the perspective of the traditionally inclined Sangha, these new 'activist' monks, however, rather contributed to the decline of Buddhism than stemming the tide. The Thingaza Sayadaw eloquently described this position in a conversation with ubiquitous Colonel Olcott who visited Rangoon in 1885:

> Great Layman, at the beginning of the rainy season, the farmer plows his large field and, at the same time, in one small corner he makes a nursery of small paddy plants. As the rain continues to fall, he anxiously digs drains around his nursery to keep away the water. In ordinary times he can manage to keep his nursery above water, but, in a year of a catastrophic deluge,

---

[5] On monastic schools and Western education, see Smith 1965, 57–66.

[6] On this issue, see the chapter "Buddhist Education" in Turner 2014, 45–74.

[7] Smith quotes Queen Victoria's proclamation of 1858 in that regard: "we do strictly charge and enjoin all those who may be in authority under us that they abstain from all interference with the religious belief of worship of any of our subjects on pain of our highest displeasure." See Smith 1965, 42.

floods will occur, the young plants in the nursery will die, and after the
floods have abated the fields will remain barren because no transplanting can
take place. Great Layman, I am the farmer, the monasteries are my nurseries,
and Lower Burma is my field. I could have dealt with an ordinary deluge of
new ideas but not with a catastrophic flood. Alas, as you have noted, my
nurseries are now underwater and I cannot hope to drain them out. (as
quoted in Turner 2014, 12–13)

While the religious vacuum left by the end of the monarchy could be
filled at least to a certain extent by the flurry of Buddhist lay associations
of local and national reach that emerged during the last decade of the
nineteenth century and the beginning of the twentieth century, the incom-
ing flood of Western ideas inundating the monasteries especially of Lower
Burma due to their proximity to Rangoon as the new administrative centre indeed proved to be impossible to drain, just as the Thingaza Sayadaw
had feared. This 'inundation' was quite a peculiar one: while the British
colonial administration was rather keen in harnessing the monks and their
influence over the people not only for religious reforms but also for modernizing the Burmese education system, thus to a certain extent encouraging younger monks to become socially and politically active, it did its very
best to discourage the same monks to involve themselves in nationalist
activities in order to prevent them from becoming "an independent political power capable of challenging the government" (Smith 1965, 54–55).
On that front, the British colonial government could draw on the support
of the majority of the senior monks leading the Burmese Sangha. A comment in the *Rangoon Gazette Weekly Budget* of 16 May 1921, for example,
claimed that the leaders of the Sangha agreed:

> that it is highly undesirable for junior monks to tour about in the country
> doing political propaganda work at the bidding of laymen and on behalf of
> secular societies entirely contrary to the spirit of the Vinaya rules; that it is
> also undesirable for laymen to persuade Buddhist monks to join them in
> undertaking political propaganda work, thereby infringing the Vinaya rules
> and bringing the Buddhist Church into disrepute, disorder and chaos.
> (Rangoon Gazette Weekly Budget, as quoted in Smith 1965, 55)

The use of the term 'undesirable' is quite interesting: it seems to allude
to the fact that the higher clergy's influence over its monks was rather
restricted and weak, as Smith points out, reminding us that "monks at the
time of their ordination gave no pledge to obey the orders of these

authorities" (Smith 1965, 56). Smith's argumentation is quite consistent with my argumentation in the fourth chapter that the Sangha is rather loosely organized, with only limited powers of the higher echelons to discipline or, in extreme cases, forcefully disrobe and dispel recalcitrant monks.

Interestingly, when it comes to open rebellions, it was not so much the younger generation of monks who took the mantle of violent anti-colonialism. Rather, this was done by some older, traditionalist monks via fomenting unrest and rallying the laity, mainly the rural one, around their cause: getting rid of the foreign oppressors with their foreign religion. Examples of such *dhammakatika* (activist) monks would be U Thawbita and U Tiloka—two extremist monks (according to my definition) who did not shy away from spreading rumours in the case of the former or encouraging their audience to refuse to pay the tax and to break the legs of tax collectors should they venture into their villages in the case of the latter (Smith 1965, 99–100). The importance of *dhammakatika* monks, both as instigators of violence and as rallying points for the people, is emphasized by Smith who opined that "[in] the anti-colonial struggle, the *pongyis* (monks) were the first nationalists" (Smith 1965, 85).[8]

Open rebellions and insurgencies were only the most visible part of the iceberg of anti-colonialism.[9] Less visible but far more durable and, thus, influential than these largely futile and costly mass uprisings were the political associations (known as *wuthanu athin* or 'heritage preservation groups') founded in the urban centres of colonial Burma by the old elites and the now rapidly expanding middle classes—the former drawing on their traditional wealth and their invaluable positions as important nodes in the still-existing patron-client networks that had kept traditional society together, while the latter enjoyed new-found wealth, courtesy of trade opportunities that emerged with Burma now being connected to the global maritime transport network. Many of these new political organizations were patterned after successful secular-nationalist movements in British India such as the Indian Congress Party. An example would be the

---

[8] Smith distinguishes between 'traditional' and 'modern' nationalism (see Smith 1965, 81). Here, he obviously means 'modern' nationalism.

[9] The probably best-known of these violent uprisings is the *Saya San Rebellion* of 1930–1932. But since the eponymous leader's connections to the sangha were rather weak (he had been a novice for several years in his youth, about three decades before the uprising), I refrained from discussing it here. For more information, see Aung-Thwin 2011.

General Council of Burmese Associations (GCBA, also known as Great
Burma Association), founded in 1920. Others however heavily drew on
religion, and, hence, on Buddhism. The first such organization—from
which the GCBA later split—was the *Young Men's Buddhist Association*
(YMBA). Founded in 1906 as an umbrella group of several smaller
Buddhist associations that emerged during the 1890s, the YMBA as a
federation of Buddhist lay followers basically was a carbon-copy of the
Sinhalese YMBA, which was founded in 1898 as a Buddhist answer to the
Christian Young Men's Christian Association (YMCA). Like the Sinhalese
YMBA, the Burmese one used Theravāda Buddhism as their ideological
vehicle in order to achieve independence from colonial rule, however,
strictly via "accepted and approved channels" (Aung-Thwin 2011, 16).
Furthermore, as Matthews (1999, 30) emphasizes, it "was also the first
religio-cultural organization to co-operate with politicized monks."

It was, however, not only 'accepted and approved channels' that the
politically active monks made use of. Some issues seemed to have come to
a head rather suddenly and in an unorganized, unplanned fashion, after
having simmered on for quite a while. An example for that is the *Shoe Issue*
of 1919 (see Turner 2014, 120–133). Monks had been incensed for quite
a while by the practice of British colonial administrators to enter pagodas
without removing their shoes or boots first, as was (and still is) polite practice. They did so even though the YMBA had made a formal request in
1916 to stop this practice, and even though one of leading monks of his
times, the Ledi Sayadaw,[10] had written a 95-page pamphlet on that matter,
titled *On the Impropriety of Wearing Shoes on Pagoda Platforms* (Smith
1965, 88). On 4 October 1919, the anger finally boiled over when some
Europeans casually entered the Eindawya pagoda in Mandalay, again without removing their footwear first. To their surprise, they were set upon by
an angry mob of monks and lay followers, and unceremoniously kicked
out. Colonial police quickly re-established order, and arrested some of the
actors, including four monks. While three of the monks got away lightly,
their leader U Kettaya was found guilty of attempted murder and was thus
handed down a life sentence (Human Right Watch 2009, 29). One month

---

[10] The Ledi Sayadaw (his Dhamma name/monk name was U Nanadhaja) was instrumental
in popularizing *Vipassana* or insight meditation—previously limited to monks and nuns and
inaccessible to lay followers. See the excellent biography of the Ledi Sayadaw from Braun
2013.

later, the British colonial government attempted to defuse the situation by issuing a written response, both to Ledi Sayadaw's pamphlet and the riot. Firstly, they explained that this European behaviour was due to culturally different ideas about proper behaviour and was not meant to cause offence. Secondly, they pointed out that this had never been a problem before, and that it was not seen as such even in the other two Theravāda countries Siam (Thailand) and Ceylon (Sri Lanka). Thirdly, however, they conceded that from now on, temples and pagodas could set their own rules regarding who was allowed to gain access, and how—with the exception of soldiers, police, and officials tasked with maintaining public order (Smith 1965, 88–89). Thus, it is fair to say that with the exception of U Kettaya being jailed for life, the Sangha had won this round. More importantly, those inclined towards political activism, either to protect Buddhism or the nation, or both, had noted that this direct and forceful approach actually worked, even though the incident in itself occurred spontaneously, without any prior planning.

The unexpected success encouraged other monks, for example U Ottama, to also start agitating against the British colonial government that was perceived as corrupting the moral values of the people, while also undermining the authority of the monks. The explanation U Ottama offered for his political activism is quite interesting. Although he believed that "[when] the Lord Buddha was alive, man had a predilection for Nirvana," he argued that "[there] is nothing left now. The reason why this is so is because the government is English." He concluded his thought saying that monks "pray for Nirvana but slaves can never obtain it, therefore they must pray for release from slavery in this life" (Rangoon Gazette Weekly Budget, 11 July and 19 September, as quoted in Smith 1965, 96). Matthews hence is right to argue that the monk "linked Buddhism with freedom from colonial rule, even claiming that the ultimate liberation in *nibbāna* was to be reached by means of the independence struggle" (Matthews 1999, 30–31). Of significance here is that U Ottama did not reject violence as a tool within this fight—rather, he seemed to have given the resort to violence religious sanction by way of reciting stories from the Buddha's previous lives (known as *Jataka* stories) in which even the Buddha resorted to it. As Smith explains, U Ottama "urged non-payment of taxes, the boycott, and other Gandhian techniques, but the possible use of revolutionary violence was also clearly implied in his message" (Smith 1965, 97). Not surprisingly, he was jailed several times for (attempted) insurrection, and actually died in jail on 9 September 1939, to become "probably

the most popular martyr of the Burmese independence movement"
(Bechert 2007, 150).

U Ottama's status as martyr of the independence movement should
however not mislead us to think that the increasing political activism
amongst the monkhood drew the applause of everyone—rather, it did not
sit well with the population at large since this open participation in anti-
colonial politics, or in social activism, was deemed to be a violation of the
monastic rules. Bechert (2007, 150) also mentions the participation of a
number of monks in the anti-Indian Indo-Burmese riots of 1938 as further damaging the reputation of the activist monks. Against the backdrop
of current anti-Rohingya violence in Burma, it is worthwhile to take a
brief look at these riots. According to the Final Report of the Riot Inquiry
of 1939 (henceforth cited after its chairman as Braund 1939), the riots
started on 26 July of that year in the shape of an initially peaceful protest
at the Shwedagon Pagoda in Rangoon attended by 10,000 people, including 1500 monks, against the pamphlet *The Abode of the Nats*, written by
an Indian Muslim, that was said to denigrate the religion (Braund 1939,
6, 12). After the protest meeting had ended, a "procession" of initially
"slightly more than a thousand of whom as many as half were *pongyis*"
moved down Pagoda Road towards the city centre. The carefully drafted
Final Report doubts that the outbreak of violence was premeditated:

> The procession developed out of the inflammatory speeches made and the
> final prompting of U Kumara [which I will discuss below]. That there were
> a good many there who were quite ready to come out and create mischief
> we do not doubt. But, on the whole, we think that the actual procession
> went further than the promoters of the meeting really intended. (Braund
> 1939, 14)

Premeditated or not, the mood of the mob grew ever more hostile, and
"[even] if the processionists were not armed when they started, a considerable number of them, as their ardour increased, equipped themselves
with sticks and green bamboos from fences and the trees in Pagoda Road
and with bricks and stones picked up on the way [while others] furnished
themselves with the side bars from the trams" (Braund 1939, 14).
Although some monks and some laypersons tried to calm down the mob,
it was to no avail: as soon as any Indians were found, they were set upon,
beaten up, or chased through the streets. The Final Report mentions evidence that proved the participation of a number of monks, also armed

with sticks, in such acts of mob violence: "For instance a man was beaten and injured by a *pongyi* with a stick and chased into the compound of the Diocesan Boys' High School. Of this there can be no doubt" (Braund 1939, 15). Nurtured by simmering communal tensions and fierce economic competition between Burmese Buddhists and Indian Muslims, and further aggravated by a persistent Indian labour migration into Burma, the riots quickly spread all over Burma and lasted until mid-August before they finally ran out of steam (Adas 1974, 207–208). About 139 Muslims, 25 Hindus, and 17 Burmese were killed during these riots; while 512 Muslims, 199 Hindus, 145 Burmese, and 19 'others' were injured (Braund 1939, 281). Amongst the economic damage done, the destruction of several mosques which were put to the torch is the most notable in our context. As the Final Report notes,

> In our evidence we have the mournful record of these so-called *pongyis* [...] up and down the country promoting meetings in their *kyaungs* for political or subversive ends, participating in rioting and, arms in their hands, leading or accompanying crowds of hooligans, committing assaults, looting and even murder and in general breaking the civil laws of their country and the laws of their own order. (Braund 1939, 277)

Although the committee cautions that only a few cases of direct participation of monks in such activities could be juristically proven, "[they] are enough to show the danger in which society, and the reputation of Buddhism itself, stands at this moment at the hands of a minority of *pseudo-pongyis* whose influence the Sangha itself is no longer strong enough to withstand" (Braund 1939, 278). What also is of note here is that most of the monks involved in these riots were organized in a group called *Tathana Mamaka Young Monks Association* (Braund 1939, 6–15). During the initial outbreak on 25 July in Rangoon, some of them—the Final Report explicitly names U Kumara, U Teza, and U Sandawuntha (Braund 1939, 13–14)—took the crucial role as 'firebrands' or rather 'fire starters,' whipping the crowd into a frenzy with their fiery sermons. As a result of the riots, another association of monks formed, named *All Burma Young Monks Association*, or *Yahanpyu Aphwe* in the Burmese version. The main objective of the group founded by monk U Zawtika was, according to Smith (1965, 189) "to unify the monkhood in the face of the threat which the Indian Muslims were thought to pose to Buddhist religion and Burmese culture." Obviously, the Sangha's tolerance for other religions, as mentioned by Symes, in the late eighteenth century had, in the case of the Muslims at least, come to an end due to what not only the monkhood but many laypersons as well perceived to be unchecked Indian immigration into Burma to the detriment of the Burmese themselves. Smith (ibid.) also points out that although the "growth of the organization was disrupted by World War II, [it] has grown substantially since independence." In our context, this is quite significant since it demonstrates beyond doubt that neither militant Buddhism nor the active involvement of monks in it is a new development, 'new' here defined as 'never seen before.' Ashin Wirathu and his fellow extremist and violently anti-Muslim monks hence stand in a tradition that can be traced back at least to 1938 and the *Tathana Mamaka Young Monks Association* and the *Yahanpyu Aphwe*.

The newly acquired role as political activists was not relinquished after the birth of an independent Burma on 4 January 1948. Until the military coup d'état in 1962 put an end to it, charismatic Prime Minister U Nu's strong piety and his Buddhist socialism[11] made it quite easy for the monks to continue to play politically active roles in the domestic affairs of the multi-ethnic new state, even though this was not necessarily his intention: Matthews (1999, 33) argues that although "U Nu wasted no time in demonstrating that one of his chief political aims was the restoration of Buddhism and the *sangha* to their pre-colonial status [...] he perhaps hoped as well to curb the influence of increasingly politicized monks." Be that as it may, his platform of Buddhist socialism indeed seemed to have appealed to the leading monks of his days, just as the fusion of Buddhism and Marxism did in Sri Lanka. As Sarkisyanz notes, "In a series of interviews they told the writer that among the living statesmen of Burma it was U Nu who (at that time, in 1959, being out of power) in their opinion was the closest approximation to the ideal of the perfect Buddhist ruler in the Ashokan tradition" (Sarkisyanz 1965, 226). That U Nu also was the driving force behind introducing the lunar weekly holiday (instead of the Western Sunday), a Sasana Council of elder monks regulating the affairs of the Sangha and, most importantly, the State Religion Promotion Act which was passed by the parliament on 29 August 1961 (an act that made Theravāda Buddhism the official state religion of Burma) made him even more popular for the Sangha, even though some monks still wanted more than that: the already mentioned Yahanpyu Aphwe, now with a

---

[11] On U NU's 'Buddhist Socialism,' see Sarkisyanz 1965, 166–179, 192–205, 210–228.

membership of more than 30,000 monks, "actively agitated for stronger legislation against anything perceived to represent a threat to Buddhism" (Matthews 1999, 34).

The political influence of activist monks started to wane after the military takeover on 2 March 1962: contrary to U Nu, and more in line with the traditional monarchs, General Ne Win as the head of state tolerated no meddling in political affairs by the monkhood. Even though he did not go as far as King Thohanbwa (reigned 1527–1542) who had several thousands of monks killed, Ne Win still initiated a 'Sangha Reform' (a campaign dubbed "Cleaning Up the Sangha," according to Aung Zaw 2013) and had them "surgically removed from the body politic, like diseased flesh," as Matthews (1999, 35) colourfully puts it. Many monasteries were raided,[12] and numerous politically active monks were forcefully disrobed and sentenced to prison, where some of them, for example Sayadaw U Nayaka, died—"after being tortured," as Houtman (1999, 220) emphasizes. Other senior monks had to endure smear campaigns that spread rumours about their conduct, such as the highly respected Mahasi Sayadaw, internationally known as the leading teacher of Vipassana meditation (Human Rights Watch 2009). The most telling examples of this 'surgical removal' would be the relentless persecution of those activist monks who participated in the *8888 Uprising* that commenced on 8 August 1988, or in the *Saffron Revolution* of August and September 2007[13]—especially those who had been active in a movement named *All Burma Monks' Alliance* (ABMA) as an umbrella organization of several smaller unions, including the re-formed (in 1988) Yahanpyu Aphwe. The remainders of ABMA went underground, while exiled monks formed a group called *International Burmese Monks Organisation* on 28 September 2007 in Los Angeles, in the hope to raise awareness on the ongoing human rights violations in Burma (DVB 2007)—however, without drawing much resonance. In more recent years, even Ashin Wirathu himself spent nine years

---

[12] British colonial police did likewise when they quelled the riots of 1938, but profusely apologized to the Sangha later on (see Braund 1939, 278–280)—unlike the Burmese military.

[13] It is tempting to offer a detailed discussion of the Saffron Revolution, but since this work is about the rise of militant Buddhism, this would be a digression. More information about this uprising, which in Burma was known as the *Golden Uprising* (the term 'revolution' comes with connotations of violence, after all), can be found in Human Rights Watch 2007 and Human Rights Watch 2009. See also Gravers 2012; U Piyanta Zawta 2009.

in jail due to his political activities,[14] while in March 2017, he was banned from publicly preaching for one year in a bid to keep the Rohingya conflict from escalating any further (DW 2017), or at least from drawing even more unwelcome international attention. What probably counted against him is that he also frequently criticizes the military which he claims is in collusion with Burmese-Muslim business elites.

To a certain extent, political activism led by monks was, however, tolerated in the restive border regions of Burma where ethnic minorities continue to contest the idea of a unified Burma under the control of a Burman (Bamar) elite, either in favour of independence or, at the very least, full autonomy in their internal affairs.[15] An example for such activities would be the Democratic Karen Buddhist Army (DKBA) founded by monk U Thuzana (himself an ethnic Karen) in 1994, which was used as a vehicle to try to, on the one hand, weaken the Christian-dominated Karen National Liberation Army (KNLA) in Karen State (Gravers 2010), and, on the other, to establish a Buddhist 'holy land' or *Buddhadesa*. Similarly, the Arakan Liberation Party (ALP, founded in 1968), whose leadership nearly exclusively consisted of monks and former monks, also targeted Muslims (Arakanese Rohingyas) to evict them from their 'sacred' Buddhist land. Again, it is evident that the extremist or militant monks around Ashin Wirathu are by no means a novel development out of sync what Western observers might deem to be 'real' Buddhism, supposed to be otherworldly and focused on meditation—stereotypes or, at best, ideal types that I already discussed in the fourth chapter.

### FIREBRANDS: LEGITIMIZING BUDDHIST EXTREMISM AND MILITANCY

We already encountered extremist and militant monks in the context of the anti-Indian Indo-Burmese riots of July and August 1938. Hence, and even though these incidents now are more than eight decades in the past, it still makes sense to start with them because the rhetoric and the slogans

[14] In 2003, he was sentenced to 25 years because of his anti-Islamic sermons but was released in 2012 in a mass amnesty.
[15] Full autonomy had been agreed in the pre-independence *Panlong Agreement* of 12 February 1947 between representatives of Burma's executive government under Aung San on the one hand, and representatives of the Chin, Kachin, and Shan ethnic minorities on the other.

used sound very similar to those used by current firebrand monks of the Ma Ba Tha (Burmese acronym for 'Patriotic Association of Myanmar')[16] and the 969 Movement. Unfortunately, the Final Report on the riots did not include the full texts of the sermons given at the Shwedagon Pagoda with the purpose of agitating the crowd. All the report has to say is that the "tone of the meeting developed into a crescendo of vituperation and abuse against Muslims in general" (Braund 1939, 13). In particular, it explicitly states:

> Of the violent speeches made that of U Teza, an Executive Member of the general Council of the Thathana Mamaka Young Sanghas' Association, was outstanding. Scarcely less abusive and violent was that of U Sandawuntha [...] Finally, the climax was reached when, after the close of the meeting, U Kumara [...] the President of the Rangoon Central Thathana Mamaka Young Sanghas' Association provoked the audience to form the procession. He suggested the procession should be taken [...] in order to show the real blood of the Burmese people who would not tolerate any insult to their race and religion. (Braund 1939, 13)

Regarding the anti-Indian contents of the sermons, the Final Report (ibid.) notes that "the speeches dwelt upon the Burmese-Muslim marriage question. There was an attempt by one speaker to move a boycott of all Muslims in Burma." Regarding the slogans chanted by the mob, the Final Report (ibid.) mentions "Assault Indians," "Boycott Boycott," and the sinister "Flaming Torch Burn Burn." Another one was "Burmese women who marry Indians: Are husbands scarce in Burma?" The Final Report also draws attention to rumours that were spread in order to further fan the flames of hate, with the most frequent being "imaginary insults to Buddhism" or stories about the "poisoning of food by Indian shopkeepers" (all quotes from Braund 1939, 275).

Many of the justifications used by the monks and the slogans chanted by the rioters sound rather familiar when compared to those used nowadays against the Rohingya. Quite instructive in this regard are the justifications given by Ashin Wirathu for the anti-Muslim agenda that this movement espouses. For example, when interviewed by Hannah Beech from the *Time* magazine at the New Masoeyein monastery in Mandalay, he stated that "[Muslims] are breeding so fast, and they are stealing our

---

[16] Ma Ba Tha was banned in 2017 but continues under the new name Buddha Dhamma Parahita Foundation, see Aung Kyaw Min 2017.

women, raping them […]. They would like to occupy our country, but I won't let them. We must keep Myanmar Buddhist." He told Beech that in his opinion, "[about] 90% of Muslims in Burma are 'radical, bad people,'" and also that "Arabs have hijacked the U.N" (as quoted in Beech 2013). He repeated this argument again and again, for example, in an interview with the *Guardian* published on 18 April 2013. On this occasion, he also said that "[we] are being raped in every town, being sexually harassed in every town, ganged up and bullied in every town. […] In every town, there is a crude and savage Muslim majority" (as quoted in Hodal 2013). Ashin Wirathu even goes as far as linking the practice of *halal* slaughter to this alleged penchant for violence, claiming that this "allows familiarity with blood and could escalate to the level where it threatens world peace" (as quoted in ibid.). Furthermore, he reiterated the claim of a linkage of events in Burma to the Middle East: "The local Muslims are crude and savage because the extremists are pulling the strings, providing them with financial, military and technical power" (as quoted in Hodal 2013).

Interestingly, it now appears as if he would have been at least partially right: as a result of yet another outbreak of anti-Rohingya violence in October 2012, a movement called *Harakah al Yakin* (Faith Movement) was founded at the end of that year, which then morphed into the *Arakan Rohingya Salvation Army* (ARSA) which went active in October 2016 with a series of coordinated attacks of around 300 to 400 persons against three border posts of the Burmese police (Winchester 2017). The ARSA is said to have connections to Rohingya living in exile in Saudi Arabia who, led by an individual named Ata Ullah abu Ammar Junjuni, would mastermind ARSA's operations within Burma. Since this view is also shared by the internationally well-respected *International Crisis Group* (see ICG 2016), it can be deemed credible. Hence, the Buddha's warning that violence begets violence seems to be fulfilling itself in Burma at the moment.

Regarding the widely believed theme of a Muslim penchant for violence implies that the resort to defensive (counter-) violence is deemed to be unavoidable by many Burmese monks and laypeople. Symptomatic for this believe is a response of a monk interviewed at Ashin Wirathu's monastery in Mandalay in November 2014. He argues as follows: "Every race has good and bad people, those who use violence and those who don't. But the Muslims are mostly violent. So we have to be careful for our own country's sake" (AJ+ 2014). The popular believe that Muslims are mostly violent is further nurtured by rumours of alleged crimes that Muslims have carried out against peaceful and unsuspecting Buddhists, with scores of gory pictures of slain monks and laypeople shown on the temple walls for good measure (ibid.). Furthermore, rumours were spread about forced conversions of Buddhist women, and sexual abuse of them by Muslim men, spread via social media or via pamphlets—one of them allegedly written by a monk using a pseudonym (Gravers 2015, 12). Although many of the pictures are crudely Photoshopped or otherwise 'doctored' by various interested parties, including the Burmese Army (see, for example, McPherson 2018), it should be noted that such rumours find ready acceptance not only by those in close orbit of Ashin Wirathu, but by many other monks and laypeople all over Burma—and, of course, in Rakhine State where the Rohingya form a 42.7 per cent minority. Even more so than in 1938, rumours and allegations of acts of gruesome violence against monks and Buddhist lay followers are formidable tools when it comes to further fanning the flames of hate—'even more so' meaning that the spread of social media in Burma as well renders the spreading of such rumours, accompanied by gory pictures, much easier now.

The claim that Arabs have hijacked the UN reinforces the theme of a Muslim threat to the survival of Burmese Buddhism, while also not so subtly insinuating that there would not be any succour from the outside. Rather, the Burmese Buddhists would stand alone—a theme reverberating through Burmese history from the times of the Pagan dynasty onwards, at least in the opinion of Thant Myint-U (2007, 59). No wonder then that Ashin Wirathu emphasized in a 90-minute anti-Muslim sermon also witnessed by Beech (2013) that "[now] is not the time for calm. [...] Now is the time to rise up, to make our blood boil." Defending Burmese Buddhism trumps everything else for him: "Taking care of our own religion and race is more important than democracy" (as quoted in Beech 2013). Ashin Wirathu basically repeated this argumentation in several interviews with Western media, even though he tried to distance himself from the picture of Burma's Osama bin Laden or the Burmese Face of Terror painted by the *Economist* and the *Time* magazine. One example is an interview by *Radio Free Asia's* Myanmar Service in June 2013, where he said that *Time* Magazine "referred to me as the 'Burmese Bin Laden' [...] but I told their reporter when they came and met me that it was the Muslims who gave me this name. I didn't refer to myself this way, but [Time] used this name in the story" (Khin Khin Ei 2013). Another one is an interview also held at his Masoeyein monastery in November 2014 that he began by claiming that "I think they intentionally singled me out to destroy me" (AJ+ 2014). Asked by the interviewer about the inflammatory nature of the statements he made in the *Time* article on Muslims as bad people, he responded that the "world take pity on the Muslims as a minority. But study them to understand how bad that small group is, how much trouble they have caused." He is then asked why his preaching is so popular nowadays in Burma, and why he thinks that his preaching is taking roots among Burmese people. Ashin Wirathu explains, "Our religion is not the only thing under threat. The whole country is. Just as they established Pakistan and Bangladesh, in the 2010s they're stepping up efforts to establish an Islamic state in Burma. So the whole country is now under threat, not only our faith" (all quotes from AJ+ 2014).

Beech's conclusion in her article on Ashin Wirathu is quite interesting since it fuses Wirathu's answers with her own Western interpretation of them:

> I ask Wirathu how he reconciles the peaceful sutras of his faith with the anti-Muslim violence spreading across his Bamar-majority homeland. "In Buddhism, we are not allowed to go on the offensive," he tells me, as if he is lecturing a child. "But we have every right to protect and defend our community." Later, as he preaches to an evening crowd, I listen to him compel smiling housewives, students, teachers, grandmothers and others to repeat after him, "I will sacrifice myself for the Bamar race." It's hard to imagine that the Buddha would have approved. (Beech 2013)

In a sense, Beech's mix of wonder, disbelief, and disapproval seems to be typical for Western assumptions of what (Theravāda) Buddhism stands for: as I already pointed out in the introduction, there is a certain reluctance to accept that violence and Buddhism are not as antithetic as we might think, and that, yes, Buddhist violent mobs actually are 'a thing.' Beech acknowledges that in her article, albeit also rather reluctantly only, it seems:

> It would be easy to dismiss Wirathu as an outlier with little doctrinal basis for his bigotry. But he is charismatic and powerful, and his message resonates. Among the country's majority Bamar ethnic group, as well as across Buddhist parts of Asia, there is a vague sense that their religion is under siege – that Islam, having centuries ago conquered the Buddhist lands of Indonesia, Malaysia, Pakistan and Afghanistan, now seeks new territory. (Beech 2013)

Indeed, it is the conviction that Buddhism is under threat that allows Ashin Wirathu and like-minded monks to justify the use of violence—a violence seen both as unavoidable and as defensive only, and thus permitted. It is quite significant that in the interview with Beech, Ashin Wirathu on the one hand readily concedes that an offensive use of violence is not permissible, but on the other emphasizes that Buddhist communities have the right to self-defence, especially if and when the survival of the religion as such is at stake. As one Burmese lay follower pointed out to me in a response to my short article on militant Buddhism in the *Conversation* (Lehr 2017), "Buddhism is not a suicidal utopianism." Even the concept of mindfulness (fashionable in the West at the moment) gets enlisted in this defensive struggle against Muslim encroachment. A transcription of a speech of Ashin Wirathu of March 2013 provided by Maung Zarni (2013) illustrates this:

> [The] Buddhist public needs to adopt a nationalist mindfulness – in virtually everything we do, that is, we must eat, sleep, see, hear, speak and breath [sic] '(Buddhist) nationalism.' [But] to my dismay, I am finding out that our Buddhist public still lacks this nationalist mindfulness. ['They'] (the Muslims) do everything with this (muslim [sic]) nationalist mindfulness. On [sic] example, in the previous military era, they flocked to the generals and through their connections, they have captured the Construction boom/market in Yangon. They didn't love the military or the generals. They collaborated with the military for their national (Muslim) interests. [Then] the Muslims approached and joined in large numbers the military's USDA/USDP party not because they understood democracy or human rights. Quite the contrary, they are the most blatant violators of religious freedoms and other human rights. (as transcribed by Maung Zarni 2013)

Ashin Wirathu then goes on to list cities, companies, or important positions in politics and the economy that are in danger of being taken over by Muslims, to then claim that current politicians are either unable or unwilling to defend the Buddhist religion. The he returns to mindfulness—also explaining the meaning of the '969' of the *969 Movement*:

> That is why we must all adopt this '969' (Buddhist) nationalist mindfulness. 9 stands for the 9 special attributes of the Lord Buddha; 6 for the special attributes of his teaching/Dharma; and 9 for the special attributes of the Sangha [...]. (as transcribed by Maung Zarni 2013)

Next, a call for specific action follows:

> [We] must do business or otherwise interact with only our kind: same race and same faith. [Your] purchases/money spent in 'their' (Muslim) shops

will benefit the Enemy. [They] take our women. [In] Rakhine State, with
their population explosion they are capturing it. And they will capture our
country in the end. [So], do business with only shops with '969' signs on
their facets. (as transcribed by Maung Zarni 2013)

Even though the accuracy of the summary transcription is questionable
since the transcriber himself hardly can be seen as neutral (he calls Ashin
Wirathu a 'fascist monk,' for example, and his sermon a 'Nazi speech'),
this sermon can be seen as fairly typical of Ashin Wirathu's preaching, in
which both religious and socio-economic justifications are fused with
some calls for immediate action in order to agitate the crowd, very similarly to the pattern used by those leading monks behind the anti-Indian
riots of 1938. This again demonstrates that Ashin Wirathu obviously is
part of a lineage of nationalist monks that can be traced back to the days
prior to independence, and maybe even to the first uprisings against the
British colonial regime immediately after the end of the monarchy. Calls
for a boycott of Muslim businesses and the claim that the Muslims take
'our' women had been included in the sermons of July and August 1938
as well, as I showed. In other sermons, Ashin Wirathu also encourages
Burmese-Buddhist parents not to allow their daughters to marry Muslim
men—again just like his predecessors of 1938 had done. The reconstruction of mindfulness into a 'nationalist' Burmese mindfulness, however,
seems to be novel—at least, I could not find any examples of a prior use of
this before Ashin Wirathu.

Also, and especially, the justification of defensive violence is neither new
nor inconsistent with Buddhist scripture—rather, as I explained in the
third chapter, this interpretation of the Buddha's teachings on that matter
became necessary with the onset of the second moment of Buddhist history and the advent of Buddhist kingdoms. Even the Buddha himself
showed some understanding for the wars conducted by his benefactor
King Pasenadi, although he warned that "killing, you gain your killer,
conquering, you gain the one who will conquer you" (Sangama Sutta SN
3.15, as translated by Thanissaro Bhikkhu 1999), pointing at the cycle of
action and reaction—the message being that violence begets violence.
Hence, and despite this warning, it is evident that even for the Buddha
himself, non-violence was not necessarily an absolute value—and this is a
point actually not only made by Western scholars specialized in Buddhist
ethics but also by many of the militant monks around Ashin Wirathu. As
such, Ashin Wirathu indeed is no "outlier with little doctrinal basis," as

Beech realized. There are certain limitations, however, which are insurmountable even for him and his compatriots: firstly, as I also argued earlier on, the Buddha's tendency to either condemn or at least deplore violence probably served as a powerful inhibitor against the emergence of a fully formulated 'Just War' doctrine as it already existed in the Brahmanism of the Buddha's days, and as it became part of Christian and Muslim theology. And secondly, it should also be noted that, compared to 'preachers of hate' from Abrahamic religions, militant monks face a difficult tightrope walk in that regard since the incitement to murder constitutes one of the four disrobing offences (pārājikas), that is offences resulting in the automatic expulsion from the monkhood that I discussed in the second chapter as well. For this reason, Ashin Wirathu and like-minded monks in Burma have to be very careful what they say and how they say it.

## EVALUATIONS: BURMESE MILITANT MONKS AND THE THEME OF BEING UNDER SIEGE

The transcription of one of Ashin Wirathu's typical sermons reveals the strong socio-economic undertones of the anti-Rohingya riots. Here, we can draw interesting parallels to the anti-Indian riots of 1938 again. The Final Report is quite candid when it comes to evaluating the triggers behind the riots:

> [The] riots were not, we think, religious riots. The real nature of the riots has, we think, tended to be obscured because the 'occasion' of the beginning of them in Rangoon had a religious flavour and because *pongyis* were generally prominent in them and Indians [...] became the particular objects of attack. [...] The riots at bottom were political and communal. Their immediate cause was we think, a complex piece of irresponsible political opportunism which saw in [the pamphlet] a pretext [...] to exploit for political ends the social and economic phenomena presented by Burma's large, industrious and useful population of Indian British Subjects. (Braund 1939, 287–288)

Quite ironically, the verdict of the Final Report can still be used about eight decades later against the backdrop of the current anti-Rohingya riots with only minor adaption required: these riots are not necessarily religious riots per se but revolve around perceived socio-economic issues. Hence, it is fair to say, without exculpating the extremist monks and even without completely exonerating Burmese Buddhism as it is practised, that Buddhism indeed plays a crucial role in these conflicts as a justification and legitimization strategy, but that there are other issues at work as well: without the underlying socio-economic problems, it would be much harder for the extremist monks to whip their listeners into a frenzy. Hence, and as I said in the introduction, Selengut (2003, 228) is quite right when he argues that "other factors like widespread poverty, grievances, and resentment against governmental authority or strong charismatic leaders" are required even if there is a doctrinal justification for violence available— not that Ashin Wirathu's preaching could be reduced to sheer opportunistic politicking, however: as we have seen, he went to jail for no less than nine years for his conviction that includes the belief that the military regime clandestinely collaborates with Muslim business elites. Hence, we still have to take seriously what he says and what he stands for, "however strange, aberrant or fanatical" this may sound to us, just as Kepel (1994, 11) encouraged us to do.

The fact that religion played an important part in the rise of nationalism but that there were other factors at work as well also is of utmost importance if we evaluate Buddhist nationalism in Burma through the lens of fundamentalism: just as Almond, Appleby, and Sivan observed in the case of Sri Lanka, this is not a 'pure' fundamentalism but a 'syncretic' one— which means a fundamentalism "in which ethnocultural or ethnonational features take precedence over religion or are inseparable" (Almond et al. 2003, 93, 110). Hence, just like in the case of Sri Lanka, I argue that when it comes to the perspective of the militant monks participating in movements linked to this 'syncretic' fundamentalism, the defence of Buddhism is inseparable with ethno-cultural, ethno-national, and even territorial (or 'ethno-territorial') aspects such as language and ethnicity that may well have had precedence for secular actors such as the leading politicians of the most relevant parties. After all, 'to be Burmese means to be Buddhist,' as we have seen, which also implies that from the monks' perspective, 'their' syncretic fundamentalism was an 'ethno-religiously pre-emptive' one seeking "to limit, suppress, or expel from the national community other ethnoreligious groupings" (Almond et al. 2003, 94).

The fact that religion and nationalism went hand in glove also did not escape the attention of some early observers of (then) current affairs in Colonial Burma. A contributor to the *Burma Observer*, for example, opined in 1922 that "[the] Burmese people cannot think of nationality apart from the religion that they hold, for it is Buddhism which has welded the Burmese together and the idea of nationhood owes its inception to Buddhism" (Burma Observer, 24 July 1922, as quoted in Smith 1965, 83). Smith agrees with this conclusion when he discusses nationalism in the colonial period, offering some convincing arguments on why this was the case. Firstly, he reminds us of the central role Theravāda Buddhism played ever since it became a de facto state religion in the times of King Anawratha as the founder of the Pagan dynasty in the eleventh century (Smith 1965, 83). Secondly, against the backdrop of Burmese history before the British colonial regime, he notes that the "Burmese had a fierce kind of national pride which enabled them to look with contempt upon other peoples, Mons, Kachins, Karens, Indians, and Chinese alike [while a] distinctive language, a common ethnic identity, some degree of political centralization, a shared history, a territorial base, the proximity of different and frequently hostile peoples, all contributed to the development of traditional Burmese nationalism" (Smith 1965, 82).[17] On the basis of these arguments, he then, thirdly, argues rather pointedly that:

[the] British were the last of a long series of external enemies which threatened Old Burma. A xenophobic traditionalist society girded up its loins and sought to protect itself with all its resources, material and spiritual (Smith 1965, 84)

Smith's argumentation is quite compelling. It can even be used, to a large extent, to explain the most current manifestation of Burmese Buddhist nationalism—although it requires some adjustment because, strictly speaking, Smith does not discuss the 'Burmese' as such, that is the citizens of the modern state of Burma regardless of their ethnicity, but the 'Burmans' as members of the ethnic group of the Bamar. Hence, he also repeats the saying that 'to be a Burman is to be a Buddhist.' During most parts of Burmese history including the British colonial interlude, the focus on the

[17] It should be noted that Smith distinguishes between 'traditional' and 'modern' nationalism—hence, his seemingly contradictory quip quoted earlier that the "[in] the anti-colonial struggle, the pongyis (monks) were the first nationalists" (Smith 1965, 85). Frank Trager (1966, 43) and Michael Mendelson (1975, 173–235), however, argue without any differentiation that Burmese nationalism commenced with the British colonial government—a view that I do not share since I see Burmese 'modern' nationalism basically as a continuation of 'traditional' nationalism with novel connotations now mixed to the 'us versus them' general theme.

Burmans makes sense—not so much, however, after independence when some of the other peoples he mentioned, such as Mons, Karen, and Kachin, found themselves to be citizens of the modern state of Burma, and, hence, as Burmese—not as Burman Burmese but as Karen Burmese and so forth, but Burmese still. The Burman contempt for other ethnic groups that he mentioned arguably is still present, and the Burmans still tend to look down on these groups, and even to fight with them in the restive border regions of their country. But as long as these ethnic groups are Buddhist, there is some grudging acceptance. This implies that the saying 'to be Burman is to be Buddhist' now has to be adapted to 'to be Burmese is to be Buddhist'—which obviously causes a problem for all those Burmese citizens who are neither Burmans nor Buddhists, but, say, Christian-Baptist Karen or Muslim Rohingya, for that matter. And here, we can revisit Smith's argument regarding the 'long series of external enemies' encountering a 'xenophobic traditionalist society girding its loins': seen from this perspective, the Rohingya, perceived as 'Bengali' and thus as foreigners, simply are yet another manifestation of external enemies who need to be repulsed. To a lesser extent, this can also be said about the ethnic minority groups of the Karen, Kachin, and Shan, or at least those of them who are not Buddhists.

However, I do not agree with Smith's argument that "Buddhism did not supply *ideas* to support the traditional Burmese nationalism [but rather] it provided an essential component in the national self-concept which helped to differentiate the Burmese from the foreigner" (Smith 1965, 86 [emphasis in the original]). As I showed, there are indeed ideas provided by Theravāda Buddhist doctrine, especially as it developed from the second moment of Buddhist history onwards. It is certainly true that "[there] is very little in the sacred texts of Buddhism to give positive support to any kind of nationalism [since doctrinal] Buddhism did not include such concepts as state, nation, race, or history, and indeed interpreted human existence in terms which made these ideas irrelevant and meaningless" (Smith 1965, 85). Nevertheless, there is the notion that self-defence is permissible if the realm, the Buddhist community, or the religion as such is under threat. And this is exactly the justification used by the militant nationalist monks around Ashin Wirathu, as we have seen, with the additional strand of dehumanizing the Muslim 'other' thrown in for good measure, reminiscent of the aforementioned Mahāvamsa passage. Of course, this 'pick and mix' approach used by militant monks also implies that it cannot be argued that Buddhism per se is prone to violence, or that all monks are supporting what Gravers (2015, 4) calls the "violent strain." I would however go a bit further than Gravers who also argues that "[although] religious phrases may be used in violent rhetoric, Buddhism in itself is not violent" (ibid.): in my opinion, these are not only phrases opportunistically used as tools in an otherwise mainly socio-political fight for influence and dominance. Rather, these justifications for violence on the basis of Buddhist doctrine point at firmly held believes of those monks—believes for which they are prepared to even go to jail.

Smith offers another interesting observation for the political monks of the colonial period: he argues that "the monks had little or nothing to lose, and hence could afford to indulge in irresponsible extremist attacks on the British government," and further, they "had no jobs, families, or material possessions which might be jeopardized by extremist politics, and so there was little need for moderation" (Smith 1965, 94). They had however their freedom and their lives to lose, as U Kettaya, U Ottama, and U Wisara found out—after all, it was their sacrifice which elevated them to nationalist martyrs, as discussed. As we saw, the same applies to modern monks like U Gambira in the case of the ABMA monks associated with the Saffron Revolution, and Ashin Wirathu in the case of the nationalist monks of Ma Ba Tha and the 969 Movement: both of them had to go to jail for their convictions, and they spent a substantial amount of time behind bars—not that surprising in the case of the former due to the anti-regime activities of the ABMA monks, somewhat more surprising in the case of the latter since his activities are in line with government policies.

## CAVEATS: VIEWS OF THE SILENT MAJORITY

Now it is time to add a caveat: not all monks are interested in political activism, no matter what the cause may be, and the majority of the Burmese Sangha is rather hostile to the ultra-nationalist activities of Ashin Wirathu and his fellow monks. First of all, the still-existing ABMA (underground in Burma, and active abroad) does not condone the activities of Ashin Wirathu, and his followers can be gleaned from a very clear statement that can be seen on ABMA's website:

> Regarding the recent incidents of sectarian violence in Burma, the ABMA does not condone or support religious discrimination or violence against any group of people. The sacred rules of Theravada Buddhism prohibit monks from supporting violence. (ABMA 2018)

A number of senior monks within Burma also openly condemn Ashin Wirathu and his like-minded fellow monks' activities basically for the same reasons. Hodal (2013), for example, cites Abbot Arriya Wuttha Bewuntha of Mandalay's Myawaddy Sayadaw monastery as saying that Ashin Wirathu "sides a little towards hate. [...] This is not the way Buddha taught. What the Buddha taught is that hatred is not good, because Buddha sees everyone as an equal being. The Buddha doesn't see people through religion." This sentiment is shared by a abbot of yet another major monastery in Mandalay interviewed in November 2014 who also explains his course of action in that regard as follows: "My intervention, working day and night, pleading with the people, brought the killings and the violence to an end briefly without spreading further. That's the outcome of our work" (AJ+ 2014). However, Sayadaw further states that "Trouble is brewing because the ruling government and the opposition don't get along. If the electoral contest between them is fair, it won't matter. If unjust means are employed, then it's bound to cause conflicts. One side will surely resort to creating sectarian conflicts." He also points out that Ashin Wirathu is not the only monk causing trouble: "If there are those who spread rumours, those of unsound minds would be inspired to act rash without thinking" (all quotes from AJ+ 2014).

Just as in the case of Sri Lanka, it is not without risk to speak up publicly against Ashin Wirathu and the other ultra-nationalist monks: quite disturbingly, especially when seen from the perspective of an apolitical monk, even fellow Buddhist monks are 'othered' if they dare to speak up against anti-Muslim activities. For example, in September 2015, Ashin Wirathu alleged that the Saffron Monks Network had helped 'Bengali Muslims' (i.e. Rohingya) to illegally cross the border from Bangladesh into Burma. U Thawbita, also known as the Bawa Alinn Sayadaw (Light of Life Sayadaw, see Mratt Kyaw Thu 2016) and one of the prominent Saffron Revolution monks, reluctantly took it upon himself to counter these allegations:

> Sayadaw U Wirathu said that monks from the 2007 Saffron Revolution helped Bengalis to enter Myanmar illegally. If there is such case, he should show the evidence, and take legal action against these monks who helped Bengalis in cooperation with the authorities concerned. But they are defaming the monks of the Saffron Revolution. The comment of U Wirathu is wrong. [...] We won't return their accusation because Buddha preached that between accuser and accused, only the accuser loses dignity. (as quoted in Maung Zaw 2015)

The silent majority of the Burmese monkhood seems to perceive political activities of any kind as an obstacle to reaching nibbāna. They do not differentiate between what Western observers might deem to be 'honourable' pro-democracy activities as undertaken by all those monks, novices, and nuns participating in the Saffron Revolution and the highly questionable (again, mainly from a Western viewpoint) nationalist-chauvinist activities of Ashin Wirathu, the 969 Movement, and the Ma Ba Tha: whatever the underlying intention may be, political activism will ultimately tie the monks engaged in them to the mundane world, to the detriment of their progress towards enlightenment. It is worthwhile to repeat the statement of an abbot of a monastery in Mandalay who was interviewed by Spiro in the 1970s. In the context of reaching nibbāna, the abbot said:

> It is like a log floating on a river – if there are no obstacles, it will eventually float to the ocean. These [politically active, PL] monks will have a hard time getting to the ocean [nirvana] because their political organizations are an obstacle. In fact, not only will they not get to the ocean for a very long time, but it is even more likely that they will become waterlogged and sink to the bottom of the river. Instead of getting to the ocean, they will end up in hell. (as quoted in Spiro 1982, 393)

This is a sentiment I found expressed as well, albeit not so eloquently, and sometimes in rather forceful terms. Those (admittedly few) Burmese monks whom I could query about this issue suggested that if it is politics in general, or social activism in particular, that motivates the younger generation of monks, then they would be better off to disrobe and leave the Sangha, in order to embark on a career as politicians or activists. After all, taking sides in politics would not only stand in their way towards nibbāna, but it could lead to bad feelings within the monkhood itself, and to the advent of factionalism. It could even result in a distortion of the Buddha's teaching by way of interpreting it (intentionally or not) in a way to make it fit to their own political ideas. To illustrate this, they explicitly mentioned the (verbal) clashes between the nationalist wings of Ma Ba Tha and the 969 Movement on the one hand, and the Saffron Monks Network on the other: indeed, these vitriolic exchanges are quite unedifying to watch, especially from the perspective of an apolitical monk from the countryside. In my opinion, their warning firmly puts Saffron Revolution monk U Igara's enthusiasm in perspective: in July 2008 (i.e. more than nine months after the violent suppression of the Saffron Revolution), he opined that "something was achieved [in September 2007]. A whole new generation of monks has been politicized. We're educating them" (as quoted in Human Rights Watch 2009, 2). In the eyes of the majority of the Burmese Sangha, the politicization of substantial parts of the monkhood is not a good thing, no matter which side one takes. But whether the views of this silent majority actually matter remains to be seen—I shall return to this issue in the concluding chapter.

## References

ABMA. 2018. About the ABMA. *All Burma Monks' Alliance*. http://allburma-monksalliance.org

Adas, Michael. 1974. *The Burma Delta: Economic Development and Social Change on an Asian Rice Frontier, 1852–1941*. Madison: University of Wisconsin Press [e-book].

Ahmed, Ibtisam. 2017. The Historical Roots of the Rohingya Conflict. *IAPS Dialogue*, October 4. https://iapsdialogue.org/2017/10/04/the-historical-roots-of-the-rohingya-crisis/

AJ+. 2014. *Myanmar's Anti-Muslim Monks* (YouTube video). November 12. https://www.youtube.com/watch?v=GtAl9zJ3t-M

Almond, Gabriel A., R. Scott Appleby, and Emmanuel Sivan. 2003. *Strong Religion: The Rise of Fundamentalisms around the World*. Chicago/London: University of Chicago Press.

Aung Kyaw Min. 2017. Ma Ba Tha to Continue Under New Name. *Myanmar Times*, May 29. https://www.mmtimes.com/national-news/yangon/26171-ma-ba-tha-to-continue-under-new-name.html

Aung-Thwin, Maitrii. 2011. *The Return of the Galon King: History, Law, and Rebellion in Colonial Burma*. Singapore: NUS Press.

Aung Zaw. 2013. The Power Behind the Robe. *The Irrawaddy*, September 20 (first published in October 2007 in the print version of *The Irrawaddy*). https://www.irrawaddy.com/from-the-archive/power-behind-robe.html

Bechert, Heinz. 2007. 'To be a Burmese is to be a Buddhist': Buddhism in Burma. In *The World of Buddhism: Buddhist Monks and Nuns in Society and Culture*, ed. Heinz Bechert and Richard F. Gombrich, 147–158. London: Thames & Hudson (reprint).

Beech, Hannah. 2013. The Face of Buddhist Terror. *Time*, July 1. http://content.time.com/time/magazine/article/0,9171,2146000,00.html

Braund, H B L. (Chairman). 1939. *Final Report of the Riot Inquiry Committee*. Rangoon: Superintendent, Government Printing and Stationery. https://ia801609.us.archive.org/22/items/in.ernet.dli.2015.206317/2015.206317.Final-Report.pdf

DVB. 2007. International Monks' Organisation Established. *Democratic Voice of Burma*, October 30. http://www.dvb.no/uncategorized/international-monks-organisation-established/607

DW. 2017. Hate Speech Myanmar Monk Banned From Preaching by Buddhist Council. *Deutsche Welle*, March 11. http://www.dw.com/en/hate-speech-myanmar-monk-banned-from-preaching-by-buddhist-council/a-37905421

Ei Ei Thu. 2017. Bagan on Way to UNESCO Listing as World Heritage Site. *Myanmar Times*, September 29. https://www.mmtimes.com/travel/bagan-way-unesco-listing-world-heritage-site.html

Gombrich, Richard F. 2006. *Theravāda Buddhism: A Social History From Ancient Benares to Modern Colombo.* 2nd ed. Abingdon/New York: Routledge.

Gravers, Mikael. 2010. The Monk in Command. *The Irrawaddy* 18 (5). http://www2.irrawaddy.org/print_article.php?art_id=18407 or at http://www.buddhistchannel.tv/index.php?id=9,9146,0,0,1,0#.U4n8ZBbIZFw

———. 2012. Monks, Morality and Military. The Struggle for Moral Power in Burma – And Buddhism's Uneasy Relation with Lay Power. *Contemporary Buddhism: An Interdisciplinary Journal* 13 (1): 1–33. https://www.tandfonline.com/doi/full/10.1080/14639947.2012.669278?src=recsys

———. 2015. Anti-Muslim Buddhist Nationalism in Burma and Sri Lanka: Religious Violence and Globalized Imaginaries of Endangered Identities. *Contemporary Buddhism: An Interdisciplinary Journal* 16 (1): 1–27. https://www.tandfonline.com/doi/full/10.1080/14639947.2015.1008090

Hodal, Kate. 2013. Buddhist Monk Uses Racism and Rumours to Spread Hatred in Burma. *The Guardian*, April 18. https://www.theguardian.com/world/2013/apr/18/buddhist-monk-spreads-hatred-burma

Houtman, Gustaaf. 1999. *Mental Culture in Burmese Crisis Politics: Aung San Suu Kyi and the National League for Democracy.* Tokyo: Institute for the Study of Languages and Cultures of Asia and Africa, Tokyo University.

———. 2000. *Human Origins, Myanmafication and 'Disciplined' Burmese Democracy.* Pekhon: Pekhon University Press.

Human Rights Watch. 2007. *Crackdown. Repression of the 2007 Popular Protests in Burma* 19 (18 (C)). https://www.hrw.org/report/2007/12/06/crackdown/repression-2007-popular-protests-burma

———. 2009. *The Resistance of the Monks. Buddhism and Activism in Burma.* Human Rights Watch, September 22. https://www.hrw.org/report/2009/09/22/resistance-monks/buddhism-and-activism-burma

Ibrahim, Azeem. 2018. *The Rohingyas. Inside Myanmar's Genocide.* London: Hurst & Company.

ICG. 2016. *Myanmar: A New Muslim Insurgency in Rakhine State.* International Crisis Group (ICG) Report No 283, 15 December. https://www.crisisgroup.org/asia/south-east-asia/myanmar/283-myanmar-new-muslim-insurgency-rakhine-state

Kepel, Gilles. 1994. *The Revenge of God. The Resurgence of Islam, Christianity and Judaism in the Modern World*. Cambridge: Polity Press.

Khin Khin Ei. 2013. Myanmar Monk Rejects Terrorist Label Following Communal Clashes. *Radio Free Asia*, June 21. https://www.rfa.org/english/news/myanmar/monk-06212013182954.html

Lehr, Peter. 2017. Militant Buddhism is on the March in Southeast Asia – Where Did It Come From? *The Conversation*, November 7. https://theconversation.com/militant-buddhism-is-on-the-march-in-south-east-asia-where-did-it-come-from-86632

Lieberman, Victor B. 1976. A New Look at the 'Sāsanavamsa'. *Bulletin of the School of Oriental and African Studies* 39 (1): 137–149.

Matthews, Bruce. 1999. The Legacy of Tradition and Authority: Buddhism and the Nation in Myanmar. In *Buddhism and Politics in Twentieth-Century Asia*, ed. Ian Harris, 26–53. London: Continuum.

Maung Zarni. 2013. Racist Leader Monk Rev. Wirathu's Speech. Summary translation to English by Maung Zarni. *M-Media*, March 24. http://www.m-mediagroup.com/en/archives/7625

Maung Zaw. 2015. Saffron Monks Fire Back at U Wirathu. *Myanmar Times*, September 11. https://www.mmtimes.com/national-news/mandalay-upper-myanmar/16440-saffron-monks-fire-back-at-u-wirathu.html

McPherson, Poppy. 2018. Myanmar Army Fakes Rohingya Photos in 'True News' Book. *Bangkok Post/Reuters*, August 31. https://www.bangkokpost.com/news/special-reports/1531606/myanmar-army-fakes-rohingya-photos-in-true-news-book

Mendelson, E. Michael. 1975. *State and Sangha in Burma: A Study of Monastic Sectarianism and Leadership*. Ithaca: Cornell University Press.

Mratt Kyaw Thu. 2016. The State of the Sangha. *Frontier Myanmar*, February 19. https://frontiermyanmar.net/en/the-state-of-the-sangha

Republic of the Union of Myanmar. 2016. The Union Report: Religion. In *The 2014 Myanmar Population and Housing Census*, Census Report Volume 2-C, July. Naypyidaw: Department of Population/ Ministry of Labour/Immigration and Population.

Sarkisyanz, Emanuel. 1965. *Buddhist Backgrounds of the Burmese Revolution*. Amsterdam: Springer.

Selengut, Charles. 2003. *Sacred Fury. Understanding Religious Violence*. Walnut Creek et al.: Altamira Press.

Smith, Donald Eugene. 1965. *Religion and Politics in Burma*. Princeton: Princeton University Press.

Spiro, Melford E. 1982. *Buddhism and Society. A Great Tradition and Its Burmese Vicissitudes*. Berkeley/Los Angeles/London: University of California Press (2nd, expanded ed.).

Symes, Michael. 1800. *An Account of an Embassy to the Kingdom of Ava, Sent by the Governor-General of India, in the year 1795. By Michael Symes, Esq. Lieut-Col. In His Majesty's 76th Regiment* [electronic book]. London: printed by W. Bulmer and Co. Cleveland-Row, St. James's; and sold by Messrs. G. and W. Nicol, Booksellers to his Majesty, Pall-Mall; and J. Wright, Piccadilly.

Thanissaro Bhikkhu, trans. 1999. Sangama Sutta: A Battle (2). *Samyutta Nikaya: The Grouped Discourses.* Access to Insight: Readings in Theravāda Buddhism. http://www.accesstoinsight.org/tipitaka/sn/sn03/sn03.015.than.html

Thant Myint-U. 2007. *The River of Lost Footsteps. A Personal History of Burma.* London: Faber & Faber.

Trager, Frank N. 1966. *Burma: From Kingdom to Republic.* London: Pall Mall Press.

Turner, Alicia. 2014. *Saving Buddhism. The Impermanence of Religion in Colonial Burma.* Honolulu: University of Hawai'i Press.

U Pyinya Zawta. 2009. Leading Saffron Monk's Memoir. *Mizzima News,* January 2. Article hosted at http://allburmamonksalliance.org/feature-articles-statements/

UNHCR. 2018. *Report of the Independent International Fact-Finding Mission on Myanmar* (advance unedited version). United Nations Human Rights Council, August 24. https://www.ohchr.org/Documents/HRBodies/HRCouncil/FFM-Myanmar/A_HRC_39_64.pdf

UNHCR Refworld. Undated. *Burma Citizenship Law (Pyithu Hluttaw Law No. 4 of 1982).* http://www.refworld.org/docid/3ae6b4f71b.html

Winchester, Mike. 2017. Birth of an Ethnic Insurgency in Myanmar. *Asia Times Online,* August 28. http://www.atimes.com/article/birth-ethnic-insurgency-myanmar/

CHAPTER 7

# Thailand: "It Is Time to Arm Thai Buddhists"

With regard to the arguments made in the chapters on Sri Lanka and Burma on the rise of extremist Buddhism, it can be said that very similar forces seem to be at work in Thailand, where 95 per cent of the people are Theravāda Buddhists: there is a lingering feeling of being under siege by Muslims as the implacable enemy of the day. In contrast to Sri Lanka and Burma, however, this feeling is largely restricted to the Deep South (the provinces of Pattani, Yala, Narathiwat, and Songkhla)[1] where the Muslims form the majority, and where a Malay-Muslim insurgency has resulted in more than 8000 deaths since 2004—including Buddhist monks and novices. However, compared to a similar feeling of being under siege by communists in the 1970s when ultra-nationalist monk Phra Kittiwutthō declared that killing communists was not a sin but the sacred duty of all Thai people, firebrand monks like Ashin Wirathu in Burma or Galagoda Aththe Gnanasara Thero in Sri Lanka are few and far between, and anti-Muslim rhetoric, although it exists, is a rather subdued affair.

---

[1] Pattani, Yala, and Narathiwat were part of the Sultanate of Patani, while Songkhla used to be the Sultanate of Singgora (Songkhla is a Thai rendering of the name). Both previously semi-independent sultanates were formally annexed by Thailand as a result of the Anglo-Siamese Treaty of 1909. Strictly speaking, the province of Satun (which also used to be a sultanate) also belongs to the Muslim-majority provinces, but since it is not part of the conflict, it can safely be disregarded in the following discussion.

© The Author(s) 2019
P. Lehr, *Militant Buddhism*,
https://doi.org/10.1007/978-3-030-03517-4_7

However, what also seems to set Thailand apart from the two other case studies is that in the Deep South, a new kind of monks seems to have emerged, even though this is either hushed up or categorically denied: the so-called *thahān phra* or soldier monks. This phenomenon of armed monks has been explored by Michael K. Jerryson (2011) and Duncan McCargo (2009, 11–32), who both conducted interviews in the conflict areas of the Deep South. Their trailblazing work is very helpful in order to start teasing out the differences of current Thai Buddhist militancy as compared to Sinhalese and Burmese forms of Buddhist militancy. But, since the arguments that will be made on the political activities of modern monks in particular and modern Thai Theravāda Buddhism in general obviously necessitate an in-depth understanding of how modern Thai Buddhism is constructed, the narrative has to start at the beginning of what is deemed to be 'modern' Buddhism, that is, just like in the previous cases, in the late nineteenth century. Again, Seneviratne's caveat mentioned in the first chapter should be kept in mind: when it comes to the tensions between doctrine and monastic life, we can only go as far as we are able to reconstruct the latter.

## FOUNDATIONS: THE RELATIONS BETWEEN SANGHA AND STATE IN THAILAND

A good starting point for a discussion of the relationship of Buddhism and the state is to remind readers that, contrary to Burma and Sri Lanka, Thailand managed to escape Western colonialism to a large extent—not completely though, since both the domestic modernizations and the foreign and security policies of Kings Mongkut (or Rama IV) and Chulalongkorn (Rama V) were deeply influenced by the urgent need to appear 'modern' in the eyes of France and Great Britain who had just swallowed Vietnam, Laos, and Cambodia (in the case of the former), and Thailand's long-time enemy Burma (in the case of the latter). But since Thailand (until 1936 Siam) served as a useful buffer state between the two colonial empires, it remained free from direct control that would have relegated the king to a largely ceremonial role, as was the case for the last Vietnamese emperors and Cambodian kings, or that would simply have abolished the monarchy, as the British did in Burma. Hence, Seneviratne's (1999, 13) claim that

> [as] a country that was not colonized by a modern European power, Thailand also reveals with great clarity the fact that modernist religious

reformism is more than simply a by-product of colonial domination [and] that Thailand's reformism is part of a general process of modernization that came into being as a result of non-colonial contact with the western world.

should be taken with a pinch of salt: it can be argued that the Siamese/ Thai modernization process also aimed at denying the colonial powers an easy excuse for carving up the kingdom and incorporating it into their colonial empires. Nevertheless, it can be argued that due to the absence of overt colonialization, the continuation of the traditional monarchy and the Sangha hierarchy, the absence of any major insurgency or domestic armed conflict (Swearer 1999, 195), and, in particular, the uninterrupted role of Buddhism as the (quasi) state religion precluded the emergence of political monks comparable to Sri Lanka and Myanmar (Spiro 1982, 391). There simply was no power vacuum to be filled comparable to the cases of Sri Lanka and Burma—not that the country escaped the politicization of the monkhood (or parts of it) for long, as we shall see. But before I start analysing contemporary monks and their stances towards social and political activities, the traditional relationship between Sangha and kingship needs to be inspected to provide some necessary context.

The first vestiges of Buddhism (probably Mahāyāna) reached Thailand, or, more precisely, the Chaophraya area, around the fifth century as in the case of Burma.[2] And very similarly, the original Buddhist lore seems to have been intertwined with Brahmanism, Hinduism, and folk religion featuring local gods, ancestors, and ghosts/spirits (phi). Theravāda Buddhism proper entered much later in the thirteenth century, coming from Sri Lanka (Baker and Phongpaichit 2005, 7–8). It quickly underwent a similar metamorphosis as the original Mahāyāna strand: as Baker and Phongpaichit point out, "[in] practice, this pure form of Theravāda was blended with other religious practices, including roles for Hindu gods, notions of supernatural power often borrowed from tantric types of Buddhism, and folk beliefs in spirits – especially in their power to foretell and influence the future" (Baker and Phongpaichit 2005, 19). But as I argued in the first chapter, worshipping gods such as Ganesh (the 'Elephant God') or Kuanjin is not inconsistent with Theravāda Buddhism as long as they are not seen as saviours who can grant access to nibbāna. Furthermore,

---

[2] As mentioned in the chapter on Burma, it is not entirely clear whether the Sasanavamsa relates to Burma or to the Thai-controlled Chaophraya valley.

as Tiyavanich (1997, 5) emphasizes, "[substantially] different forms of Buddhism existed" within the different regions that belonged to the Siamese kingdom, with each "of these Buddhist traditions [...] differently influenced by the many different forms of indigenous spirit worship and by the Mahayana and Tantric traditions that flourished prior to the fourteenth century." This also implies that many different monastic lineages or *nikayas* existed, with different interpretation of what the right practice (orthopraxis) should be and how the monastic discipline should be observed.

The relationship between the Sangha and the royal courts was similar to the situation in Sri Lanka and Burma: in the traditional Buddhist polity as defined by Tambiah (1978, 111–112), a strong relationship between the monastic order and the state existed. The kings provided protection and patronage, while the Sangha offered religious support for them, for example, by likening them to cakkavattins ('wheel turners') and dhamma-rajas (righteous rulers) as described in the first chapter. On the role of the kings as protectors of the religion, Tambiah illustrates this willingness to take up arms in defence of the Buddha's teaching quite nicely:

> It has been the custom of kings from old time to preserve the Buddhist religion and to further its prosperity. The way of doing this was by keeping cohorts of good soldiers to form an army, and by the accumulation of weapons, with the royal power at the head. Thereby he vanquished all his enemies in warfare, and he prevented the Buddhist religion from being endangered by the enemy, as kings have always done. (as quoted in Tambiah 1976, 162)

Regarding the religious support offered by the Sangha to the kings, it should be noted that this was not only lip service and empty pro-monarchy propaganda developed to keep the peasants at bay—for whom the monks often played the role of arbitrators in conflicts with officialdom, by the way (Suksamran 1979, 80–84). Rather, "[some] monasteries kept chronicles which judged each ruler, praising those who defended the [realm] skilfully, ruled their people with fairness and compassion, and of course patronized the Sangha" (Baker and Phongpaichit 2005, 20). In any case, again we see the two pillars, monarchy and monkhood, at work to keep the realm together, drawing on the support of the people who can be seen as the third pillar. Hence, Tambiah's eloquently expressed argument rings true: "Early Buddhism forged a macroconception that yoked religion (*sasana*) and its specialized salvation seekers, the monks in their collective identity as sangha, with a socio-political order of which kingship was the articulating principle" (Tambiah 1976, 5). Both pillars, monarchy and Sangha, had a mutual interest of weeding out any potential challengers: "Siamese kings and high-ranking monks saw it as their duty to collect and edit Buddhist texts, rewrite Buddhist history, purge the community of monks (Sangha) of corrupt persons, and reign in renegade independent-minded practitioners" (McDaniel 2006, 102). It should however be noted that in the early times of Thai history, several kingdoms fought for supremacy against each other: Mueang Nua (northern cities) centred first on Sukhothai, then on Phitsanulok; Lan Xang (lit. 'One Million Elephants') centred on Vientiane (nowadays Laos); Lan Na ('One Million Rice Fields') centred on Chiang Mai ('New Town'); and Xian (Siam, as the Portuguese rendered this Chinese name) centred on Ayutthaya. Similar to Burma which faced a similar endemic struggle for dominance, this occasionally also affected the monkhood since temples were deemed to be fair game in these wars. Thus, they were frequently plundered and destroyed in the process, and monks were either killed or forced to flee.

The monks were not always innocent victims in these bitter internal wars. Rather, an increasing factionalism within the Sangha, quite fragmented due to the lack of a firm hierarchy on the one hand and the difficulty of communication on the other, invariably enabled the various contenders for the crown to find the required support from at least one major temple situated on their territory. An example for such a conspiration is narrated in the *Royal Chronicles of Ayutthaya*: When in 1561, Prince Si Sin tried to seize the throne from King Maha Chakkrapat, the abbot of Wat Pa Kaeo, Phra Phanarat, "provided an auspicious moment" for that venture, thus throwing in his lot with the prince. Unfortunately for both, the auspicious moment turned out to be rather inauspicious in the end: the prince got shot dead in the ensuing battle, and the abbot was swiftly executed. As the Chronicle states, "[when] the King learned that the Reverend Phanarat of Pa Kaeo Monastery had really fixed an auspicious moment for Prince Si Sin, he had [him] taken to be executed and impaled at the public execution grounds along with the corpse of Prince Si Sin" (Cushman and Wyatt 2006, 41–42). Apart from occasionally being conspirators, a number of monks even actively took part in these wars, either as combatants or as spies. Regarding the active participation in a conflict, the *Royal Chronicles of Ayutthaya*, for example, note that during the war with Hongsawadi, 1563 to 1564, [the Reverend] "Maha Nak, who was a monk at Phukhao Thòng Monastery, left the monkhood and agreed to erect a stockade to protect the naval forces" (Cushman and Wyatt 2006, 32). In that case, the senior monk disrobed first before doing his bit for his king, Maha Chakkrapat, in the king's first war against the (equally Theravāda Buddhist) Burmese invaders under King Bayinnaung and was thus technically not a monk when he did so. Whether he reordained afterwards, or what generally happened to him, is not mentioned in the chronicle. Regarding the use of monks as spies, this seems to have been a common practice in this war as well as in all subsequent Burmese-Siamese wars as well, although it is hard to say whether these spies were 'real' monks or just soldiers disguised as such. How endemic this practice was on the Burmese side (which probably made more use of it than the Siamese/Thai side) is even today illustrated by the Thai monks' practice to shave their eyebrows: this non-doctrinal habit was introduced during one of those wars (it is difficult to establish with any degree of precision which one) in order to better tell the 'good' Thai monks from the spying 'bad' Burmese monks (Pannapadipo 2005, 29–30; Palmisano 2013).

After Ayutthaya had finally established its supremacy, the monkhood fared better, and the temples and monasteries prospered, for example, under the reign of King Borommakot (r. 1733–1758) who was honoured with the title of Thammaracha for his efforts (Baker and Phongpaichit 2005, 20–21). However, in contrast to their Burmese counterparts, the kings of Ayutthaya in general seemed to have been less interested in showering the monkhood with lavish royal patronage: as Baker and Phongpaichit state, the construction of new temples and monasteries, and the repair of older ones, was predominantly initiated and funded by the aristocracy, while the kings focused on patronizing Brahmanism due to its importance for court ritual and royal prestige (Baker and Phongpaichit 2005, 20). They also draw attention to King Narai (r. 1656–1688) who threw down the gauntlet to the Sangha in a literary work titled 'Can monks question kings?'—a prerogative that monks probably took for granted ever since the times of King Pasenadi (Prasenajit) of Kosala. Narai was not the only one in that regard: King Taksin (r. 1767–1782) also attempted to rein in the Sangha by bringing it under his personal control, even going as far as giving lectures to monks and demanding them to acknowledge that he had already reached the first of the four stages to enlightenment, and thus to declare him a *sotāpanna* or 'stream-winner.'[3] Those monks who refused "were demoted in status, and hundreds

---

[3] Also frequently translated as 'stream enterer.' The following stages are 'once-returner', 'never-returner', arahant/arhat.

were flogged and sentenced to menial labour" (Wyatt 2003, 127). Taksin's maltreatment of monks played a crucial role in the decision taken by a faction of the leading aristocrats to remove him from the throne and to have him executed. One of his generals, General Chao Phraya Chakri, was subsequently crowned king and ascended the throne under the name of Phra Phutthayotfa Chulalok, in the West better known as Rama I.

## RECONSTRUCTIONS: THE GRADUAL POLITICIZATION OF THE THAI SANGHA

The kings of the new Chakri dynasty lost no time in modernizing and Westernizing the country, for example, by gradually turning Thailand into a market economy, and by even more gradually replacing hereditary rulers and governors with secular bureaucrats trained in Bangkok and appointed by the court. As for the dynasty's moral legitimacy, it still drew on the Ayutthayan brand of Buddhist kingship, according to which the king was seen as a Bodhisatta, which means "a spiritual superhuman being who had accumulated great merit over previous lives, been reincarnated in order to rule with righteousness, and would become a Buddha in the future" (Baker and Phongpaichit 2005, 31). In the process, Ayutthayan King Borommakot Thammaracha "was idealized as the model king, and other late Ayutthayan monarchs condemned as poor rulers," with the overall aim to establish the new dynasty "as defenders of Buddhism against the destructive (though Buddhist) Burmese. [Even the] conquests of Lao and Khmer territories were justified as saving these peoples from less perfectly Buddhist governance" (Baker and Phongpaichit 2005, 32)—an interesting allusion to the malleable boundaries of the term 'defensive' as in 'defensive violence,' as I already discussed.

A monarchy that shored up its legitimacy by emphasizing its role as the defenders of Buddhism naturally depended on a Sangha congenial to this lofty aim—'congenial' first of all meaning that it was supporting the king, and, secondly, that it upheld the Buddha's teaching and the *Vinaya* rules of conduct. Arguably, the Sangha had suffered since the downfall of Ayutthaya, and then again in the last years of King Taksin's rule when many of the monks were forcibly disrobed and condemned to hard labour for their refusal to accept him as a sotāpanna. For the first king of the new Chakri dynasty, Phra Putthayotfa Chulalok (Rama I), this presented him with the perfect excuse to purify the Sangha, as many of his predecessors had done. The purification of the Sangha however was only the beginning: in the process of modernization and Westernization, both monarchy and Buddhism were largely stripped of their mystical and mythological elements, in particular, during the reigns of King Mongkut (Rama IV, reigned 2 April 1851–1 October 1868) and King Chulalongkorn (Rama V, reigned 1 October 1868–23 October 1910).[4] In a sense, Buddhism was essential-ized, as it was in Sri Lanka. However, and this is quite a crucial difference, in Siam/Thailand, this was done as a 'top-down' process, inaugurated by the monarchy. The major guiding force behind this essentialization of Thai Buddhism was King Mongkut who spent no less than 27 years in the monkhood as a fully ordained monk with the ordination name of Vajirayan before he was crowned king in 1851. Although he seemed to have genu-inely enjoyed the monastic life, he certainly did not like the lax practice of many of the monks he met, especially the habit not to involve themselves in worldly affairs. In Vajirayan's view, "true Buddhism was supposed to refrain from worldly matters and confine itself to spiritual and moral affairs" (Winichakul 1994, 39).

In 1833, Vajirayan's new 'Buddhist orthodoxy movement' crystallized into the *Thammayuttika Nikai* (Pali: Dhammayuttika Nikaya; 'Order adhering to the Dhamma') or Thammayut for short, whose strict monas-tic discipline mirrored that of an abbot of a Mon monastery near Bangkok which Vajirayan had visited in 1830 (Tiyavanich 1997, 6). In contrast to the monks of the other lineages or nikayas which I mentioned earlier, Thammayut monks are meant to focus on the study of Pali scripture and on becoming masters of the Vinaya instead of practising meditation or involving themselves in this-worldly activities, including menial works like cleaning their own living quarters, maintaining their temples, or washing their own robes (Tiyavanich 1997, ibid.)—tasks that monks of the other lineages, now lumped together as *Mahanikai* (Pali: Maha Nikaya, mean-ing 'Great Collection' or 'Great Order'), are used to carrying out without qualms. The rural Mahanikai monks I met, for example, did all these things and more, like growing their own vegetables, repairing their *kutis* (huts), repainting *naga* statues or temple buildings, or even constructing new buildings for the temple with the assistance of their lay followers. They reminded me that in the olden days, temple schools did not only teach how to read and write plus basic arithmetic, but also practical things like husbandry, carpentry, boat-building, and the like, depending on the region.

---

[4] On Mongkut's reforms, see, for example, Kirsch 1975.

Under Vajirayan's reign as King Mongkut, and accelerated by one of his sons Prince Wachirayan (Vajirananavarorasa) who later became the Supreme Patriarch, Thammayut expanded all over Thailand, thus also serving as a vehicle for the centralization of the Thai state: while in the times of the Ayutthayan kings who basically ruled as suzerains over a number of small kingdoms and principalities, a decentralized monkhood with its own regional traditions, languages, and practices was not a problem, this was no longer the case in a time of nation-building and centralization. As Tiyavanich (1997, 8) puts it, "[in] creating a modern Thai state the Bangkok authorities needed not only a common language but a common religion." To ensure at least a similar (albeit not exactly the same) practice adhered to by both the monks of the 'modern' Thammayut lineage and the 'old' Mahanikai collection of lineages, a centralized hierarchy enforcing a modicum of orthopraxy was required as well. The Sangha Act of 1902 saw to this by setting up an ecclesiastical-bureaucratic hierarchy under the control of a government-appointed Supreme Patriarch (*Somdet Phra Sangharat* or Sangharaja) presiding over the *Mahatherasamakhom* ('Council of Elders,' also known as 'Supreme Council'). Tiyavanich (1997, 8–9) further explains that "[formerly] autonomous Buddhist monks belonging to diverse lineages became part of the Siamese religious hierarchy with its standard texts and practices, whereas previously no single tradition had predominated. This modern ecclesiastical system brought the hitherto unorganized sangha into line with the civilian government hierarchy."[5]

With a formal hierarchical control established over the far-flung temples and monasteries, and with the traditional monarchy still intact, there obviously was no space similar to Sri Lanka or Burma, which was conducive to the emergence of political monks or activist monks. However, the rapid Westernization and modernization of Thailand brought with it not only the influx of large bodies of technical expertise, but also of Western political ideas, especially as regards parliamentary democracy. Political unrest

---

[5] There still are some variants which are not, or at least not entirely, under a centralized control, for example, the so-called *khruba* (lit. 'venerable teachers') in the shape of 'charismatic holy men' with huge numbers of followers in Thailand's north and northeast, following the tradition of Lanna Buddhism (see Cohen 2017). U Thuzana belongs to this tradition (see Buadaeng 2017). Furthermore, there is the *Santi Asoke* (lit. 'peaceful Ashoka'), established in 1975 (see Essen 2004), and also Wat Phra Dhammakaya and its controversial (and now fugitive) abbot Luang Por Dhammajayo (see Scott 2009).

among the elite eventually led to the 1932 Revolution and the overthrow
of the traditional absolute monarchy in favour of a parliamentarian one
with only residual powers left for the monarch. Despite persistent attempts
of the Sangha hierarchy to prevent this, the monkhood—and as in the
cases of Sri Lanka and Burma, especially the younger monks—did not
remain unaffected. Kenneth Landon vividly describes this development as
follows:

> The new political ideas penetrated into the temple grounds... Novices and
> young monks were sometimes requested not to leave the temple grounds
> during the period of revolutionary activity. The pull was too great, however.
> The roads of Bangkok were dotted with yellow robes during the exciting
> days. Some temples forbade discussion of political subjects. There were peo-
> ple who suggested that a democratic form of government was needed in the
> temples as well as elsewhere. To this some of the head priests agreed. Many
> more objected. (Kenneth Landon, as quoted in Suksamran 1982, 41)

Some democratic changes were finally introduced by the Sangha Act of
1941. It reduced the powers of the Supreme Patriarch and the Council of
Elders, and also brought the administrative structure of the Sangha in line
with the changes on the side of the secular government. For us, these are
not relevant.[6] What is relevant is that the only papered-over antagonism
between the more traditional Mahanikai monks and the modernist
Thammayut monks came to the fore again since the former, although
forming about 93 per cent of the monkhood, found themselves largely
frozen out from the levers of power within the Sangha hierarchy by the
minority of elitist and urbanite Thammayut monks. Another Sangha Act
was required to rectify these issues. The new act came in 1962 against the
backdrop of the Vietnam War and the threat of communism in Thailand
as well.[7] In order to combat this threat, Field Marshall Sarit Thanarat, the
leader of the military regime which had taken over in 1958 via a coup
d'état, drew on the two powerful symbols of Thai identity, the monarchy
and Buddhism. Regarding Buddhism and the Sangha, Sarit "considered
that if the Sangha was to be an effective tool for national achievement, it

[6] On these changes, see, for example Suksamran 1982, 42–44. The text of the act can be
found in Mahāmakuta Educational Council 1989, 19–33.
[7] The text of the Sangha Act of 1962 can be found in Mahāmakuta Educational Council
1989, 35–46.

must be strong, disciplined, and well organized" (Suksamran 1982, 46). Hence, the authority of the Supreme Patriarch and the Council of Elders was restored, while dissenting monks, in particular progressive monks deemed to be communist sympathizers, were removed from their positions and forced to disrobe.[8] After having thus brought the Sangha back under firm state control, the military regime then made good use of suitable monks as tools in nation-building and modernization programmes, especially in the more remote areas of the countryside.

The majority of the monks actually were not overly keen to participate in the government-supported shift towards this-worldly activities including nation-building efforts. Indeed, the drive for "this-worldly activities for monks was articulated more fervently by the laity than the monks themselves" (Seneviratne 1999, 14). It was, however, supported by a number of 'modernizing monks' who agreed with the government that such activities were unavoidable due to the challenges faced by Thailand in general, and its monarchy and religion in particular (Suksamran 1982, 53). After all, Thailand in the 1960s and 1970s still was in the early stages of development, and many rural areas were yet to benefit from any measures inaugurated in that regard. Hence, especially in the north-east (Isan) with its own tradition, culture, and language, dissident groups had emerged, "some with a tinge of Marxism," as Tanham (1974, 34) quips. The Communist Party of Thailand (CPT) adroitly exploited this situation, planning for an uprising, or 'People's War' in their parlance, from 1961 onwards. Under the impression of the worsening situation in Indochina, it made eminent sense both for the government and the Sangha to marshal the power and reputation of the monkhood to prevent a conflagration of the Indochina Wars to Thailand as well. Thus, when the military government launched several programmes geared towards nation-building and national development during the early 1960s, among them were the *Thammathūt* ('Dhammic Ambassador') and *Thammacārik* ('Wandering Dhamma') programmes[9] which attracted many of the activist (young) monks. The objectives of these projects were at least threefold: first, to improve the living conditions on the countryside; second, to revive or strengthen the population's belief in Buddhist morality and values; and,

---

[8] On the persecution of Phra Phimolatham (alternatively: Phimontham) as the most prominent victim, see, for example, Jackson 1989, 94–112; Ford 2017, 95–103.

[9] On these programmes, see, for example, Suksamran 1979, 187–204.

third, to use this revived Buddhist morality as a formidable bulwark against the spread of communism (Keyes 1999, 6).

Although these programmes certainly had at least some impact, they proved to be too little, too late: on 7 August 1965, the long-planned communist uprising broke out. Tanham cautions that "[not] all the violence was communist, to be sure; it included banditry and cattle rustling and non-communist dissidence," to then add "but we have it on communist word as well as from observers in the field that communist violence in the Northeast did increase markedly in late 1965" (Tanham 1974, 42). The communist uprising quickly spread all over the country. It took the Royal Thai Army, supported by the Royal Thai Police and a number of volunteer forces, until 1973 to suppress the uprising in a mix of a 'soft' approach that included rural development programmes as well as psychological operations (Psyops), and a 'hard' approach based on military operations—the latter predominant during the brutal final phase in 1972 to 1973. In the febrile atmosphere during this insurgency, communists and suspected communist sympathizers alike were regularly 'othered' as enemies of the state and treated as such. This 'othering' was also extended to those intellectuals and students in Bangkok who had turned against the military regime (since 9 December 1963 under Field Marshal Thanom Kittikachorn) and its systematic abuse of power. Although not only intellectuals and students but rather the bulk of the Thai society as such turned against the regime, it was mainly the demonstrations of students of Bangkok's Thammasat University from early 1973 onwards that gradually brought the regime to its knees. When on 6 October 1973, several student activists and some teachers were arrested by the police for distributing leaflets demanding a new constitution, the situation quickly escalated, and the regime saw itself faced by mass demonstrations of up to 500,000 people. On 14 October 1973, a clash between demonstrators and police and army units resulted in the death of more than 70 people—an incident that, as Keyes (1999, 7) says, "was greatly shocking to the majority of Thai including the king." The following day, the regime collapsed, and Thanom, together with his Deputy Prime Minister Field Marshal Praphas Charusatien, went into exile. A democratic interlude began that lasted about three years until October 1976.

For us, these developments are of importance because they resulted in the emergence of a flurry of ultra-nationalist, extreme right-wing movements that, against the backdrop of the war in Indochina and, in 1975, the defeat of the Western-aligned non-communist states of South Vietnam,

Laos, and Cambodia by the communists, saw it as their duty to protect Thailand from a similar fate. Probably the best-known of these movements are the *Luksua Chaoban* (Village Scouts), organized in small cells, mainly active in the countryside and tasked with 'ferreting out' suspected communist supporters (Wyatt 2003, 291) and the *Krathing Daeng* (Red Gaurs), a paramilitary organization centred on Bangkok and mainly consisting of vocational students, school dropouts, and unemployed young men on the one hand, and veterans from the Indochina wars on the other (Suksamran 1982, 79). This paramilitary organization did not emerge spontaneously but was set up after the October 1973 uprising by the Royal Thai Army's Internal Security Operations Command (ISOC) as an early counter-weight against the student movement, and subsequently equipped with small arms and grenades. The most important organization in our context, however, is *Nawaphon* or 'New Force Movement' (alternatively: 'Ninth Force,' 'Nine New Forces')—a movement set up in 1974 by Wattana Keowimol, former head of the Thai Students Association in the United States (Leifer 1995, 170). Like the Village Scouts and the Red Gaur, it also enjoyed covert support from ISOC. Its membership of low-level government officials and public officers was "based mainly on networks of personal connections in the bureaucracy" (Wyatt 2003, 291). Since Nawaphon aimed at achieving national security "by virtuously following the Buddhist Middle Way to political, economic and social prosperity" (Suksamran 1982, 80), it also attracted a fair number of monks.[10] Why these monks joined is easy to explain: the events in Cambodia after the victory of the Red Khmer, characterized by Ian Harris as the 'unravelling of the Buddhist state' and the 'destruction of institutional Buddhism' in the country (Harris 2013, 12, 118), convinced them that communism, especially the brutal Red Khmer version of it, did indeed pose a mortal danger to Buddhism in general, and the monkhood in particular. Furthermore, the forced abdication of Laotian King Sisavang Vatthana on 2 December 1975[11] and the subsequent abolition of the Laotian monarchy (Kershaw 2001, 83–88) also convinced them that the Thai monarchy would suffer a

---

[10] According to Suksamran 1982, 81 (fn. 68), Kittiwuttho claimed that "over ten thousand monks joined the movement."

[11] Sisavang Vatthana's year of death is disputed: depending on the source, he was either executed in 1977, or died of malaria in 1978, or in March 1980, or as late as 1984 in 'Camp Number One,' a detention centre in Sam Neua. See, for example, Kershaw 2001, 86.

similar fate after a communist coup in Thailand. Thus, it was imperative to crush similar movements in Thailand before they became too strong.

The Nawaphon monks' open participation in pro-regime and anti-student demonstrations during 1975 and 1976, in particular the very public participation of Phra Kittiwutthō (Kittiwuthō Bhikkhu, born 1936), put the Supreme Patriarch (Sangharāt) and the Supreme Council in a quandary. In November 1974, the Supreme Council had explicitly ruled that for monks, it was forbidden to participate in political rallies, be it actively or passively, or to recommend specific parties to their followers. This decision was taken on the grounds that "monks must be impartial and demonstrate to every pious Buddhist without discrimination their loving-kindness and compassion" (Suksamran 1982, 102). The Council order further explained that in "a political election, for example, there is a winner and a loser... Taking sides in any political election would only be harmful to the prestige of monks. People would no longer respect them" (ibid.). Although the decision was aimed mainly at progressive monks leaning towards the political left, they were now forced to take an equally public stand regarding the participation of Phra Kittiwutthō and fellow Nawaphon monks in pro-government demonstrations of the political right. The Supreme Patriarch, pressed by liberal newspapers, however, only went as far as clarifying that Kittiwutthō's activities probably constituted only minor infractions of the monastic code that could be dealt with by a simple reproach (*tamni*), but added that "[if] the facts be that Kittiwutthō acted to protect the country, that is a good purpose; but I do not see that what he did was of any utility and also as monks it is not necessary to act like this" (as quoted in Keyes 1999, 11–12). Apart from this mild reproach, no further action was taken until mid-June 1976, and Kittiwutthō's notorious interview on the killing of communists.

## MARA: PHRA KITTIWUTTHŌ'S 'HOLY WAR' AGAINST COMMUNISM

I already pointed out how difficult it can be for Buddhist monks not only to condone violence, but to openly instigate their followers to carry out such acts without falling foul of committing a disrobing offence. In this context, the use of denigrating terms such as 'dogs' for the Rohingya Muslims in Burma can be seen as an attempt to dehumanize them because violence meted out against non-humans is considered a lesser sin in

Buddhism, as discussed. Dehumanizing the 'other' hence is the second strand of the justification of violence within Theravāda Buddhism ever since the beginning of the second moment of Buddhist history. In a Sinhalese context, the advice to King Dutugāmunu in the Mahāvamsa did exactly that. Although the Mahāvamsa as a specifically Sinhalese chronicle does not play a role regarding the justifications of violence in Thailand, a very similar approach was chosen by Phra Kittiwutthō to justify and legitimize violence against Thai communists, real or perceived.

Little is known about Phra Kittiwutthō's early life, and what has been reported can probably be dismissed as a post hoc "hagiographic treatment" that omitted relevant but awkward details rather than a fact-based biography (Keyes 1999, 4; Ford 2017, 266). What is clear is that from early on in his ecclesiastical career, he was an activist monk with substantial oratory skills and charisma, espousing the opinion that "members of the sangha should not remain in their temples waiting for the laity to seek them out for purposes of merit making"—rather, he suggested that monks "should go out to propagate the dhamma, the way of the Buddha, to guide those who are Buddhists in finding moral bases for their actions and to convert those who are not Buddhists" (Keyes 1999, 5; Suksamran 1982, 94). With this activist interpretation of the role of a modern monk, he fitted in rather well with the *Thammathūt* and *Thammacārik* programmes, inaugurated by the Thai government during the 1960s, and also with the Asia Foundation's *Thammaphatthanā* ('Dhammic Development') project. Initially, and unlike fellow monks participating in these programmes, he seemed not to have harboured any overtly anti-communist convictions. This changed, however, in the aftermath of the 'October 1973 Revolution,' that is, the collapse of the military government of Field Marshal and Prime Minister Thanom Kittikachorn, and the start of the democratic interlude that for Kittiwutthō must have looked like a prelude to a communist takeover.

Of particular interest here is Kittiwutthō's construction of communists not only as political opponents who could be defeated via a political discourse but as the implacable embodiments of *Mara* ('the Evil One') who had to be physically removed from the body politic since they adhered to an ideology "that negated virtue (kwamdi) and aimed at the destruction of society, the happiness of mankind, and religion [and] was thus the most dangerous and direct enemy of Buddhism" (Suksamran 1982, 139). For Kittiwutthō, there was not the slightest doubt that these ruthless Thai communists would try to break the bond between the people and the monks by discrediting the latter, by distorting the teachings of the Buddha, and even by using 'disguised monks,' that is, communist infiltrators who ordained as monks to work as the 'enemy from within' in order to sow discord within the Sangha itself, aside from indoctrinating unsuspecting lay followers with communist propaganda in their sermons. Obviously, with the inclusion of 'disguised monks' under the label of communism, Kittiwutthō also used the communist danger to take aim at all those 'progressive monks' who dared to criticize the government and, thus, the established order.

Since communism posed such a mortal danger to Thai nation, religion, and monarchy, compromising was not an option—communism could only be stopped by taking decisive action against the ideology as well as those subscribing to it. In his speeches, Kittiwutthō made clear that this was "the responsibility of every Thai, whether he be monk or layman, rich or poor" (Suksamran 1982, 142). For his fellow monks, he had a special message:

> We must decide now what we shall do in the face of communist danger ... our nation, religion and monarchy are in danger of being destroyed ... One thing is definite – the monks must not sit in the monastery seeking personal salvation and waiting for the laity to seek them out ... How can one seek after *Nibbana* when a gun is pointed at one's throat? ... Can we sit and do nothing while the country is being destroyed and while the communists are constantly attacking Buddhism? Are we going to let our country to be ruled by the communists by not helping? Are we going to let our people be enslaved as in Laos and Cambodia? (as quoted in Suksamran 1982, 147)

His recommendation was that just like the communists, the monks should reach out to the villagers as well, "but use the Dhamma as a guide" and "the people's respect for and confidence in the monkhood to persuade them to their views" (Suksamran 1982, 147–148). The theme of fighting against Mara aside, his suggestions are reminiscent of those developed by Anagārika Dharmapāla in Ceylon/Sri Lanka, and by various Burmese monks such as U Kumara, U Teza, and U Sandawuntha in 1938 prior to independence, or Ashin Wirathu today. From a comparative perspective, these calls to action in Sri Lanka and Burma offer an interesting benchmark: as we have seen, in both cases, Muslims were very effectively 'othered' by describing them as implacable enemies of Buddhism, hell-bent in wiping it out in Sri Lanka and Burma as they had done in Pakistan and India before. However, Dharmapāla and his Burmese counterparts usually left it there, shying away from directly justifying the recourse to physical violence. Even firebrand monk Ashin Wirathu astutely refrains from openly committing such a blatant *pārājika* offence, and only recommends 'firm action' against Muslims, also occasionally describing them as 'dogs' and, thus, as non-human beings. It is then left to the lay followers to connect the dots. This is where Kittiwutthō stands out: as Suksamran sees, it, he went on to declare a 'holy war' on communists. How far Kittiwutthō was prepared to go became clear in the now notorious interview in June 1976, published by the magazines *Prachachart* and *Chaturat*:

> I think we must do this [i.e., killing], even though we are Buddhists. But such killing is not the killing of persons (*khon*). Because whoever destroys the nation, religion and the monarchy is not a complete person, but mara (evil). Our intention must not be to kill people but to kill the Devil. It is the duty of all Thai. (as quoted in Suksamran 1982, 150)

Since for Phra Kittiwuthō, these communists as the personified evil were "not complete persons," killing them was only a comparatively small sin:

> It is like [...] when a fish is killed to make a stew to place in the alms bowl for a monk. There is certainly demerit in killing the fish, but we gain much greater merit from placing [the stew] in the alms bowl of the monk. (Keyes 1999, 14)

It speaks for the resilience of Thai Buddhism that despite the fear of an imminent communist revolution in Thailand, Kittiwutthō's callousness reminiscent of the argumentation used in the Mahāvamsa drew the ire of the vast majority of the Thai public. Typical for the outrage he had sparked was the liberal magazine *Prachachart's* accusation that he had obviously founded a new religion—"one predicated on killing" (Suksamran 1982, 150). Furthermore, "[many] cartoonists illustrated Kitthiwuttho wearing a grenade rosary in place of the customary Buddhist beads and preaching how to kill communists" (ibid.). His call to violence was also condemned by many of his contemporary monks, in particular, by the progressive ones who called him "a villain in a yellow robe" (Suksamran 1982, 151) and even equated him with Dewathat (Devadatta), a cousin of the Buddha who created a (temporary) schism while the Buddha was still alive and was thus sent straight to hell. The outrage even culminated in calls that he should be forcefully disrobed since he had openly committed a serious *pārājika* offence. Kittiwutthō avoided an expulsion from the Sangha by qualifying his statements in another major sermon held on 2 July 1976, which also found nationwide coverage. In this sermon, he claimed that he was speaking metaphorically (Ford 2017, 267) and that it was not the (literal) death of individual communists that he had preached, but the (virtual) death of communism as an ideology:

> [It] is true that I said killing communists is not demeritorious, and I stick to it [...] What I meant by 'communist' is an ideology. It is the ideology which uses killing as a means to attain governmental power, as Mao-Tze Tung said 'power must be attained through the barrel of a gun'. Wherever this ideology pervades, there is massive killing. [...] ... Communism is a complex compound of false consciousness, delusion, greed, jealousy, malevolence and anger. It is not a person or a living animal. Thus killing communism is killing ideology (*latthi*), hence it is not demeritorious. (as quoted in Suksamran 1982, 153)

Kittiwutthō reminded his audience of the *Kesi Sutta*. In this sutta, Kesi the horse-trainer admits that it is his practice to kill an untameable horse to avoid a disgrace to the lineage of his teachers. He then asks the Buddha as "the unexcelled trainer of tameable people" how he would deal with those untameable ones who would not submit to the Buddha's teaching. The Buddha responds that he would kill such a person. When the astonished Kesi blurts out that this surely would not be the proper conduct for the Buddha, the Buddha elaborates as follows:

> It is true, Kesi, that it's not proper for a Tathagata to take life. But if a tameable person doesn't submit either to a mild training or to a harsh training or to a mild & harsh training, then the Tathagata doesn't regard him as being worth speaking to or admonishing. His knowledgeable fellows in the holy life don't regard him as being worth speaking to or admonishing. This is what it means to be totally destroyed in the Doctrine & Discipline, when the Tathagata doesn't regard one as being worth speaking to or admonishing, and one's knowledgeable fellows in the holy life don't regard one as being worth speaking to or admonishing. (Kesi Sutta, as translated by Thanissaro Bhikkhu 1997)

Kittiwutthō then went on to interpret the exchange between Kesi and the Buddha as follows:

The Buddha kills and discards, but the word 'kill' according to the principle of the Buddha is killing according to the Dhamma and Vinaya of Buddhism. To kill and discard by not teaching is the method of killing. It does not mean that the Buddha ordered the killing of persons. But he ordered the killing of the impurities (*kilesa*) of people. (as quoted in Suksamran 1982, 153)

In the light of the statements he made in the interview, in particular the parts where he declared that communists as individuals would be the embodiments of evil, and his likening them to fish killed for making curry, Kittiwuttho's reinterpretation is not convincing. The very title of his sermon, *Ka Kommunit Mai Bap*, that is 'killing communists is not reprehensible,' told a different story in any case—well understood by his followers, who probably mostly remembered the title of the sermon and not the contents of it. Hence, Satha-Anand (2014, 184) regards Kittiwuttho's use of the sutta as a "dangerous game of meaning manipulation." Nevertheless, this qualification of his original argumentation, and the fact that may senior members of the Sangha hierarchy as well as the political elite shared his views, proved to be sufficient to stop an investigation against him by the Sangha dead in its tracks. Of interest for us is that his reinterpretation of his original message puts him in line with those militant monks in Sri Lanka and Burma who, while shying away to exhort their followers to kill, nevertheless legitimized the recourse to violence, including lethal violence, in order to protect the Buddhist state and Buddhism as such. Kittiwuttho's further clarification in early July 1976 made this even clearer: here, he stated that while monks 'kill' communists by refusing to teach them, soldiers would do so by using arms—and they would be morally right to do so, since "to kill some 5,000 people to secure and ensure the happiness of 42 million Thais" would be "an act of sacrificing the lesser good for the common good" as compromising with communists would be impossible:

If we want to preserve our nation, religion, and monarchy, we sometimes have to sacrifice certain *sila* (rules of morality) for the survival of these institutions. If we are cautious in keeping to the rules of morality, then these three institutions will not survive. I ask you to ponder this; how would you choose between the violation of the prohibition of killing and the survival of the nation, religion, and the monarchy. (as quoted in Suksamran 1982, 155)

In this 'lesser good versus greater good' argumentation that sounds very utilitarian and realpolitikal (to use the Western political terms), we find one of the two central themes that we have already found when examining the legitimization strategies of militant monks in Sri Lanka and Burma as well as various monks in history: since the Buddhist nation, and Buddhism as such, is in grave danger, the recourse to violence is justified, nay, even the moral duty since it is for the common good, and the preservation of the teachings of the Buddha. As Satha-Anand (2014, 183) sees it, "[once] nationalism is put at the highest point on a scale of values, the violation of the first Buddhist precept is re-defined as an act of 'sacrifice.'" The Burmese Buddhist lay follower who told me that Buddhism is not a suicidal utopianism would certainly agree with Kittiwuttho's reasoning— and so would probably all those contemporary militant monks in Burma and Sri Lanka, just that the current enemies are not the communists but the Muslims. But still, of all the leading militant monks we have encountered thus far, Kittiwuttho is the only one who very openly offered a general justification and legitimization of violence in a carte blanche way against a specific set of 'others' as the targets of such violence. He even went as far as turning the Buddhist version of 'thou shalt not kill' on its head, transforming it into a 'thou shalt kill' command:

> The Thai must kill communists. Anyone who wants to gain merit must kill communists. The one who kills them will acquire great merit, and the merit acquired from such killing will help preserve the religion for as long as 5,000 or even 10,000 years... If the Thai do not kill them, the communists will kill us. (as quoted in Suksamran 1982, 155)

Suksamran (1982, 156–157) is certainly not wrong to argue that Kittiwuttho's message found a ready audience in the febrile atmosphere of these years, culminating in the aforementioned crackdown of 6 October 1976. This notwithstanding, his sermons did not culminate in a school of thought inspired by him like the Sinhalese *Jathika Chintanaya* or 'National Thought' inspired by Dharmapāla and Rahula. Rather, Kittiwuttho was gradually sidelined, with the commonly shared understanding that as a monk, he had gone too far. Some scandals revolving around allegations of 'sexual misconduct' and connections to the Thai underworld further undermined his credibility (Ford 2017, 284). Hence, when the communist peril was over, Kittiwuttho disappeared from the headlines for good, and his message of hate and violence disappeared with him as well.

Open and very visible participation of monks in political demonstrations again resurfaced more than four decades later during the clashes between loosely organized factions colloquially known as Yellow Shirts and Red Shirts starting in 2005. The most prominent example for such activist monks is ultra-royalist 'yellow monk' Phra Buddha Issara, one of the leaders of the anti-Yingluck Shinawatra (at that time Thai prime minister) demonstrations organized by the People's Democratic Reform Committee (PDRC) as part of the Bangkok Shutdown Movement of 2013/2014. He became notorious partly because of the activities of his own private 'body guards' who in February 2014 even had the temerity to briefly detain two undercover police officers they had spotted in the crowd of spectators, and 'divested' them of their pistols—an offence that in May 2018 finally led to the monk's arrest under the charge of running an illegal organization (The Nation 2018). More typical in my opinion, however, were the numerous less prominent monks who reluctantly felt compelled to take a side to declare themselves either 'red monks' or 'yellow monks,' often egged on by their own followers and probably against their better judgement. Hence, it is not very surprising that the bulk of the monks who chose a side opted for the red side: firstly, the majority of Thai monks come from the northern and north-eastern parts of Thailand where the Red Shirts find the bulk of their political support; secondly, the values of their respective 'flocks' quite often also has an impact on the values of the monks in question. Yet, the anecdotal evidence I garnered in Bangkok in late April/early May 2010 during the Red Shirt anti-government protests in Lumphini Park and then again during the Yellow Shirt Shutdown Bangkok Restart Thailand Movement of 2013 and 2014 indicates that many of these monks were mainly driven by motivations best described as 'pastoral care' for their 'flocks,' not necessarily by a firm political conviction of the monks themselves (see also Dubus 2017, 36–39). Sometimes however, the reasons offered seemed to be a bit contradictory, and at least some vague political convictions, or sympathy for the demands of their lay followers, shone through.

Symptomatic for this is one 'red monk' interviewed by the *Star Online* during the height of the bitter political struggle. He argued that he only took part in rallies of the Red Shirts as an observer: "I have learnt to stay above it. I know it. I see it. I understand it but I won't be it" (Habib et al. 2010). Then, however, he conceded that "[you] can't change society outside only but change them also from the inside" (ibid.)—a slightly convoluted statement that indicates, at least in my opinion, that this monk was not as neutral an observer as he thought he would be. Nevertheless, the few 'red' and even fewer 'yellow monks' I had the opportunity to chat with would probably have agreed with Phra Suwichano, at that time chief of training at the Maha Chulalongkorn Buddhist University, who pointed out that monks in Thailand should stay out of politics (Habib et al. 2010), or with the highly regarded intellectual monk Phra Paisal who bluntly argued that in his opinion, "many monks nowadays do not follow the right principles. They base their judgements more on their personal feelings rather than dharma. This is not dharmocracy, but rather egocracy" (McCargo 2012b, 633). But since this leads too far from my own research interest, I will leave this 'red versus yellow' issue open—of importance for us is the fact that even though a number of rather outspoken, activist monks took part on either side of the bitter political divide, none of them even remotely went as far as constructing the 'other' side as embodiments of Mara who had to be physically removed from the Thai body politic. Such a blatant 'othering,' however, is visible in Thailand's Deep South as the home of a slow-moving Muslim insurgency—at least to a certain extent.

## GUNS: MILITANT BUDDHISM IN THE DEEP SOUTH

As we have seen in the case studies on Sri Lanka and Burma, the 'othering' of Muslims is one of the current core themes of militant Buddhism: Muslims are constructed as the implacable enemies of Buddhism, keen to destroy Buddhist nations and to turn them into yet another part of the Darul Islam—a narrative more often than not based on and 'proven' by a rather selective reading of history. Such a narrative also exists in Thailand, and it actually precedes the current wave of Malay-Muslim separatism in Thailand's Deep South that started in January 2004, albeit not the origins of this conflict that can be traced back to the rebellions of 1903 and 1922 in response to heavy-handed Thai nation-building efforts (Pitsuwan 1985, 29, 51–61). The anti-Muslim narrative in question featured prominently in a book published in 2002 by an ultra-conservative monk, Phra Dhammapitaka, who attacked Islam as well as Christianity, contrasting their monotheistic lack of tolerance, their propensity for religious violence and religious persecution, and their coerced conversions with the superior (in his view) Buddhist values, especially the absence of any attempt "to transform the different others into one's image" (Satha-Anand 2014, 188). Regarding the Muslims, Phra Dhammapitaka had the following to say:

Around AD 1200 the Muslim Turkish army invaded the areas of Northeast Asia which was the centre of Buddhism at that time. After taking control over the cities, Islam was propagated. The Muslim Turkish army had burned down Buddhist monasteries and Buddhist universities, killing monks and laypeople, forcing them to convert to Islam. (as quoted in Satha-Anand 2014, 187)

It should be noted that Dhammapitaka's intention was not to instigate violence against Muslims or Christians (who he criticized for the crusades), but to celebrate Buddhist tolerance. Nevertheless, it is rather telling that his attacks against the Muslims followed an argumentative pattern which is already familiar to us from the other two case studies: obviously, this particular selective reading of history also belongs to the repertoire of Thai Buddhists, ready to be used whenever there is a need for it. This was the case after the Malay-Muslim separatism in the Deep South flared up again in January 2004. Until today, the number of victims has surpassed the mark of 8000—about double as much as the death toll of the Irish Republican Army (IRA) during the (in-) famous *Troubles*. As regards monks and novices as victims, the first one was an elderly monk who was killed on 22 January 2004 in Narathiwat, followed two days later by two monks and a novice in Yala (McCargo 2009, 14). Much more than the killing of civilians, these attacks against monks and novices seriously aggravated the conflict. After all, monks and novices (and also nuns) have a special significance within the Thai society, as explained, which means attacking them is attacking one of the pillars of the Thai state, and thus seen as an extraordinary provocation.

To a certain extent, the measures taken against this new—or rather, renewed—threat posed by a Muslim separatist insurgency echoed those employed against the communist threat of the 1970s. Paramilitary units were deployed in the Deep South, Buddhist militias similar to the Red Gaurs of old were formed in the shape of the Volunteer Defence Force (*Kong Asa Raksa Dindaen* or *Or Sor* according to the Thai acronym), and suitable weapons (such as assault rifles) were handed out to interested members of the Buddhist public living in the most exposed parts of the three affected provinces Pattani, Yala, and Narathiwat who were willing to join the Village Development and Self-Defence (*Chor Ror Bor*) programme (ICG 2007, 13–14). And, just like in the 1970s, there was the fear of being overwhelmed by an implacable enemy—a fear very similar to Phra Kittiwutthō's provocative question in the 1970s quoted by Suksamran

(1982, 147) "how can one seek after *Nibbana* when a gun is pointed at one's throat?"

This fear initially only affected Buddhist-Muslim relations in the Deep South, but then gradually spread to other parts of Thailand as well, for example, the north-east and, as some scholars claim, even in Bangkok. In the case of the north-east, the "shrinking space for tolerance in Thai Buddhism" (Satha-Anand 2003) manifested itself, for example, in unexpected public protests in Chiang Mai against plans to build a *halal* industrial estate, even though Muslim *halal* businesses are not exactly new in this city where Muslims have been part of the community for hundreds of years. Nevertheless, local Buddhists saw these plans as a direct attack against their Buddhist culture. The *Bangkok Post*, for example, quotes a senior monk from a local temple as saying that "[we] have been living together peacefully for more than 720 years under the rich and strong Lanna heritage. [...] The establishment of the halal industrial estate will have a negative effect on the traditional lifestyle, customs and local environment. It's a big loss for the spiritual and cultural identity of Lanna" (Yongcharoenchai 2016). But, as the *Bangkok Post* found out, this blatant case of bigotry only seemed to be the tip of an iceberg of rumours that, amongst others, claimed that "the halal project had a hidden agenda to move more than 5,000 Muslim families from Pattani to Chiang Mai" (ibid.). Unsurprisingly, some nervous villagers feared that the conflict in the Deep South would also travel with those families to Chiang Mai: "'I don't want our peaceful Buddhist town turned into a violent war zone like the deep South,' said one villager, Yai. 'I have nothing against Muslims, but none of us want any outsiders to come in and change our way of life'" (as quoted in ibid.).

The same 'I have nothing against Muslims but...' reasoning also seems to have affected cosmopolitan Bangkok, as Satha-Anand claims, for example, as regards the objection of what he calls 'ultra-rightist Buddhist groups' to the provision of Muslim prayer rooms at the Hua Lamphong main railway station (Satha-Anand 2003). Personally, I cannot confirm Satha-Anand's observations: those Muslims I met over the years in the vicinity of the Masjid Mirsasuddeen in Silom Soi 20, Bang Rak, did not feel targeted directly or indirectly, although these are anecdotal impressions only and not representative. Furthermore, in a conversation with me on 18 August 2013, Surin Pitsuwan, former Minister of Foreign Affairs, later ASEAN Secretary General, and himself a Muslim, also expressed some doubts in that regard. Again, however, this is an anecdotal evidence only that does not necessarily contradict Satha-Anand's findings.

Be that as it may, even in the conflict zone itself, that is the three provinces Pattani, Yala, and Narathiwat, and unlike in the case of Kittiwutthō, the fear of Muslims is mainly expressed by way of low-level grumbling within parts of the Buddhist population or by monks in temples in Muslim-majority or remote areas, but not via public sermons by firebrand monks that exaggerate the threat posed by the Muslim insurgents, nor even went as far as dehumanizing them as Kittiwutthō did with the communists. One of the few examples to the contrary would be Phra Apichart Punnajanto, then head of monk preachers at Wat Benchamabopit (also known as the "Marble Temple'). This monk called upon his followers on various social media outlets to burn down a mosque for each monk killed by Muslim-Malay separatists in Thailand's restive Deep South:

> It is time to arm Thai Buddhists. [...] Time for compassion has run out. If a monk is killed in the deep South, a mosque must be burned down in exchange. Starting from the North, we must chase away this cult from every area until there is no one in that cult left. We will oppose its attempt to enter our area through all means. (Ekachai 2015)

Somewhat below the threshold of inciting hate, there were many more sermons that simply painted a rather gloomy picture of the Deep South as a future Muslim province if the Thai state and the Thai Buddhists would not take swift and firm action to defeat the insurgency, which at least one monk whose sermon was recorded on a DVD denounced as a "hellish doctrine" (McCargo 2009, 16; also see McCargo 2012a, 22–26). And sure enough, as McCargo (2009, 18–21, 2012a, 26–30) also reports, there also were a number of anonymous leaflets purportedly distributed by both sides, but probably penned by military intelligence officers "aimed to strengthen the determination of local Buddhists to resist violence caused by Muslims" (McCargo 2009, 21). But still, charismatic extremist monks on par with cold-war monk Phra Kittiwutthō, or with Galagoda Aththe Gnanasara Thero in Sri Lanka and Ashin Wirathu in Burma, did not emerge.

The main reason for this general absence of public incendiary sermons that condemn Muslims as it is habitually done by Sinhalese or Burmese extremist monks probably is that unlike in the cases of the Sinhalese and Burmese Sanghas, the better organized and far more hierarchical Thai

Sangha usually reacts swiftly to suppress any activities of a blatantly political nature—especially if said monks enjoy a huge followership on social media. Ultra-nationalist monk Phra Apichart Punnajanto found out in September 2017 how swiftly the Sangha could (finally) move after he called upon his followers on various social media outlets to burn down a mosque for each monk killed by Malay-Muslim separatists in Thailand's restive Deep South one time too often. Two years before, in 2015, he narrowly escaped punishment by temporarily closing down his Facebook page that contained the offending messages. In 2017, the emergence of video clips and DVDs that were widely disseminated, however, meant that now there was enough proof against him to speedily disrobe him for a very public and blatant pārājika offence and to expel him from the Thai Sangha for good (The Nation 2017). Phra Apichart's brazen call for a tit-for-tat response to acts of anti-Buddhist violence committed by members of an amorphous Muslim insurgency in the Deep South is, after all, not in the interest of the Thai government which attempts, at least on an 'on again, off again' basis, to peacefully solve or defuse the conflict. Ratcheting up the violence via fiery sermons is thus seen as counter-productive. Other and more subtle means were, and still are, preferred when it comes to the task of protecting the lives of monks and novices, especially those living in remote temples in the three most affected provinces: Yala, Narathiwat, and Pattani.

Such crackdowns do not only affect monks preaching hatred against Muslims, by the way, but basically all monks who dare to publicly meddle in politics. Former PDRC-supporting monk Phra Buddha Issara would be one of the most prominent recent cases in that regard, as already mentioned, and so would be Luang Por Nen Kham Chattiko—a jet-setting monk who owned a private jet, several luxury cars, and other items not normally associated with monks, before he was forced to disrobe and sentenced to 114 years jail (reduced to 20 years as per Thai law) on 9 August 2018 (*Thai PBS* 2018). Another and even more spectacular case would be the forced disrobing and arrest of Phra Prom Dilok (abbot of Wat Sam Phraya) and his secretary, and of Phra Phrom Sitthi (abbot of Wat Sa Ket) and his three assistant abbots. Another prominent monk who would have suffered the same fate, Phra Phrom Metee, assistant abbot of Wat Samphanthawong, managed to escape to Germany where he applied for political asylum. Phra Phrom Dilok and Phra Phrom Metee had been members of the Sangha's Supreme Council before their fall from grace, and thus belonged to the most influential clerics of the Thai Sangha. All of them (apart from fugitive Phra Phrom Metee) also were first summarily disrobed, and then arrested and charged with embezzlement of temple funds to the tune of 130 million baht (Ngamkhan 2018). Needless to say, their royally bestowed monastic ranks were revoked as well.

The latest amendment of the Sangha Act of 1962, passed in July 2018, now allows the summary dismissal of the 20 members of the Sangha Council as the highest governing body under the order of the king. On the one hand, this amendment can be seen as a further centralization of the current military government's power, but on the other, it also reveals a certain scepticism whether the Sangha hierarchy as it stands is able to purge errant monks on its own, especially errant high-ranking monks accused of corruption and/or meddling in political affairs (Tonsakulrungruang 2018). Even one rather senior and famous monk, Phra Paisal Visalo, abbot of the Sukato Forest Monastery, opined quite candidly that "[in] the Thai monastic tradition, there is no space for self-reform. Be it in Sri Lanka, in Burma or in Thailand, *sangha* reform has always come from the king" (as quoted in Dubus 2017, 26). The abbot also acknowledges that the "*sangha* has become too close to the state, the central power" (as quoted in Dubus 2017, 27)—an argument that I have made several times by now. But since following this treat would lead us too far off the topic, I will leave it there without further comment.

As I already mentioned, certain 'other means' are applied by the Thai state to protect temples and monks in the Deep South. The most obvious choice is to deploy police forces or army units to guard the temples, and to escort the monks on their alms rounds early in the morning. Although the open presence of police and army units on temple grounds severely diminishes the temple's sacred character, most abbots and senior monks of those temples that are most exposed to attacks from Muslim insurgents grudgingly accept the necessity of such measures, which, depending on the severity of the threat, could also include the ban of morning alms rounds if they are perceived to be too risky, or even in the 'hardening' of temple buildings via sand bags and access controls (see, for example, Jerryson 2011, 127–139). Security measures however do not seem to stop there; rather, persistent rumours have it that there also are active soldiers ordained as monks and deployed to certain temples, bringing their arms with them: usually, one pistol in the typical satchel monks wear when leaving the temple grounds, and one assault rifle in the particular monk's kuti (hut). In Thai, the term for these soldier monks is *thahān phra*.

Officially, these monks do not exist. The Thai National Office for Buddhism, for example, dismisses their existence out of hand. But rumours persist, and while McCargo (2009, 24) mentions no less than 75 soldier monks who "were ordained at one Pattani temple in 2005, then assigned to various temples around the province", Jerryson (2011, 116–123) even was lucky enough to encounter and to interview such a 'soldier monk,' who he gave the pseudonym 'Phra Eks.' Unfortunately, I was not so successful myself, but some of 'my' monks, especially those rural monks also living in the South of Thailand, readily acknowledged the existence of soldier monks when I mentioned them during our conversations. The pattern usually was the following:

Q:   'Have you heard of 'soldier monks'?
A:   *Knowing nod* 'Those in the (Deep) South?'

The urban monks living in Bangkok whom I met over the last couple of years, however, seemed to be genuinely unaware of the existence of such soldier monks and had not even come across any rumours about them. They also seemed to be genuinely shocked about the sheer allegation that such monks could exist—after all, and as already discussed in the third chapter, the Buddha himself explicitly ruled out the ordination of soldiers. Whenever the existence of soldier monks was acknowledged (the further south I went, the more likely this was), I usually asked some follow-on questions regarding what 'my' monks thought about them. At times, all I got was an extended and decidedly awkward silence followed by a swift change of topic, for example, on how I was getting on with my meditation practice. Those who did answer my questions all expressed a deep disquiet regarding such activities, and a firm belief that these soldier monks were no 'real' monks. Again, one reason offered was that the ordination of soldiers was forbidden by the Buddha. Another one was that these 'soldier monks' explicitly lied to their preceptor—that is, the senior monk who ordained them—and to the monks present at the ordination ceremony: if they would have admitted that they were active soldiers, then their ordination would certainly have been refused, in their opinion. After all, two of the 13 questions during the ordination procedure are 'are you a free man' and 'are you free from government service?' (Buddhanet 2008), which means active soldiers actually have to lie twice, which in the firm opinion of the thudong monks rendered the whole ordination invalid from the very beginning. One of the thudong monks, at that time the head monk of a small temple where they temporarily stayed during Buddhist Lent (*pansa*), pensively added:

If the people can no longer belief the monk, then they will not come to the temple anymore. Because they tell the monks everything: all their problems, all the bad things they have done. Sometimes they talk about fighting. Sometimes they talk about stealing things. Sometimes they talk about taking drugs. But if a soldier can be monk, then why can't a police officer be monk too? Nobody will trust the monks anymore.[12]

Coincidentally, the thudong monk's fears as regards police officers in saffron robes proved to be eerily predictive. Soon after my return to Bangkok on 2 August, a new story made its rounds about a recent police sting operation: in order to bust a drug-dealing monk in a temple somewhere in Lopburi, a police officer disguised himself as a monk. The drug-dealing monk was duly arrested as soon as he handed over the drugs to his 'fellow' monk. Although in that case, the police officer only disguised as a monk and did not even temporarily ordain as such, I found the story quite remarkable in the context of the thudong monk's comments.

To return to the topic of soldier monks, Jerryson (2011, 122) asks soldier monk Phra Eks whether he thought that military monks were necessary, and was told that "[without] Buddhism to teach and guide people, it would be a nation filled with selfish people." Jerryson, pointing out that Phra Eks' "rationalization is one of prima facie; the ideological threat of moral turpitude overturns the interdiction against violence" (ibid.), then carries on discussing the phenomenon of military monks in other Buddhist traditions, looking at Chinese, Tibetan, and Japanese militarized monks (Jerryson 2011, 123–125). He offers a very tempting argument:

> The rationale for many of these monks was that their conduct, while unethical, was necessary in this deteriorated state of the world. To put it quite simply, an armed monk was better than no monks at all. (Jerryson 2011, 124–125)

Of course, one could dismiss this argument with the remark that comparing contemporary Theravāda Thai military monks with medieval Mahāyāna Japanese monks would be a bit like explaining developments in, say, a Protestant district in modern-day England by drawing on Catholic

---

[12] Personal conversation in late July 2018 in a temple in Chaiya District, Surat Thani Province.

sects in medieval Italy or Spain. However, Jerryson quotes a senior Thai monk who admits that it "is beneficial to have military monks in order to protect the religion," and that without military monks, temples would be destroyed, with the effect that Buddhism would vanish from the area (Jerryson 2011, 126). Again, this is a very tempting argument, especially when examined in the light of prima facie duties mentioned by Jerryson. Since this issue is of importance here, it is worthwhile to briefly recapitulate my discussion of prima facie duties of the second chapter on the basis of Hallisey's argumentation. As we remember, Hallisey, referring to W. D. Ross' understanding of prima facie duties,[13] argues that the concept "does not suggest that some moral principles are more important than others [and] also eschews any attempt to discover any consistency in the things we take to matter morally" (Hallisey 1996, 38–39). He then uses the well-known *Mangalasutta* (lit.: 'Discourse on Blessings') as an example to illustrate his reasoning. This sutta contains a list of 38 prima facie duties, including some common-sense recommendations such as living in a suitable locality, supporting mother and father as well as caring for one's wife and children; some other geared towards the Noble Eightfold Path, for example, to associate with the monks, abstain from intoxicants, or to lead a chaste life (Mangalasutta, as translated by Narada Thera 1994). But as Hallisey points out, some of the recommendations of the Mangalasutta contradict themselves: for example, the recommendation to live a chaste life is difficult to reconcile with the one on caring for one's wife and children. Hence, Hallisey draws the following conclusion:

> It is precisely this inclusiveness that prevents us from taking the items on the list as together providing a portrait of an ideal moral agent, such as we might find in a virtue-theory of ethics. [...] Indeed, rather than the outline of any particular underlying ethical theory, the impression that one takes away from this list [...] is that all sorts of things matter [...] but in a way that is not structured by systematic consistency. (Hallisey 1996, 39–40)

If we follow Hallisey, then we could indeed argue that both Phra Eks and the senior monk quoted by Jerryson are right: most certainly, without

[13] A 'prima facie' duty is a duty that is obligatory unless it is overridden or trumped by another duty. As Garrett (2004) explains, "[an] example of a prima facie duty is the duty to keep promises. 'Unless stronger moral considerations override, one ought to keep a promise made.'"

monks, temples would fall in disrepair or even be destroyed, and Buddhism would thus vanish from the affected area. It thus follows that indeed, "an armed monk was better than no monks at all" (Jerryson 2011, 124–125), and that ordaining active soldiers as monks—even though explicitly forbidden by the Buddha—would be the better course of action. We could even go one step further and again draw on Carl Schmitt's suggestion of the existence of an *Ausnahmezustand* or 'state of exception' which Jerryson (2018, 459) discussed in the context of Sinhalese Buddhist extremism: surely, ordaining active soldiers as monks with the laudable aim to protect Buddhists and Buddhism would be entirely justified from this perspective. It is however quite significant that when I asked 'my' monks whether it would indeed be better to have armed monks than no monks at all, none of them was willing to accept this reasoning. They went as far as acknowledging that some temples would need to be protected either by soldiers or by the police, and that in certain areas, monks would have to accept to be accompanied by soldiers or police even for the daily alms round. But when it came to the question of ordaining soldiers as monks, they did not budge: for them, that was morally wrong, even repulsive. In the opinion of the thudong monks in particular, there were already enough 'bad monks' in the ranks of the Thai Sangha who should be disrobed—having soldier monks on top of that would only further erode the Thai people's trust in the monkhood.

Interestingly, there may no longer be an urgent need for soldier monks. Research conducted by one of my students for his MLitt dissertation indicates that as early as 2006, the perception of the Muslim community in the Deep South regarding the activities of the insurgents changed drastically:

> During 2004–2007, the local community had shared the sentiment of the insurgents. However, after this period the support reduced for certain attacks. [...] The community no longer found the previous tactics of the insurgents, which included beheadings, to be acceptable [...] while the local Ulama began to express that the insurgents' previous actions were against the Islamic rules of engagement. (Gyte 2018, 42)

One remembers that even Al Qaeda thought beheadings to be un-Islamic when Abu Musab al-Zarqawi's Al Qaeda in Iraq (AQI), basically the predecessor of today's Islamic State of Iraq and Syria (ISIS), carried out a number of such gruesome acts, which were videotaped and published. One of the core arguments in Al Qaeda's Ayman al-Zawahiri's letters to al-Zarqawi that beseeched him to stop such activities was that they would result in a loss of support because of their barbaric and decidedly un-Islamic nature. While AQI, and later on ISIS, carried on regardless for a variety of reasons, the potential loss of support from their community (which the insurgents in the Deep South need to survive) obviously prompted the insurgents to change their tactics—including abandoning their beheading attacks targeting monks and novices, while at least reducing their attacks against temples. This is not to say that no such incidents occur any longer: since the various cells of this only loosely organized insurgency operate independently from each other, it basically depends on the local cell in question on which tactics are used and which are not. Nevertheless, and quite ironically, it could well be that soldier monks were introduced just at the moment when they actually were no longer required. Hence, this blatant violation of monastic rules may well have been futile in the end.

## Evaluations: No Country for Militant Monks

It is time now for some concluding remarks. To begin with, let us revisit Almond, Appleby, and Sivan's concept of a 'syncretic' fundamentalism as opposed to a 'pure' one. As we recall, they defined syncretic fundamentalism as one "in which ethnocultural or ethnonational features take precedence over religion or are inseparable" (Almond et al. 2003, 93, 110). While in the cases of Sri Lanka and Burma, I accepted the idea that there is, indeed, such a syncretic fundamentalism at work without any qualifications, I would, in the case of Thailand, argue that if such a fundamentalism is present at all, then it is only restricted to the Deep South, while all other parts of Thailand remain either less affected or completely unaffected by it. Why this is the case can be answered in different ways. First of all, the insurgency in the Deep South so far has not spread to other parts of Thailand and seems to be well contained and localized at the moment. Hence, and despite the fact that since 2004, more than 8000 people have lost their lives, this conflict did not manage to trigger a nationwide anti-Muslim sentiment that could be whipped into a frenzy by militant monks. Unlike the Rohingyas in neighbouring Burma, the Malay-Muslims of the Deep South usually are also not labelled as illegal immigrants and thus foreigners, but seen as Thai citizens as well.

A second answer, linked to the first one, can be found if we turn to the national level. In the case of Burma, important secular political stakeholders, especially the still all-powerful army (Tatmadaw), tolerate the activities of the militant monks since they fit rather well with their own political agenda. This is, however, not the case in Thailand where neither the Sangha hierarchy nor the government is prepared to tolerate the meddling in political affairs of firebrand monks, for a variety of reasons which I discussed above. For example, whipping Buddhist ultra-nationalists into a frenzy is usually deemed to be counter-productive by the government since this would not make the on-again, off-again talks with the insurgents, brokered by the good offices of Malaysia, any easier. To put it bluntly, while in neighbouring Burma, the government sees the solution of the Rohingya conflict simply in evicting these 'foreigners,' the Thai government sees a solution to the insurgency in the Deep South in negotiations with these Muslim 'fellow citizens', and in defusing and de-escalating the conflict as much as possible.

Finally, in the previous chapter on Burma I already quoted Spiro (1982, 392), as saying that despite being highly articulate and seemingly ever-present, politically active monks actually are a fairly small minority, usually to be found only in the cities or in major temples, while being notably absent in the villages. In my opinion, Spiro's comment derived from his interviews with monks in Burma three decades ago can still be used in the context of Thailand at the end of the second decade of the twenty-first century: indeed, the monks I met also opined that involving themselves in politics, or even in social work, would stand between them and the chance of reaching nibbāna. They usually also held rather dim views on social work that many Western observers cite when it comes to the (perceived) positive aspect of Thai Buddhism—for example, the activities of environmentalist or 'ecology' monks (*phra nak anuraksa*) geared to protect the dwindling Thai national forests (see, for example, Darlington 1998, 2000), or the hands-on drugs prevention programmes of Wat Tham Krabok in Saraburi Province (more information at Wat Thamkrabok 2015), or the social reforms in the tradition of Buddhadasa Bhikkhu (see, for example, Ito 2012 and Jackson 2003)—not because they thought such activities to be bad, but because any form of political activism is detrimental for monks. This frequently expressed opinion means that I can also relate to the faint air of disappointment Spiro alludes to when narrating the first response of an abbot he interviewed in Mandalay: "I thought you were interested in nirvana; those [political monks'] organizations have nothing to do with attaining nirvana" (Spiro 1982, 393). Very similarly, those rural monks I spoke to, and in particular the thudong monks, were, without exception, utterly uninterested in all things political, up to the point of politely but firmly turning the conversation to other matters. Most importantly, they were absolutely not prepared to see the conflict in the Deep South in terms of an impending Muslim invasion that would spell an end to Thai Buddhism and were thus also not of the opinion that a defensive war would be necessary and justifiable. One older monk from the South compared the insurgency to the communist uprising in the 1960s and 1970s and opined that while in the days of the communists, and the downfall of Buddhism in Cambodia and Laos, there was a danger that had to be countered, just as Phra Kittiwutthō had claimed, this was manifestly not the case today. He even went as far as arguing that if the Deep South would break away from Thailand, this still would not bring about an end of Buddhism there—after all, he argued, there are many Buddhist temples on the other side of the border in present-day Malaysia. To appropriate the title of the book of Irving Chan Johnson (2010), the *Buddha on Mecca's Verandah* seems to thrive in a Muslim environment, and Thai Buddhists can live there in peace—so, why not Malay-Muslims in Thailand? In my opinion, this is a fair summing-up on 'my' monks' view of the situation, with the very clear connotations that there was nothing to worry about, and that Thai Buddhism was not under siege.

## REFERENCES

Almond, Gabriel A., R. Scott Appleby, and Emmanuel Sivan. 2003. *Strong Religion: The Rise of Fundamentalisms Around the World*. Chicago/London: University of Chicago Press.

Baker, Chris, and Pasuk Phongpaichit. 2005. *A History of Thailand*. Cambridge et al.: Cambridge University Press.

Buadaeng, Kwanchewan. 2017. A Karen Charismatic Monk and Connectivity Across the Thai-Myanmar Borderland. In *Charismatic Monks of Lanna*, ed. Paul T. Cohen, 149–170. Copenhagen: NIAS Press.

Buddhanet. 2008. Ordination Procedure in the Theravada Tradition. *Buddhist Studies: Monastic Community*. https://www.buddhanet.net/e-learning/buddhistworld/ordination1.htm

Cohen, Paul T., ed. 2017. *Charismatic Monks of Lanna*. Ed. T. Cohen, 149–170. Copenhagen: NIAS Press.

Cushman, Richard D., and David K. Wyatt. 2006. *The Royal Chronicles of Ayutthaya. A Synoptic*. Trans. Richard D. Cushman and Ed. David K. Wyatt. Bangkok: The Siam Society.

Darlington, Susan M. 1998. The Ordination of a Tree: The Buddhist Ecology Movement in Thailand. *Ethnology* 37 (1): 1–15.

———. 2000. Rethinking Buddhism and Development: The Emergence of Environmentalist Monks in Thailand. *Journal of Buddhist Ethics* 7 (online version).

Dubus, Arnaud. 2017. *Buddhism and Politics in Thailand*. IRASEC's Short Books 40. Bangkok: IRASEC. http://www.irasec.com/ouvrage144

Ekachai, Sanitsuda. 2015. Nip Unholy Hate Speech in the Bud. *Bangkok Post*, November 4. https://www.bangkokpost.com/opinion/opinion/753808/nip-unholy-hate-speech-in-the-bud

Essen, Juliana. 2004. Santi Asoke Buddhist Reform Movement: Building Individuals, Community and (Thai) Society. *Journal of Buddhist Ethics* 11: 1–20.

Ford, Eugene. 2017. *Cold War Monks. Buddhism and America's Secret Strategy in Southeast Asia*. New Haven/London: Yale University Press.

Garrett, Jan. 2004. *A Simple and Usable (Although Incomplete) Ethical Theory Based on the Ethics of W. D. Ross*. August 10. http://people.wku.edu/jan.garrett/ethics/rossethc.htm

Gyte, Joseph. 2018. *Thailand's Deep South Insurgency: Declining Violence, but Why?* Unpublished MLitt Dissertation, University of St Andrews.

Habib, Shahanaaz, Teh Eng Hock, and Brian Moh. 2010. Staying Neutral Is Hard for Monks. *The Star Online*, April 19. https://www.thestar.com.my/news/nation/2010/04/19/staying-neutral-is-hard-for-monks/

Hallisey, Charles. 1996. Ethical Particularism in Theravāda Buddhism. *Journal of Buddhist Ethics* 3: 32–43.

Harris, Ian. 2013. *Buddhism in a Dark Age. Cambodian Monks Under Pol Pot*. Chiang Mai: Silkworm Books.

ICG. 2007. *Southern Thailand: The Problem with Paramilitaries*. Asia Report No. 140, October 23. https://www.crisisgroup.org/asia/south-east-asia/thailand/southern-thailand-problem-paramilitaries

Ito, Tomomi. 2012. *Modern Thai Buddhism and Buddhadāsa Bikkhu. A Social History*. Singapore: NUS Press.

Jackson, Peter A. 1989. *Buddhism, Legitimation and Conflict: The Political Functions of Urban Thai Buddhism*. Social Issues in Southeast Asia. Singapore: ISEAS.

———. 2003. *Buddhadāsa: Theravada Buddhism and Modernist Reform in Thailand*. Bangkok: Silkworm Books.

Jerryson, Michael K. 2011. *Buddhist Fury: Religion and Violence in Southern Thailand*. Oxford et al.: Oxford University Press.

———. 2018. Buddhism, War, and Violence. In *Oxford Handbook of Buddhist Ethics*, ed. Daniel Cozort and James M. Shields, 453–478. Oxford: Oxford University Press.

Johnson, Irving Chan. 2010. *The Buddha on Mecca's Verandah. Encounters, Mobilities, and Histories Along the Malaysian-Thai Border*. Chiang Mai: Silkworm Books.

Kershaw, Roger. 2001. *Monarchy in South-East Asia. The Faces of Tradition in Transition*. London/New York: Routledge.

Keyes, Charles F. 1999. Political Crisis and Militant Buddhism in Contemporary Thailand. Rev. ed., original version published in *Religion and Legitimation of Power in Thailand, Burma and Laos*, ed. Bardwell Smith, 147–164. Chambersburg: Anima Books 1978. http://www.academia.edu/8987102/Political_Crisis_and_Militant_Buddhism_in_Contemporary_Thailand_rev_1999_

Kirsch, Thomas A. 1975. Modernizing Implications of Nineteenth Century Reforms of the Thai Sangha. *Contributions to Asian Studies* VIII: 8–23.

Leifer, Michael. 1995. *Dictionary of the Modern Politics of South-East Asia*. London/New York: Routledge.

Mahāmakuta Educational Council. 1989. *Acts of the Administration of the Buddhist Order of Sangha in Thailand. B.E. 2445, B.E. 2484, B.E. 2505*. Bangkok: Mahāmakuta Educational Council, The Buddhist University. https://sujato.files.wordpress.com/2010/07/sangha-acts.pdf

McCargo, Duncan. 2009. The Politics of Buddhist Identity in Thailand's Deep South: The Demise of Civil Religion? *Journal of Southeast Asian Studies* 40 (1): 11–32. http://www.polis.leeds.ac.uk/assets/files/Staff/mccargo-pol-buddhism-south-2009.pdf

———. 2012a. *Mapping National Anxieties: Thailand's Southern Conflict*. Singapore: NIAS Press.

———. 2012b. The Changing Politics of Thailand's Buddhist Order. *Critical Asian Studies* 44 (4): 627–642. http://www.polis.leeds.ac.uk/assets/files/Journal%20articles/CAS-Buddhism-McCargo-December-2012.pdf

McDaniel, Justin. 2006. Buddhism in Thailand: Negotiating the Modern Age. In *Buddhism in World Cultures: Comparative Perspectives*. Religion in Contemporary Cultures, ed. Stephen C. Berkwitz, 101–128. Santa Barbara: ABC CLIO.

Ngamkhan, Wassayos. 2018. Senior Monks Defrocked After Raids. Phra Buddha Isara Among Those Nabbed. *Bangkok Post*, May 25. https://www.bangkokpost.com/news/general/1472209/senior-monks-defrocked-after-raids

Palmisano. 2013. How to Become a Thai Monk: Preparation, Part 2. *Thai Language Blog*, October 26. https://blogs.transparent.com/thai/how-to-become-a-thai-monk-preparation-part-2/

Pannapadipo, Phra Peter. 2005. *Phra Farang: An English Monk in Thailand*. London: Arrow Books.

Pitsuwan, Surin. 1985. *Islam and Malay Nationalism: A Case Study of the Malay-Muslims of Southern Thailand*. Bangkok: Thai Khadi Research Institute, Thammasat University.

Satha-Anand, Suwanna. 2003. Buddhist Pluralism and Religious Tolerance in Democratizing Thailand. In *Philosophy, Democracy and Education*, ed. Philip Cam, 193–213. Seoul: Korean National Commission for UNESCO.

———. 2014. The Question of Violence in Thai Buddhism. In *Buddhism and Violence: Militarism and Buddhism in Modern Asia*, ed. Vladimir Tikhonov and Torkel Brekke, paperback ed., 175–193. New York/London: Routledge.

Scott, Rachelle L. 2009. *Nirvana for Sale? Buddhism, Wealth, and the Dhammakaya Temple in Contemporary Thailand*. New York: State University of New York Press.

Seneviratne, H.L. 1999. *The Work of Kings. The New Buddhism in Sri Lanka*. Chicago/London: University of Chicago Press.

Spiro, Melford E. 1982. *Buddhism and Society. A Great Tradition and Its Burmese Vicissitudes*. 2nd expanded ed. Berkeley/Los Angeles/London: University of California Press.

Suksamran, Somboon. 1979. *Buddhism and Politics: The Political Roles, Activities and Involvement of the Thai Sangha*. PhD Dissertation, University of Hull. https://core.ac.uk/download/pdf/2731851.pdf?repositoryId=127

———. 1982. *Buddhism and Politics in Thailand*. Singapore: Institute for Southeast Asian Studies.

Swearer, Donald K. 1999. Centre and Periphery: Buddhism and Politics in Modern Thailand. In *Buddhism and Politics in Twentieth-Century Asia*, ed. Ian Harris, 194–228. London: Continuum.

Tambiah, Stanley J. 1976. *World Conqueror and World Renouncer. A Study of Buddhism and Polity in Thailand Against a Historical Background*. Cambridge et al.: Cambridge University Press.

———. 1978. Sangha and Polity in Modern Thailand: An Overview. In *Religion and Legitimation of Power in Thailand, Laos and Burma*, ed. Bardwell L. Smith, 111–133. Chambersburg: Anima Books.

Tanham, George K. 1974. *Trial in Thailand*. New York: Crane, Russak & Company.

Thai PBS. 2018. Former 'Nen Kham' Gets 114 Years for Cheating. *Thai PBS*, August 9. http://englishnews.thaipbs.or.th/former-nen-kham-gets-114-years-for-cheating/

Thanissaro Bhikkhu. 1997. Kesi Sutta: To Kesi the Horsetrainer. *Anguttara Nikaya: The Further-factored Discourses*. Access to Insight: Readings in Theravāda Buddhism. https://www.accesstoinsight.org/tipitaka/an/an04/an04.111.than.html

The Nation (Bangkok). 2017. Anti-Islam Extremist Monk Forced to Disrobe. *The Nation*, September 21. http://www.nationmultimedia.com/detail/national/30327286

———. 2018. Phra Buddha Isara Arrested After Commando Raid of Temple. *The Nation*, May 25. http://www.nationmultimedia.com/detail/national/30346206

Tiyavanich, Kamala. 1997. *Forest Recollections. Wandering Monks in Twentieth-Century Thailand*. Chiang Mai: Silkworm Books.

Tonsakulrungruang, Khemtong. 2018. Thailand's Sangha: Turning Right, Coming Full Circle. *New Mandala*, August 07. http://www.newmandala.org/thailands-sangha-turning-right-coming-full-circle/

Wat Thamkrabok. 2015. Drugs & Alcohol Detoxification and Rehabilitation. https://wat-thamkrabok.org

Winichakul, Thongchai. 1994. *Siam Mapped: A History of the Geo-Body of a Nation*. Honolulu: University of Hawaii Press.

Wyatt, David K. 2003. *Thailand: A Short History*. 2nd ed. Chiang Mai: Silkworm Books.

Yongcharoenchai, Chaiyot. 2016. Bigotry on the Boil over Halal Project. *Bangkok Post*, March 13. https://www.bangkokpost.com/news/special-reports/895308/bigotry-on-the-boil-over-halal-project

CHAPTER 8

# Comparative Analysis: "Buddhism Is Not a Suicidal Utopianism"

In this chapter, I will discuss, compare, and contextualize the findings of the three cases studies, on the basis of the general discussion in the introduction and the two main research questions.[1] The 'thick descriptions' of the previous three chapters will be investigated for similarities and dissimilarities in the first step, to then use the general framework established in the introduction to situate them in the broader context of religion and politics in general, and in the narrower regional context in particular. For that purpose, the arguments put forward by Toft, Philpott, and Khan, as well as Selengut's call for a holistic approach that includes case-specific factors such as religious, historical, and sociological conditions will be revisited. But before I do so and discuss the activities of the extremist or militant monks, that is the 'dark monks' as some Thai monks of the forest tradition called them, I would like to emphasize that we are talking about a minority here—yes, a very vocal and outspoken one that does not shy away from (negative) headlines, and a very dangerous one to boot as the Sinhalese monk Watareka Vijitha Thera (who was abducted and assaulted) would probably agree, but a minority nevertheless. Seen from this perspective, I tend to agree with Keyes (1999, 3) who reminds us that

[1] These were: Q1 How can the rise of militant Theravada Buddhism based on the notion of a Buddhist 'holy war' against 'others' (mostly Muslims at the moment) be explained? And Q2 'How, why, and for what goals' do Theravada Buddhist religious actors 'involve themselves' in politics?

© The Author(s) 2019
P. Lehr, *Militant Buddhism*,
https://doi.org/10.1007/978-3-030-03517-4_8

"Theravāda Buddhism has traditionally been seen as a refuge of peace from a world of incessant conflict or as a source of strength for those who would restore peace in a mundane world. It has rarely been seen as a basis for the taking up of arms and destroying one's enemies." I also sympathize with Jarni Blakkarly who, rather convincingly, argues:

> It does not take much knowledge of Buddhism to realise just how irreconcilable the thinking of Buddhist extremists [sic] groups are with what the Buddha Gotama taught and the way Buddhism is practiced throughout most of the world. (Blakkarly 2015)

And yet, during my research, I heard time and again that I would be missing the point—mostly so because I am basically a follower of Western-constructed, essentialized Theravāda Buddhism who takes the luxury of ignoring the stark realities of the Age of Suffering, and the impossible choices that are on offer. The warning that 'Buddhism is not a suicidal utopianism' also still rings in my ears. Hence, I have to accept that there are other interpretations of Buddhism which are not so contemplative, and even violent, if need be—which in any case is why I embarked on this voyage into this aspect of Buddhism in the first place, and why I adopted a socio-theological approach that takes the protagonists and their aims and objectives seriously and not just as some unfortunate aberrations "of activist groups [...] deviant from the religious norm and therefore uncharacteristic of true religion" (Juergensmeyer 2017, 16) we can easily ignore.

## Basics: Similarities and Dissimilarities

Let us commence by briefly repeating some basic facts that I touched upon in the case studies. To start with some statistics, it is worthwhile to repeat that in the three countries, Theravāda Buddhists form the absolute majority of the population by a wide margin: about 70 per cent in the case of Sri Lanka (with 22 million people the smallest of the three countries), 88 per cent in the case of Burma (with a population of 54 million), and a whopping 95 per cent in Thailand (with a population of nearly 70 million). In comparison, the Muslims as the currently most frequently targeted 'others' in the three countries are small minorities only; while Muslims in Sri Lanka are just shy of 10 per cent (9.7 per cent, to be precise), they only amount to 4.3 per cent in the cases of Burma and Thailand. In the case of Sri Lanka, we should, however, also mention the presence of

12.6 per cent Hindus and of 7.4 per cent Christians—as we have seen, the Hindu Tamils form the 'original other,' while (Evangelical) Christians often are targeted as well. In the other two cases, the numbers of followers of other religions are marginal: Burma reports 6.3 per cent Christians and 1.6 per cent unspecified others, while Thailand 1.17 per cent Christians and 0.03 per cent Hindus.

Regarding demographics, it also needs to be emphasized that none of the three countries is ethnically homogenous. Sri Lanka, for example, is the home of 75 per cent Sinhalese, 15.4 per cent Tamils (both Sri Lankan and Indian), and 9.2 per cent Sri Lankan Moors. In the case of Burma, 68 per cent are Bamar (Burmans), 9 per cent Shan, 7 per cent Karen, 4 per cent Rakhine, and 2 per cent Mon. Thailand features about 76.5 per cent ethnic Thais (Central Thais, North-eastern Thais/Khon Isan, Northern Thais/Khon Muang, and Southern Thais), 14 per cent Thai Chinese, and 3 per cent Thai Malays, the remainder being Karen, Khmer, Mon, and hill tribes. This ethnic heterogeneity, most pronounced (and violent) in Burma, also explains the still ongoing nation-building processes that come with a strong ethno-nationalist, or even ethno-chauvinist, flavour, in which Buddhism plays a major role, as discussed. After all, the vast majority of the dominant ethnic groups in all three countries are Buddhists.

It is also of significance that the various 'others' in the shape of non-Buddhist minority ethnic groups are geographically concentrated, which means that in certain regions of the three countries, they either form the majority or at least a formidable minority group able to challenge the dominant ethnic group in one way or another, be it as formidable voting blocs for a political party or as the supporters of a separatist movement. In the case of Sri Lanka, the Sri Lankan (mainly Hindu) Tamils are concentrated in the north and east of the island, while the Muslims are mainly found in the north-western and north-eastern coastal regions, in the latter case forming a bridge between the two Hindu Tamil majority regions. Unsurprisingly, these were the areas in which the Liberation Tigers of Tamil Eelam (LTTE) tried to establish its own *Tamil Eelam*,[2] either as a separate state or at least an autonomous region. In Burma, the dominant ethnic group of the Bamar is situated centrally in the Irrawaddy river basin, while all other ethnic groups are mainly situated at the hilly

---

[2] 'Eelam' is the Tamil name for Sri Lanka.

and mountainous fringes of the country. In the case of the Rohingya in Rakhine State (Arakan), they formed (before the current conflict) a sizeable minority of 42.7 per cent, not necessarily threatening but at least challenging the political dominance of the 52.2 per cent of Buddhist Rakhines. As regards Thailand, the various Thai ethnic groups, predominantly Buddhist, form the majority in basically all parts of the kingdom, with the sole exception of the Deep South, that is, the provinces of Narathiwat, Pattani, Yala, and Songkhla plus Satun,[3] where Malay Muslims are the majority.

Furthermore, all three states, and especially all three Buddhist majorities, had or still have to face insurgencies in the shape of competing ethno-nationalist movements. In Sri Lanka, it was mainly the LTTE who fought for Tamil Eelam as a homeland for the Tamils. Although the LTTE were a secular movement with somewhat vague Marxist underpinnings and definitely not an ethno-religious (Hinduist) movement, the fact that the majority of the Tamils either fighting for the LTTE or living in areas controlled by the LTTE were (a) not Sinhalese but Tamils, and (b) not Buddhists but mainly Hindus with some Muslim Tamils present as well, did not escape the Sinhalese-Buddhist majority of Sri Lanka, especially not those who were members of the Sri Lankan armed forces who suffered grievous losses in the many set-piece battles of the three so-called *Eelam Wars* until the LTTE could finally be defeated in May 2009. More than 100,000 people had been killed by then, and about one million civilians had been displaced. What certainly helped constructing the LTTE as an implacable enemy that posed a mortal danger not only to the Sinhalese majority but to Buddhism in general were the attacks of LTTE hit squads and suicide bombers (known as Black Tigers) against Buddhist temples (for example, the Tooth Temple in Kandy) and against monks and novices which the LTTE saw as symbols and representatives of the state, and thus as 'fair game.'

In the case of Burma, it can be said that it is by far the worst off of the three countries as regards the geographical spread and sheer size of insurgencies and separatist movements. From independence onwards, most non-Bamar (non-Burman) ethnic groups fought their own wars of independence against the Burman-Buddhist majority. As of today, basically all border areas of Burma are conflict zones in which brutal civil wars with

---

[3] As mentioned in the chapter on Thailand, Satun does not belong to the conflict zone.

utter disregard for human rights conventions are fought, especially so Kachin State (on the border to China and India), Kayah State (on the border to Thailand), Karen/Kayin State (also on the border to Thailand), Rakhine State (border to Bangladesh), and Shan State (border to China, Laos, and Thailand). The combined estimated numbers of casualties are even higher than those in Sri Lanka: about 250,000 people have been killed so far, and about one million of civilians displaced—and these numbers do not yet include the Rohingya conflict which also displaced nearly a million of people. Most of the ethno-national movements have established their own statelets and field their own armed (guerrilla) forces, in the case of the Shan State funded by the drugs trade since this state forms part of the infamous *Golden Triangle* (see, for example, Chin 2009). The Rohingya, who have now (in 2016) formed the *Arakan Rohingya Salvation Army* (ARSA) after previous attempts of collective self-defence have failed, are a latecomer in that regard.

In Thailand, a Malay-Muslim insurgency flared up again in January 2004 that has cost more than 8000 lives by now. Although regionally contained—the insurgents usually do not strike outside of the Deep South—and although far less severe than the civil wars in Sri Lanka or Burma, the spate of arson and bombing attacks against temples on the one hand, and beheading attacks on monks and novices on the other, during the first years of the renewed conflict also triggered a feeling of Buddhism and the nation under threat. Again, the targeting rationale of the separatist insurgents can be explained by the fact that like in the case of the civil war in Sri Lanka, temples and monks were seen as symbols and representatives of the state and thus fair game. But as I argued in the chapter on Thailand, the perception of being under siege was also mainly restricted to the Deep South, and much less virulent in other parts of Thailand. The end of beheading attacks targeting monks and novices due to a pushback against such gruesome tactics from within the Muslim community and the majority of Muslim clerics may help to defuse the conflict to some extent, but that remains to be seen. It is also important to note that, contrary to the Sri Lankan case where militant monks simply seem to have shifted the focus from Tamils to Muslims after the LTTE had finally been defeated in early 2009, or the Burmese case where militant Buddhism targeting perceived Muslim outsiders (Rohingya) as well as non-Buddhist insurgents in the contested Golden Triangle seems to have been a permanent feature, militant Buddhism in Thailand all but vanished after the decline of the Communist Party of Thailand (CPT) in the late 1970s, and only resurfaced when the Muslim insurgency flared up again. Even so, it currently is a rather subdued affair as compared to Sri Lanka and Burma.

## NARRATIVES: THE THEME OF BEING 'UNDER SIEGE' AND THE JUSTIFICATION OF (DEFENSIVE) VIOLENCE[4]

It should be abundantly clear by now that in the three Theravāda countries Sri Lanka, Burma, and Thailand, Buddhists constitute the vast majority of the population: 70 per cent in the case of Sri Lanka, 88 per cent in the case of Burma, and a massive 95 per cent in the case of Thailand. Hence, we would thus be excused for thinking that there is nothing to worry about: Buddhism obviously is safe and secure, and so is the Buddhist majority of those countries. However, this is not the perception of the militant monks. As we have seen, they are convinced that the opposite is true: Buddhism is under siege, and in grave danger of being wiped out. To explain this, they point out that 'yes, we are a majority in our country and "they" (the Muslims, in the case of Sri Lanka, also Hindu Tamils) are a minority only—but on the other side of our borders, there is plenty more of them.' Especially in Sri Lanka and Burma, the notion that the Muslim (or Hindu) minority present in their country is just the avant-garde of an imminent invasion, and that firm action has to be taken to prevent 'them' from taking over Buddhist lands and eradicating Buddhism is very strong indeed. After all, there are only about 150 million Theravāda Buddhists worldwide (of about 500 Buddhists in total), surrounded by 1.8 billion Muslims (the 2.3 billion Christians are currently not seen as a major threat, with the exception of Evangelical Christians who are a minority only) (numbers from Sherwood 2018). Apart from sheer numbers, the feeling of being under siege is aggravated by the fact that, as Keyes (2016, 41) notes, there "is no concept in Buddhism comparable to the Islamic *ummah*, or community of all believers, or to the Christian *catholic* in its basic sense of a universal church." This implies that the extremist monks of the three countries perceive "themselves more and more as the defenders of a threatened faith and an island of conservative tradition in a hostile and changing world," as Thant Myint-U (2007, 59) argued in the case of Burma. Unsurprisingly, the militant monks see their communities as tar-

---

[4] This chapter draws on my article "Militant Buddhism is on the march in Southeast Asia – where did it come from?" See Lehr 2017.

gets of a relentless 'Holy War,' and see it as their right, nay, as their duty, to respond in kind with their own variant of 'Holy War.' As Gravers (2015, 2) adds, this perception of fighting a 'Holy War' against an implacable enemy "is embedded in an imaginary of a world engulfed in a decline of both morality (*sila*) and knowledge of the doctrine (*dhamma*), as related in Buddhist cosmological narratives of the impermanence of the Buddha's teachings." This also implies that, to a certain extent, fighting this 'Holy War' can also be seen as an attempt to at least slow down, if not stop, the decay and, thus, the inevitable disappearance of the Buddha's teachings as envisioned and predicted by the Buddha himself.

The conceptualization of *dhamma* in this context is quite interesting. Although probably not too many political monks would nowadays subscribe to Sinhalese monk Vijayavardhana's claim that democracy is "a leaf taken from the book of Buddhism," and even fewer to his second claim that "Marxism is a leaf taken out from the book of Buddhism – a leaf torn out and misread" (Vijayavardhana 1953, 595–596), many of them still see the *dhamma* "as a democratic sharing of moral values, such as loving kindness and compassion, which is translated into a modern form of mutual help and security," as Gravers (2015, 3) explains in the context of the Burmese case, to then draw on Foucault's concept of *political spirituality* in order to put it in the correct theoretical framework. Understanding the *dhamma* as a call for political action, or at least as a justification for such, thus allows political monks to embark on exactly that: political action for the betterment of the people as such.

Furthermore, the conviction that Buddhism is under threat also allows them, or at least the militant, ultra-nationalist monks of all three Theravāda countries which I examined, to justify the resort to violence as well: although even the most belligerent of the militant monks readily concede that an offensive use of violence should never be allowed, they never fail to point out that peaceful and non-violent Buddhist communities have the right to self-defence, especially if and when the survival of the religion as such is at stake. As I already mentioned in the chapter on Burma, this point was forcefully made to me in a private communication by a Burmese lay follower who declared that "Buddhism is not a suicidal utopianism." Jerryson (2018, 459) frames this conviction in a more academic way by drawing attention on German philosopher and political scientist Carl Schmitt's suggestion of an *Ausnahmezustand* (state of exception) that basically justifies any action taken by the state in such a situation no matter what the law says, according to the German principle *Not kennt kein Gebot* or 'necessity knows no laws.' This line of argumentation is not new, as we have seen: as soon as Buddhist states came into being, the monkhood had to find ways to justify violence, including war, waged by the notionally righteous and virtuous ruler against an opponent—after all, it was his benevolence and the law and order created by him that enabled them to survive as a monastic order. By bestowing their rulers with titles that fused their temporal and spiritual authority, the respective Sanghas not only legitimized these wars, but virtually sanctified them—at least when it came to wars against the forces of non-believers. Hence, it can be argued that in the case of Theravāda Buddhism, most wars can be contributed to a "closely aligned monasticism and state" (Jerryson 2018, 455).[5] Regarding internal wars, for example the clashes between various contenders for the crown after the death of a king, an increasing factionalism within the monkhood certainly facilitated the task of sanctioning violence within their respective polity as well. Interestingly, even the Buddha himself showed some understanding for the wars conducted by his benefactor King Pasenadi (Prasenajit) of Kosala against his nephew King Ajātasattu: instead of condemning them straight away, he only warned that 'killing, you gain your killer, conquering, you gain the one who will conquer you,' pointing at the cycle of action and reaction—the message being that violence begets violence. This warning notwithstanding, the point can be made that even for the Buddha, non-violence was not necessarily an absolute value—and this is a point forcefully made by many of the militant monks.

Of interest here is the blurring of the boundaries between external and internal foes. This is particularly the case for the Muslims: the minorities present within the borders of Sri Lanka, Burma, and, to a lesser extent, Thailand are framed as 'avant-gardes' or 'fifth columns' clandestinely weakening the defences of the Buddhist majorities to prepare for the day when the 'jihad' starts. As I have demonstrated, the theme of being under siege by a faceless and numerous Muslim enemy can be traced back in all three cases to the destruction of the centres of Buddhist learning in India,

---

[5] Jerryson's argument in the original context is a wider one since he covers all strands of Buddhism: "Most Buddhist-inspired wars are either the result of a closely aligned monasticism and state, or a movement that contains millenarian elements." The latter, however, play a much less pronounced role in Theravāda Buddhism as they do in the other strands, with the exception of the recurring messianic revolts in the area straddling nowadays Thailand and Laos mentioned by him and discussed in the previous chapter on Thailand.

including the vast monastery and university of Nalanda, by several waves of Muslim armies between the eleventh and the thirteenth centuries. In all three cases, this theme has been used for nationalist purposes: in Sri Lanka at the turn of the nineteenth century by Anagārika Dharmapāla who explicitly blamed the Muslims for wiping out Buddhism in India, and currently by various monks associated with the Bodu Bala Sena (BBS); in Burma by monks of the Ma Ba Tha, and especially so by Ashin Wirathu; in Thailand by Phra Dhammapitaka in 2002 and now also by a few like-minded monks in the Deep South.

On several occasions in this book, I have drawn attention to the importance of Sri Lanka's Mahāvamsa since it offers a well-known precedent on which to fall back when it comes to sanctioning, or at least post hoc legitimizing, violence meted out by the state against non-believers. Indeed, as Seneviratne argued, this is the hegemonic text for Sri Lanka. But as we have seen, similar justification strategies emerged in Burma and in Thailand as well. In the present context, it is important to repeat what Seneviratne says about the Sangha of King Dutthagamani's days—the Sangha that came up with this particular strand of legitimizing violence against non-believers. Seneviratne argues as follows:

> Whether fictional or true, what the story reflects on the Sangha is clear: its culture did not have effective mechanisms for imbuing itself with the universalist values of tolerance, nonviolence, and pluralism that we readily infer from the ethical theories of Buddhist compendia and celebrate as the achievement of the Ashokan Buddhist state. Thus, in the Sangha or at least in a decisive section of its membership in the Buddhist state as it blossomed in early medieval Sri Lanka, we are able to isolate a crucial variable inhibitive of the development of civility. (Seneviratne 1999, 21)

This is quite an important argument to make. As I explained in Chap. 4 on monks in the age of dukkha, using Satha-Anand's 'Three Moments in Buddhist History' (Satha-Anand 2014, 175) as the most convenient periodization of Buddhist history for my purpose, the Sangha's stance towards, and argumentation around, violence and non-violence had to change over time by sheer necessity: during the lifetimes of the Buddha, the Sangha had to function in an environment still largely defined by Brahmanism and of states dominated by Brahmanism, while from the times of Emperor Ashoka Maurya onwards, the Sangha found itself operating in a Buddhist realm which often had to defend itself against neighbouring kingdoms and empires which may or may not have been Buddhist as well. As the Sangha of these days soon found out, this was a very mixed blessing indeed: on the one hand, it certainly allowed Buddhism in general, and the monastic order in particular, to prosper, with major temples and even individual monks frequently being bestowed with generous gifts and honours by a grateful king. On the other hand, the monkhood quickly realized that it was time and again called upon by the kings to shore up the (often questionable) legitimacy of their rule, and to sanction the (equally questionable) endemic wars their rulers waged, both external wars such as in the case of the Burmese-Siamese Wars, or internal wars as in the case of contested succes- sions. Against this backdrop, it was not necessarily sheer opportunism that drove monks like those probably fictional ones of the Mahāvamsa to come up with credible explanations for the king's campaigns, but immensely practical and realpolitikal considerations aimed at ensuring the survival of the monkhood as such, and also of one's individual self in case a monk in question was called upon to advise the ruler. One could even say that the Sangha in question did not have much of a choice. In any case, Seneviratne concludes his rather devastating judgement on the inability of the medieval Sangha to contribute to the development of civility as follows:

> Differently stated, the much-written-about cultural role of the Sangha in Buddhist kingdoms involved, amidst many positive contributions, a paro- chializing and hegemonizing tendency which could only have had a chilling effect on the possibility of working out effective cultural linkages in the arduous task of constructing a civil society. (Seneviratne 1999, 21)

This deep-seated Theravāda-Buddhist parochialism which Thant Myint-U deplores in the case of Burma as well, contributed immensely to this per- ception of being under siege, surrounded by a hostile world full of ene- mies. In our times of the third moment of Buddhist history, this parochial perspective of the Sangha only worsened, as discussed. Hence, I agree with Seneviratne's verdict that

> [just] as the politico-ethical potential that was realized in Asokan Buddhism failed to suffuse the medieval flowering of Buddhism in Sri Lanka with the golden glow of its civility, reformist Buddhism of modern times failed to take the path that would have ultimately led to a civil society. Instead, it launched itself on a trajectory that has plunged the society in darkness. (Seneviratne 1999, 21)

But still, sanctioning the violent and not always morally justifiable actions of one's ruler or one' state driven by the conviction that Buddhism is under siege is one thing—actively encouraging one's followers to commit acts of violence in defence of the religion is something completely different. As we have seen, of all the leading militant monks we have encountered in the chapters on Sri Lanka, Burma, and Thailand, Kittiwutthō is the only one who (before his unconvincing retraction) very openly offered a general justification and legitimization of violence and killing in a carte blanche way against 'othered' people—in his case, Thai communists. By contrast, the monks of the Sinhalese Mahāvamsa legitimization of violence did so in a somewhat dispassionate and detached 'post hoc' way after the violence had been committed, while militant monks in Sri Lanka and Burma usually leave it to their followers to link the themes of justified defensive actions on the one hand, and the 'othering' of the chosen target group on the other. The reluctance to openly condone violence against people shows that compared to 'preachers of hate' from Abrahamic religions, militant monks face a difficult tightrope walk in that regard since the incitement to murder constitutes one of the four disrobing offences (pārājikas), that is, offences resulting in the automatic expulsion from the monkhood. Even instigating one's followers to use violence against objects can have harsh consequences for a monk. For example, and as mentioned in Chap. 7 on Thailand, in September 2017, ultra-nationalist Thai monk Phra Apichart Punnajanto was forced to disrobe because he had publicly demanded that for each monk killed in Thailand's Deep South, a mosque should be torched. Most militant monks are thus very careful in avoiding open calls to violence; instead, they somewhat ambiguously preach 'passive resistance': not buying from Muslims, not selling to Muslims, not fraternizing with Muslims, not allowing one's children to marry Muslims. They leave it to their followers, especially those organized in pro-state vigilante groups or Buddhist militias, to draw the proper conclusions, and to connect the dots.

There is, however, more than meets the eye in these Buddhist versions of holy wars. In a sense, I think that it is entirely justifiable to generalize the verdict of the Final Report of 1939 on the anti-Indian riots of July and August 1938 in (Colonial) Burma. As I already mentioned in Chap. 6 on Burma, the authors of the Final Report rather astutely argued as follows: "The riots at bottom were political and communal. Their immediate cause was we think, a complex piece of irresponsible political opportunism"—an opportunism that made good use of a convenient pretext to exploit socio-economic issues for political reasons (Braund 1939, 287–288). This is also the reason why I argued that if we can talk about the existence of Buddhist fundamentalism in the three countries at all, then it should be rather seen as a 'syncretic fundamentalism' as opposed to a 'pure fundamentalism'—syncretic fundamentalism defined as one "in which ethnocultural or ethnonational features take precedence over religion or are inseparable" (Almond et al. 2003, 93, 110). Again, that does not mean that the radical and extremist monks are not serious as regards their demands, but it implies that other subtexts are present as well, revolving around exactly this opportunism just mentioned. One of them is a fairly obvious one, and relates to the collapse of the traditional states that allowed the monks so inclined to become political entrepreneurs and activists in their own right in a now vastly larger political arena. A second one revolves around the relationship between monks and their lay followers on the local level. A third one focusses on the relationship between traditional monks and modern monks.

Regarding the first subtext of the collapse of the traditional states, in two of the three countries I examined, that is Sri Lanka and Burma, historical and political discontinuities as a result of British colonialization played a major role in triggering a process of first gradual, then rapid, politicization of the monkhood—or at least parts of it. As we have seen, in both countries, Theravāda Buddhism lost its pre-eminent place in society that it had so far enjoyed, as well as the royal patronage that went with it. Hence, the Sanghas in question saw their traditional prerogatives threatened by the new secular colonial regimes which did not necessarily see Buddhism as a socio-political force to be reckoned with. With these new colonial regimes, a wave of Western Christian missionaries entered the countries as well to look for converts, which finally drove the monks over the proverbial brink. But again, referring to the defence of their pre-eminent role now threatened by the encroachment of others is not sufficient to explain the gradual politicization of parts of the Sanghas. After all, in both countries, the leading forces of this reaction to the encroachment of Western (colonial) secularism on the governmental level and of Christian missions on the societal mainly were the younger monks. Not yet monks long enough to be set in their ways, and socialized into a now rapidly changing society, they developed a political awareness, while some of them even turned into social agents and political entrepreneurs in their own right.

The politicization of an increasing number of monks was facilitated by the abolition of the traditional monarchy on the one hand, and the subsequent absence of a Supreme Patriarch on the other—an office that in both countries had been tied to the court, and hence was abolished together with it. The quintessence of this was that no traditional power stood between the political monks and their agitations. This was not the case for Thailand: since the country escaped the fate of being colonized, both monarchy and the office of the Supreme Patriarch remained intact, thus precluding the emergence of political monks similar to Myanmar and Sri Lanka. Furthermore, since Theravāda Buddhism never lost its pre-eminence for these very reasons, the most important reason for their emergence, that is the defence of the religion, initially did not manifest itself (Spiro 1982, 391–392). It did so, however, during the Cold War and under the impression of the communist takeover in the equally Buddhist monarchies of Cambodia and Laos just across the border in the mid-1970s: since Thailand was at that time also fighting against a communist uprising, militant monks emerged who took it upon themselves to fight against communism in defence of monarchy and religion, the most prominent being Phra Kittiwutthō, who also went farthest as regards the justification of violence, and even of killing.

Regarding the second subtext, that is the relationship between monks and lay followers, I argued in the case studies that this is not a one-way street. Rather, the laity has certain expectations of the monk regarding not only his conduct but also his preaching, and his mediation and arbitration of local conflict if and when required. This also means that the monk, especially one who stays with a certain community for years, also sees himself as their protector, defending them against an overbearing state. It is thus quite logical that the monk, and his opinion, is, to a great extent, influenced by the community he serves. In the case of Thai extremist monk Phra Kittiwutthō, Keyes (1999, 10) alludes to this connection when he argues that "it is important to note that his support was drawn from much the same class of people as became supporters of the Nawaphon movement." The same argument can be made for the various Red Shirt- and Yellow Shirt-affiliated monks whom I encountered in Bangkok between 2010 and 2014 during the height of the political crisis that still besets Thailand. In the case of Burmese monks, Kyaw Yin Hlaing draws some interesting conclusions that connect the dots quite convincingly:

A monk is likely to be an opponent of the state if most of his lay disciples are individuals with strong anti-state sentiments or citizens who are politically and economically worse off under the existing political system. Similarly, if a monk has senior government officials and supporters of the government as his lay disciples, he is more likely to act like a supporter of the state. The monk who has major [lay disciples] both in the state and non-state sectors tries to appease both sides by participating in state-sponsored religious ceremonies and by expressing his support for democracy through private interaction with [lay disciples] from the non-state sector. (Kyaw Yin Hlaing 2008, 133–134)

This argumentation resonates rather well with Braund's comment made in 1939 on the 'irresponsible political opportunism' of the extremist monks he and his fellow commissioners investigated: just like their secular counterparts, that is politicians, politically active monks tend to cater to the needs and demands of their followers. When it comes to the framing of these demands, whatever these may be, the monks quite naturally fall back on religious, that is Buddhist, imagery and symbolism in order to do so. Interestingly, most of the secular politicians in the three Theravāda countries do likewise—not necessarily because of their own piety or any genuine religious concerns they have but because the religio-political culture of the state makes it a logical choice to also use religious (Buddhist) symbolism. After all, religious affiliation is a powerful tool when it comes to 'othering' parts of the population and turning this part into a potentially hostile 'them,' while appealing to all those who subscribe to the chosen religion, thus turning them into 'us.' Hence, Holt's argument that Buddhist movements such as the BBS in Sri Lanka or the Ma Ba Tha "may be led or orchestrated by Buddhist monks, but their aims are almost purely economic and political in nature" (Holt 2016, 9) is quite a compelling one—at least at first glance. His second argument that "militant groups like the BBS arose in a specific political context [and] there seems to be little doubt that they were allowed to operate with impunity or given cover by the state's security forces" (ibid.) also is quite compelling, although it is much stronger in the case of Sri Lanka and Burma, while not entirely convincing in the case of Thailand where the state continues to crack down at least on those political active monks who become too influential, and thus too dangerous as potential rallying points for the opposition. Holt's third argument that there was (and actually still is) "a considerable amount of collusion in play between [...] Buddhist monastic interests and the [...] Buddhist business community" (ibid.) also is quite convincing, again with some caveats thrown in for the Thai case.[6] His argumentation complements Selengut's point that "other factors like widespread poverty, grievances, and resentment against governmental authority or strong charismatic leaders" (Selengut 2003, 228) are required to trigger religious violence even if a doctrine justifying religious violence is present.

The third subtext concerns the relationship between tradition and modernity, or, more precisely, between traditional monks and modern monks. Here, it also quickly emerges that between the black of the one position and the white of the other, there are actually a few shades of grey that render the drawing of boundaries quite challenging. Gravers describes the issue as follows, after having discussed Jonathan Friedman's (1994) notion of globalized identity politics that also affects fundamentalism and nationalism:

> I suggest that the Buddhist monks rather ascribe to a hybrid (localized) identification, which amalgamates traditional Buddhist cosmological imaginary and a modern moral imaginary of the world order. Thus, I hesitate to view traditionalism and modernism as polar points of identification. The nationalist Buddhist monks in Burma and Sri Lanka are neither anti-democratic nor anti-modern; instead, they have an ethnicized perception of those for whom democracy works and whom it includes—thus, challenging Western conceptions of democracy. (Gravers 2015, 2)

This also implies that the difference between, say, the peaceful Saffron Revolution monks of 2007 and the current militant anti-Muslim monks in Burma is not necessarily as vast and irreconcilable as it seems at first glance, and that demonstrating against a military regime that is seen to be oppressive and not Buddhist enough in its politics in 2007 does not necessarily contradict anti-Muslim agitation just a couple of years later when seen through Graver's lens of an 'ethnicized perception': the beneficiaries in both cases are the Burmese Buddhists—and maybe even only the Burman Buddhists, that is the ethnic group of the Bamar. In the words of Freeman:

---

[6] Holt only advances these three arguments for the case of Sri Lanka and Sinhalese Buddhism—widening it to the other two Theravādin countries, however, is entirely possible in order to suss out similarities and dissimilarities, which is why I've done so.

> It would be too simplistic [...] to suggest that there was no ideological
> overlap between the Saffron monks and their more nationalistic brethren.
> While many Saffron monks have spoken out against religious violence and
> in favour of reconciliation, they may share some views with nationalists,
> especially when it comes to the Rohingya. [...] The view that Rohingya are
> outsiders is hardly a rare one, even among pro-democracy activists. (Freeman
> 2017)

Likewise, adopting environmentalism as part of one's political programme,
as the *Jāthika Hela Urumaya* (National Sinhala Heritage Party or JHU)
did in Sri Lanka, does also not necessarily mean that this comes part and
parcel with an inclusive understanding of democracy regardless of ethnicity or religion, or with any nod to democracy at all. After all, even in a
Western context, environmentalist ideas can be found on the extreme left
and the extreme right of the political spectrum. All taken together, it
would thus be a bit too hasty and too simplistic to think in black and white
categories when it comes to the evaluation of the political actions of activist monks—although admittedly, extremist monks as the Buddhist equivalents to Christian or Muslim 'preachers of hate' make this simple splitting
rather easy.

I would however like to add a warning here—a warning which I already
briefly mentioned in the case study on Sri Lanka and which also explains
why I just cautioned that Holt's arguments make sense 'at first glance': if
we unduly focus on all the non-religious aims and objectives, which means
on economic and political ones, we are in danger of imagining the monks
as nothing more but convenient handmaidens, or 'useful tools,' in the
service of others. In my opinion, this view would be either too simplistic as
well or too apologetic or both because opportunistic politically active, and
in particular the extremist, monks may well be (just like all other political
entrepreneurs), but they most certainly have an agenda of their own. And
this is why I argued in the introduction that we need to complement
Selengut with Kepel who emphasized that "we have to take seriously both
what they are saying and the alternative societies they are trying to build"
(Kepel 1994, 11). This then begs the question of what the monks want—a
question arguably much easier asked than answered. And with that question in mind, it is time now to revisit Juergensmeyer's concept of 'cosmic
wars' (Juergensmeyer 2003, 148–166), since this is at least part of the
answer.

## COSMOLOGIES: PARALLELS WITH OTHER RELIGIONS

In his book *Terror in the Mind of God*, Juergensmeyer (2003) discusses "images of divine warfare" in the context of Christian Identity activism—and violence—in the USA. He calls these acts 'cosmic wars,' describing them thus:

> They evoke great battles of the legendary past, and they relate to metaphysical conflicts between good and evil. Notions of cosmic war are intimately personal but can also be translated to the social plane. What makes religious violence particularly savage and relentless is that its perpetrators have placed such religious images of divine struggle – cosmic war – in the service of worldly political battles. For this reason, acts of religious terror serve not only as tactics in a political strategy but also as evocations of a much larger spiritual confrontation. (Juergensmeyer 2003, 149–150)

Gravers (2015, 4) adds that these cosmic wars "signify imaginaries of endangered identities and appeal to a fundamental ontological fear and thus often carry legitimized violence." This ontological fear in conjunction with the notion of a larger-than-life spiritual confrontation thus allows a Muslim cleric to claim that "Islam is under attack" (Juergensmeyer 2008, 1). It also allows "Jewish militants in Israel, Hindu and Sikh partisans in India, Buddhist fighters in Sri Lanka, and members of Christian militias in the United States" (ibid.) to make the same claim.

As regards the nature of the cosmic war that in Juergensmeyer's opinion reaches from the 'intimately personal' to the 'social plane,' Yishai Schlissel, Paul Jennings Hill, Nathuram Godse, and Thalduwe Somarama Thero, all discussed in Chap. 2 on holy wars, are examples for the former, while Muslim mobs in Bangladesh hacking atheist bloggers to death, and Buddhist mobs in Sri Lanka and Burma are examples for the latter. These few examples also demonstrate that 'cosmic wars' can be waged, and indeed are waged, by the followers of any religion, depending on the circumstances and regardless of the respective religion's professed abstention from violence. I should add against the backdrop of the current hardening of religious positions, and their reframing as 'cosmic wars' that also justify the use of violence, that this is not the first time such reframing occurs. I already mentioned the crusades, for example. A lesser known but very similar reaction to the perceived 'encroachment of others' in premodern times is that of Persian Zoroastrianism in the third century CE, which also targeted Buddhism amongst other beliefs for basically the same reasons as described above. Peter Frankopan, in his fascinating book *The Silk Road*, explains this rather eloquently after having described the demolition and ransacking of Jewish, Buddhist, Manichaean, and other places of worship:

> One of the reasons why Zoroastrianism became so embedded in the consciousness and identity of third-century Persia was as a reaction to the inroads being made by Christianity, which had started to spread alarmingly along the trade routes – just as Buddhism had done in the east. [...] Stamping out alternative cosmologies went hand in hand with the fervent Zoroastrianism that characterized the resurgence of Persia. A state religion was starting to emerge, one that identified Zoroastrian values as synonymous with Persian and provided what has been called 'a supporting pillar of Sasanian kingship.' (Frankopan 2016, 34–35, 39)

Again, here is the hostile 'other' seemingly hell-bent to wipe out one's own sacred tradition, and, hence one's own way of life—which is why this implacable enemy needs to be swiftly dealt with without mercy before it is too late. Indeed, the Zoroastrian priests would very probably have supported Ashin Wirathu's exhortation that this was not the time for peaceful and quiet meditation but for firm action. Needless to say, in both the militant Buddhist and the fervent Zoroastrianist cases, this also resulted in the emergence of an "increasingly strident and self-confident priesthood whose role extended deep into the spheres of politics" (Frankopan 2016, 39–40)—an argument which reminds us again of Selengut's warning that the theme of 'cosmic war' alone is insufficient to explain their move 'deep into the spheres of politics.'

If we compare militant Buddhism with militant versions of other religions, it becomes obvious that there are parallels, and that the mechanics employed are basically the same: either a religious 'other' or, even better, an 'ethno-religious other' is identified, turned into a convenient scapegoat, and blamed for a wide range of problems on the economic, political, and societal planes. 'They steal our jobs' is frequently mentioned, 'they steal our women' also is quite popular, and 'they are responsible for the moral decay' also is an often-made argument—we have seen all these claims uttered by various militant monks. The same argumentation can be found in the speeches and publications of Islamist clerics, and of fundamentalist-Christian preachers. The 'other' depends on the location of these preachers of hate—in the case of Islamist, or more pre-

cisely Salafist-Jihadist clerics, the 'other' consists of all sorts of unbelievers including secular Western nations, and also those within the own
ranks deemed to be heretics. In the case of fundamentalist Christians,
and also of secular right-wing demagogues, the 'other' includes the
Muslims who are perceived as trying to destroy Western civilization. In
the case of militant Hinduism, better known as Hindutva, the 'other'
consists of all non-Hindus, but mainly of Muslims and Christians. And
in the case of the militant monks, the 'other' mainly consists of Muslims
at the moment since they are deemed to wage a holy war against
Buddhism for centuries now—although in Sri Lanka, Hindus and
Christians alike are also othered if need be. In a sense, what we see here
seems to be Huntington's 'clash of civilizations' at work in the shape of
several holy wars linked to each other and fuelling each other (see
Huntington 1993; Huntington 1996). In the case of the current
Rohingya conflict in Burma, this linkage is blatantly obvious: from the
perspective of militant Buddhists, the Muslim Rohingya are foreign
'Bengalis' or 'Bangladeshis' who have illegally migrated into Rakhine
State as an avant-garde of the looming jihad. Hence, waging a defensive
holy war against them is the right course of action in order to stop them
before it is too late. On the other side, militant Muslims perceive the
brutal persecution and eviction of Rohingya as a brazen Burmese-
Buddhist attempt to seize Muslim territories, and to roll back the Dar
al-Islam. From their perspective, embarking on a defensive jihad thus is
perfectly justified. Of significance here is that both sides see themselves
as threatened by the other, and hence as the righteous defenders fighting
for a just cause, and certainly not as the offenders encroaching on territories that do not belong to them. Again, as I already argued in previous
chapters, what constitutes a defensive holy war and what constitutes an
offensive one lies in the eyes of the beholder.

There is yet another but less obvious parallel that should be mentioned
at least briefly, since this also partially answers the 'what do the monks
want' question, and this is the idea of 'holy lands' which need to be protected and defended against internal as well as external enemies. Notions
of such 'holy lands' conceptualized as sacred spaces populated by devout
people forming an ideal society are well known from the three revealed
Abrahamic religions. Modern examples would be the attempt to create a
Jewish sacred space by way of the State of Israel (Bar 2008), or the
Taliban's attempt to turn Afghanistan into an Islamic emirate. Most
recently, the Islamic State of Iraq and Syria (ISIS) tried the same within the

borders of their self-proclaimed caliphate. But the notion of 'holy lands' conceptualized as sacred spaces also exists in Theravāda Buddhism in the shape of a *Buddhadesa* or 'Buddha-Land.'[7] Anagārika Dharmapāla, for example, clearly conceptualized Sri Lanka as the 'sacred island' of Buddhism, which explains why he tried to cajole his fellow Sinhalese Buddhists into improving their moral standards: he firmly believed that "with a return to the righteous Buddhist way of life, progress will occur, and the country will be prosperous" (Seneviratne 1999, 32). Similar notions seem to exist within the Burmese variant of Buddhist ultra-nationalism, although these are much less pronounced than in the case of Dharmapāla's ideology. In my opinion, the idea of a *Buddhadesa* currently is most visible in the border areas of Burma and Thailand as an area of operation of charismatic monks known as *khrubas* (venerated teachers) such as U Thuzana,[8] who I already briefly mentioned in the chapters on Burma and Thailand.

As in the case of many other famous monks, most existing biographies are more or less hagiographies celebrating the monk's life. This is also the case for the only biography that has (to my knowledge) been translated into English, and which is therefore "the main reference for scholars who have studied U Thuzana," as Buadaeng (2017, 150, fn. 5) laconically states, even more so since this biography is available online now. The author of the biography, Myaing Nan Shwe, admits quite frankly in his foreword that "[this] book is not a biography […,] in fact it is a personal record of Sayadaw's life experiences" (Myaing Nan Shwe 1999, 1). Nevertheless, Myaing Nan Shwe's book is indeed a valuable source for the purpose at hand.

Of interest to us is that U Thuzana (born 1949), an ethnic Karen himself, briefly served in the Christian-dominated Karen National Liberation Army (KNLA) as part of the equally Christian-dominated Karen National Union (KNU) before he was ordained as a monk. During this compulsory service, he "found many zedis, stupas, shrines and pagodas […] which were ravaged by time immemorial. [He] moved with piety and determined

---

[7] This topic was brought to my attention in a two-hour conversation with a senior monk in a major temple in Bangkok in January 2018.

[8] According to Myiang Nan Shwe (1999, 10), 'Thu Za-na' means 'Virtuous and Upright.' For his followers, he is better known as the Myaing Gyi Ngu Sayadaw (lit. 'the revered monk from Myaing Gyi Ngu—a special region of the Karen/Kayin State).

to rebuilt [sic] religious edifices when opportunities arise [sic]" (Myaing Nan Shwe 1999, 14–15). The first opportunity arose in 1976. From then on, U Thuzana, a monk for seven years by then with a reputation for ascetic meditation practice, made good use of the rising number of followers to renovate derelict stupas, pagodas, and temples in the Karen region controlled by the Christian-dominated KNU. Initially, both the KNU as the political organization and the KNLA as its military wing tolerated his activities, even though the rising number of Buddhist followers must have led to some suspicion. In particular, the KNLA feared that pagodas situated on hills, and thus visible from a long range, could be used as reference points for the Burmese Army's artillery units. Hence, when in 1989, U Thuzana set his sights on renovating a pagoda on a hill near the KNLA headquarters at the town of Manerplaw, they refused to give permission for that venture (Myaing Nan Shwe 1999, 109–114). From a military point of view, their refusal made eminent sense—not so, however, for U Thuzana and his followers who felt increasingly discriminated against by mainly the Christian officers of the KNLA, and also by the KNU whose official religious education programme was exclusively Christian (Myaing Nan Shwe 1999, 157; also see the statement of the DKBA in Myaing Nan Shwe 6–7),[9] and thus began to think about a split. Finally, in December 1994, and after a series of mistreatments U Thuzana's followers allegedly had to suffer at the hands of Christian KNLA officers, the bulk of the Buddhist units left the KNLA and reorganized themselves as the Democratic Karen Buddhist Army (DKBA) (Rand 2009, 111–112).

U Thuzana himself left the DKBA after only one year in 1995, unwilling to get dragged into their deadly war against the KNLA, usually fought in cooperation with the Burmese army against their fellow Karen. Unlike U Gambira and Ashin Wirathu, for example, he does not seem to be interested in overtly political activities prone to draw the attention of regional and international media, even though what he does and what he stands for is of an eminently political nature—not only for Burmese (Karen) Buddhism, but also for Thai Buddhism, at least for North-eastern Thai Lanna Buddhism. After all, the realization of his vision of a *Buddhadesa* or (Holy) Buddhist Land revolves around the active cooperation of the

---

[9] In the English translation, the DKBA acknowledgement appears unpaginated between the paginated foreword (ends at page 6) and the first chapter of the also paginated book (starts at page 7).

people inhabiting its potential borders. To explain this, we need to briefly return to the theme of the decline of the *dhamma* that was already mentioned earlier in the chapter.

There are basically two views why this decline happens, as Cohen explains: "one (emphasized in the scholastic texts) that treats the decline and disappearance of the Dhamma as an inexorable process impervious to human action and the other, expressed in narrative accounts, that attributes the decline of Buddhism to human failings and which, in theory, could be prevented or at least prolonged" (Cohen 2017, 11). For that, however, a moral change is required, or what Cohen calls an "'active utopianism', that is, an ideal society that can only be achieved through moral change and deliberate collective action" (Cohen 2017, 11–12). Cohen's 'active utopianism' by way of a 'deliberate collective action' can, in my opinion, be generalized to cover all other 'holy land' ideas irrespective of religion, or secular ideology for that matter: a new society has to be built from scratch, and that requires the active participation of the society in question.

This of course begs a flurry of questions, most importantly in our context the question of what happens to all the 'others' who for one reason or another fail to take part in this 'active utopianism'—for example, because they happen to follow another religion, or no religion at all. Whatever their particular reason to not take part in the 'holy land' venture may be, it is clear that from the perspective of all those who subscribe to this 'cosmological imaginary,' as Gravers (2015) calls it, or to this 'sacred ideology,' as I would call it, they stand in the way of realizing this lofty goal. In the case of the *Buddhadesa* ideology in the border areas of Burma and Thailand, this already resulted in the exertion of a certain amount of pressure on people unwilling to join this kind of devout collective action either to toe the line and become vegetarians as one visible element of this heightened sense of morals, or to move away from the now 'purified' and 'sacred' space. In the case of Sri Lanka and Anagārika Dharmapāla's fusion of Sinhalese ethno-nationalism and Buddhism, it resulted in a vilification of the Tamil Hindu and Tamil Muslim 'others'—after all, their continued presence on Sri Lanka as the 'sacred island' forms a major obstacle on the road to the creation of a Sinhalese-Buddhist *dhammadīpa*, as discussed. In the Islamist case of the Taliban in Afghanistan and ISIS in Iraq and Syria, it resulted in a harsh application of sharia law, and the execution of recalcitrants. In the quasi-secular case of the Red Khmer, Khmer communism as their 'sacred ideology' also imbued with a modicum of Buddhist 'pure land' concepts (see Harris 2013, 51–63) resulted in the death of about one-third of the population (Sharp 2005). In these cases, Cohen's 'active utopianism' morphed into a 'lethal utopianism': either you take active part in it or you die. But since following this track would lead us too far away from the topic, I shall leave it here.[10]

## EPIPHENOMENA: HOW 'BUDDHIST' IS BUDDHIST VIOLENCE?

The argumentation above finally leads me to two crucial questions at the very heart of the rise of militant Buddhism topic—questions that I may well have partially answered in the previous parts as well as in this chapter, but which I have not yet fully addressed: first of all, how 'Buddhist' is Buddhist violence? And secondly, how come that militant Buddhism so far managed to escape the attention of, and hostility from, a Western audience which still seems to be all too willing to ignore Buddhist mobs even though they are indeed 'a thing,' as we have seen? Blakkarly (2015) raises a similar question, pointing out that "it is worth asking why these acts of violence have not tainted the way the West sees Buddhism?" And further: "many white atheists who are implacably opposed to religion speak approvingly of Buddhism and are increasingly willing to attend Vipassana meditation retreats. So why are we prepared to dissociate some religions from acts of violence, and not others?" If these questions sound strange, let me illustrate them with a quote from Juergensmeyer's numerous articles on religious violence. In the context of a discussion of the American public's willingness to label Islam rather than Christianity a 'terrorist religion,' he highlights an interesting 'tit-for-tat' pattern:

> The arguments that agree – or disagree – with this position often get mired in the tedious task of dredging up scriptural or historical examples to show the political or militant side of Islam (or, contrarily, of other religions like Christianity, Judaism, or Hinduism). The opponents will challenge the utility of those examples, and the debate goes on. (Juergensmeyer 2017, 14)

So far, I have done a fairly decent (I hope) job of 'dredging up scriptural or historical examples' to highlight how extremist or militant Buddhist monks in Sri Lanka, Burma, and Thailand justify and legitimize what they

---

[10] Comparing 'holy lands' and their conceptualization as sacred spaces currently forms part of a new research project I am involved in.

or their lay followers do in order to protect Buddhism, deemed to be under siege. Very probably, I will find opponents who challenge my examples, my interpretation of scripture, and especially the conclusions I arrive at—the, at times, scathing responses to the articles I wrote on this topic are indicative for that. Juergensmeyer is not finished yet, however:

> The arguments would not be necessary, however, if one did not assume that religion [here, Buddhism] is responsible for acts of public violence in the first place. (Juergensmeyer, ibid.)

Strictly speaking, this is not correct: even if one assumes that religion is not responsible for acts of public violence, it would still make sense to see what kind of scriptural or historical examples are used in order to 'bestow' totally secular aims and objectives, whatever they may be, with a thin veneer of 'holy war' legitimacy, even if only to make these acts of violence appear to be more honourable and dignified than a mere, naked grab for secular power. Nevertheless, it is important to answer the question of just how 'Buddhist' these manifest cases of Buddhist violence in Sri Lanka, Burma, and Thailand are. As often, there are basically three positions: the 'black' one maintaining that religion (Buddhism) is the problem, the 'white' one asserting that religion (Buddhism) is not the problem but rather the victim, and the 'grey' one arguing that religion is not necessarily the problem but nevertheless 'problematic' (Juergensmeyer 2017, 11, 14, 17).

Regarding the position that religion is not the problem, or at least not the main problem, this still seems to be the mainstream platform within international relations, as I already pointed out: in all three leading paradigms (Realism, Liberalism, Constructivism), religion, if acknowledged at all, "is seen as an epiphenomenon – it represents something other than what it appears to be – and as such [...] it could not be a real cause for conflict" (McTernan 2003, 23). Such scholars would be quick to point at the secular aims and objectives that became apparent in all three case studies, which can mainly be subsumed under the label 'socio-economic issues.' Some Buddhist scholars would also eagerly point at faults in the interpretation of scriptural Buddhism the extremist monks draw upon to legitimize the resort to violence—the claim that these monks misinterpret scripture either willfully or due to their ignorance is one that I have heard several times, and not only from Western scholars of Buddhism, but also from some Thai academics as well as scholar monks. Simply dismissing extremist monks like Galagoda Aththe Gnanasara Thero, Ashin Wirathu, or Phra Apichart Punnajanto as outliers with little doctrinal basis for their bigotry (to paraphrase Beech 2013), however, is not good enough when it comes to countering these preachers of hate—after all, as Beech admitted, their message resonates. In any case, as Dawson (2017, 40) notes, "[faulty] theology is not a reliable indicator of degree of religiosity or the primacy of religion in someone's motivations." Since Theravāda Buddhism revolves around orthopraxis much more than around orthodoxy, it would be quite difficult to decide what is faulty or not, unless a blatant *Parājikā* offence has been committed—and this also is quite difficult to prove.

Another line of reasoning frequently applied in order to defend religion as 'not the problem' is to dismiss the extremist monks as 'handmaidens of power' or mere 'tools' for someone else, that is secular stakeholders such as politicians or, maybe, economic interests. Here, we could adapt the quote from McTernan to state that for those defenders of religion (or Buddhism), the extremist monks 'represent someone other than themselves,' thus again dismissing the monks and their messages while also insulating the 'real' religion (Buddhism) against their nefarious non-doctrinal activities. Whether this argumentation is successful or not arguably depends on a case-by-case investigation—there certainly are monks who act on behalf of their clientele, as I discussed and explained above. But extending this argument so far that it includes all extremist monks, even monks as influential as Gnanasara Thero or Ashin Wirathu, thus reducing them to mere tools as well, fails to convince me: yes, they are part of a vast network including powerful figures from the government, the military, and the economic sector, and work in conjunction with them. But the Burmese Ma Ba Tha and 969 Movement now cooperate more or less closely with the BBS in Sri Lanka, while also organizing conferences in Thailand—which indicates that the extremist monks are establishing themselves as powerful political actors in their own right. It is also true that not all of these extremist monks are in possession of a detailed blueprint for the time when they have won and the 'other' has been defeated. Just like Al Qaeda's political ideas of a future caliphate are rather vague and nebulous, so are the plans for a future 'dharmacracy'—if such a political construct is intended at all. If we take a look at the '12 points' platform of the JHU in Sri Lanka, for example, this looks pretty much like a restoration of the traditional Buddhist polity—albeit without a king as the Dhammaraja, but a democratic government of sorts instead. In other cases however, the defence of Buddhism, and the restoration of the traditional state, seems to be religio-political aim and objective enough—a state also interpreted as a righteous one, with Buddhism enjoying the status of the pre-eminent religion but not necessarily being in the (political) driving seat. Hence, to argue that Theravāda Buddhism is not the problem certainly is indefensible—rather, it has to be acknowledged that it either is 'the problem,' or is at the very least 'problematic' since, arguably, when instrumentalized by extremist monks, it results in the outbreak of (secular) latent conflicts. Since these latent conflicts would sooner or later find expression via a different and probably secular ideology even if extremist monks would never have emerged in the first place, it is probably best to see Theravāda Buddhism as 'problematic' but not as the sole 'problem.' But I shall leave this to the readers to decide for themselves.

## CONCLUSION: THE UNSUSTAINABILITY OF 'DHARMACRACY'

After having discussed and analysed the activities of the three 'saffron armies' and their political impact, it is time now for a return to the caveat with which I opened this chapter: just as in the case of other religions and their respective preachers of hate, these very vociferous and also quite media-savvy ultra-nationalist militant monks also known as 'war monks' or 'war mongers' are not the majority, despite all their posturing and bluster. Rather, during my research for this project, I realized that an assessment made by Spiro for the situation in Burma in the 1970s still largely holds true:

> Although political monks are highly articulate, and although, having achieved influence and notoriety, they manage to convey the impression – thereby enhancing their power – that they represent vast numbers of monks, they are in fact a very small minority, even in the cities. In the villages, of course, they are almost nonexistent. (Spiro 1982, 392)

Spiro's comment still is valid more than three decades later: indeed, the monks I interviewed also opined that involving themselves in politics, or even in social work, would stand between them and the chance of reaching nibbāna. Also still valid is Jackson's comment on the persistent tensions between monks and politics:

> [An] explicit political role for Theravada Buddhist monks is ultimately unsustainable. This is because the ethical legitimacy – which monks confer on the state in politically stable periods and which also draws them into the political arena in times of crisis – is founded upon the notion of worldly renunciation and retreat from the spiritually polluting influence of involvement in lust-driven political conflicts. Theravada Buddhist theocracies are inherently unstable in the long run because of the contradiction between

monks' active political involvement and a notion of political legitimacy defined in terms of world renunciation. (Jackson 1989, 152)

In my opinion, this is even more the case for extremist or militant monks due to their justification and legitimization of violence, all the casuistry around that notwithstanding—after all, theirs is a continuous tightrope walk, with the possibility of being summarily disrobed because of having committed a 'disrobing' or *Pārājika* offence. The problem with this position, however, is that if we accept the argument of the unsustainability of what Peter Schalk (1990) called a 'dharmacracy' due to the inherent 'world conqueror versus world renouncer' tension, then we also would have to accept, at least to a large extent, the argument that extremist monks, just like other political monks, are merely a 'tool of politics,' 'stage props,' or 'handmaiden of power' in the service of others, as Seneviratne (1999, 17, 279) puts it. And further, we would have to concede that the current international relations paradigm that sees religion as an epiphenomenon only would still make sense. Personally, I am doubtful of all that. But as I just said, I shall leave that to the readers to decide for themselves.

## REFERENCES

Almond, Gabriel A., R. Scott Appleby, and Emmanuel Sivan. 2003. *Strong Religion: The Rise of Fundamentalisms Around the World*. Chicago/London: University of Chicago Press.

Bar, Gideon. 2008. Reconstructing the Past: The Creation of Jewish Sacred Space in the State of Israel, 1948–1967. *Israel Studies* 13 (3): 1–21. https://www.jstor.org/stable/30245829?seq=1#metadata_info_tab_contents.

Beech, Hannah. 2013. The Face of Buddhist Terror. *Time*, July 1. http://content.time.com/time/magazine/article/0,9171,2146000,00.html

Blakkarly, Jarni. 2015. Buddhist Extremism and the Hypocrisy of 'Religious Violence'. *ABC Religion and Politics*, May 29. http://www.abc.net.au/religion/articles/2015/05/29/4245049.htm

Braund, H.B.L. (Chairman). 1939. *Final Report of the Riot Inquiry Committee*. Rangoon: Superintendent, Government Printing and Stationery. https://ia801609.us.archive.org/22/items/in.ernet.dli.2015.206317/2015.206317.Final-Report.pdf

Buadaeng, Kwanchewan. 2017. A Karen Charismatic Monk and Connectivity Across the Thai-Myanmar Borderland. In *Charismatic Monks of Lanna*, ed. Paul T. Cohen, 149–170. Copenhagen: NIAS Press.

Chin, Ko-Lin. 2009. *The Golden Triangle. Inside Southeast Asia's Drug Trade*. Ithaca/London: Cornell University Press.

Cohen, Paul T. 2017. Charismatic Monks of Lanna Buddhism. In *Charismatic Monks of Lanna*, ed. Paul T. Cohen, 1–25. Copenhagen: NIAS Press.

Dawson, Lorne L. 2017. Discounting Religion in the Explanation of Homegrown Terrorism: A Critique. In *The Cambridge Companion to Religion and Terrorism*, ed. James R. Lewis, 32–45. New York: Cambridge University Press.

Frankopan, Peter. 2016. *The Silk Roads: A New History of the World*. Paperback ed. London et al.: Bloomsbury.

Freeman, Joe. 2017. The 'Good Monk' Myth. *The Atlantic*, September 29. https://www.theatlantic.com/international/archive/2017/09/saffron-revolution-good-monk-myth/541116/

Friedman, Jonathan. 1994. *Cultural Identity and Global Process*. London et al.: Sage Publications.

Gravers, Mikael. 2015. Anti-Muslim Buddhist Nationalism in Burma and Sri Lanka: Religious Violence and Globalized Imaginaries of Endangered Identities. *Contemporary Buddhism: An Interdisciplinary Journal* 16 (1): 1–27. https://www.tandfonline.com/doi/full/10.1080/14639947.2015.1008090.

Harris, Ian. 2013. *Buddhism in a Dark Age. Cambodian Monks Under Pol Pot*. Chiang Mai: Silkworm Books.

Holt, John C. 2016. Introduction. In *Buddhist Extremists and Muslim Minorities: Religious Conflict in Contemporary Sri Lanka*, ed. John C. Holt, e-book version ed., 1–17. New York City: Oxford University Press.

Huntington, Samuel P. 1993. The Clash of Civilizations? *Foreign Affairs* 72 (3 Summer): 22–49.

———. 1996. *The Clash of Civilizations and the Remaking of World Order*. New York: Simon & Schuster.

Jackson, Peter A. 1989. *Buddhism, Legitimation and Conflict: The Political Functions of Urban Thai Buddhism (Social Issues in Southeast Asia)*. Singapore: ISEAS.

Jerryson, Michael K. 2018. Buddhism, War, and Violence. In *Oxford Handbook of Buddhist Ethics*, ed. Daniel Cozort and James M. Shields, 453–478. Oxford: Oxford University Press.

Juergensmeyer, Mark. 2003. *Terror in the Mind of God. The Global Rise of Religious Violence*. 3rd ed. Berkeley/Los Angeles/London: University of California Press.

———. 2008. *Global Rebellion. Religious Challenges to the Secular State, from Christian Militias to al Qaeda*. Berkeley: University of California Press.

———. 2017. Does Religion Cause Terrorism? In *The Cambridge Companion to Religion and Terrorism*, ed. James R. Lewis, 11–22. New York: Cambridge University Press.

Kepel, Gilles. 1994. *The Revenge of God. The Resurgence of Islam, Christianity and Judaism in the Modern World*. Cambridge: Polity Press.

Keyes, Charles F. 1999. Political Crisis and Militant Buddhism in Contemporary Thailand (Revised edition, Original Version Published in *Religion and*

*Legitimation of Power in Thailand, Burma and Laos*, ed. Bardwell Smith, 147–164. Chambersburg: Anima Books 1978). http://www.academia. edu/8987102/Political_Crisis_and_Militant_Buddhism_in_Contemporary_ Thailand_rev_1999

Keyes, Charles. 2016. Theravada Buddhism and Buddhist Nationalism: Sri Lanka, Myanmar, Cambodia, and Thailand. *The Review of Faith & International Affairs* 14 (4): 41–52.

Kyaw Yin Hlaing. 2008. Challenging the Authoritarian State: Buddhist Monks and Peaceful Protests in Burma. *Fletcher Forum of World Affairs* 32 (1 Winter): 125–144. http://heinonline.org/HOL/Page?handle=hein.journals/forwa32& div=12&g_sent=1&casa_token=&collection=journals#.

Lehr, Peter. 2017. Militant Buddhism Is on the March in Southeast Asia – Where Did It Come From? *The Conversation*, November 7. https://theconversation. com/militant-buddhism-is-on-the-march-in-south-east-asia-where-did-it- come-from-86632

McTernan, Oliver. 2003. *Violence in God's Name: Religion in an Age of Conflict.* Maryknoll/London: Orbis Books.

Myaing Nan Shwe. 1999. *Myaing Gye: Ngu Sayadaw. A Jahan who Shines the Light of Dhamma.* Trans. Shin Khay Meinda. Myaing Gyi Ngu Special Region, Karen State (DKBA): Mann Ba Nyunt Pe. http://www.burmalibrary.org/docs11/U_ Thuzana%27s_Book-red.pdf

Rand, Nelson. 2009. *Conflict. Journeys Through War and Terror in Southeast Asia.* Bangkok: Maverick House.

Satha-Anand, Suwanna. 2014. The Question of Violence in Thai Buddhism. In *Buddhism and Violence: Militarism and Buddhism in Modern Asia*, ed. Vladimir Tikhonov and Torkel Brekke, paperback ed., 175–193. New York/London: Routledge.

Schalk, Peter. 1990. Articles 9 and 18 of the Constitution as Obstacles to Peace. *Lanka* 5 (December): 280–292.

Selengut, Charles. 2003. *Sacred Fury. Understanding Religious Violence.* Walnut Creek et al.: Altamira Press.

Seneviratne, H.L. 1999. *The Work of Kings. The New Buddhism in Sri Lanka.* Chicago/London: University of Chicago Press.

Sharp, Bruce. 2005. Counting Hell: The Death Toll of the Khmer Rouge in Cambodia. *Cambodia: Beauty and Darkness.* http://www.mekong.net/cam- bodia/deaths.htm

Sherwood, Harriet. 2018. Religion: Why Faith Is Becoming More and More Popular. *The Guardian*, August 27. https://www.theguardian.com/ news/2018/aug/27/religion-why-is-faith-growing-and-what-happens- next?CMP=Share_iOSApp_Other

Spiro, Melford E. 1982. *Buddhism and Society. A Great Tradition and Its Burmese Vicissitudes.* 2nd exp. ed. Berkeley/Los Angeles/London: University of California Press.

Thant Myint-U. 2007. *The River of Lost Footsteps. A Personal History of Burma*. London: Faber & Faber.

Vijayavardhana, D.C. 1953. *Dharma-Vijaya (Triumph of Righteousness) or The Revolt in the Temple*. Colombo: Sinha Publications.

# CHAPTER 9

# Outlook: How to Deal with War Monks?

As the case studies demonstrated, militant, extremist, and ultra-nationalist Buddhist violence is not a new phenomenon, but rather an overlooked and under-reported one that was largely ignored by international media for quite a while. In the era of modern media and modern social media such as global television, Twitter, Facebook, or YouTube, this is, however, no longer possible: militant Buddhist violence and its current Islamophobia is out there for everybody to see. In the case of anti-Muslim violence in Burma, this already led to a backlash: Islamist groups such as al Qaeda, Islamic State of Iraq and Syria (ISIS), the Taliban in Pakistan, and the Indonesian Jemaah Islamiyyah (JI) issued statements threatening to attack Burmese Buddhists in retaliation for what they see as a 'state-sponsored murder' of Muslims. The torching of Buddhist temples in Bangladesh (October 2012) and the bomb explosions in one of the holiest sites of Buddhism, the Bodh Gaya temple complex in Bihar (July 2013), indicate that a tit-for-tat cycle of violence may be in the offing. Be that as it may, for the time being it can be expected that the sound of war drums gets even louder: as Ashin Wirathu said, this is not the time for calm meditation.

There is much more to be said about the rise of militant Theravāda Buddhism, its impact on the affected region of South and Southeast Asia, how the militant monks relate to the moderate and unpolitical monks, how the militant form networks across national border, and how this militancy should be framed. As discussed, it can be explained in ethno-religious

P. Lehr, *Militant Buddhism*,
https://doi.org/10.1007/978-3-030-03517-4_9

or socio-cultural/socio-economic terms, and it can thus be seen, follow-ing Almond et al. (2003, 93, 110), as a 'syncretistic fundamentalism' as opposed to a 'pure' one. Hence, we can indeed ask the question on how Buddhist this Buddhist violence actually is. If we were so inclined, we could even explain it away as an epiphenomenon that does not really mat-ter—something that "represents something other than what it appears to be – and as such, they maintain, it could not be a real cause for conflict" (McTernan 2003, 23). But if we adopt the perspective of the militant monks active in Sri Lanka, in Burma, and, to a lesser extent, in Thailand, it emerges that this conflict is first of all about religion, and the defence of the Dhamma—not about the control of resources or any worldly goods. For these monks, their actions constitute a defensive 'holy war' or 'Dhamma Yudha' in response to a perceived aggressive jihad against Buddhism—an offensive jihad that has been waged for centuries, with the destruction of the famous Buddhist library in Nalanda/Bihar at the end of the twelfth century, and the destruction of the famous Bamiyan Buddhas in March 2001 as just two of the most notorious 'milestones.' This some-what simplistic and biased reading of history, reminiscent of Huntington's 'clash of civilizations,' reinforces the militant monks' belief that now is not the time for peaceful meditation but for firm action—in Burma, in Sri Lanka, and, again to a lesser extent, in Thailand. The Buddha's warning that violence begets violence seems to have fallen on deaf ears for the time being, and the war drums are getting louder still. So, how should we deal with these 'war monks'? Are there any feasible ways to silence them?

## LAW: BRINGING THEM TO JUSTICE

As we saw in the case of Thailand, one way would be to simply force them to disrobe and bring them to justice for incitement of hate or whatever the relevant paragraph of the country's criminal code would be. This however requires the cooperation of the Sangha hierarchy and the state in question, which in the cases of Burma and Sri Lanka is difficult to obtain: a few notable examples to the contrary notwithstanding (even Ashin Wirathu spent 7 years in jail for spreading anti-Muslim hatred before he was released under an amnesty, see Hodal 2013), militant monks are not normally cen-sored or arrested but tolerated. After all, the monks' views are often shared by the mainly Buddhist politicians and the bulk of their equally Buddhist voters. Even if a government would be prepared to crack down on extrem-ist monks, in a majority Buddhist environment, doing so is a risky strategy for the incumbent government since this could lose them the next elections. As a result, even well-intended politicians usually remain studiously silent on the topic. Burma's Aung San Suu Kyi, until recently one of the West's most celebrated heroes, is a telling case in point. In sum, in both Burma and Sri Lanka, the political will to crack down on extremist monks is very weak, if existent at all. Again, the situation in Thailand is different since the well-entrenched military government does not tolerate any meddling in political affairs by monks, whatever they stand for—especially not if these monks have a large following that could be turned into a political pressure group.

## MEDIA: DENYING THEM THE 'OXYGEN OF PUBLICITY'

Another way to deal with extremist monks and their sermons of hate would be to deny them what former British Prime Minister Margret Thatcher called 'the oxygen of publicity'—for example, by shutting down their Facebook or Twitter accounts. In the case of Burma's war monks, Facebook actually tried to silence Ashin Wirathu as a 'hate figure' and Ma Ba Tha as a 'hate organization.' But, as Lee Short points out, by trying to do so, "Facebook runs the risk of being seen as a foreign tool for silencing 'patriotic' voices and exacerbating an already existing nationalist persecution complex" (Short 2018). And further, "As decades of censorship and repression in Myanmar showed, [...] silencing people often gives them martyr status" (ibid.). This, of course, also raises the broader question of whether we should entrust big companies like Facebook, Twitter, Google, or others the power to decide what can and what cannot be said and published. In any case, experience shows that shutting down their accounts and their voices for good is very difficult, if not impossible. For example, when on 27 August 2018, Facebook shut down the account of Burmese Senior General Min Aung Hlaing after the UNHCR's Independent International Fact-Finding Mission on Myanmar had explicitly named him as one of the "alleged perpetrators of serious human rights violations and crimes under international law" (UNHCR 2018, 17, also see Long 2018), the Senior General was back online a mere 48 hours later, this time hosted by the Russian Facebook equivalent VKontakte (VK) (Moe Myint 2018). This shows how difficult it is in a world dominated by social media to drown out the noise of the war drums, which still keeps getting louder.

In this context, in the previous chapter (and in several others before), I have made the point that extremist monks are not just some misfits that can easily be ignored. This begs the question that whether simply ignoring them is actually an option that we could choose. After all, this would also be a potential way to deny them the oxygen of publicity. Sanitsuda Ekachai raised the same question when she wondered how to respond to Phra Apichart Punnajanto's message of hate, but answered it in the negative:

> Many believe we should not give him the attention he seeks. It is also just one monk's view. Furthermore, more discussions will most likely trigger resentment and anger from Muslims, many of whom – like the monk – operate with ethnic and racial chauvinism, not their prophet's peaceful teachings. So why let ourselves be this monk's tool to intensify religious division? Just ignore him and let his ugly proposal die a natural death in social media. I disagree. Phra Apichart's mosque-burning idea may be just his personal one. But fear and prejudice against Islam and Muslims in the Buddhist clergy are certainly not. (Ekachai 2015)

Basically, what she means is that such preachers of hate should be challenged, preferably on the same social media platforms they use to disseminate their vitriolic sermons. This is not only a recommendation for members of the general public, but most importantly a clarion call for fellow monks, especially the senior clergy. As Ekachai (ibid.) points out, "silence can only be interpreted as tacit support." I agree with her position: it would be really helpful if the Sangha hierarchy in all three countries would condemn such messages of hate in no uncertain terms instead of keeping their silence. And not only that, extremist monks should swiftly be disrobed and expelled. But, as I already stated, in most cases, this is more or less wishful thinking since, indeed, there seems to be tacit support for such monks, and tacit approval of their messages—not only within the Sangha hierarchy but also within the state as such. As regards the general public, we know all too well that in the age of 'fake news' and troll farms, this is akin to 'mission impossible.'

First of all, it is well-nigh impossible to penetrate the walls of the 'echo chambers' in which the extremist monks and their equally extremist followers can be found; secondly, challenging these extremists may well come with personal danger, as the case of the outspoken Sinhalese moderate monk Watareka Vijitha Thera demonstrates: was "kidnapped, disrobed and assaulted [after having] been threatened and attacked on previous occasions after having spoken against the BBS for spreading hate and inciting communal disharmony" (Tegal 2014; also see BBC 2014). As regards the disapproval of the silent majority of the monks of all three Sanghas, this does not really matter—history shows that silent majorities hardly ever matter. In the case of the silent majority of monks, this silence is rather ambiguous in any case since it may just mean that these silent monks are detached from politics in general, be they progressive or regressive, left or ultra-right. To put it rather bluntly, the majority of monks' silence does not amount to a clear condemnation of the ultra-nationalist positions of the extremist monks.

## REFORMATION: BACK TO CHARISMATIC DEVOTION

Originally, this gloomy outlook was exactly how I intended to conclude this book. However, there is more to be said here on how to deal with 'war monks' from the Theravāda Buddhist side of view—even though it sounds a bit preposterous for a political scientist and lay Buddhist to offer recommendations for, shall we say, 'demilitarizing' Theravāda Buddhism. Having said that, I perfectly agree with Seneviratne who, in 1999, asked quite a pertinent question after having explained why the Buddhist Sangha had been manifestly unable to meaningfully contribute to the development of a civil society, and why it rather had "plunged society in darkness." Seneviratne's question is as follows:

[Given] Buddhism's universalism, which gives it an unprecedented initial push to enable the building of a civil society, is it possible to imagine a Buddhist state in which the Sangha reverts to the profile it enjoyed in the proto-Buddhist Asokan state? (Seneviratne 1999, 21–22)

He juxtaposes the Sangha of the proto-Buddhist state that he sees as one that is "free, propertyless, and charismatic" with that of the "established, landed, and routinized Sangha" that developed from the onset of the second moment in Buddhist history onwards:

The first, while in fact highly conscious of group belongingness especially arising out of charismatic devotion to the founder, professes openness and tolerance and stands for ideals which are always articulated in universalist terms. The second, ensconced in privilege and bounty and committed to their perpetuation, is allied in mutual interest with a dominant linguistic, regional, ethnic, or other parochial group. (Seneviratne 1999, 23–24)

Now, from my own experience with Thai ascetic monks, I cannot help but point out that Seneviratne seems, on this occasion, to treat the Sangha as a monolithic block—at least, 'my' monks most certainly neither enjoyed nor craved anything connected to "privilege and bounty." And they are not just the exception to the rule. Nevertheless, Seneviratne is not wrong either. He could have asked yet another question that might have helped answering the first one: what could monastic Theravāda Buddhism learn from other main strands of Buddhism that did not (yet) develop a similar penchant for parochial, ethno-national violence framed in Buddhist terms? And, further, is it possible to delink monastic Theravāda Buddhism from being embraced by, and reciprocally embracing, the state? Seneviratne (1999, 22) himself discusses the Indian Buddhist renaissance inaugurated by Bhimrao Ramji Ambedkar in search for an answer, pointing out that "neither in the Asokan nor the Ambedkarist versions is Buddhism an 'establishment'." However, Ambedkar's revived Buddhism came with a very distinctive purpose: emancipating the lowest castes of India, formerly known as 'untouchables' and then as 'Dalits' by offering them an escape from the Hindu caste system to a casteless (at least notionally) Buddhism. In a sense, it can thus be argued that Ambedkar's laudable effort has at least some connotations of 'liberation theology,' to borrow this term from Latin American Catholicism for a moment. It is thus unlikely that Ambedkar's Buddhism would have even a fleeting chance to be at least looked into—as far as this is possible at all in an institutionalized, post-charismatic (to use Max Weber's categorization) Sangha in Sri Lanka, Burma, or Thailand. Rather, we have to look for local attempts to break free from the state and its suffocating embrace on the one hand, and from involvement in power politics and identity politics on the other.

Whether any of these reform movement will ever gain traction is difficult to predict. However, if we look at the experiences with earlier reform movements situated outside of the mainstream Sangha and its various branches, then it is difficult to remain optimistic. We are probably better advised not to put our hopes too high. After all, 'Theravāda' means the 'teachings of the elders'—a term that already comes with distinctive conservative undertones, even though what goes today as Theravāda more or less are reconstructions that do not go further back in time than the late nineteenth century, as we have seen. Even so, Carrithers (2007, 133) is quite right to argue that Theravāda "would best be thought of as that school which, as Buddhism grew and expanded, continually inclined toward the conservative choice, the preservation of an archaic view of

Doctrine and of the Order of monks, the Sangha." If we adopt this viewpoint, and I certainly do, then we have to concede that a fundamental reform of Theravāda Buddhism, as suggested above, is not possible—if we take the monastic structure away from it, then Theravāda would simply stop being Theravāda. The only reformation that I deem possible is the development of a stricter hierarchy similar, for example, to that of the Catholic Church. In enforcing not only orthopraxy but also orthodoxy on the monkhood, dissident monks could be more effectively dealt with. But even that is beset with many problems—starting with the observation that such reforms have been attempted time and again, never worked out as hoped, and rather sooner than later simply dissipated. And most of the time, it was actually the state behind such reforms, and not the Sangha—an issue that throws us back to the argument I made earlier: currently, in Burma and Sri Lanka, there is a manifest lack of political will to crack down on extremist monks. Furthermore, and quite ironically, as we can see in the case of the current turmoil in the strictly hierarchical Catholic Church, that is, the ongoing revolts against Pope Francis, dissident voices can be stifled for a while but never completely shut down. It seems to be in the human nature that some adopt more conservative, even extremist, positions than others. Hence, developing a stricter hierarchy within the three Sanghas would certainly not be a panacea but more realistically create a number of different problems.

## VERDICT: NOT THE TIME FOR QUIET MEDITATION

As I see it, and this is indeed a rather pessimistic view, we reached several dead ends here: firstly, as it stands, neither the Sangha hierarchy nor the state in Sri Lanka, Burma, and (to a lesser degree) Thailand is interested in cracking down hard on extremist monks: maybe on progressive monks on the political left, but certainly not on the extremist monks of the ultra-right. Secondly, denying these monks the oxygen of publicity is difficult, to say the least: shutting down websites and profiles is only a very temporary solution, and sometimes it seems that it takes these monks and the organizations they belong to only a couple of hours to be back in business. Thirdly, challenging the views of these monks and their followers comes with severe personal risks, of which being mercilessly trolled is probably the most harmless. Fourthly, the reform of the Sangha is certainly a fascinating topic for conferences and academic publications, but when it comes to tangible action, then 'don't hold your breath,' as the saying goes. And fifthly and

LEHR

finally, meekly repeating again and again that these monks are a minority only (as I admittedly did), or denying their existence in the first place, does not help either: a minority they may well be—but they are a vociferous one, whose message of hate obviously gains traction. Thus, for the time being, I fear that we are stuck with these Buddhist variants of the preachers of hate we know from other religions, just as we are stuck with Islamist or Fundamentalist-Christian clerics peddling messages of hate. In my opinion, it is time for the secularists to accept that the age of secularism is over, and that this century will see a return of religion as a factor that cannot possibly be ignored—neither in domestic politics nor in international relations. This also implies that it is time to revisit Max Weber's category of *Wertrationalität* or 'value rationality' as opposed to *Zweckrationalität* or 'purposive rational- ity' (Weber 1967): if actors are mainly driven by (religious) absolute values and not by (secular) negotiable aims and objectives, then we really need a paradigm shift in international relations theory, as Shah and Philpott (2011, 51) suggested, in order to accommodate (at least as regards international relations theory) the changing rationales that would then dominate inter- national-level politics. And since, at least in my opinion, organized and politicized religions have seldom been a force for good over the millennia, maybe it is also time to take yet another critical look at Huntington's 'clash of civilisations' hypothesis (Huntington 1993, 1996)—maybe this much criticized concept simply was ahead of its time when it was published, and maybe its time has now come. Be that as it may, and as I already stated, for the time being, the sound of war drums (*bheri-ghosa*) is getting ever louder—not only in Theravāda Buddhism, but in other religions as well.

## REFERENCES

Almond, Gabriel A., R. Scott Appleby, and Emmanuel Sivan. 2003. *Strong Religion: The Rise of Fundamentalisms Around the World*. Chicago/London: University of Chicago Press.

BBC. 2014. Sri Lanka Moderate Monk Critical of anti-Muslim Violence Beaten. *BBC News Asia*, June 19. http://www.bbc.co.uk/news/world-asia-27918343

Carrithers, Michael B. 2007. They Will Be Lords Upon the Island: Buddhism in Sri Lanka. In *The World of Buddhism: Buddhist Monks and Nuns in Society and Culture*, ed. Heinz Bechert and Richard F. Gombrich, 133–146. Reprint, London: Thames & Hudson.

Ekachai, Sanitsuda. 2015. Nip Unholy Hate Speech in the Bud. *Bangkok Post*, November 4. https://www.bangkokpost.com/opinion/opinion/753808/nip-unholy-hate-speech-in-the-bud

Hodal, Kate. 2013. Buddhist Monk Uses Racism and Rumours to Spread Hatred in Burma. *The Guardian,* April 18. https://www.theguardian.com/world/2013/apr/18/buddhist-monk-spreads-hatred-burma

Huntington, Samuel P. 1993. The Clash of Civilizations? *Foreign Affairs* 72(3): 22–49.

———. 1996. *The Clash of Civilizations and the Remaking of World Order.* New York: Simon & Schuster.

Long, Kayleigh. 2018. Mea Culpa? Facebook Covers Its Tracks in Myanmar. *Asia Times,* August 27. http://www.atimes.com/article/mea-culpa-facebook-covers-its-tracks-in-myanmar//

McTernan, Oliver. 2003. *Violence in God's Name: Religion in an Age of Conflict.* Maryknoll/London: Orbis Books.

Moe Kyint. 2018. Military Chief Wastes No Time Finding New Home on Social Media. *The Irrawaddy,* August 29. https://www.irrawaddy.com/news/military-chief-wastes-no-time-finding-new-home-social-media.html

Seneviratne, H.L. 1999. *The Work of Kings. The New Buddhism in Sri Lanka.* Chicago/London: University of Chicago Press.

Shah, Timothy S., and Daniel Philpott. 2011. The Fall and Rise of Religion in International Relations. In *Religion and International Relations Theory,* ed. Jack Snyder, 24–59. New York/Chichester: Columbia University Press.

Short, Lee. 2018. Facebook Tries to Silence Myanmar's Hateful Monks. *Asia Times,* July 5. http://www.atimes.com/article/facebook-tries-to-silence-myanmars-hateful-monks/

Tegal, Megara. 2014. The Burning Fires of Aluthgama. *The Sunday Leader,* June 22. http://www.thesundayleader.lk/2014/06/22/the-burning-fires-of-aluthgama/

UNHCR. 2018. Report of the Independent International Fact-Finding Mission on Myanmar (Advance Unedited Version). United Nations Human Rights Council, August 24. https://www.ohchr.org/Documents/HRBodies/HRCouncil/FFM-Myanmar/A_HRC_39_64.pdf

Weber, Max. 1967. *The Religion of India: The Sociology of Hinduism and Buddhism.* Trans. and Ed. Hans H. Gerth and Don Martindale. New York/London: The Free Press/Collier-Macmillan.

# BIBLIOGRAPHY

Abeysekara, Ananda. 2001. The Saffron Army, Violence, Terror(ism): Buddhism, Identity, and Difference in Sri Lanka. *Numen* 48 (1): 1–46.

ABMA. 2018. About the ABMA. *All Burma Monks' Alliance.* http://allburma-monksalliance.org

Acharya, Amitav, and Barry Buzan. 2010. Conclusion: On the Possibility of a Non-Western International Relations Theory. In *Non-Western International Relations Theory. Perspectives on and Beyond Asia*, ed. Amitav Acharya and Barry Buzan, 221–238. London/New York: Routledge.

Adas, Michael. 1974. *The Burma Delta: Economic Development and Social Change on an Asian Rice Frontier, 1852–1941* (e-book). Madison: University of Wisconsin Press.

Aeusrivongse, Nidhi. 2004. Understanding the Situation in the South as a 'Millenarian Revolt'. *Kyoto Review of Southeast Asia.* https://kyotoreview.org/issue-6/understanding-the-situation-in-the-south-as-a-millenarian-revolt/

AFP. 2018. Myanmar lures Bangladesh Buddhists to Take over Rohingya Land: Officials. *Agence France Press*, April 2. https://www.bangkokpost.com/news/world/1439458/

Ahmed, Ibtisam. 2017. The Historical Roots of the Rohingya Conflict. *IAPS Dialogue*, October 4. https://iapsdialogue.org/2017/10/04/the-historical-roots-of-the-rohingya-crisis/

AJ+. 2014. *Myanmar's Anti-Muslim Monks* (YouTube video). November 12. https://www.youtube.com/watch?v=GtAl9zJ3t-M

Allen, Charles. 2013. *Ashoka: The Search for India's Lost Emperor.* Paperback ed. London: Abacus.

© The Author(s) 2019
P. Lehr, *Militant Buddhism*,
https://doi.org/10.1007/978-3-030-03517-4

Almond, Gabriel A., R. Scott Appleby, and Emmanuel Sivan. 2003. *Strong Religion: The Rise of Fundamentalisms Around the World*. Chicago/London: University of Chicago Press.

Anālayo, Bhikkhu. 2007. The Arahant Ideal in Early Buddhism – The Case of Bakkula. *Indian International Journal of Buddhist Studies* 8: 1–21.

———. 2010. Once Again on Bakkula. *Indian International Journal of Buddhist Studies* 11: 1–28.

Anand, Dibyesh. 2011. *Hindu Nationalism in India and the Politics of Fear*. New York/Basingstoke: Palgrave Macmillan.

Ariff, Yusuf. 2017. Ven. Akmeemana Dayarathana Thero Arrested. *Adaderana*, October 2. http://www.adaderana.lk/news/43336/ven-akmeemana-dayarathana-thero-arrested

Ashin Yevata. 2010. *Revolution of the Monks*. Great Britain: Amazon

Augustine of Hippo (St Augustine). Undated. Contra Faustum Manichæum, Book 22. 69–76. *Early Church Texts*. http://www.earlychurchtexts.com/public/augustine_war_contra_faustum.htm

Aung Kyaw Min. 2017. Ma Ba Tha to Continue Under New Name. *Myanmar Times*, May 29. https://www.mmtimes.com/national-news/yangon/26171-ma-ba-tha-to-continue-under-new-name.html

Aung Zaw. 2013. The Power Behind the Robe. *The Irrawaddy*, September 20 (first published in October 2007 in the print version of *The Irrawaddy*). https://www.irrawaddy.com/from-the-archive/power-behind-robe.html

Aung-Thwin, Maitrii. 2011a. *The Return of the Galon King: History, Law, and Rebellion in Colonial Burma*. Singapore: NUS Press.

———. 2011b. The Limping Monk and the Deaf King: Peasant Politics, Subaltern Agency, and the Postcolonial Predicament in Colonial Burma. In *New Perspectives on the History and Historiography of Southeast Asia: Continuing Explorations*, ed. Michael A. Aung-Thwin and Kenneth R. Hall, 201–228. London/New York: Routledge.

Baker, Chris, and Pasuk Phongpaichit. 2005. *A History of Thailand*. Cambridge et al.: Cambridge University Press.

Bandara, Veedeya. 2012. On National Consciousness (Jathika Chinthanaya) and Democracy. *Colombo Telegraph*, June 15. https://www.colombotelegraph.com/index.php/on-national-consciousness-jathika-chinthanaya-and-democracy/

Bar, Gideon. 2008. Reconstructing the Past: The Creation of Jewish Sacred Space in the State of Israel, 1948–1967. *Israel Studies* 13 (3): 1–21. https://www.jstor.org/stable/30245829?seq=1#metadata_info_tab_contents

Barnett, Michael. 2011. Another Great Awakening? International Relations Theory and Religion. In *Religion and International Relations Theory*, ed. Jack Snyder, 91–114. New York/Chichester: Columbia University Press.

Bartholomeusz, Tessa. 1999. First Among Equals: Buddhism and the Sri Lankan State. In *Buddhism and Politics in Twentieth-Century Asia*, ed. Ian Harris, 173–193. London: Continuum.

———. 2002. *Defense of Dharma: Just-War Ideology in Buddhist Sri Lanka*. London/New York: Routledge.

Bartholomeusz, Tessa J., and Chandra de Silva, eds. 1993. *Buddhist Fundamentalism and Minority Identities in Sri Lanka*. Albany: State University of New York Press.

BBC. 2007. Q&A: Protests in Burma. *BBC News Asia-Pacific*, October 2. http://news.bbc.co.uk/1/hi/world/asia-pacific/7010202.stm

———. 2014a. Sri Lanka Muslims Killed in Aluthgama Clashes with Buddhists. *BBC News Asia*, June 16. http://www.bbc.co.uk/news/world-asia-27864716

———. 2014b. Sri Lanka Moderate Monk Critical of Anti-Muslim Violence Beaten. *BBC News Asia*, June 19. http://www.bbc.co.uk/news/world-asia-27918343

———. 2014c. Sri Lanka Charges Moderate Monk Critical of Anti-Muslim Violence. *BBC News Asia*, June 25. http://www.bbc.co.uk/news/world-asia-28023701

———. 2015. Bangladesh Blogger Niloy Neel Hacked to Death in Dhaka. *BBC News Asia*, August 7. http://www.bbc.co.uk/news/world-asia-33819032

———. 2018. Sri Lanka Hardline Monk Gnansara Jailed for Intimidation. *BBC News Asia*, June 14. https://www.bbc.co.uk/news/world-asia-44479610

Bealey, Frank. 1999. *The Blackwell Dictionary of Political Science*. Oxford: Blackwell.

Bechert, Heinz. 1995. *When Did the Buddha Live? The Controversy on the Dating of the Historical Buddha*. Delhi: Sri Satguru Publications.

———. 2007. 'To Be a Burmese Is to Be a Buddhist': Buddhism in Burma. In *The World of Buddhism: Buddhist Monks and Nuns in Society and Culture*, ed. Heinz Bechert and Richard F. Gombrich, 147–158. Reprint, London: Thames & Hudson.

Bechert, Heinz, and Richard F. Gombrich, eds. 2007. *The World of Buddhism: Buddhist Monks and Nuns in Society and Culture*. Reprint, London: Thames & Hudson.

———. 2008. *Der Buddhismus. Geschichte und Gegenwart*. 3rd ed. München: Verlag C. H. Beck.

Beech, Hannah. 2013. The Face of Buddhist Terror. *Time*, July 1. http://content.time.com/time/magazine/article/0,9171,2146000,00.html

Berger, Peter L. 1968. A Bleak Outlook Is Seen for Religion. *New York Times*, February 25.

———. 1999a. The Desecularization of the World: An Overview. In *The Desecularization of the World: Resurgent Religion and World Politics*, ed. Peter Berger, 1–18. Washington, DC: Eerdmans/Ethics and Public Policy Center.

————., ed. 1999b. *The Desecularization of the World: Resurgent Religion and World Politics*. Washington, DC: Eerdmans/Ethics and Public Policy Center.

Bigandet, Paul A. 1912. *The Life or Legend of Gaudama, the Buddha of the Burmese*. 2 vols. London: Trübner.

Bischoff, Roger. 1995. Buddhism in Myanmar: A Short History. *Buddhanet's Book Library*. Kandy: Buddhist Publication Society. http://www.buddhanet.net/pdf_file/bud-myanmar.pdf

Biver, Emilie. 2014. *Religious Nationalism: Myanmar and the Role of Buddhism in Anti-Muslim Narratives. An Analysis of Myanmar's Ethnic Conflicts Through the Lens of Buddhist Nationalism*. Unpublished MSc Thesis, Lund University.

Blackton, Charles S. 1970. The Action Phase of the 1915 Riots (The 1915 Riots in Ceylon: A Symposium). *Journal of Asian Studies* 29 (2): 235–254.

Blakkarly, Jarni. 2015. Buddhist Extremism and the Hypocrisy of 'Religious Violence'. *ABC Religion and Politics*, May 29. http://www.abc.net.au/religion/articles/2015/05/29/4245049.htm

Bob, Yonah Jeremy. 2016. Life Sentence for Jerusalem Pride Parade Stabber Who Killed Teen Girl. *Jerusalem Post*, June 26. http://www.jpost.com/Israel-News/Life-sentence-for-Jerusalem-pride-parade-stabber-who-killed-teen-girl-457749

Bodhi Bhikkhu. 2000. *The Connected Discourses of the Buddha. A Translation of the Samyutta Nikāya*. Somerville: Wisdom Publications.

Brahmavamso, Ajahn. 1996. Vinaya: The Four Disrobing Offences. *Newsletter*, April–June. Perth: The Buddhist Society of Western Australia. http://www.budsas.org/ebud/ebsut019.htm

Braun, Erik. 2013. *The Birth of Insight: Meditation, Modern Buddhism, and the Burmese Monk Ledi Sayadaw*. Chicago: Chicago University Press.

Braund, H.B.L. (Chairman). 1939. *Final Report of the Riot Inquiry Committee*. Rangoon: Superintendent, Government Printing and Stationery. https://ia801609.us.archive.org/22/items/in.ernet.dli.2015.206317/2015.206317.Final-Report.pdf

Buadaeng, Kwanchewan. 2017. A Karen Charismatic Monk and Connectivity Across the Thai-Myanmar Borderland. In *Charismatic Monks of Lanna*, ed. Paul T. Cohen, 149–170. Copenhagen: NIAS Press.

Bucknell, Roderick, and Chris Kang. 2013. *The Meditative Way: Readings in the Theory and Practice of Buddhist Meditations*. New York/London: Routledge.

Buddha Dharma Education Association/Buddhanet. 2008. Unit Six: The Four Immeasurables. *Buddhist Studies, Secondary Level*. http://www.buddhanet.net/e-learning/buddhism/bs-s15.htm

Buddhanet. 2008. Ordination Procedure in the Theravada Tradition. *Buddhist Studies: Monastic Community*. https://www.buddhanet.net/e-learning/buddhistworld/ordination1.htm

Buddharakkhita Acharya, trans. 1996a. Buddhavagga: The Buddha (Dhammapada 179–196). *Dhammapada: The Buddha's Path of Wisdom*. Access to Insight: Readings in Theravāda Buddhism. http://www.accesstoinsight.org/tipitaka/kn/dhp/dhp.14.budd.html

Buddharakkhita, Acharya. 1996b. Dandavagga: Violence. *Dhammapada: The Buddha's Path of Wisdom*. Access to Insight: Readings in Theravāda Buddhism. http://www.accesstoinsight.org/tipitaka/kn/dhp/dhp.10.budd.html

Bullit, John. 2005. The Five Precepts: *pañca-sila*. Access to Insight: Readings in Theravāda Buddhism. http://www.accesstoinsight.org/ptf/dhamma/sila/pancasila.html

Burmanet News. 2008. Statement by the All Burma Monks' Association. *Burmanet News*, June 18. http://www.buddhistchannel.tv/index.php?id=51,6662,0,0,1,0#.Wr-7pK3MxE4

Carrithers, Michael B. 2007. They Will Be Lords Upon the Island: Buddhism in Sri Lanka. In *The World of Buddhism: Buddhist Monks and Nuns in Society and Culture*, ed. Heinz Bechert and Richard F. Gombrich, 133–146. Reprint, London: Thames & Hudson.

———. 2008. 'Sie werden die Herren der Insel sein': Buddhismus in Sri Lanka. In *Der Buddhismus. Geschichte und Gegenwart*, ed. Heinz Bechert and Richard F. Gombrich, 3rd ed., 140–168. München: Verlag C. H. Beck.

Catholic Herald. 2016. Fr Hamel Was Martyred 'In Odium Fidei', Says Archbishop Fischer. *Catholic Herald*, July 27. http://www.catholicherald.co.uk/news/2016/07/27/fr-hamel-was-martyred-in-odium-fidei-says-archbishop-fisher/

Chakrabongse, H.R.H. Prince Chula. 1960. *Lords of Life: The Paternal Monarchy of Bangkok, 1782–1932. With the Earlier and More Recent History of Thailand*. London: Alvin Redman.

Chandraprema, C.A. 1991. *Sri Lanka, the Years of Terror: The J.V.P. insurrection, 1987–1989*. Colombo: Lake House Bookshop.

Chin, Ko-Lin. 2009. *The Golden Triangle. Inside Southeast Asia's Drug Trade*. Ithaca/London: Cornell University Press.

Chongcharoen, Piyarach. 2018. Battered Young Novice Dies. *Bangkok Post*, August 24. https://www.bangkokpost.com/news/crime/1527714/battered-young-novice-dies

Cimatu, Henri R. 2014. Buddhist Extremists Accused of Persecuting Sri Lankan Christians. *World-Wide Religious News*, July 25. https://wwrn.org/articles/43062/

Clarkprosecutor.org. Undated. *Paul Jennings Hill*. http://www.clarkprosecutor.org/html/death/US/hill873.htm

Cohen, Paul T. 2017. Charismatic Monks of Lanna Buddhism. In *Charismatic Monks of Lanna*, ed. Paul T. Cohen, 1–25. Copenhagen: NIAS Press.

Colombo Page. 2013. Buddhist Extremists Group in Sri Lanka Overpower Evangelical Christians. *Colombo Page News Desk*, June 16. http://www.colombopage.com/archive_13A/Jun16_1371391544KA.php

Colombo Telegraph. 2014. Unedited Full Video: BBS Gnanasara's Pre-Riots Speech (Video). *Colombo Telegraph*, June 19. https://www.colombotelegraph.com/index.php/unedited-full-video-bbs-gnanasaras-pre-riots-speech/

Coningham, R.A.E., et al. 2013. The Earliest Buddhist Shrine: Excavating the Birthplace of the Buddha, Lumbini (Nepal). *Antiquity* 87: 1104–1123. https://www.cambridge.org/core/journals/antiquity/article/earliest-buddhist-shrine-excavating-the-birthplace-of-the-buddha-lumbini-nepal/903386 47E132E7B20420CCC9C847E237

Cook, Joanna. 2014. *Meditation in Modern Buddhism. Renunciation and Change in Thai Monastic Life*. Paperback ed. New York: Cambridge University Press.

Croissant, Aurel. 2007. Muslim Insurgency, Political Violence, and Democracy in Thailand. *Terrorism and Political Violence* 19 (1): 1–18. https://www.uni-heidelberg.de/imperia/md/content/fakultaeten/wiso/ipw/croissant/publications/croissant_2007_muslim_insurgency.pdf

Cushman, Richard D., and David K. Wyatt. 2006. *The Royal Chronicles of Ayutthaya. A Synoptic Translation by Richard D. Cushman*. Ed. David K. Wyatt. Bangkok: The Siam Society.

Darlington, Susan M. 1998. The Ordination of a Tree: The Buddhist Ecology Movement in Thailand. *Ethnology* 37 (1): 1–15.

———. 2000. Rethinking Buddhism and Development: The Emergence of Environmentalist Monks in Thailand. *Journal of Buddhist Ethics* 7 (online version).

Davis, S. 1991. 'Et Quod Vis Fac.' Paul Ramsey and Augustinian Ethics. *The Journal of Religious Ethics* (Special Focus Issue: The Ethics of Paul Ramsey) 19 (2): 31–69.

Dawson, Lorne L. 2017. Discounting Religion in the Explanation of Homegrown Terrorism: A Critique. In *The Cambridge Companion to Religion and Terrorism*, ed. James R. Lewis, 32–45. New York: Cambridge University Press.

de Choisy, François-Timoléon. 1995. *Journal du Voyage de Siam. Présenté at annoté par Dirk van der Cruysse*. Paris: Fayard.

De Silva, K.M. 1981. *A History of Sri Lanka*. London: C. Hurst.

De Silva, Chandra R. 1998. The Plurality of Buddhist Fundamentalism: An Inquiry into Views Among Buddhist Monks in Sri Lanka. In *Buddhist Fundamentalism and Minority Identities in Sri Lanka*, ed. Tessa J. Bartholomeusz and Chandra de Silva, 53–73. Albany: State University of New York Press.

De Silva, Nilika. 2001. Sri Lankans – Independent or Dependent on Alcohol? *Sunday Times* (Colombo), February 4. http://www.sundaytimes.lk/010204/plus3.html

Deegalle, Mahinda. 2003. Theravada Attitudes to Violence. *Journal of Buddhist Ethics* 10: 81–93.

———. 2004. Politics of the Jathika Hela Urumaya Monks: Buddhism and Ethnicity in Contemporary Sri Lanka. *Contemporary Buddhism. An Interdisciplinary Journal* 5 (2): 83–103. https://doi.org/10.1080/14639940 42000319816.

———. 2006. Introduction. In *Buddhism, Conflict and Violence in Modern Sri Lanka*, ed. Mahinda Deegalle, 1–21. London/New York: Routledge.

———. 2013. Sinhala Ethno-Nationalisms and Militarization. In *Buddhism and Violence: Militarism and Buddhism in Modern Asia*, ed. Vladimir Tikhonov and Torkel Brekke, 15–36. New York/London: Routledge.

Dewasiri, Nirmal Ranjith. 2016. *New Buddhist Extremism and the Challenge to Ethno-Religious Coexistence in Sri Lanka*. Colombo: International Centre for Ethnic Studies, October. http://ices.lk/wp-content/uploads/2016/12/New-Buddhist-Extremism-and-the-Challenges.pdf

Dhammasami, Khammai. 2004. *Between Idealism and Pragmatism. A Study of Monastic Education in Burma and Thailand from the Seventeenth Century to the Present*. Unpublished PhD Dissertation, Faculty of Oriental Studies, University of Oxford, Oxford.

Dharmadasa, K.N.O. 1974. A Nativistic Reaction to Colonialism: The Sinhala-Buddhist Revival in Sri Lanka. *Asian Studies Journal* 12 (1): 159–179. http://www.asj.upd.edu.ph/mediabox/archive/ASJ-12-1-1974/dharmadasa-nativistic%20reaction%20colonialism%20singhala%20buddhist%20revival%20sri%20lanka.pdf

Dharmapala, Anagarika. 1893. Introductory Note to *The Kinship Between Hinduism and Buddhism: A Lecture Delivered in the Town Hall, Calcutta, Oct. 24th, 1892*, by Henry Steel Olcott. Calcutta: Maha Bodhi Society.

Dubus, Arnaud. 2017. *Buddhism and Politics in Thailand (IRASEC's Short Books 40)*. Bangkok: IRASEC. http://www.irasec.com/ouvrage144

Durkheim, Emile. 1995. *The Elementary Forms of Religious Life*. Translated and with an Introduction by Karen E. Fields. New York: The Free Press.

DVB. 2007. International Monks' Organisation Established. *Democratic Voice of Burma*, October 30. http://www.dvb.no/uncategorized/international-monks-organisation-established/607

DW. 2017. Hate Speech Myanmar Monk Banned from Preaching by Buddhist Council. *Deutsche Welle*, March 11. http://www.dw.com/en/hate-speech-myanmar-monk-banned-from-preaching-by-buddhist-council/a-37905421

Easwaran, Eknath, trans. 2007. *The Bhagavad Gita*. Tomales: Nilgiri Press.

Ei Ei Thu. 2017. Bagan on Way to UNESCO Listing as World Heritage Site. *Myanmar Times*, September 29. https://www.mmtimes.com/travel/bagan-way-unesco-listing-world-heritage-site.html

Ekachai, Sanitsuda. 2015. Nip Unholy Hate Speech in the Bud. *Bangkok Post*, November 4. https://www.bangkokpost.com/opinion/opinion/753808/nip-unholy-hate-speech-in-the-bud

Escobar, Pepe. 2018. Will the Putin-Xi Era Supersede the Western Liberal (Dis)order? *Asia Times Online*, March 25. http://www.atimes.com/article/will-putin-xi-era-supersede-western-liberal-disorder/

Farook, Latheef. 2012. Attack on Dambulla Mosque: Latest Hooliganism Under Organized 'Hate Muslim' Campaign. *Colombo Telegraph*, April 29. https://www.colombotelegraph.com/index.php/attack-on-dambulla-mosque-latest-hooliganism-under-organized-hate-muslim-campaign/

Fernando, P.T.M. 1970. The Post Riots Campaign for Justice. (The 1915 Riots in Ceylon: A Symposium). *Journal of Asian Studies* 29 (2): 255–266.

Fernando, Jude Lal. 2013. *Religion, Conflict and Peace in Sri Lanka: The Politics of Interpretation of Nationhoods*. Berlin et al.: LIT Verlag.

Ford, Eugene. 2017. *Cold War Monks. Buddhism and America's Secret Strategy in Southeast Asia*. New Haven/London: Yale University Press.

Forum Weltkirche. Undated. Sri Lanka: Das Ende der Religionsfreiheit. *Forum Weltkirche*. http://www.forum-weltkirche.de/de/artikel/17862.sri-lanka.html

Frankopan, Peter. 2016. *The Silk Roads: A New History of the World*. Paperback ed. London et al.: Bloomsbury.

Freeman, Joe. 2017. The 'Good Monk' Myth. *The Atlantic*, September 29. https://www.theatlantic.com/international/archive/2017/09/saffron-revolution-good-monk-myth/541116/

Friedman, Jonathan. 1994. *Cultural Identity and Global Process*. London et al.: Sage Publications.

Fu, Charles Wei-hsun, and Sandra A. Wawrytko, eds. 1991. *Buddhist Ethics and Modern Society: An International Symposium*. New York/Westport/London: Greenwood Press.

Galtung, Johan. 1969. Violence, Peace, and Peace Research. *Journal of Peace Research* 6 (3): 167–191.

Garg, Ganga Ram. 1992. Adam's Bridge. *Encyclopaedia of the Hindu World, A-Aj*. New Delhi: South Asia Books.

Garrett, Jan. 2004. *A Simple and Usable (Although Incomplete) Ethical Theory Based on the Ethics of W. D. Ross*. August 10. http://people.wku.edu/jan.garrett/ethics/rossethc.htm

Gethin, Rupert. 2004. Can Killing a Living Being Ever Be an Act of Compassion? The Analysis of the Act of Killing in the Abhidhamma and Pali Commentaries. *Journal of Buddhist Ethics* 11: 167–202.

Gokhale, Balkrishna Govind. 1965. The Early Buddhist Elite. *Journal of Indian History* XLII (2): 391–402.

Gombrich, Richard F. 1966. The Consecration of a Buddhist Image. *Journal of Asian Studies* 26 (1): 23–36.

———. 1992. Dating the Buddha: A Red Herring Revealed. In *The Dating of the Historical Buddha/Die Datierung des Historischen Buddha, Part 2*, ed. Heinz Bechert, 237–262. Göttingen: Vandenhoeck & Ruprecht.

———. 2006. *Theravāda Buddhism: A Social History from Ancient Benares to Modern Colombo*. 2nd ed. Abingdon/New York: Routledge.

———. 2007. Buddhism in Ancient India: The Evolution of the Sangha. In *The World of Buddhism: Buddhist Monks and Nuns in Society and Culture*, ed. Heinz Bechert and Richard F. Gombrich, 77–89. Reprint, London: Thames & Hudson.

———. 2008a. Einleitung: Der Buddhismus als Weltreligion. In *Der Buddhismus. Geschichte und Gegenwart*, ed. Heinz Bechert and Richard F. Gombrich, 3rd ed., 15–32. München: Verlag C. H. Beck.

———. 2008b. Der Buddhismus im alten und mittelalterlichen Indien: Sinn und Aufgabe des Sangha. In *Der Buddhismus: Geschichte und Gegenwart*, ed. Heinz Bechert and Richard F. Gombrich, 3rd ed., 71–93. München: Verlag C. H. Beck.

Gopin, Marc. 2000. *Between Eden and Armageddon: The Future of World Religions, Violence, and Peacemaking*. Oxford/New York: Oxford University Press.

Grant, Patrick. 2009. *Buddhism and Ethnic Conflict in Sri Lanka*. Albany: State University of New York Press.

Gravers, Mikael. 2010. The Monk in Command. *The Irrawaddy* 18 (5, May). http://www2.irrawaddy.org/print_article.php?art_id=18407 or at http://www.buddhistchannel.tv/index.php?id=9,9146,0,0,1,0#.U4n8ZBbIZFw

———. 2012. Monks, Morality and Military. The Struggle for Moral Power in Burma – And Buddhism's Uneasy Relation with Lay Power. *Contemporary Buddhism: An Interdisciplinary Journal* 13 (1): 1–33. https://www.tandfonline.com/doi/full/10.1080/14639947.2012.669278?src=recsys

———. 2015. Anti-Muslim Buddhist Nationalism in Burma and Sri Lanka: Religious Violence and Globalized Imaginaries of Endangered Identities. *Contemporary Buddhism: An Interdisciplinary Journal* 16 (1): 1–27. https://www.tandfonline.com/doi/full/10.1080/14639947.2015.1008090

Griswold, Eliza. 2015. Is This the End of Christianity in the Middle East? *The New York Times Magazine*, July 22. www.nytimes.com/2015/07/26/magazine/is-this-the-end-of-christianity-in-the-middle-east.html?_r=3

Gunaratna, Rohan. 1995. *Sri Lanka: A Lost Revolution? The Inside Story of the JVP*. 2nd ed. Kandy: Institute of Fundamental Studies.

Gyte, Joseph. 2018. *Thailand's Deep South Insurgency: Declining Violence, but Why?* Unpublished MLitt Dissertation, University of St Andrews.

Habib, Shahanaaz, Teh Eng Hock, and Brian Moh. 2010. Staying Neutral Is Hard for Monks. *The Star Online*, April 19. https://www.thestar.com.my/news/nation/2010/04/19/staying-neutral-is-hard-for-monks/

Hallisey, Charles. 1996. Ethical Particularism in Theravāda Buddhism. *Journal of Buddhist Ethics* 3: 32–43.

Hansard. 1916. Ceylon (Temperance Movement). *Hansard Commons Sittings, Oral Answers to Questions.* May 25. https://api.parliament.uk/historic-hansard/commons/1916/may/25/ceylon-temperance-movement

Harris, Elizabeth J. 1994. *Violence and Disruption in Society. A Study of the Early Buddhist Texts.* The Wheel Publication No. 392/393. Kandy: Buddhist Publication Society.

Harris, Ian. 1995. Getting to Grips with Buddhist Environmentalism: A Provisional Typology. *Journal of Buddhist Ethics* 2: 173–190.

———. 2005. *Cambodian Buddhism. History and Practice.* Chiang Mai: Silkworm Books.

———. 2012. Buddhism, Politics and Nationalism. In *Buddhism in the Modern World*, ed. David L. McMahan, 1177–1194. Oxon: Routledge.

———. 2013. *Buddhism in a Dark Age. Cambodian Monks Under Pol Pot.* Chiang Mai: Silkworm Books.

Harris, John. 2018. In Sri Lanka, Facebook's Dominance Has Cost Lives. *The Guardian*, May 6. https://www.theguardian.com/commentisfree/2018/may/06/sri-lanka-facebook-lives-tech-giant-poor-countries?CMP=share_btn_fb

Harvey, Godfrey E. 1925. *History of Burma: From the Earliest Times to 10 March 1824.* London: Frank Cass & Co.

Harvey, Peter. 2000. *An Introduction to Buddhist Ethics: Foundations, Values and Issues.* Cambridge: Cambridge University Press.

Haynes, Jeffrey. 2013. *An Introduction to International Relations and Religion.* 2nd ed. Harlow et al.: Pearson.

Head, Jonathan. 2007. The Hardship that Sparked Burma's Unrest. *BBC News*, October 2. http://news.bbc.co.uk/1/hi/world/asia-pacific/7023548.stm

Heslop, Luke A. 2014. On Sacred Ground: The Political Performance of Religious Responsibility. *Contemporary South Asia* 22 (1): 21–36. https://www.tandfonline.com/doi/abs/10.1080/09584935.2013.870975

Higgs, Roberts. 2005. How Many Divisions Does the Pope Have? *The Independent Institute Newsroom*, April 11. http://www.independent.org/newsroom/article.asp?id=1492

Hill, Paul. 2003. *Mix My Blood with the Blood of the Unborn* (unedited version). August. http://www.armyofgod.com/PaulHillMixMyBloodPDF.html

Hodal, Kate. 2013. Buddhist Monk Uses Racism and Rumours to Spread Hatred in Burma. *The Guardian*, April 18. https://www.theguardian.com/world/2013/apr/18/buddhist-monk-spreads-hatred-burma

Hoffman, Bruce. 1997. The Confluence of International and Domestic Trends of Terrorism. *Terrorism and Political Violence* 9 (2): 1–15.

Holt, John C. 2016a. Introduction. In *Buddhist Extremists and Muslim Minorities: Religious Conflict in Contemporary Sri Lanka*, ed. John C. Holt, 1–17 (e-book version). New York City: Oxford University Press.

———. 2016b. A Religious Syntax to Recent Communal Violence in Sri Lanka. In *Buddhist Extremists and Muslim Minorities: Religious Conflict in Contemporary Sri Lanka*, ed. John C. Holt, 194–210 (e-book version). New York City: Oxford University Press.

Horner, I.B., trans. 1938. *The Book of the Discipline (Vinaya-Pitaka): Suttavibangha*. Sacred Books of the Buddhists. 3 vols., vol. XXIII, ed. Rhys Davids. London: Humphrey Milford.

Houtman, Gustaaf. 1999. *Mental Culture in Burmese Crisis Politics: Aung San Suu Kyi and the National League for Democracy*. Tokyo: Institute for the Study of Languages and Cultures of Asia and Africa, Tokyo University.

———. 2000. *Human Origins, Myanmafication and "Disciplined" Burmese Democracy*. Pekhon: Pekhon University Press.

Human Rights Watch. 2007. *Crackdown. Repression of the 2007 Popular Protests in Burma*. Vol. 19, No. 18 (C), December. https://www.hrw.org/report/2007/12/06/crackdown/repression-2007-popular-protests-burma

———. 2009. *The Resistance of the Monks. Buddhism and Activism in Burma*. Human Rights Watch, September 22. https://www.hrw.org/report/2009/09/22/resistance-monks/buddhism-and-activism-burma

Huntington, Samuel P. 1993. The Clash of Civilizations? *Foreign Affairs* 72 (3): 22–49.

———. 1996. *The Clash of Civilizations and the Remaking of World Order*. New York: Simon & Schuster.

Ibrahim, Azeem. 2018. *The Rohingyas. Inside Myanmar's Genocide*. London: Hurst & Company.

ICG. 2007. *Southern Thailand: The Problem with Paramilitaries*. Asia Report No. 140, October 23. https://www.crisisgroup.org/asia/south-east-asia/thailand/southern-thailand-problem-paramilitaries

———. 2014. *Myanmar: The Politics of Rakhine State*. Asia Report No. 261, October 22. http://www.crisisgroup.org/~/media/Files/asia/south-east-asia/burma-myanmar/261-myanmar-the-politics-of-rakhine-state.pdf

———. 2016. *Myanmar: A New Muslim Insurgency in Rakhine State*. International Crisis Group (ICG) Report No 283, December 15. https://www.crisisgroup.org/asia/south-east-asia/myanmar/283-myanmar-new-muslim-insurgency-rakhine-state

Ito, Tomomi. 2012. *Modern Thai Buddhism and Buddhadāsa Bikkhu. A Social History*. Singapore: NUS Press.

Jackson, Peter A. 1989. *Buddhism, Legitimation and Conflict: The Political Functions of Urban Thai Buddhism.* Social Issues in Southeast Asia. Singapore: ISEAS.

———. 1997. Withering Centre, Flourishing Margins: Buddhism's Changing Political Roles. In *Political Change in Thailand: Democracy and Participation,* ed. Kevin Hewison, 75–93. London: Routledge.

———. 2003. *Buddhadāsa: Theravada Buddhism and Modernist Reform in Thailand.* Bangkok: Silkworm Books.

Jayawardena, Kumari. 1970. Economic and Political Factors in the 1915 Riots (The 1915 Riots in Ceylon: A Symposium). *Journal of Asian Studies* 29 (2): 223–233.

Jenkins, Stephen. 2011. On the Auspiciousness of Compassionate Violence. *Journal of the International Association of Buddhist Studies* 33 (1–2): 299–331. http://archiv.ub.uni-heidelberg.de/ojs/index.php/jiabs/article/view/9284

Jerryson, Michael K. 2011. *Buddhist Fury: Religion and Violence in Southern Thailand.* Oxford et al.: Oxford University Press.

———. 2014. A Path to Militant Buddhism: Thai Monks as Representations. In *Buddhism and Violence: Militarism and Buddhism in Modern Asia,* ed. Vladimir Tikhonov and Torkel Brekke, paperback ed., 75–94. New York/Abingdon: Routledge.

———. 2018. Buddhism, War, and Violence. In *Oxford Handbook of Buddhist Ethics,* ed. Daniel Cozort and James M. Shields, 453–478. Oxford: Oxford University Press.

Jerryson, Michael K., and Mark Juergensmeyer, eds. 2010. *Buddhist Warfare.* Oxford/New York: Oxford University Press.

Jeyaraj, D.B.S. 2014. The Assassination of Prime Minister S. W. R. D. Bandaranaike 55 Years Ago. http://dbsjeyaraj.com/dbsj/archives/33515

Johnson, Irving Chan. 2010. *The Buddha on Mecca's Verandah. Encounters, Mobilities, and Histories Along the Malaysian-Thai Border.* Chiang Mai: Silkworm Books.

Johnson, Todd M., and Brian J. Grim. 2013. *The World's Religions in Figures: An Introduction to International Religious Demography.* Hoboken: Wiley-Blackwell.

Jordt, Ingrid. 2008. Turning over the Bowl in Burma. *Religion in the News* 10 (3, Winter). http://www.trincoll.edu/depts/csrpl/RINVol10No3/turning%20 over%20the%20bowl.htm

Juergensmeyer, Mark. 2003. *Terror in the Mind of God. The Global Rise of Religious Violence.* 3rd ed. Berkeley/Los Angeles/London: University of California Press.

———. 2008. *Global Rebellion. Religious Challenges to the Secular State, from Christian Militias to al Qaeda.* Berkeley: University of California Press.

————. 2017. Does Religion Cause Terrorism? In *The Cambridge Companion to Religion and Terrorism*, ed. James R. Lewis, 11–22. New York: Cambridge University Press.

Juergensmeyer, Mark, and Mona Kanwal Sheikh. 2013. A Sociotheological Approach to Understanding Religious Violence. In *Oxford Handbook of Religion and Violence*, ed. Mark Juergensmeyer, Margo Kitts, and Michael Jerryson, 620–643. Oxford: Oxford University Press.

Kathirithamby-Wells, J., and Clare Hall. 1999. The Age of Transition: The Mid-Eighteenth to the Early Nineteenth Centuries. In *Cambridge History of Southeast Asia, Vol. One, Part Two. From c. 1500 to c. 1800*, ed. Nicholas Tarling, 228–275. Cambridge: Cambridge University Press.

Kawanami, Hiroko, and Geoffrey Samuel, eds. 2013. *Buddhism, International Relief Work, and Civil Society*. New York: Palgrave Macmillan.

Kearney, Robert N. 1970. Introduction (The 1915 Riots in Ceylon: A Symposium). *Journal of Asian Studies* 29 (2): 219–222.

Kemper, Steven. 2015. Rescued from the Nation: Anagarika Dharmapala and the Buddhist World (Online). Chicago: Chicago Scholarship, May

Kent, David W. 2010. Onward Buddhist Soldiers: Preaching to the Sri Lankan Army. In *Buddhist Warfare*, ed. Michael K. Jerryson and Mark Juergensmeyer, 157–177. Oxford/New York: Oxford University Press.

Kepel, Gilles. 1994. *The Revenge of God. The Resurgence of Islam, Christianity and Judaism in the Modern World*. Cambridge: Polity Press.

Kershaw, Roger. 2001. *Monarchy in South-East Asia. The Faces of Tradition in Transition*. London/New York: Routledge.

Keyes, Charles F. 1999. Political Crisis and Militant Buddhism in Contemporary Thailand (Revised edition, original version published in *Religion and Legitimation of Power in Thailand, Burma and Laos*, ed. Bardwell Smith, 147–164. Chambersburg: Anima Books 1978). http://www.academia.edu/8987102/Political_Crisis_and_Militant_Buddhism_in_Contemporary_Thailand_rev_1999_

————. 2007. Monks, Guns, and Peace: Theravāda Buddhism and Political Violence. In *Belief and Bloodshed. Religion and Violence Across Time and Tradition*, ed. James K. Wellman, 145–163. Lanham et al.: Rowman & Littlefield.

Keyes, Charles. 2016. Theravada Buddhism and Buddhist Nationalism: Sri Lanka, Myanmar, Cambodia, and Thailand. *The Review of Faith & International Affairs* 14 (4): 41–52.

Khantipalo Bhikkhu. 1986. *Aggression, War, and Conflict: Three Essays*. Bodhi Leaf No. 108. Kandy: Buddhist Publication Society. http://www.bps.lk/olib/bl/bl108-p.html

Khin Khin Ei. 2013. Myanmar Monk Rejects Terrorist Label Following Communal Clashes. *Radio Free Asia*, June 21. https://www.rfa.org/english/news/myanmar/monk-06212013182954.html

Kirsch, Thomas A. 1975. Modernizing Implications of Nineteenth Century Reforms of the Thai Sangha. *Contributions to Asian Studies* VIII: 8–23.

Kitiarsa, Pattana. 2006. Magic Monks and Spirit Mediums in the Politics of Thai Popular Religion. *Inter-Asia Cultural Studies* 6 (2): 209–226.

———. 2012. *Mediums, Monks, and Amulets. Thai Popular Buddhism Today.* Chiang Mai: Silkworm Books.

Kyaw Aye. 1984. The Sangha Organization in Nineteenth Century Burma and Thailand. *Journal of the Siam Society* 72 (1–2): 166–196.

Kyaw Yin Hlaing. 2008. Challenging the Authoritarian State: Buddhist Monks and Peaceful Protests in Burma. *Fletcher Forum of World Affairs* 32 (1): 125–144. http://heinonline.org/HOL/Page?handle=hein.journals/forwa32& div=12&g_sent=1&casa_token=&collection=journals#

Lamotte, Etienne. 2007. The Buddha, His Teachings, and His Sangha. In *The World of Buddhism: Buddhist Monks and Nuns in Society and Culture*, ed. Heinz Bechert and Richard F. Gombrich, 41–58. Reprint, London: Thames & Hudson.

Landesamt fuer Verfassungsschutz Baden-Wuerttemberg/Germany. 2006. *Rechtsextremismus.* Stuttgart, March.

Lehr, Peter. 2013. Between Dhamma-Ghosa and Bheri-Ghosa: Militant Buddhism in Burma. *South Asia Democratic Forum (SADF) Bulletin*, No 10, November 4. http://sadf.eu/home/wp-content/uploads/2013/11/think-southasia10.pdf

———. 2016. Holy Wars Along the Maritime Silk Road: Extremist Islamism, Hinduism, and Buddhism. In *ASEAN Looks West: ASEAN and the Gulf Region*, ed. Wilfried A. Herrmann and Peter Lehr, 115–140. Bangkok: White Lotus Press.

———. 2017. Militant Buddhism Is on the March in Southeast Asia – Where Did It Come from? *The Conversation*, November 7. https://theconversation.com/ militant-buddhism-is-on-the-march-in-south-east-asia-where-did-it-come-from-86632

———. 2018. Diskurse der Gewalt: Gewalttätiger Buddhismus und extremist-ischer Islamismus in Burma. In *Jahrbuch Terrorismus 2017/2018*, ed. Stefan Hansen and Joachim Krause, 114–141. Opladen/Berlin/Toronto: Verlag Barbara Budrich.

Leifer, Michael. 1995. *Dictionary of the Modern Politics of South-East Asia.* London/New York: Routledge.

Lieberman, Victor B. 1976. A New Look at the 'Sāsanavamsa'. *Bulletin of the School of Oriental and African Studies* 39 (1): 137–149.

Lochtefeld, James G. 2002. *The Illustrated Encyclopedia of Hinduism: A-M.* New York: Rosen Publishing Group.

Long, Kayleigh. 2018. Mea culpa? Facebook Covers Its Tracks in Myanmar. *Asia Times*, August 27. http://www.atimes.com/article/mea-culpa-facebook-covers-its-tracks-in-myanmar//

Loy, David. 1982. Enlightenment in Buddhism and Advaita Vedanta: Are Nirvana and Moksha the Same? *International Philosophical Quarterly* 23 (1): 65–74. http://buddhism.lib.ntu.edu.tw/FULLTEXT/JR-AN/26715.htm

Lukes, Steven. 1973. *Individualism.* Oxford: Oxford University Press.

Mahāmakuta Educational Council. 1989. *Acts of the Administration of the Buddhist Order of Sangha in Thailand. B.E. 2445, B.E. 2484, B.E. 2505.* Bangkok: Mahāmakuta Educational Council, The Buddhist University. https://sujato.files.wordpress.com/2010/07/sangha-acts.pdf

Marty, Martin E. (with Jonathan Moore). 2000. *Politics, Religion and the Common Good. Advancing a Distinctly American Conversation About Religion's Role in Our Shared Life.* San Francisco: Jossey-Bass Inc.

Mascaró, Juan, trans. 2003. *The Bhagavad Gita.* Reprint, London et al.: Penguin Books.

Matthews, Bruce. 1999. The Legacy of Tradition and Authority: Buddhism and the Nation in Myanmar. In *Buddhism and Politics in Twentieth-Century Asia,* ed. Ian Harris, 26–53. London: Continuum.

Maung Zarni. 2013. Racist Leader Monk Rev. Wirathu's Speech. Summary Translation to English by Maung Zarni. *M-Media,* March 24. http://www.m-mediagroup.com/en/archives/7625

Maung Zaw. 2015. Saffron Monks Fire Back at U Wirathu. *Myanmar Times,* September 11. https://www.mmtimes.com/national-news/mandalay-upper-myanmar/16440-saffron-monks-fire-back-at-u-wirathu.html

McCargo, Duncan. 2004. Buddhism, Democracy and Identity in Thailand. *Democratization* 11 (4): 155–170.

———. 2009. The Politics of Buddhist Identity in Thailand's Deep South: The Demise of Civil Religion? *Journal of Southeast Asian Studies* 40 (1): 11–32. http://www.polis.leeds.ac.uk/assets/files/Staff/mccargo-pol-buddhism-south-2009.pdf

———. 2012a. *Mapping National Anxieties: Thailand's Southern Conflict.* Singapore: NIAS Press.

———. 2012b. The Changing Politics of Thailand's Buddhist Order. *Critical Asian Studies* 44 (4): 627–642. http://www.polis.leeds.ac.uk/assets/files/Journal%20articles/CAS-Buddhism-McCargo-December-2012.pdf

McDaniel, Justin. 2006. Buddhism in Thailand: Negotiating the Modern Age. In *Buddhism in World Cultures: Comparative Perspectives.* Religion in Contemporary Cultures, ed. Stephen C. Berkwitz, 101–128. Santa Barbara: ABC CLIO.

McMahan, David L. 2012. Buddhist Modernism. In *Buddhism in the Modern World,* ed. David L. McMahan, 159–176. Oxon: Routledge.

McPherson, Poppy. 2018. Myanmar Army Fakes Rohingya Photos in 'True News' Book. *Bangkok Post/Reuters,* August 31. https://www.bangkokpost.com/news/special-reports/1531606/myanmar-army-fakes-rohingya-photos-in-true-news-book

McTernan, Oliver. 2003. *Violence in God's Name: Religion in an Age of Conflict.* Maryknoll/London: Orbis Books.

Mendelson, E. Michael. 1975. *State and Sangha in Burma: A Study of Monastic Sectarianism and Leadership.* Ithaca: Cornell University Press.

Moe Kyint. 2018. Military Chief Wastes No Time Finding New Home on Social Media. *The Irrawaddy*, August 29. https://www.irrawaddy.com/news/military-chief-wastes-no-time-finding-new-home-social-media.html

Moran, Michael. 2006. The Pope's Divisions. *CFR Analysis Brief*, February 3, at http://www.cfr.org/religion/popes-divisions/p9765

Mratt Kyaw Thu. 2016. The State of the Sangha. *Frontier Myanmar*, February 19. https://frontiermyanmar.net/en/the-state-of-the-sangha

Myaing Nan Shwe. 1999. *Myaing Gye: Ngu Sayadaw. A Jahan Who Shines the Light of Dhamma.* Trans. Shin Khay Meinda. Myaing Gyi Ngu Special Region, Karen State (DKBA): Mann Ba Nyunt Pe. http://www.burmalibrary.org/docs11/U_Thuzana%27s_Book-red.pdf

Nānamoli, Bhikkhu, and Bhikkhu Bodhi. 2005. *The Middle Length Discourses of the Buddha: A Translation of the Majjhima Nikāya.* 3rd ed. Somerville: Wisdom Publications.

Nanamoli Thera. 1994. Cula-kammavibhanga Sutta: The Shorter Exposition of Kamma. *Tipitaka, Majjhima Nikaya.* Access to Insight: Readings in Theravāda Buddhism. http://www.accesstoinsight.org/tipitaka/mn/mn.135.nymo.html

Narada Thera. 1994. Mangalasutta: Blessings. *Tipitaka, Khuddakapatha.* Access to Insight: Readings in Theravāda Buddhism. http://www.accesstoinsight.org/tipitaka/kn/khp/khp.5.nara.html

Narayan Swami, M.R. 2004. *Tigers of Lanka, from Boys to Guerrillas.* Colombo: Vijitha Yapa Publications.

Naughton, John. 2018. Facebook's Global Monopoly Poses a Deadly Threat in Developing Nations. *The Guardian*, April 29. https://www.theguardian.com/commentisfree/2018/apr/29/facebook-global-monopoly-deadly-problem-myanmar-sri-lanka

Neher, Charles. 1985. Buddhism and Politics in Thailand: A Study of Sociopolitical Change and Political Activism in the Thai Sangha (Book Review). *Journal of Asian Studies* 44 (2): 474–475.

Ngamkhan, Wassayos. 2018. Senior Monks Defrocked After Raids. Phra Buddha Isara Among Those Nabbed. *Bangkok Post*, May 25. https://www.bangkokpost.com/news/general/1472209/senior-monks-defrocked-after-raids

Nietzsche, Friedrich. 2006 (orig. 1882). *The Gay Science.* In *The Nietzsche Reader*, ed. Keith A. Pearson and Duncan Large, 207–237. Malden/Oxford/Carlton: Blackwell.

Nilsen, Marte. 2014. Military Temples and Saffron-Robed Soldiers: Legitimacy and the Securing of Buddhism in Southern Thailand. In *Buddhism and Violence:*

*Militarism and Buddhism in Modern Asia,* ed. Vladimir Tikhonov and Torkel Brekke, paperback ed., 37–53. New York/Abingdon: Routledge.

Nuhman, M.A. 2016. Sinhala Buddhist Nationalism and Muslim Identity in Sri Lanka: One Hundred Years of Conflict and Coexistence. In *Buddhist Extremists and Muslim Minorities: Religious Conflict in Contemporary Sri Lanka,* ed. John C. Holt, 18–53 (e-book version). New York City: Oxford University Press.

Nye, Joseph S., Jr. 2004. *Soft Power: The Means to Success in World Politics.* New York: Perseus Books.

Obeyesekere, Gananath. 1970. Religious Symbolism and Political Change in Ceylon. *Modern Ceylon Studies* 1 (1): 43–63.

———. 1975. Sinhalese-Buddhist Identity in Ceylon. In *Ethnic Identity: Cultural Continuities and Change,* ed. George de Vos and Lola Romanucci-Ross, 231–258. Palo Alto: Mayfield Publishing.

———. 1991. Buddhism and Conscience: An Exploratory Essay. *Daedalus* 120 (3, Summer): 219–239.

———. 2011. Foreword. In *In My Mother's House: Civil War in Sri Lanka,* Thiranagama, Sharika (author), xi–xvi. Philadelphia: University of Pennsylvania Press.

Olcott, Henry Steel. 1893. *The Kinship Between Hinduism and Buddhism.* Calcutta: Maha Bodhi Society.

Palmisano. 2013. How to Become a Thai Monk: Preparation, Part 2. *Thai Language Blog,* October 26. https://blogs.transparent.com/thai/how-to-become-a-thai-monk-preparation-part-2/

Pannapadipo, Phra Peter. 2005. *Phra Farang: An English Monk in Thailand.* London: Arrow Books.

Parnwell, Michael, and Martin Seeger. 2008. The Relocalization of Buddhism in Thailand. *Journal of Buddhist Ethics* 15: 79–176. www.thaibuddhism.net/pdf/parnwell-seeger.pdf

Peiris, Gopitha. 2006. Most Venerable Hikkaduwe Sri Sumangala Nayaka Thera remembered. *Daily News Online,* April 29. www.archives.dailynews.lk/2006/04/29/fea05.asp

Perera, Edward. 1915. *Memorandum upon Recent Disturbances in Ceylon.* London: Edward Hughes & Co. https://ia801401.us.archive.org/5/items/memorandumuponre00pererich/memorandumuponre00pererich.pdf

Perera, Ajith P. 2008. As Buddhists, Should We Further Milk Local Talibans? *Dare to Be Different* (Blog), September 12. https://bandaragama.wordpress.com/tag/ven-gangodawila-soma-thero/

Pitsuwan, Surin. 1985. *Islam and Malay Nationalism: A Case Study of the Malay-Muslims of Southern Thailand.* Bangkok: Thai Khadi Research Institute, Thammasat University.

Premasiri, P.D. 2006. A 'Righteous War' in Buddhism? In *Buddhism, Conflict and Violence in Modern Sri Lanka,* ed. Mahinda Deegalle, 78–85. London/New York: Routledge.

Prothero, Stephen. 1995. Henry Steel Olcott and 'Protestant Buddhism'. *Journal of the American Academy of Religion* LXIII (2): 281–302.

Qutb, Sayyid. 2003. *Milestones*. Chicago: Kazi Publications.

Rahula, Walpola. 1974. *The Heritage of the Bhikkhu: A Short History of the Bhikkhu in Educational, Cultural, Social, and Political Life*. New York: Grove Press.

Rajapakse, C.V. 2003. Ven. Migettuwatte Gunanada Thera, the Indomitable Orator. *Daily News*, January 25. www.archives.dailynews.lik/2003/01/25/fea05.html

Ranatunga, D.C. 2003. That Controversial Clash. *Sunday Times Plus*, August 24. www.sundaytimes.lk/030824/plus/9.html

Ranawaka, Patali Champika. 2013. *Al Jihad Al Qaeda Islam muladharmavadaye varthamanaya ha anagataya*. Mudungoda: Tharanga (original ed. 2003). https://www.scribd.com/document/226004818/Al-jihad-Al-Qaeda

Rand, Nelson. 2009. *Conflict. Journeys Through War and Terror in Southeast Asia*. Bangkok: Maverick House.

Republic of the Union of Myanmar. 2016. The Union Report: Religion. In *The 2014 Myanmar Population and Housing Census*. Census Report Volume 2-C. Naypyidaw: Department of Population, Ministry of Labour, Immigration and Population, July.

Reuters. 2018. German far-Right Protesters Clash with Leftists After Chemnitz Stabbing. *Reuters*, August 27. https://www.reuters.com/article/us-germany-chemnitz/german-government-condemns-far-right-demo-in-eastern-city-after-fatal-dispute-idUSKCN1LC1DD

RFA. 2008. Burma Monks' Leader Urges Resistance. *Radio Free Asia*, Myanmar Service, March 18. https://www.rfa.org/english/news/myanmar/burma-monkleader-03182009112622.html

Rhys Davids, Thomas W., trans. 1890. *The Questions of King Milinda. Part I*. Sacred Books of the East, ed. Henry E. Palmer and F. Max Müller, vol. 35. Oxford: Clarendon Press. http://www.sacred-texts.com/bud/milinda.htm

Rhys Davids, Thomas W., and Hermann Oldenberg, trans. 1881. *Vinaya Texts Part I: The Patimokkha, The Mahāvagga, I-IV*. Sacred Books of the East, ed. Henry E. Palmer and F. Max Müller, vol. 13. Oxford: Clarendon Press. https://archive.org/details/1922707.0013.001.umich.edu

Rhys Davids, Thomas W., and Rhys Davids, Caroline Augusta Foley, trans. 1921. Cakkavatti Sihanada Suttanta. In *Dialogues of the Buddha, Translated from the Pali of the Digha Nikaya by T.W. and C.A.F. Rhys-Davids Part III*. Online version at Buddhist Library Online. http://buddhistlibraryonline.com/index.php/dighanikaya/pathikavaggapali/dn26-cakkavatti-sutta/66-cakkavatti1

Riza, Raashid. 2012. Bigoted Monks and Militant Mobs: Is This Buddhism in Sri Lanka Today? *Groundviews. Journalism for Citizens*, April 23. http://groundviews.org/2012/04/23/bigoted-monks-and-militant-mobs-is-this-buddhism-in-sri-lanka-today/

Robinson, Paul F. 2003. *Just War in Comparative Perspective*. London/New York: Ashgate.

Rogers, John D. 1989. Cultural Nationalism and Social Reform: The 1904 Temperance Movement in Sri Lanka. *The Indian Economic and Social History Review* 26 (3): 319–341. http://journals.sagepub.com/doi/pdf/10.1177/001946468902600303

Roshanth, M. 2015. We Have Never Been Anti-Tamil Ven. Athuraliye Rathana Thera. *Daily Mirror (Sri Lanka)*, March 16. https://www.pressreader.com/sri-lanka/daily-mirror-sri-lanka/20150316/281698318226334

Rubenstein, Richard. 2001. The Temple Mount and My Grandmother's Paper Bag. In *Jewish-Muslim Encounters: History, Philosophy, and Culture*, ed. Charles Selengut, 141–164. St Paul: Paragon.

Sachi Sri Kantha. 2005. Sinhalese-Muslim Riots of 1915: A Synopsis. *Ilankai Tamil Sangam* (website). http://www.sangam.org/articles/view2/?uid=1060

Samuels, Jeffrey. 2004. Toward an Action-Oriented Pedagogy: Buddhist Texts and Monastic Education in Contemporary Sri Lanka. *Journal of the American Academy of Religion* 72 (2): 955–971.

Sanitsuda, Ekachai. 2001. *Keeping the Faith: Thai Buddhism at the Crossroads*. Bangkok: Post Books.

Sarkisyanz, Emanuel. 1965. *Buddhist Backgrounds of the Burmese Revolution*. Amsterdam: Springer.

Satha-Anand, Suwanna. 2003. Buddhist Pluralism and Religious Tolerance in Democratizing Thailand. In *Philosophy, Democracy and Education*, ed. Philip Cam, 193–213. Seoul: Korean National Commission for UNESCO.

———. 2014. The Question of Violence in Thai Buddhism. In *Buddhism and Violence: Militarism and Buddhism in Modern Asia*, ed. Vladimir Tikhonov and Torkel Brekke, paperback ed., 175–193. New York/London: Routledge.

Schalk, Peter. 1990. Articles 9 and 18 of the Constitution as Obstacles to Peace. *Lanka* 5 (December): 280–292.

———. 2017. The LTTE: A Nonreligious, Political, Martial Movement for Establishing the Right of Self-Determination of Ilattamils. In *The Cambridge Companion to Religion and Terrorism*, ed. James R. Lewis, 146–157. New York: Cambridge University Press.

Schedneck, Brooke. 2011. Constructions of Buddhism: Autobiographical Moments of Western Monks' Experiences of Thai Monastic Life. *Contemporary Buddhism. An Interdisciplinary Journal* 12 (2): 327–346.

Schonthal, Benjamin. 2016. Configurations of Buddhist Nationalism in Modern Sri Lanka. In *Buddhist Extremists and Muslim Minorities: Religious Conflict in Contemporary Sri Lanka*, ed. John C. Holt, 97–115 (e-book version). New York City: Oxford University Press

Scott, Rachelle L. 2009. *Nirvana for Sale? Buddhism, Wealth, and the Dhammakaya Temple in Contemporary Thailand*. New York: State University of New York Press.

Sedgwick, Mark. 2015. Jihadism: Narrow and Wide: The Dangers of Loose Use of an Important Term. *Perspectives on Terrorism* 9 (2): 34–41. http://www.terrorismanalysts.com/pt/index.php/pot/article/view/417

Selengut, Charles. 2003. *Sacred Fury. Understanding Religious Violence.* Walnut Creek et al.: Altamira Press.

Seneviratne, H.L. 1989. Identity and the Conflation of Past and Present. *Social Analysis: The International Journal of Social and Cultural Practice* 25: 3–17, Identity, Consciousness and The Past: The South Asian Scene, September. https://www.jstor.org/stable/23163047?seq=1#page_scan_tab_contents

———. 1999. *The Work of Kings. The New Buddhism in Sri Lanka.* Chicago/London: University of Chicago Press.

Shah, Timothy S., and Daniel Philpott. 2011. The Fall and Rise of Religion in International Relations. In *Religion and International Relations Theory*, ed. Jack Snyder, 24–59. New York/Chichester: Columbia University Press.

Sharp, Bruce. 2005. Counting Hell: The Death Toll of the Khmer Rouge in Cambodia. *Cambodia: Beauty and Darkness.* http://www.mekong.net/cambodia/deaths.htm

Sherwood, Harriet. 2018. Religion: Why Faith Is Becoming More and More Popular. *The Guardian*, August 27. https://www.theguardian.com/news/2018/aug/27/religion-why-is-faith-growing-and-what-happens-next?CMP=Share_iOSApp_Other

Short, Lee. 2018. Facebook Tries to Silence Myanmar's Hateful Monks. *Asia Times*, July 5. http://www.atimes.com/article/facebook-tries-to-silence-myanmars-hateful-monks/

Shwe Lu Maung (alias Shahnawaz Khan). 2005. *The Price of Silence: Muslim-Buddhist War of Bangladesh-Myanmar – A Social Darwinist's Analysis.* Columbia: DewDrop Arts and Technology.

Silva, Kalinga Tudor. 2016. Gossip, Rumour, and Propaganda in Anti-muslim [sic] Campaigns of the Bodu Bala Sena. In *Buddhist Extremists and Muslim Minorities: Religious Conflict in Contemporary Sri Lanka*, ed. John C. Holt, 119–137 (e-book version). New York City: Oxford University Press

SITE. 2017. *Al-Qaeda Central Urges Muslims to Financially, Militarily, and Physically Support Their Brethren in Myanmar.* Country Report Burma, SITE Intelligence Group, September 19.

Sivaraksa, Sulak. 1991. Buddhist Ethics and Modern Politics: A Theravāda Viewpoint. In *Buddhist Ethics and Modern Society: An International Symposium*, ed. Charles Wei-hsun Fu and Sandra Wawrytko, 159–166. New York/Westport/London: Greenwood Press.

———. 2012. *Conflict, Culture, Change: Engaged Buddhism in a Globalizing World.* Bangkok: Suksit Siam Publications.

Smith, Donald Eugene. 1965. *Religion and Politics in Burma.* Princeton: Princeton University Press.

Snyder, Jack. 2011. Introduction. In *Religion and International Relations Theory*, ed. Jack Snyder, 1–23. New York: Columbia University Press.

Spiegel Online. 2016. Papst über Terrorismus: 'Nicht richtig, den Islam mit Gewalt gleichzusetzen'. *Spiegel Online*, August 1. http://www.spiegel.de/panorama/papst-franziskus-islam-und-gewalt-nicht-gleichsetzen-a-1105568.html

Spiro, Melford E. 1982. *Buddhism and Society. A Great Tradition and Its Burmese Vicissitudes*. 2nd expanded ed. Berkeley/Los Angeles/London: University of California Press.

———. 1996. *Burmese Spiritualism*. Piscataway: Transaction Publishers.

Sri Lanka Mirror. 2017. Monks Behind Attacks on Muslim Shops Identified! *Sri Lanka Mirror*, October 3. https://srilankamirror.com/news/5153-monks-behind-attacks-on-muslim-shops-identified

Strong, John S. 1983. *The Legend of King Aśoka*. Princeton: Princeton University Press.

———. 2015. *Buddhisms: An Introduction*. London: Oneworld Publications.

Sugunasiri, Suwanda H.J. 2013. Devolution and Evolution in the *Aggañña* Sutta. *Canadian Journal of Buddhist Studies* 9: 17–104.

Suksamran, Somboon. 1979. *Buddhism and Politics: The Political Roles, Activities and Involvement of the Thai Sangha*. PhD Dissertation, University of Hull. https://core.ac.uk/download/pdf/2731851.pdf?repositoryId=127

———. 1982. *Buddhism and Politics in Thailand*. Singapore: Institute for Southeast Asian Studies.

Sumedho, Ajahn. n.d. *The Four Noble Truths*. Hemel Hempstead: Amaravati Publications. https://web.archive.org/web/20150325013823/http://www.buddhanet.net/pdf_file/4nobltru.pdf

Sunday Herald (Colombo). 2008. Rise of 'War Monk' Sparks Fear of Bloodier Conflict. *Herald Scotland*, March 2. http://www.heraldscotland.com/news/12768721.Rise_of__apos_war_monk_apos__sparks_fears_of_bloodier_conflict/

Swearer, Donald K. 1995. *The Buddhist World of Southeast Asia*. 2nd ed. Chiang Mai: Silkworm Books.

———. 1999. Centre and Periphery: Buddhism and Politics in Modern Thailand. In *Buddhism and Politics in Twentieth-Century Asia*, ed. Ian Harris, 194–228. London: Continuum.

Symes, Michael. 1800. *An Account of an Embassy to the Kingdom of Ava, Sent by the Governor-General of India, in the Year 1795. By Michael Symes, Esq. Lieut-Col. In His Majesty's 76th Regiment* (electronic book). London: printed by W. Bulmer and Co. Cleveland-Row, St. James's; and sold by Messrs. G. and W. Nicol, Booksellers to his Majesty, Pall-Mall; and J. Wright, Piccadilly.

Tadjbakhsh, Shahrbanou. 2010. International Relations Theory and the Islamic Worldview. In *Non-Western International Relations Theory. Perspectives on and Beyond Asia*, ed. Amitav Acharya and Barry Buzan, 174–196. London/New York: Routledge.

Tambiah, Stanley J. 1970. *Buddhism and the Spirit Cults in North-East Thailand.* Cambridge Studies in Social Anthropology, No. 2. Cambridge: Cambridge University Press.

———. 1976. *World Conqueror and World Renouncer. A Study of Buddhism and Polity in Thailand Against a Historical Background.* Cambridge et al.: Cambridge University Press.

———. 1978. Sangha and Polity in Modern Thailand: An Overview. In *Religion and Legitimation of Power in Thailand, Laos and Burma,* ed. Bardwell L. Smith, 111–133. Chambersburg: Anima Books.

———. 1984. *The Buddhist Saints of the Forest and the Cult of Amulets.* Cambridge Studies in Social and Cultural Anthropology. Cambridge: Cambridge University Press.

———. 1992. *Buddhism Betrayed? Religion, Politics, and Violence in Sri Lanka.* Chicago/London: University of Chicago Press.

———. 1996. *Leveling Crowds. Ethnonationalist Conflicts and Collective Violence in South Asia.* Berkeley: University of California Press.

Tanham, George K. 1974. *Trial in Thailand.* New York: Crane, Russak & Company.

Taub, Amanda, and Max Fisher. 2018. Where Countries Are Tinderboxes and Facebook Is a Match. *New York Times,* April 21. https://www.nytimes.com/2018/04/21/world/asia/facebook-sri-lanka-riots.html

Taylor, Alan. 2001a. *American Colonies: The Settling of North America.* New York: Penguin Press.

Taylor, J.L. 2001b. Embodiment, Nation, and Religio-Politics in Thailand. *South East Asia Research* 9 (2): 129–147.

Tegal, Megara. 2014. The Burning Fires of Aluthgama. *The Sunday Leader,* June 22. http://www.thesundayleader.lk/2014/06/22/the-burning-fires-of-aluthgama/

Terwiel, Barend J. 2011. *Thailand's Political History. From the 13th Century to Recent Times.* Bangkok: River Books.

———. 2012. *Monks and Magic. Revisiting a Classic Study of Religious Ceremonies in Thailand.* 4th rev. ed. Copenhagen: NIAS Press.

Thai PBS. 2018. Former 'Nen Kham' Gets 114 Years for Cheating. *Thai PBS,* August 9. http://englishnews.thaipbs.or.th/former-nen-kham-gets-114-years-for-cheating/

Thanissaro Bhikkhu. 1994. Kalama Sutta: To the Kalamas. *Anguttara Nikaya: The Further-factored Discourses.* Access to Insight: Readings in Theravāda Buddhism. https://www.accesstoinsight.org/tipitaka/an/an03/an03.065.than.html

———. 1997a. Samaññaphala Sutta: The Fruits of the Contemplative Life. *Dhīkha Nikaya: The Long Discourses.* Access to Insight: Readings in Theravāda Buddhism. http://www.accesstoinsight.org/tipitaka/dn/dn.02.0.than.html

————. 1997b. Kakacupama Sutta: The Simile of the Saw. *Majjhima Nikaya: The Middle-length Discourses*. Access to Insight: Readings in Theravāda Buddhism. http://www.accesstoinsight.org/tipitaka/mn/mn.021x.than.html

————. 1997c. Kesi Sutta: To Kesi the Horsetrainer. *Anguttara Nikaya: The Further-factored Discourses.* Access to Insight: Readings in Theravāda Buddhism. https://www.accesstoinsight.org/tipitaka/an/an04/an04.111.than.html

————, trans. 1998. Yodhajiva Sutta: To Yodhajiva (The Warrior). *Samyutta Nikaya: The Grouped Discourses*. Access to Insight: Readings in Theravāda Buddhism. http://www.accesstoinsight.org/tipitaka/sn/sn42/sn42.003.than.html

————, trans. 1999a. Sangama Sutta: A Battle (2). *Samyutta Nikaya: The Grouped Discourses*. Access to Insight: Readings in Theravāda Buddhism. http://www.accesstoinsight.org/tipitaka/sn/sn03/sn03.015.than.html

————. 1999b. Sakkha-Pañha Sutta: Sakkha's Questions. *Digha Nikaya: The Long Discourses*. Access to Insight: Readings in Theravāda Buddhism. http://www.accesstoinsight.org/tipitaka/dn/dn.21.2x.than.html

————, trans. 2001. Sangama Sutta: A Battle (1). *Samyutta Nikaya: The Grouped Discourses*. Access to Insight: Readings in Theravāda Buddhism. http://www.accesstoinsight.org/tipitaka/sn/sn03/sn03.014.than.html

————, trans. 2007. Bhikkhu Pātimokkha: The Bhikkhus' Code of Discipline. *Vinaya Pitaka: The Basket of the Discipline*. Access to Insight: Readings in Theravāda Buddhism. http://www.accesstoinsight.org/tipitaka/vin/sv/bhikkhu-pati.html#pr

————, trans. 2008. Maha-cattarisaka Sutta: The Great Forty. *Majjhima Nikaya: The Middle-length Discourses*. Access to Insight: Readings in Theravāda Buddhism. http://www.accesstoinsight.org/tipitaka/mn/mn.117.than.html

Thant Myint-U. 2007. *The River of Lost Footsteps. A Personal History of Burma.* London: Faber & Faber.

The Economist. 2013. Fears of a New Religious Strife: Buddhism Vs. Islam in Asia. *The Economist Online*, July 27. https://www.economist.com/news/asia/21582321-fuelled-dangerous-brew-faith-ethnicity-and-politics-tit-tat-conflict-escalating

The Nation (Bangkok). 2017. Anti-Islam Extremist Monk Forced to Disrobe. *The Nation*, September 21. http://www.nationmultimedia.com/detail/national/30327286

————. 2018. Phra Buddha Isara Arrested After Commando Raid of Temple. *The Nation*, May 25. http://www.nationmultimedia.com/detail/national/30346206

Thurman, Robert. 1997. The Dalai Lama on China, Hatred, and Optimism. *Mother Jones*, November/December. http://www.motherjones.com/politics/1997/11/dalai-lama

Tikhonov, Vladimir. 2013. Introduction. In *Buddhism and Violence: Militarism and Buddhism in Modern Asia*, ed. Vladimir Tikhonov and Torkel Brekke, 1–12. New York/London: Routledge.

Tikhonov, Vladimir, and Torkel Brekke, eds. 2013. *Buddhism and Violence: Militarism and Buddhism in Modern Asia*. New York/London: Routledge.

Tiyavanich, Kamala. 1997. *Forest Recollections. Wandering Monks in Twentieth-Century Thailand*. Chiang Mai: Silkworm Books.

———. 2005. *The Buddha in the Jungle*. Chiang Mai: Silkworm Books.

Toft, Monica Duffy. 2011. Religion, Rationality, and Violence. In *Religion and International Relations Theory*, ed. Jack Snyder, 115–140. New York/Chichester: Columbia University Press.

Toft, Monica Duffy, Daniel Philpott, and Timothy S. Shah. 2011. *God's Century. Resurgent Religion and Global Politics*. New York/London: W. W. Norton & Company.

Tonsakulrungruang, Khemtong. 2018. Thailand's Sangha: Turning Right, Coming Full Circle. *New Mandala*, August 07. http://www.newmandala.org/thailands-sangha-turning-right-coming-full-circle/

Trager, Frank N. 1966. *Burma: From Kingdom to Republic*. London: Pall Mall Press.

Turnell, Sean, and Alison Vicary. 2008. Parching the Land? The Chettiars in Burma. *Australian Economic Review* 48 (1): 1–25. https://onlinelibrary.wiley.com/doi/pdf/10.1111/j.1467-8446.2007.00232.x

Turner, Alicia. 2014. *Saving Buddhism. The Impermanence of Religion in Colonial Burma*. Honolulu: University of Hawai'i Press.

Tylor, Edward B. 1871. *Primitive Culture. Researches into the Development of Mythology, Philosophy, Religion, Art, and Custom*. Vol. 1. London: John Murray.

U Gambira. 2007. What Burma's Junta Must Fear. *Washington Post*, November 4. http://www.washingtonpost.com/wp-dyn/content/article/2007/11/02/AR2007110201783.html

U Pyinya Zawta. 2009. Leading Saffron Monk's Memoir. *Mizzima News*, January 2. Article hosted at http://allburmamonksalliance.org/feature-articles-statements/

UNHCR. 2014. *Violations of Muslims' Civil & Political Rights in Sri Lanka. Annex 1 – Attacks Against Muslims*. Stakeholder Report, UN Human Rights Committee, Secretariat for Muslims, September 9. http://tbinternet.ohchr.org/Treaties/CCPR/Shared%20Documents/LKA/INT_CCPR_CSS_LKA_18205_E.pdf

———. 2018. *Report of the Independent International Fact-Finding Mission on Myanmar* (advance unedited version). United Nations Human Rights Council, August 24. https://www.ohchr.org/Documents/HRBodies/HRCouncil/FFM-Myanmar/A_HRC_39_64.pdf

UNHCR Refworld. Undated. *Burma Citizenship Law (Pyithu Hluttaw Law No. 4 of 1982)*. http://www.refworld.org/docid/3ae6b4f71b.html

Vijayavardharna, D.C. 1953. *Dharma-Vijaya (Triumph of Righteousness) or The Revolt in the Temple.* Colombo: Sinha Publications.

Walshe, Maurice. 1995. *The Long Discourses of the Buddha. A Translation of the Dīgha Nikāya.* Somerville: Wisdom Publications.

Wat Thamkrabok. 2015. Drugs & Alcohol Detoxification and Rehabilitation. https://wat-thamkrabok.org

Weber, Max. 1967. *The Religion of India: The Sociology of Hinduism and Buddhism.* Trans. and ed. Hans H. Gerth and Don Martindale. New York/London: The Free Press/Collier-Macmillan.

Wellman, James K., ed. 2007. *Belief and Bloodshed. Religion and Violence Across Time and Tradition.* Lanham et al.: Rowman & Littlefield.

Wells, Kenneth E. 1975. *Thai Buddhism: Its Rites and Activities.* Bangkok: Suriyabun Publishers.

Wenk, Klaus. 1968. *The Restoration of Thailand Under Rama I, 1782–1809.* The Association for Asian Studies: Monographs and Papers, No. XXIV. Tucson: The University of Arizona Press.

Wickremeratne, Ananada. 1995. *Buddhism and Ethnicity in Sri Lanka: A Historical Analysis.* New Delhi et al.: Vikas Publishing House.

Wijayaratna, Mohan. 1990. *Buddhist Monastic Life: According to the Texts of the Theravāda Tradition.* Cambridge et al.: Cambridge University Press.

Wijenayake, Walter. 2008. Ven Migettuwatte Gunananda. *The Island Online,* September 20. www.island.lk/2008/09/20/features3.html

Wilkinson, Paul. 2001. *Terrorism Versus Democracy: The Liberal State Response.* 1st ed. London: Frank Cass.

Williams, Joe. 2015. Victim of Jerusalem Pride Attack Dies of Injuries. *Pink News,* August 2. https://www.pinknews.co.uk/2015/08/02/victim-of-jerusalem-pride-attack-dies-of-injuries/

Winchester, Mike. 2017. Birth of an Ethnic Insurgency in Myanmar. *Asia Times Online,* August 28. http://www.atimes.com/article/birth-ethnic-insurgency-myanmar/

Winichakul, Thongchai. 1994. *Siam Mapped: A History of the Geo-Body of a Nation.* Honolulu: University of Hawaii Press.

Withnall, Adam. 2018. Sri Lanka Declares State of Emergency over Fears Anti-Muslim Attacks in Kandy Could Spread. *The Independent,* March 6. http://www.independent.co.uk/news/world/asia/sri-lanka-state-emergency-anti-muslim-kandy-attacks-spread-buddhist-central-hill-town-a8241811.html?utm_campaign=Echobox&utm_medium=Social&utm_source=Facebook

Wyatt, David K. 2003. *Thailand: A Short History.* 2nd ed. Chiang Mai: Silkworm Books.

Yongcharoenchai, Chaiyot. 2016. Bigotry on the Boil over Halal Project. *Bangkok Post,* March 13. https://www.bangkokpost.com/news/special-reports/895308/bigotry-on-the-boil-over-halal-project

# INDEX[1]

---

[1] Note: Page numbers followed by 'n' refer to notes.

© The Author(s) 2019
P. Lehr, *Militant Buddhism*,
https://doi.org/10.1007/978-3-030-03517-4

## B

Babbar Khalsa, 13
Bamar (Burman), 159, 174, 178, 183, 233, 245
Bamiyan Buddhas, 17, 262
Bandaranaike, Sirimavo (Prime minister), 20, 56, 125, 126
Bandaranaike, Solomon West Ridgeway Dias (Prime minister), 125
Bayinnaung (Toungoo Dynasty) (King), 198
Bhagavad Gita, 49, 50, 60
Bheri-ghosa, 1–10, 268
Bhikkhu (monk), 55, 56, 88
*Bhikkhu Pātimokkha* (code of monastic discipline), 55–56, 61, 139
Bimbisāra of Magadha (Indian King), 61, 102
Binderbaht (pindapāta), 89
Bodawpaya (Konbaung Dynasty) (King), 161
Bodh Gaya (Temple in Bihar), 3, 261
Bodhisattva, 16
*Bodu Bala Paura* (Buddhist Shield), 145
Bodu Bala Sena (BBS), 9, 119, 127, 138–141, 146, 149, 239, 244, 255, 264
Borommakot Thammaracha (Kingdom of Ayutthaya) (King), 199
Brahmanism, 46, 49, 60, 124, 160, 181, 195, 198, 239
Brahmin, 65, 102
Britton, John, Dr., 19, 28
Buddha, 5, 8, 15, 32, 32n16, 32n17, 33, 36, 45–57, 45n1, 59, 61–67, 70–72, 74, 75, 84–86, 84n3, 90, 91, 93n12, 94, 97n15, 99–103, 100n19, 111, 115, 116, 118, 121, 126, 129, 135, 137, 141–143, 150, 169, 176,
178–181, 186, 187, 196, 199, 207–212, 220, 223, 226, 232, 237–239, 262
Buddhadasa Bhikkhu, 225
*Buddhadesa* (Buddha Land), 150, 174, 250–252
Buddha Issara, Phra, 213, 218
Buddhist Catechism, 123, 124
Buddhist ethics, 36, 51, 54, 74, 180
Buddhist Lent (pansa), 94, 95, 220
Buddhist Marxism, 133
Buddhist nationalism, 71, 124, 125, 127, 131, 134, 143, 144, 144n12, 179, 182, 183
Buddhist polity, 103, 196, 255
Buddhist socialism, 111, 132, 133, 172
Buddhist Taliban, 151
Burman (Bamar), 159, 162, 164, 174, 183, 184, 233, 245
Burmese, 1n1, 3, 9, 34, 36, 38, 46, 83, 84, 85n4, 99, 104, 105, 116, 157, 157n1, 159–163, 164n4, 165, 166, 168, 170–172, 173n12, 175–185, 183n17, 187, 188, 194, 198, 199, 208, 212, 217, 235, 237, 243, 245, 250, 251, 261, 263

## C

Cakkavattin (Chakravartin), 65, 68, 69, 103, 104, 164, 196
Cakkavatti Sihanāda Sutta, 65, 68, 70
Castes, 49, 67, 102, 111, 148, 266
Catholics, 7, 15n3, 18, 20, 33, 38n21, 85, 87n5, 100n19, 108, 118, 122, 141, 144n12, 145, 146, 221, 236, 267
Christian fundamentalism, 1, 19, 145
Christianity, 3, 4, 13, 15n3, 18, 25, 32, 33, 87, 107, 118, 124, 129, 136, 214, 248, 253

CPSIA information can be obtained
at www.ICGtesting.com
Printed in the USA
LVHW081012101119
636873LV00014B/1455/P